Introduction to the Administration of Criminal Justice

Introduction to the Administration of Criminal Justice

an overview of the criminal justice system and its components

2nd Edition

THOMAS F. ADAMS
Chairman, Administration of Justice
Santa Ana College

PRENTICE-HALL, INC., Englewood Cliffs, N.J. 07632

Library of Congress Cataloging in Publication Data

Adams, Thomas Francis, (date)
Introduction to the administration of criminal justice.

(Prentice-Hall series in criminal justice)
Published in 1974 under title: Introduction to the administration of justice.
Includes bibliographies and index.
1. Criminal justice, Administration of—United States. I. Title.
KF9223.A927 1980 364'.973 79-24974
ISBN 0-13-477794-8

Prentice-Hall Series in Criminal Justice
James D. Stinchcomb, *Editor*

10 9

Printed in the United States of America

Prentice-Hall International, Inc., *London*
Prentice-Hall of Australia Pty. Limited, *Sydney*
Prentice-Hall of Canada, Ltd., *Toronto*
Prentice-Hall of India Private Limited, *New Delhi*
Prentice-Hall of Japan, Inc., *Tokyo*
Prentice-Hall of Southeast Asia Pte. Ltd., *Singapore*
Whitehall Books Limited, *Wellington, New Zealand*

Dedicated to Brian D. Adams
My son and good friend

Contents

Preface

The system of criminal justice administration is directly involved in the maintenance of ordered liberty in the United States of America. As the peacekeepers for society, the three components of the criminal justice system —police, courts, corrections—directly affect the daily lives of every woman, man, and child in this society. It is imperative that this awesome system be thoroughly understood by the people it serves. It is my sincere wish that you, the student, have such an understanding as a result of reading this text and listening to the explanations of your instructors.

This second edition has been almost completely rewritten, and the sequence of some of the chapters changed so that the study of the text is a natural sequence of events as you are exposed to the justice system. The first two chapters are devoted to an overview of the total criminal justice system and all of its parts, plus the constitutional basis for creation of the system. Also included in the second chapter is a very brief synopsis of some of the more significant court cases involving constitutional issues in police and court procedures. Although there is certainly no attempt to replace a good criminology text or course on the subject, I do believe that it is necessary to devote some time and space to the topics of the scope or extent of crime and its challenge, and some of the more prevalent explanations of crime and its causes. It seems futile to discuss the administration of the criminal justice system without defining our terms and discussing what it is that necessitates operation of the system in the first place.

A short chapter on the evolution of criminal justice provides a little historical background for the next four chapters, which are devoted to an explanation of what the criminal justice system is, what its component parts are, and how it operates in our modern society. Selection, education, and training in Chapter Ten, and the coverage of ethics, professionalism, and the public image involve moral and ethical issues on how the professional should perform in private as well as in public. The student who is preparing for entrance exams and interviews while seeking employment in the criminal justice professions will find the material in Chapter Ten particularly helpful.

The final chapter in this book has to be completed by the student, because it is still being written. It is impossible to close out the study of the progress of the dynamic and ever-changing justice system. Although there had been earlier studies and investigations of the system, none went into such detail or covered such breadth as the President's Crime Commission in 1965-67. Upon that august body's recommendations, the Omnibus Crime Bill and various other legislation caused the expenditure of literally billions of dollars in the forms of grants and led to extensive studies of procedures and equipment and implementation of many types of new equipment and methods of carrying out the age-old activities of the criminal justice system. Many projects, studies, and innovations in procedure, and changes in attitudes have been made possible by these grants. We have just scratched the surface in discussing these topics in Chapter Twelve of this book.

In addition to the President's Crime Commission's recommendations, another committee, the National Advisory Commission on Criminal Justice Standards and Goals recommended specific goals and plans for action to reach those goals. Based upon the information you read in the last chapter of this book, including the recommendations of those two august bodies, as well as other sources, you will be able to compare the past with the present as far as your own local criminal justice agencies are concerned. You will also see and read about trends for the future. Of particular interest is the list of exemplary programs originally tried in one or more agencies, then found applicable to many other jurisdictions, and subsequently initiated in places other than where they were first put into action. Exemplary programs make it possible for a much greater portion of the people to benefit from federally funded studies that only benefited the grant recipients and the people they served at first. Eventually, many experimental programs will become standard operational procedure in many agencies throughout the nation. Only then will we be able to see widespread results from the President's Crime Commission and the billions of dollars dispensed during subsequent years via enabling legislature including the Omnibus Crime Bill.

At the end of each chapter you will find Exercises and Study Questions, Recommended Semester/Term Projects and (publications) Suggested for Additional study. Please make liberal use of these aids and I guarantee the text will have more meaning to you as a serious student of the criminal justice system. The exercises and study questions, you will probably discover, will be similar to those that your instructor will ask on graded quizzes and exams. The recommended projects are a mere beginning; you or your instructor may think of different and/or more appropriate projects for you to work on. Our recommendations are primarily designed to stimulate the thought processes. The lists of additional sources for study are by no means complete; many of the later books or publications are not listed, and your own preferences or those of your instructor are bound to produce lists that you will find more suitable for your own studies. To that I say Bravo! Originality and initiative in going down your own avenues of study should enhance your understanding of the criminal justice system and related topics.

This text is just the beginning, an introduction to the fascinating study of the criminal justice system. Please consider it as you would a guided tour, then go back on your own and visit in your studies those areas that interest you most.

T. F. Adams
Santa Ana, California

1

Introduction to Criminal Justice: The System

INTRODUCTION

The criminal justice system throughout the United States is actually a conglomorate of systems. It is unique because of the governmental relationships in the U.S. political system. There are literally thousands of independent yet interrelated agencies with similar or identical responsibilities linked together into what appear to the casual observer to be a garbled collection of different bureaucracies.

There are three major components of the system of criminal justice. Those three are most commonly referred to as (1) police, or law enforcement, (2) courts, and (3) corrections. The police component consists of federal, state, and local agencies responsible for protection, investigation, and law enforcement. The courts component comprises the judicial systems of all strata of government and includes the prosecuting attorneys and defense attorneys, as well as quasi-judicial (arbitration, fact-finding, investigating) agencies and the courts, which referee and regulate many aspects of the system. Corrections includes the local, state, and federal agencies of probation and parole as well as the various correctional institutions throughout the country. Although there are three major components of the criminal justice system, another major branch of government cannot be overlooked: the legislative bodies that promulgate the laws which serve as the tools of the criminal justice professions. Actually, then, there are four major components that make the criminal justice system work. They are (1) legislation, (2) police, (3) courts, and (4) corrections.

In this chapter we shall briefly define the goals and objectives of these four components of the system and explore their interrelationships in order to understand how this remarkable system works, in spite of—or perhaps because of—its limitations and in accordance with legal and constitutional parameters provided for its operation.

IS CRIMINAL JUSTICE A SYSTEM?

Systems specialists are reluctant to attach the title *system* to the criminal justice agencies and their affiliates for a variety of reasons. Foremost among those reasons is their belief that a system is more well-defined and that there is more cohesiveness and uniformity, a more solid basis for the interrelationships of the various units.

The system of criminal justice has often been labeled a "nonsystem" because so many of the agencies are totally autonomous and independent, although their legal responsibilities and/or geographical jurisdictions may be continguous, or in some cases overlap. An example of such criticism may be found in a committee report of the American Bar Association:

> The American criminal justice system is rocked by inefficiency, lack of coordination, and an obsessive adherence to outmoded practices and procedures. In many respects, the entire process might more aptly be termed a non-system, a feudalistic confederation of several independent components often working at cross purposes. A disproportionate allocation of funds to police works to the detriment of other constituent agencies, such as the courts and correction facilities.[1]

Although not as critical of the effectiveness of the system, a federal commission report similarly appraised the agency relationships in the svstem:

> This study finds that, generally, the collective operations of police, public prosecutors, public defense counsels, courts and corrections establishments do not constitute a well articulated system. Those operations do not reflect clearly assigned responsibilities, supported by ample and strategic allocation of resources and affording—indeed, guaranteeing—protection for all citizens. While this report necessarily focuses on the intergovernmental relations problems impinging on the criminal justice system, no analysis of its institutional parts can, or should, avoid the basic judgment that much of it, in fact, is a "non-system." Police, prosecution, courts, and corrections function too frequently in isolation, or in ways that are counterproductive to each other.[2]

Having completed a sabbatical study of what has happened to the criminal justice system since the President's Crime Commission reports were released in 1967, and reviewing what improvements, if any, have occurred as a result of extensive federal funding since that time, I was impressed with the lack of change in the "nonsystem" status. Methods and hardware have improved, but each government continues to appear to be fiercely dedicated to retaining its own autonomous individuality, a concept fostered by the American system of government.

[1]American Bar Association Special Committee on Crime Prevention and Control, *New Perspectives on Urban Crime* (Chicago: American Bar Association, 1972), p. 7.

[2]Advisory Commission on Intergovernmental Relations, *State-Local Relations in the Criminal Justice System* (Washington, D.C.: Government Printing Office, 1971), p. 13.

Looking at the system as it is, however, one does find many smoothly functioning interrelated activities of many different agencies. The human circulatory and respiratory systems have their irregularities and dysfunctions, yet they are still quite effective in serving the purposes for which they are intended. Considering that fact—that systems of the body have imperfections yet seem to accomplish their basic objectives of making the body function—the justice system adequately qualifies for designation as a "system."

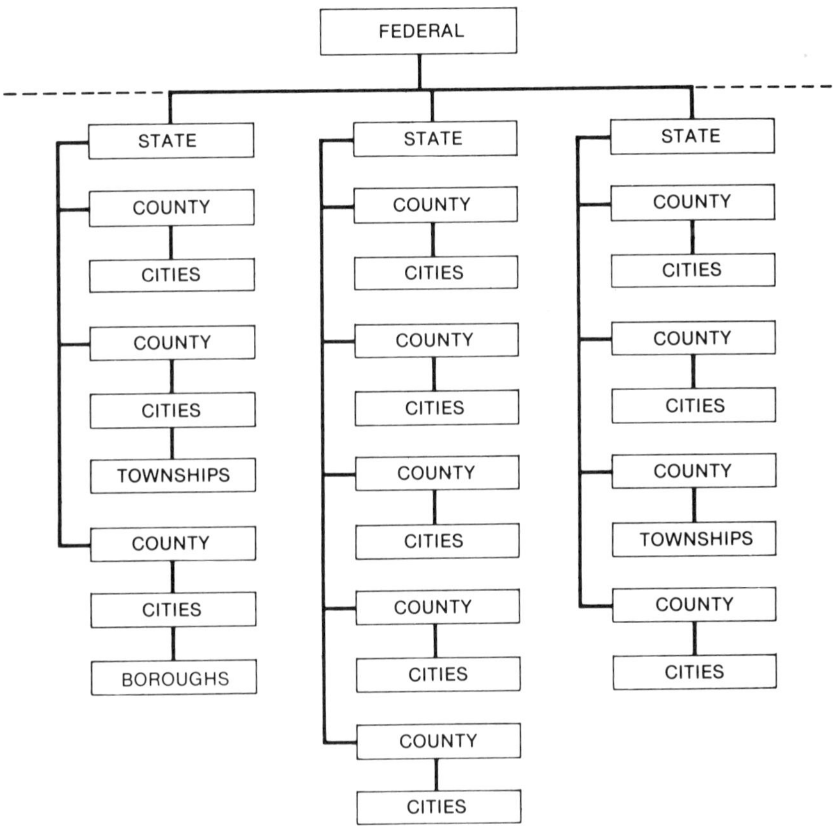

Figure 1-1 The Nonexistent Police System. Constant referral to "levels" of government lead the observer to believe that the cities, boroughs, and townships are supervised by county governments, and, in turn, that county governments are superior in the system to all other governments in the county. Actually, there is no hierarchy, and each of the governments is autonomous (there are exceptions, of course).

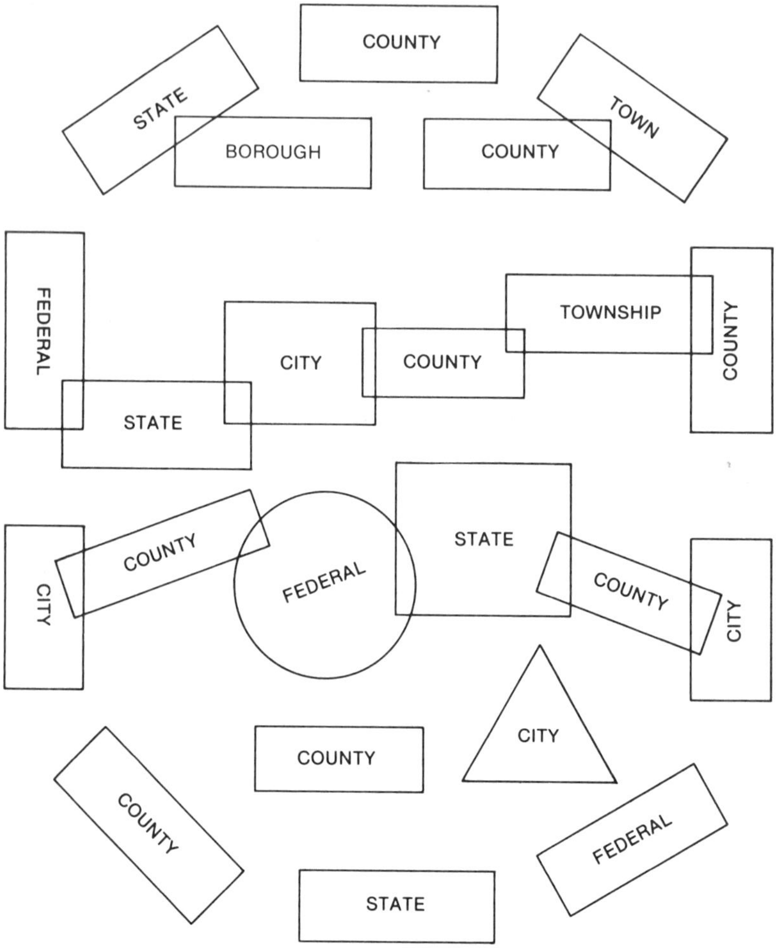

Figure 1-2 The Police System as It Is. Each agency is virtually autonomous. However, some jurisdictions overlap in authority-responsibility relationships to their constituencies.

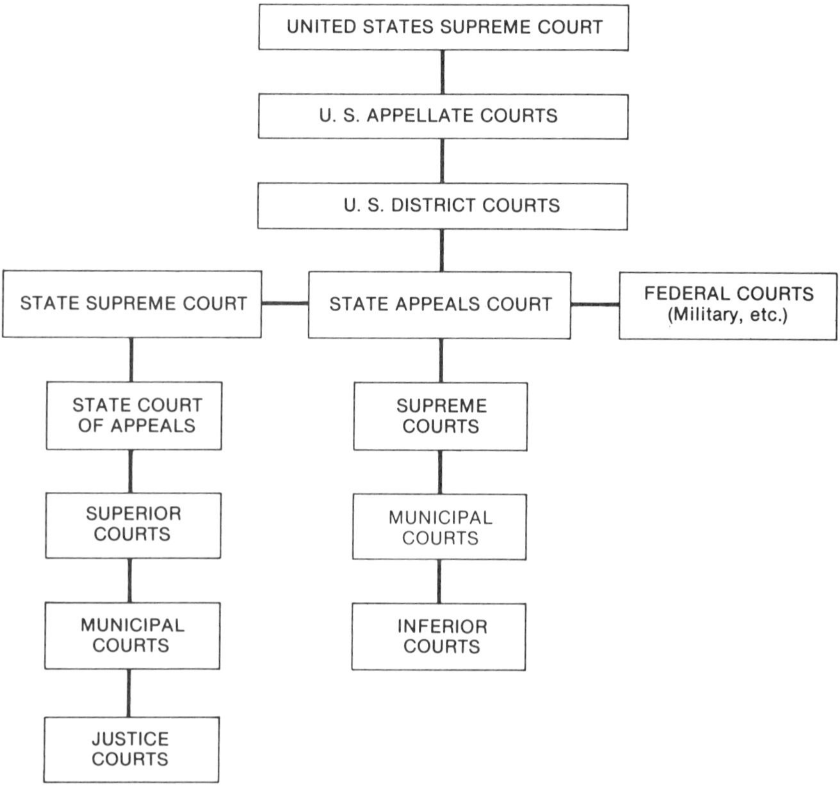

Figure 1-3 Nonexistent Court System as Perceived by the Uninformed. There appears to be a superior-subordinate relationship throughout the court system.

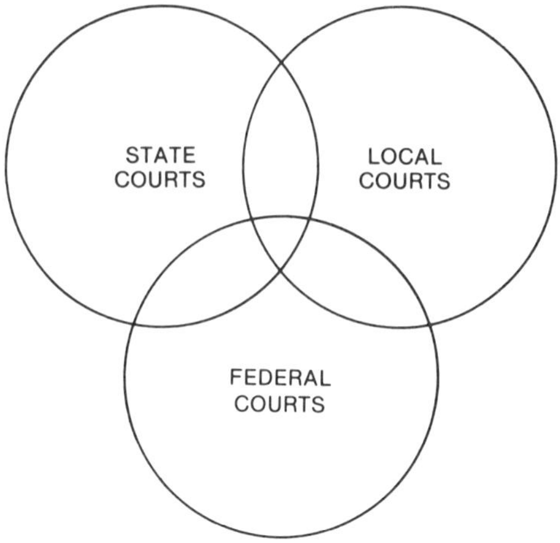

Figure 1-4 The U.S. Court Systems as They Are. Each functions as a separate entity, yet there are overlapping jurisdictions. The U.S. Supreme Court resolves constitutional matters.

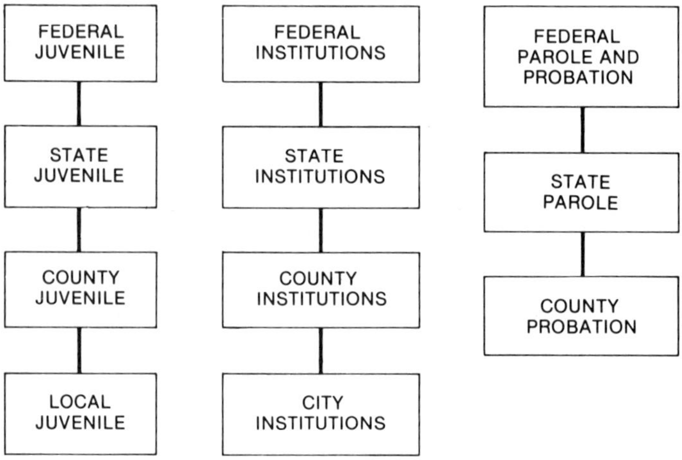

Figure 1-5 Nonexistent Corrections System.

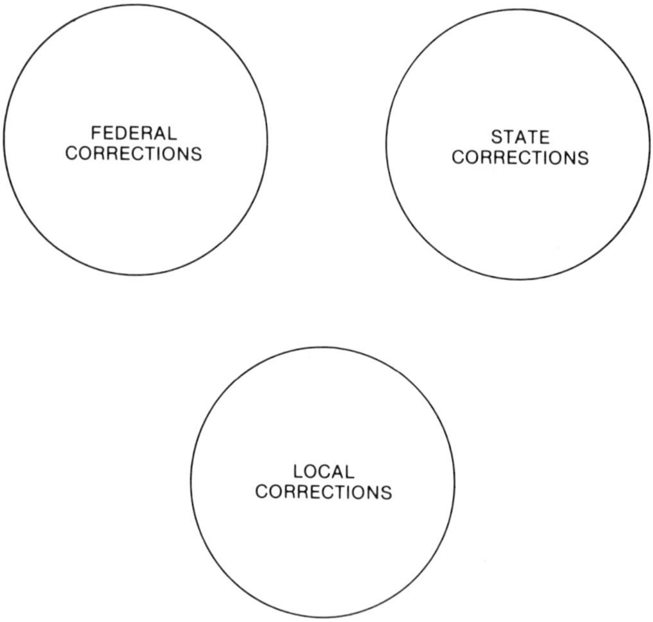

Figure 1-6 The U.S. Corrections Systems. Each system is autonomous.

Throughout the fascinating array of individuals and the agencies that employ them, there runs a common gold thread of public service with what appears to be an unattainable goal of a society free from crime and justice for the greatest percentage of people served. As the circulatory system has a goal of keeping the body functioning as efficiently as possible, the criminal justice system's goal is to keep humanity functioning as efficiently as possible.

COMPONENTS OF THE SYSTEM

Legislature

Based upon the provisions and limitations of the United States Constitution and the constitutions of all the individual states, the various legislative bodies create the laws and agencies responsible for the enforcement of those laws. Virtually every government has its own lawmaking authority, regardless of level of government. The result is an array of separate sets of laws for federal, state, and local governments to be enforced by the executive branch of each government through their respective police agencies. Police power is the term which describes the power of government to make these laws through legislative action, and the enforcement of those laws through executive action.[3]

Police

Although many laws are enacted by one legislative body, such as federal or state legislature, many of those laws may be enforced by the police of any of the government levels regardless of geographic or legal jurisdictions. Thus, it is not unusual for state and local agencies to arrest violators of federal laws, and it is most usual for local police officers to arrest for state law violations. Because of their specialized nature, or the way the laws themselves are written, there are many laws that provide for their investigation and enforcement exclusively by specified police agencies. The result is a great number of separate police agencies throughout the country—many with vast geographical jurisdictions but with very narrow legal jurisdictions—with the power to investigate and enforce just a few specific laws.

For whatever reasons they have, which are probably as numerous as there are legislators, different legislative bodies create laws that are similar to laws passed by other legislative bodies. Consequently, there are many police agencies actually duplicating the activities of each other. For example, gun control may be a taxation matter enforced by the Treasury

[3]See Chapter 2 for a more detailed examination of the phenomenon known as *police power*.

Department and a national security matter enforced by the Federal Bureau of Investigation; alcoholic beverage control at the state level involves control of licensed bars and their employees, while the same laws are enforced by local police agents for control of criminal behavior of the customers in the licensed bars. Attempts are continuously made to keep duplication to a minimum, but in actual practice the key to police effectiveness is in the cooperative efforts of the individual agents themselves.

Objectives of the Police In order to accomplish their goals of maintaining peace and tranquility in a state of ordered liberty, basic objectives of the police include the following:

- Create a feeling of ever-presence of the uniformed patrol force by maintaining visibility in the community through motorized or foot patrols.
- Provide benevolent services in cooperation with other agencies, such as giving directions and information concerning the community and its facilities, providing emergency counseling services, rescue and emergency first aid assistance, and generally assisting people in matters consistent with the police goals.
- Perform crisis-intervention activities for the purpose of minimizing criminal conduct, with particular emphasis on domestic and neighborhood disputes.
- Attend public gatherings to ascertain that such gatherings are lawful and not infringing on the rights of others, and to assure the right of those individuals in attendance to peacefully assemble.
- Investigate allegations of criminal behavior and take appropriate steps to identify, arrest, and bring to a fair trial the alleged perpetrators of those crimes.
- Enforce the laws and ordinances of the federal, state, and local goverment which are charged to the department for enforcement. Cooperate with other government agencies in enforcement of the laws charged to those agencies.
- Investigate the causes of traffic collisions and take appropriate action to reduce or eliminate such accidents, including reporting engineering or educational problems to the appropriate persons and enforcing traffic laws, including the arrest of violators.
- Investigate conditions and other matters related to licensing and other regulatory concerns of the jurisdiction and make appropriate reports to other responsible agencies.
- Direct vehicular and pedestrian traffic to expedite its flow with the greatest degree of efficiency and safety to all concerned.
- Maintain a peaceful and crime-free community through crime prevention and repression activities, public information, and preventive maintenance techniques.
- Investigate complaints and handle calls for police intervention in matters that involve the legal and traditional responsibilities of the department.
- Maintain, through investigation and enforcement activities, an effective balance of vice control in accordance with prevailing community standards.

- Perform as effectively as possible in activities to discover delinquent and predelinquent behavior of juveniles and take direct action to deter development of criminal and other asocial behavior patterns.
- Interact with as many individuals and groups in the community to explain the goals and objectives of the department and to secure their advice and assistance.
- Maintain a property and evidence storage facility to assure procedurally correct presentation of physical evidence in court and return of lost and stolen property to lawful owners.
- Prepare essential reports and records and those that are required by law and provide appropriate information to legally authorized persons.

The preceding list is only a sample of the total statement of objectives for any given police agency. For the sheriff's department, objectives will be necessary to cover the functions of operation of the county jail and serving as bailiff in the courts.

Objectives for each agency in the police component of the criminal justice system will vary from jurisdiction to jurisdiction, depending on laws and traditions. The local agencies will have much broader lists of objectives, while the various state and federal agencies will be much more restrictive. Although agencies of state police may have—and usually do—statewide jurisdiction, their legal responsibilities are much more restrictive, such as state highways, or state-licensed doctors, or state-licensed on-sale and off-sale liquor establishments and their employees. Federal agencies may have jurisdictions spanning the entire United States, plus U.S.-licensed ships on the high seas, or U.S. citizens abroad, but their laws to enforce may be restricted to taxation or customs or immigration or narcotic drug control.

Federal agencies with police responsibilities include the following:

Secret Service. A branch of the Treasury Department charged with protection of the President, Vice-President, various other officials and their families, and enforcement of laws involving U.S. currency and other specified documents.

Internal Revenue Service. A tax-related police agency.

Bureau of Alcohol, Tobacco, and Firearms. Involved with taxation laws as a branch of the Treasury Department, but also actively involved in bomb-related crimes.

Drug Enforcement Administration. Control of legal and illegal drug production and distribution throughout the world.

Federal Bureau of Investigation. Concerned with national security and several dozen highly specialized laws, including unlawful flight to avoid prosecution, transporting stolen cars across state lines, kidnaping and transporting victims across state lines, federal bank robbery statutes.

State police agencies include the following:

Alcoholic Beverage Control. Concerned with liquor licensees.

Highway Patrol. Investigation of highway safety and collision.

Motor Vehicles. Regulation of licensed drivers, automobiles, car dealers.

Consumer Affairs. Enforcement of professional standards and laws related to various professions, such as doctors, nurses, insurance agencies.

Parks and Recreation.

Fish and Game.

There are literally hundreds more throughout the various states. We shall cover more of those agencies and their responsibilities in Chapter 6.

The police component of the criminal justice system involves at least fifty federal agencies, several hundred state agencies, and close to 40,000 local agencies directly involved in law enforcement in the United States.[4] According to the Federal Bureau of Investigation annual crime statistics report, *Crime in the United States 1977,*[5] 98 percent of the population was served by approximately 15,000 agencies contributing to that report. With more than twice that 15,000 not reporting to the FBI with their crime statistics but only 4 percent of the population not covered by reporting agencies, it appears that there must be considerable overlapping in geographic jurisdiction among the police agencies in the nation.

The Courts

The courts throughout the United States are—like the police—organized (or "disorganized") in a fashion similar to the interrelationships of the local, state, and federal governments, each operating within its own separate sphere of authority and responsibility. The local courts at the municipal and county level, numbering into the many thousands, have primary jurisdiction over criminal cases of misdemeanor and felony categories that involve municipal, county, and state laws. An appeals process through progressively higher court levels provides for certain issues to be appealed through the state court system to the state supreme court, and, in some cases, to the U.S. Supreme Court.

The federal court system consists of the U.S. Supreme Court, the appellate courts, the military courts, and the district courts. Jurisdiction of the Supreme Court includes appeals in matters of constitutionality, controversies involving certain public officials, and other matters in which a state is a party to a legal action. The courts of appeal, eleven in number, hear appeals from the district courts. Other special purpose appeals courts include the Court of Systems and Patent Appeals and the Court of Military

[4]President's Commission on Law Enforcement and the Administration of Justice, *Task Force Report: The Police* (Washington, D.C.: Government Printing Office, 1967), p. 7.

[5]Federal Bureau of Investigation, *FBI Uniform Crime Reports* (Washington, D.C.: Government Printing Office, 1968), pp. 1–2.

Appeals. At the trial level in federal courts are ninety-three district courts, the Court of Claims, Customs Court, and Courts Martial for the military services.

State court systems have several levels of jurisdiction, ranging from the small township justice court to the state supreme court. At the local level is the justice court, the city court, or the municipal court. The exact type and designation varies from state to state. The smaller or less populous court district may call for a designation of lesser stature than a court district with a greater population, with the justice court being the lower designation and the municipal court the higher designation. These courts handle misdemeanor criminal cases, small claims, which is a do-it-yourself court involving damages or loss up to about $750 or $1,000 (attorneys are not allowed to represent clients), and other civil cases involving less than $3,000 to $5,000 (which varies from state to state, depending on the laws governing the courts' limitations in the respective states). The higher category of these two courts—municipal court—usually handles the preliminary hearing phase of the felony crime process to determine whether the case should be tried in superior court.

Superior court is the trial court for the county or parish for all felony offenses; this court also serves as an appeals court for cases decided upon in the lower courts and handles litigation involving greater amounts of damages sought for redress than the lower courts can handle. Juvenile court is usually a separate part of the civil division of the superior court, and the probation officer of the county and his/her deputies serve under direction of the presiding judge of the superior court as well. Special departments of the superior court include probate to handle matters involving wills and related administrative matters, guardianship, domestic relations, adoptions, and a psychiatric department to deal with matters involving the mentally ill and others needing treatment, including addicts, inebriates, and mentally disordered sex offenders.

The grand jury, a vestige of the eleventh-century English criminal justice system, performs a quasi-judicial role in the courts component of modern United States criminal justice. Appointed by the court to serve for a specified period of time, usually not more than one year, grand juries operate for both federal and state judicial systems. Initially recommended by judges, then selected by lot, these individuals, who allegedly represent the communities they serve, investigate various matters and recommend actions that should be taken to improve community and government operations. In criminal matters, the prosecutor (district or county attorney, or other government prosecutor) presents evidence and introduces witnesses to the grand jury. The jurors make whatever inquiries they consider essential and in accordance with prescribed procedures as interpreted to them by the prosecutor. Their vote determines whether or not certain people should be held to answer in superior court for the charges they specify. In the absence of such a grand jury proceeding, this function is performed by a municipal court judge in a preliminary hearing. When remanded by the grand jury, the action is called an *indictment.* When remanded to the higher court by a lower court judge, the action is called an *information.* In either case the district prosecutor handles the prosecution.

In addition to the formalized court system, many states have an assortment of other bodies that perform judicial roles. Arbitration boards in matters of liability claims and various types of disputes between people make decisions that have the same effect as though they were made by a court. Commissions charged with professional and vocational standards appoint hearing officers, who take testimony and examine evidence to make recommendations to the commission, which, in turn, takes action that likewise has a courtlike effect, such as the temporary or permanent loss of a license and the right to continue practicing in that profession or occupation.

Court officers include all of the attorneys who practice law in the courts. Prosecutors, who represent the People through the respective governments, are charged with proving guilt in accordance with the Constitution, and they include the Attorney General of the United States and the respective states, U.S. attorneys, corporation counsels, district attorneys, county and city prosecutors, and others with similar responsibilities. The accused are assured legal counsel by virtue of the Fifth and Sixth Amendments to the Constitution, which provide for "due process" and representation by counsel.[6]

In the event the defendant is indigent and cannot provide for his own counsel, one will be provided by the court for him. In order to provide competent counsel for indigent defendants on a consistent basis, the professional, government-employed public defender has taken his place as a regular member of the criminal justice system.

Each court has a bailiff. The function of the bailiff is to maintain order; to protect the judge, the accused, the witnesses, and everyone else in the courtroom. The bailiff is a peace officer who carries out the directions of the judge and various other related duties, including routine security procedures in the courtroom and court house. In the California Superior Court the bailiff is usually the sheriff, in municipal court the marshal serves as bailiff, and in the justice court the constable serves in that capacity. The multifaceted roles of these officers will be explained in more detail in a later section of this text.

In many states the probation officer and his/her deputies serve at the pleasure of the superior court. Their role is to conduct presentence inves-

[6]See Articles V and VI of the Bill of Rights. For further elaboration and detailed explanation of these rights see Gideon V. Wainright (372 U.S. 335), Escobedo v. Illinois (378 U.S. 478), Massiah v. United States (377 U.S. 210), Miranda v. Arizona (384 U.S. 436); and for an elaboration of this right to emphasize a juvenile's rights under similar conditions see Gault v. Arizona (387 U.S. 1).

tigations, make recommendations to the court regarding decisions relative to confinement and alternatives with a view to punishment and rehabilitation, and supervise those individuals who have been placed on probation with a specified program of supervised freedom as prescribed by the court.

The district courts of appeal meet at various locations throughout the state, sometimes on a circuit-court basis, meeting for several months each year at several locations. Cases originating in the municipal courts and justice courts are taken, on appeal, through the superior court to the district courts of appeal. Except when otherwise provided, appeals from superior court are likewise taken to the district courts of appeal. The appellate courts hear cases on appeal in criminal matters, contested elections, eminent domain, and various contested matters of civil law.

The state supreme court is the highest court in most states provided for by the several state constitutions, with jurisdiction generally as follows:

- In all superior court cases in equity.
- In cases at law involving title or possession of real estate, tax legality, impost, assessment, toll, or municipal fine.
- In all probate matters as provided by law.
- In criminal cases in which a sentence of death has been prescribed, and the automatic appeal examines only questions of law.
- Over writs of mandamus, certiorari, prohibition, habeas corpus, and all other necessary writs.
- Over matters before the district courts of appeal when the Supreme Court orders such matters to be transferred to it from that court.
- Over applicants to the State Bar when found qualified by the Bar Examiners of the State Bar and in matters of disciplinary action on recommendation of the Board of Governors of the State Bar.[7]

Still to be considered along with the courts component of the criminal justice system, yet separate and distinct from it, is the Court of Impeachment, which consists of the U.S. Senate. Other ministerial matters of the courts are related to such bodies as a judicial council, which is concerned with policy matters of the practices and procedures in the courts; and the Commission on Judicial Qualifications and Judicial Council, which is concerned with qualification and appointment of competent judges, and their retention or removal for cause.

Corrections

The corrections component of the criminal justice system serves a population that is extremely difficult to define in terms of numbers and percentages, because of the highly transient nature of the processes and the individuals involved. In 1967 the President's Crime Commission reported

[7]California State Constitution, Article VI, Sections 3, 4, 21, and 612.

that correctional institutions of various types throughout the country "admit, control, and release an estimated 3 million individuals each year."[8] The same report estimated that approximately one-third or more of that amount, or approximately 1.4 million, were in institutions, and the balance were on parole or probation. A Bureau of Prisons report showed a 20,000 increase of inmate population in federal and state institutions from 1939 to 1970.[9] During those years, the United States population increased by nearly 70 million, while the inmate population per 100,000 total U.S. population went down from 137.1 to 96.7. Numbers of probationers and parolees are even more difficult to ascertain. For the purpose of this basic orientation to the corrections component of the system, I suggest that it is safe to estimate that approximately two-thirds of the individuals served by the component are either outside the institutions in a probation or parole status. Although more recent inmate and probation-parole statistics may show a more drastic number of "clients" because of court reactions to "leniency" charges, the ratio of 2 to 1 is not likely to change appreciably.

The Federal correctional institution system consists of forty-five facilities, including six penitentiaries (Florence, Arizona; El Paso, Texas; Chicago, Illinois; New York, New York; Terminal Island, California; San Diego, California), a medical center in Springfield, Missouri; a behavioral research center; intermediate and short-term adult institutions; centers for young adults, youths, and juveniles; and community treatment centers. Throughout the United States there are approximately 432 correctional institution systems, including over 1,200 separate facilities for adults and juveniles.[10] As of March 1970, there were 4,037 locally administered jails meeting the definition of "any facility operated by a unit of local government for the detention or correction of adults suspected or convicted of crime and which has authority to detain longer than 48 hours."[11] On a specific census date reported in that same document, there were 160,863 persons held in those institutions for juveniles and adults. Probation and parole systems in the United States, many operating as combination probation and parole organizations, including the federal probation system totalled 1,647 in 1966.[12] More recent statistics, showing slightly different numbers, have been collected by various study groups, but the information above appears to be most reliable until the 1980 census data is released.

[8]President's Commission on Law Enforcement and the Administration of Justice, *Task Force Report: Corrections* (Washington, D.C.: Government Printing Office, 1967).

[9]Federal Bureau of Prisons, "National Prisoner Statistics: Prisoners in State and Federal Institutions for Adult Felons. 1968, 1969, 1970," p. 2.

[10]Herman Piven and Abraham Alcabes, *The Crisis of Qualified Manpower for Criminal Justice: An Analytic Assessment with Guidelines for New Policy* (Washington, D.C.: Government Printing Office, 1969), vol. 2, *Correctional Institutions,* p. 7.

[11]Federal Bureau of Prisons: *Biennial Report 1970–71*, p. 24.

[12]Piven and Alcabes, *The Crisis of Qualified Manpower for Criminal Justice: An Analytic Assessment with Guidelines for New Policy,* vol. 1, *Probation/Parole,* p. 6.

It is evident that the term *corrections* encompasses a multitude of functions, people, concepts, and ideals. Corrections generally involves the rehabilitation—or correcting—phase of the process through which an individual must proceed once he has been determined guilty of a crime and inducted into the justice system. There are three basic parts to this component, although the first and third are quite similar. Those three parts are probation, institutions, and parole.

Probation

Probation involves the placement of a convicted offender (or an adjudicated delinquent juvenile) under supervision in the community in lieu of incarceration, under conditions prescribed by the court, and under the control of a probation officer. Probation involves a suspension of sentence, or part of it, and it is conditional for a specified period of time. Probation may actually be granted in place of a prison sentence, during which time the individual may be sentenced to a short term in a county jail followed by a period of time under supervised liberty. Conditions of probation are prescribed by the court and agreed to by the probationer as a condition of the assignment to probation. The conditions may include any or all of the following:

1. Observing all laws.
2. Keeping and developing good habits.
3. Keeping a good work or school record.
4. Associating only with approved persons.
5. Changing marital status only after consultation with the probation officer.
6. Abiding by all of the restrictions imposed by the judge who granted probation.

Correctional Institutions

Juvenile Institutions Juveniles are detained in a variety of places, but they are not considered as having been convicted at any time if processed through the juvenile courts and the juvenile justice system, which, in most states, is separate and distinct from the part of the system that adjudicates and processes adults (in California, for example, the juvenile court is a noncriminal division of each county's superior court, and the probation departments operate under the jurisdiction of the presiding judge of the superior court with special liaison responsibilities to the juvenile court judge).

The philosophy of the juvenile courts has been to return the child to his parents as soon as possible whenever practicable. First and minor offenders may be returned home with no incarceration, or they may be remanded to the custody of county probation officials or a state institution.

When the court remands the juvenile to custody for his first time, he may go to a local juvenile home or a camp of some type. Subsequent incarcerations for the juvenile repeater may result in his being sent to a state institution or camp for a longer period of time and then eventually home again for probation or parole.

Adult Institutions Adults are sentenced either to a city or county jail or to a state or federal penal institution for a prescribed period of time. Jail sentences are set by the judge for a specific period of time, and the defendant serves that time, less good behavior and earned time off for such voluntary acts as donating blood. Some states have "straight" sentences for felony imprisonment in state institutions that are prescribed by the judge in the same manner as one would be sent to the county jail. Other states have the "indeterminate sentence" that provides for the judge remanding the subject to prison for "the sentence prescribed by law," which is later established by a corrections board or similar committee.

The purpose for sentencing a convicted person to prison include (1) rehabilitation, (2) segregation or isolation from society, (3) retribution, and (4) the community's revenge.

Parole

Paroles are granted by federal, state, or county boards from the various institutions. Following release from prison, the parolee from a federal or state prison is placed under the supervision of a parole officer. A county jail parolee may be placed under the supervision of a probation officer. The role of the parole officer is basically the same as that of a probation officer in most cases. Both probation officer and parole officer, or "agent," are case managers who serve as "change agents" with the principal objective of assisting the individuals under their supervision to rehabilitate themselves and redirect their lives in more meaningful and lawful pursuits to avoid repeating their crimes and having to return to the courts as defendants.

The distinction between probation and parole is that in the case of parole the individual is considered "still in custody" and only on leave from the institution during the period of time he is on his good behavior. He lives under the threat of immediate return to prison if he does not live according to the strict rules that are prescribed for him. The conditions of parole are also similar to those for the person on probation, but the two should not be confused. Probation refers to the term spent by the individual in lieu of a term of imprisonment. Parole follows imprisonment and is merely considered as a continuation of that prison sentence while outside the walls of the institution. Recent developments, however, have made it necessary for more formal procedures to be followed, including hearings with representation by counsel, prior to return to prison for parole violations.

Another distinction between parole and probation is that parole is supervised by a parole or corrections board or department, an arm of the executive branch of government; while probation is a process controlled by the judicial branch of government through its agents, the probation officers.

In many jurisdictions, there is also a conditional release granted the convicted person prior to the completion of a sentence known as parole, which is administered by the County Sheriff and a county parole board consisting of a judge, chief of police, and others from the local community. In jurisdictions where this occurs, the county jail misdemeanor convictee appears before a local parole board and appeals for a portion of his or her sentence to be spent back in the community under supervision. Although it is designated as parole, supervision of these individuals is performed by the local county probation officer. Goals of corrections include (1) prevention of criminal behavior and (2) correction of violators.

DOES THE CRIMINAL JUSTICE SYSTEM GET RESULTS?

In this chapter we have briefly explored the goals and objectives of the criminal justice system. Several years ago, the following statements were made by a committee of the American Bar Association:

> The increasing incidence of violent crime in the streets of our great cities, . . . has begun to create doubts that our criminal justice apparatus, as now constituted, can adequately satisfy those essential goals of a free society.
>
> Two very broad options are open to us as a nation. We could permit the governmental machinery for the administration of justice to continue to deteriorate, relegating us ultimately to primitive self-help crime control remedies. Lynch mobs and vigilante groups are no strangers in American history. Such an option is abhorrent and the very antithesis of our democratic system. Rather, we must renew our commitment to achieve crime control by orderly and lawful means through the criminal justice process. Such a commitment requires more than the expression of noble ideas. It requires strong and immediate action to reexamine critically the criminal justice process and to reshape it into an effective deterrent to violent crime in our city streets.[13]

Referring to its statement of concern for the health of our nation as well as an estimated $16 billion per year loss by the business community, the Committee for Economic Development issued the following appraisal of our criminal justice system.

> The Committee believes that the ineffectiveness of the present structure is rooted in the organizational and administrative chaos that characterizes the nation's uncoordinated system of criminal justice, and in the management weaknesses prevailing in agencies at all levels. The Committee therefore proposes a complete administrative overhaul of the criminal justice system and a redis-

[13]ABA Special Committee, *New Perspectives on Urban Crime,* p. 9.

tribution of responsibility functions, and financial support among the various levels of government.[14]

The American Bar's Committee on Crime Prevention and Control offered its explanation of reasons for the "failure of the existing criminal justice system and its bankrupt crime control policies":

1. An antiquated, inefficient system without coordination that is overburdened with a heavier case load than it could handle.
2. A spiraling heroin addiction epidemic that contributes directly to urban crime and the overloading of the system.
3. A slow motion justice that defeats the goals of the system and demeans the entire process in the eyes of the public.[15]

The same committee of the Bar Association presented an example of the inadequacy of the system as follows:

> Even if a criminal is apprehended, his chances of being seriously disciplined are low. According to New York City's Criminal Justice Plan for 1971: "... Of those arrested in 1968, the last year for which complete data is available for felonies or misdemeanors, only 32 percent were found guilty of *any charge.* Of the remainder, 56 percent were acquitted or had their cases dismissed, 11 percent failed to appear for trial and one percent received other dispositions. Of those found guilty, only 7.4 percent received any sentences of over one year in jail and only 50 percent were sentenced to any further time in jail." When considered with the low probability of arrest for most crimes, these figures make it clear that the *crime control system* in New York poses little threat to the average criminal.[16]

The committee suggested that the so-called system of criminal justice be converted into a real system:

> The nation's criminal justice apparatus must be converted at all levels of government from a diffuse group of agencies, each acting without regard on a coordinated basis to achieve the common goal of crime control. The key word is "system," for the Task Force Report on Law and Law Enforcement to the National Commission on the Causes and Prevention of Violence has aptly described the present criminal justice process as a "non-system" of criminal justice.[17]

Along positive lines made about as many years ago, the Correctional Planning Guide, published in 1969, included the following statement:

> Despite the seriousness of the crime problem today and the increasing challenge in the years ahead, the central conclusion of the Commission is that a

[14]Committee for Economic Development, *Reducing Crime and Assuring Justice, A Statement on National Policy,* prepared by The Research and Policy Committee (New York: Committee for Economic Development, 1972), p. 7.

[15]ABA Special Committee, *New Perspectives on Urban Crime,* p. 7.

[16]ABA, *New Perspectives on Urban Crime,* p. 7.

[17]*Ibid.,* p. 13

significant reduction in crime is possible if the following objectives are vigorously pursued:

First, society must seek to prevent crime before it happens by assuring all Americans a stake in the benefits and responsibilities of American life, by strengthening law enforcement, and by reducing criminal opportunities.

Second, society's aim of reducing crime would be better served if the system of criminal justice developed a far broader range of techniques with which to deal with individual offenders.

Third, the system of criminal justice must eliminate existing inequities if it is to achieve its ideals and win the respect and cooperation of all citizens.

Fourth, the system of criminal justice must attract more people and better people—police, prosecutors, judges, defense attorneys, probation and parole officers, and corrections officials with more knowledge, expertise, initiative, and integrity.

Fifth, there must be much more operational and basic research into the problems of crime and criminal administration, by those both within and without the system of criminal justice.

Sixth, the police, courts, and correctional agencies must be given substantially greater amounts of money if they are to improve their ability to control crime.

Seventh, individual citizens, civic and business organizations, religious institutions, and all levels of government must take responsibility for planning and implementing the changes that must be made in the criminal justice system if crime is to be reduced.[18]

Essential to the achievement of these objectives is the need to overcome the fragmentation, disunity, and operations of programs at cross-purposes by the multitude of agencies and jurisdictions that are essential supports to law enforcement and corrections.

Throughout the next few chapters of this text and the time that follows in the classroom, you, the reader-student, should determine whether the various components of the criminal justice system have advanced toward more effective accomplishment of their objectives and attainment of their goals. Depending on where you live and/or where you are doing your studying, you may find that there is a wide variance between there and elsewhere in the nation.

SUMMARY

In this chapter we have examined the three basic components of the criminal justice system: (1) police, (2) courts, and (3) corrections, with an additional look at the additional component—legislation. The goals and objectives of each component and the entire system were covered as well.

[18]Law Enforcement Assistance Administration, *Correctional Planning and Resource Guide* (Washington, D.C.: Government Printing Office, 1969), p. 3.

Now that you have been introduced to the system, you should be looking into the criminal justice agencies in your own jurisdiction and compare them with your studies as you go along.

EXERCISES AND STUDY QUESTIONS

1. Sketch a diagram showing how the criminal justice system is organized in the state where you live.

2. Why is the criminal justice system so often referred to as a "non-system?" Is the label appropriate? Why? Why not?

3. What are the three principal components of the criminal justice system?

4. What is the component of government that could be considered the "fourth component" of the criminal justice system?

5. List at least two objectives for each of the three criminal justice system components.

6. Which type police agency has the greater scope of law enforcement responsibilities—state or federal?

7. What are the three subunits of the corrections component of the criminal justice system?

8. Describe the differences and similarities of probation and parole.

9. What is the legal basis for the criminal justice system?

10. Explain why we sometimes have laws that duplicate at federal, state, and local levels.

11. Name at least five state police agencies in your state and describe their functions.

12. List at least five federal police agencies and describe their functions.

13. What is the purpose of small claims court?

14. What is the function of the grand jury?

15. Which amendment to the Constitution provides for representation by counsel?

16. As an officer of the court, what are the duties of the probation officer?

17. What is the function of the bailiff in court?

18. What percentages of people under the jurisdiction of the corrections component of the criminal justice system are estimated to be out on probation and parole?

19. What are the four purposes for sentencing a convicted person to a correctional institution?

20. What are the two goals of corrections listed in the text?

RECOMMENDED SEMESTER/TERM PROJECTS

1. Write a five-hundred-word essay on where you believe the criminal justice system is today, compared with your appraisal of where it should be.

2. Interview at least three representatives from each of the three components of the criminal justice system (a total of at least nine persons). Based upon your interviews, write an opinion paper on what improvements you believe are necessary to raise each of the three components (police, courts, corrections) to the level where you think they should be by the end of next year (or some other target date).

3. Draw a complete diagram showing all three components of the criminal justice system components in the state where you live and how they interface with each other.

SUGGESTED FOR ADDITIONAL STUDY

CARTER, ROBERT M., RICHARD A. MCGEEM, and E. KIM NELSON, *Corrections In America.* Philadelphia: J. B. Lippincott Company, 1975.

CLEGG, REED K., *Probation and Parole Principles and Practices* (4th Ptg.) Springfield, Ill.: Charles C. Thomas, Publisher, 1975.

DUFFEE, DAVID, FREDERICK JUSSEY, and JOHN KRAMER, *Criminal Justice: Organization, Structure, and Analysis.* Englewood Cliffs, N.J.: Prentice-Hall, Inc., 1978.

NEWMAN, DONALD J., *Introduction to Criminal Justice.* Philadelphia: J.B. Lippincott Company, 1975.

PRESIDENT'S COMMISSION ON LAW ENFORCEMENT AND THE ADMINISTRATION OF JUSTICE, *Challenge of Crime In a Free Society.* Washington, D.C.: Government Printing Office, 1967. See Also the related *Task Force Reports* of this commission.

SILVER, ISADORE, ed., *The Crime Control Establishment.* Englewood Cliffs, N.J.: Prentice-Hall, Inc., 1974.

UNITED STATES CONSTITUTION and Constitutions of the state(s) in which you live and/or study.

2

Constitutional Considerations in Justice Administration

INTRODUCTION

The criminal justice system is authorized by the constitutions of the United States and the respective fifty states of the nation. In this chapter, we shall review the basic documents which serve as the sources for creation of the laws and agencies that make those laws, the agencies that enforce the laws, and the agencies that interpret the laws. These documents include—in addition to the constitutions—the Declaration of Independence and the Common Law, which is expressed in court decisions that either affirm or reaffirm the law, or declare its unconstitutionality.

The material covered in this chapter is in condensed form, compared with the many volumes that address the same subjects. However, you should have a general feeling for the philosophy and legality of the constitutional aspects of criminal justice when you complete the chapter.

DECLARATION OF INDEPENDENCE

When John Hancock and his colleagues signed the Declaration of Independence on July 4, 1776, it included an extensive list of grievances against the tyranny of King George III. The purpose of the document was to declare the independence of the Colonies from England and the King's oppression. The document also included a statement supporting the new nation's secession from the mother country that in effect stated that governments should not be changed for "light and transient causes," but "when a long train of abuses and usurpations, pursuing invariably the same Object evinces a design to reduce them under absolute Despotism, it is their right, it is their duty, to throw off such Government, and to provide new Guards for their future security." The Declaration reflected the philosophy of the men who fashioned the framework for the newly formed independent government: "We hold these truths to be self-evident, that all men are created equal, that they are endowed by their Creator with certain unalienable Rights, that among these are Life, Liberty, and the pursuit of Happiness.—That to secure these rights, Governments are instituted among Men, deriving their just powers from the consent of the governed. . . ."

The statesmen who took part in the framing of the Declaration of Independence also set about the task of establishing the new government of the United States of America with the following selfless pledge: "And for the support of this Declaration, with a firm reliance on the protection of Divine Providence, we mutually pledge to each other our Lives, our Fortunes and our sacred Honor." Those same men had very definite ideas as to the rights and privileges of the individual in this great new country and his relationship with his government "of the people, by the people, and for the people." The purpose of government is to insure all people in the nation that they shall equally enjoy the rights of "Life, Liberty and the pursuit of Happiness." That the right of the government to govern comes from the will of the people was also pointed out in the document.

U.S. Constitution

The people in the United States of America have the fundamental right to be free and enjoy their liberties but also the right to be secure and have protection against others who would interfere with their rights to "Life, Liberty, and the pursuit of Happiness." When the authors of the United States Constitution met, they obviously had those rights in mind, as reflected in the Preamble:

> We the people of the United States, in Order to form a more perfect Union, establish Justice, insure domestic Tranquility, provide for the common defence, promote the general Welfare, and secure the Blessings of Liberty to ourselves and our Posterity, do ordain and establish this Constitution for the United States of America.

By virtue of police power, the nation's hundreds of thousands of local, state, and federal criminal justice professionals have the responsibility and the authority to maintain an ordered liberty through the exercise of their respective duties. They must enforce the Constitution, and they, too, must be governed by its requirements. In their respective duties, the individuals in the justice system should be guided by this statement by Justice Brandeis in *Olmstead* v. *United States.*[1] Frequently referred to in recent cases, this has been considered a guiding view in judicial philosophy. Justice Brandeis wrote these words in his dissenting opinion:

> Decency, security and liberty alike demand that government officials shall be subjected to the same rules of conduct that are commands to the citizen. In a government of laws, existence of the government will be imperilled if it fails to observe the law scrupulously. Our Government is the potent, the omnipresent teacher. For good or for ill, it teaches the whole people by its example. Crime is contagious. If the Government becomes a lawbreaker, it breeds contempt for law; it invites every man to become a law himself; it invites anarchy. To declare

[1]277 U.S. 438,485.

> that in the administration of the criminal law the end justifies the means—to declare that the Government may commit crimes in order to secure the conviction of a private criminal—would bring terrible retribution. Against that pernicious doctrine this Court should resolutely set its face.

Police Power

The term *police power* inspires visions of uniformed police officers performing their various duties of chasing traffic violators and catching armed robbers while they are holding their victims hostage. It seems natural to associate the word "police" with the symbolic police officer, who visually represents to so many people all of government and its authority. Actually, the term *police power* encompasses much more than the police. *Police power* is that constitutionally authorized power of government to enact and enforce laws to regulate the conduct of the people who are within the jurisdiction of that government.

Police power rests primarily with the respective states, which are sovereign in the United States' system of government. It is the power of the legislative branch of government to make laws that provide for the public health, welfare, prosperity, morality, and safety. Enforcement of the laws is carried out by the executive branch of government through its investigative and enforcement arms. Adjudication is accomplished in the courts by the prosecution and defense under supervision and arbitration of the judiciary. Most criminal law is the responsibility of state and local governments, and the federal government reserved for itself only limited police powers.

The police power of the federal government is described in Article I, II, III, and IV of the United States Constitution, which reserve to Congress the powers to make laws, and the powers to enforce them. Article I, Section 8, states that Congress shall have the power to

> ... lay and collect taxes ... regulate commerce with foreign nations, and among the several states ... establish a uniform rule of naturalization, and uniform laws on the subject of bankruptcies ... fix the standard of weights and measures ... provide for the punishment of counterfeiting the securities and current coin of the United States ... [provide for copyright and patent laws] ... define and punish piracies and felonies committed on the high seas and offenses against the law of nations ... make rules for the government and regulation of the land and naval forces ... [exercise laws and enforcement within the District of Columbia] ... and ... make all laws which shall be necessary and proper for carrying into execution the foregoing powers, and all other powers vested by this Constitution in the government of the United States, or in any department or officer thereof.

This portion of the Constitution is probably the most significant clause of all in that it prescribes police power of the federal government.

Section 9 of Article I includes provisions that the "privilege of the writ of habeas corpus shall not be suspended, unless when in cases of rebellion or invasion the public safety may require it." The same section provides that "no bill of attainder (extinction of civil rights and capacities of a person upon sentence of death or outlawry) or ex post facto law shall be passed."

Article II, Section 3, includes the requirement that the President of the United States "shall take care that the laws be faithfully executed, and shall commission all the officers of the United States." Section 4 states: "The President, Vice President and all civil officers of the United States, shall be removed from office on impeachment for, and conviction of, treason, bribery, or other high crimes and misdemeanors."

Article III, Section 1, prescribes the powers of the U.S. Courts. Section 2 states: "the judicial power shall extend to all cases, in law and equity, arising under this Constitution, the laws of the United States . . . [and] to all cases of admiralty and maritime jurisdiction." The same section of Article III provides: "In all the other cases before mentioned, the Supreme Court shall have appellate jurisdiction, both as to law and fact, with such exceptions, and under such regulations as the Congress shall make." Section 3 of Article III defines treason and provides for its punishment.

Article IV, Section 2, provides that "the citizens of each state shall be entitled to all privileges and immunities of citizens in the several states." This was later expanded and reaffirmed under Section 1 of the Fourteenth Amendment many years later in 1868:

> All persons born or naturalized in the United States, and subject to the jurisdiction thereof, are citizens of the United States and of the state wherein they reside. No state shall make or enforce any law which shall abridge the privileges or immunities of citizens of the United States; nor shall any state deprive any person of life, liberty, or property, without due process of law; nor deny to any person within its jurisdiction the equal protection of the laws.

Section 2 of Article IV also provides for the interstate rendition, or extradition process: "A person charged in any state with treason, felony, or other crime, who shall flee from justice, and be found in another state, shall on demand of the executive authority of the state from which he fled, be delivered up, to be removed to the state having jurisdiction of the crime."

The police power of the several states is authorized by Article X of the Bill of Rights, also known as the Tenth Amendment to the Constitution, which was ratified on December 15, 1791, just four years after the establishment of the Constitution. That article provides: "The powers not delegated to the United States by its Constitution, nor prohibited by it to the states, are reserved to the states respectively, or to the people." Limitations on that power were expressed in the Fourteenth Amendment again, and in Section 2 of Article IV of the Constitution itself.

STATE CONSTITUTIONS

The various state constitutions are separate and distinct from the United States Constitution. For many years, it was the interpretation of the Supreme Court that the specific provisions of the Constitution, particularly the Bill of Rights, applied only to judicial affairs of the United States courts and not to the individual states. During the past three decades, however, there have been some significant changes. The philosophy during recent years has been that the United States Constitution and its Amendments are to be enforced by state legislation and by the state judicial and police officers. This trend will be particularly noticeable when we discuss the provisions of the Bill of Rights.

The state constitutions are each original documents and vary in language and total content, but they are basically similar in that they set forth the mechanics for the government, and they also include sections that are similar to the first ten amendments to the United States Constitution, the Bill of Rights. For example, the California Constitution contains a Declaration of Rights in Article I. Some of the sections deal with the following rights:

> *Section 1.* All men are by nature free and independent, and have certain inalienable rights; among which are those of enjoying and defending life and liberty; acquiring, possessing, and protecting property; and pursuing and obtaining safety and happiness.

This section provides for the police power of the state, and case decisions have held that the exercise of police power by a state is solely for the welfare of the *public* as opposed to individuals. Persons and property are subject to certain restraints and burdens to secure the general welfare of the state.

> *Section 2.* All political power is inherent in the people. Government is instituted for the protection, security, and benefit of the people, and they have the right to alter or reform the same whenever the public good may require it.

Cases related to this section point out that an individual who becomes a member of the society under our form of constitutional government does surrender some of his personal rights but only to the extent that such relinquishment may be necessary for the common good.

Section 3 declares that the State of California is an inseparable part of the American Union, and the Constitution of the United States is the supreme law of the land. State sovereignty is defined as the role of the states and their relationship with the federal government.

> To the Federal Government is delegated the exercise of certain rights or powers of sovereignty; and the exercise of all other rights of sovereignty, except as expressly prohibited, is reserved to the people of the respective states, or vested by them in their local governments.

Section 4 provides for religious freedom, and Section 5 provides that the privileges of the writ of habeas corpus shall not be suspended except when such suspension shall be necessary because of a rebellion or invasion. Section 6 prohibits excessive bail, unusual punishment, and the detention of witnesses in places where criminals are imprisoned.

Other sections of the California constitution bear a remarkable resemblance to certain portions of the United States Constitution, and are duplicated—in philosophy rather than in exact words or the same location in the documents—in numerous other constitutions. These provide for the right to trial by jury, freedom of speech and of the press, and the right to assemble and petition. Due process of law and its administration according to the legal and proper rules is required by the Constitution, as are the right to a speedy trial and protection against unreasonable search and seizure.

STATE POLICE POWER AS INTERPRETED BY THE COURTS

An early case involving state police powers may be found in a Supreme Court case that examined interstate commerce: *New York, New Haven,* and *Hartford Railroad Company* v. *New York:* 165 United States, 628 (1897). The issue involved a New York State law forbidding use of coal or wood stoves or furnaces for heating passenger coaches on all trains operating in the state. In sustaining the statute, the Court applied five main tests:

1. Was the nature of the subject being regulated such that it would require uniform national regulations? The Court found "not necessarily" though it was a matter on which governments might be expected to legislate.
2. Had Congress enacted legislation with which the New York statute was in conflict? The Court said "No."
3. Did the matter concern the health, safety, morals, convenience, or welfare of the inhabitants of New York State—in other words, did it come with the police power of the state? The Court ruled "Yes."
4. Did the state statute apply to both interstate and intrastate commerce, or did it discriminate against interstate commerce? The law did not single out and unreasonably burden interstate commerce, according to the Court.
5. Was the regulation reasonable, or did it impose an unreasonable burden on interstate commerce? Justice Harlan wrote, "While the Laws of the States must yield to acts of Congress passed in execution of the powers conferred upon it by the Constitution, the mere grant to Congress of the power to regulate commerce did not, of itself and without legislation by Congress, impair the authority of the States to establish such reasonable regulations as were appropriate for the protection of the health, lives and safety of their people."[2]

[2]Jewell Case Phillips, Henry J. Abraham, and A. M. Ewing Cortez, *Essentials of National Government,* 3rd ed. (Cincinnati: Van Norstrand Reinhold Co., 1971), pp. 348–349.

THE BILL OF RIGHTS

The first ten amendments to the U.S. Constitution are better known as the Bill of Rights and were added to the original document just a few months after ratification of the Constitution itself. They include some of the inalienable rights that were alluded to in the Declaration of Independence written several years earlier. They should be zealously guarded by everyone in the United States, particularly the local police departments who have the sworn duty to preserve the public peace and to protect lives and property. One very important fact that should never be overlooked with respect to the Bill of Rights is that along with the rights goes a corresponding set of responsibilities to assure liberty to others as well as to self. Madison said: "Liberty may be endangered by the abuses of liberty as well as by the abuses of power." And Oliver Wendell Holmes, Jr. illustrated the premise that all rights are relative, not absolute, and must be exercised within limits, by stating that freedom of speech does not include the right to falsely shout, "Fire!" in a crowded theater.

> *Article I.* Congress shall make no law respecting an establishment of religion, or prohibiting the free exercise thereof; or abridging the freedom of speech, or of the press; or the right of the people peaceably to assemble, and to petition the Government for a redress of grievances.

Free speech is limited in such cases when such speech or publications are obscene, or tend to disturb the peace, or advocate the overthrow of the established government. The freedom also does not include speech or publications that are designed or intended to incite to treason, rebellion, the commission of crimes, of disobedience of or disrespect for the law. A person may speak of his intense hatred, but he may not incite others to commit such acts as to riot. People may assemble to picket in a peaceful manner and shall not be inhibited except when they commit some criminal act, such as trespass on private property, or do malicious mischief to personal property, or when their gathering purpose shows evidence of changing its nature to one with the purpose of committing some criminal act. In the latter case, the assembly becomes an unlawful assembly.

The police role with respect to Article I involves one of visiting or observing an assemblage of people to ascertain its lawful nature. The police are responsible for the maintenance of peace, and there may be good cause for the officers to remain present or nearby to assure the continued peaceful and lawful nature of the assembly. Published material is of no official concern to the police unless there is a violation of the law involved. The police are not censors, nor should they be. It is merely the responsibility of the police to enforce the law as it is written and intended. Pornography is illegal filth in the eyes of some individuals but expressive art in the eyes of others. Just exactly where the separation lies between what is pornographic and what is acceptable is a matter of interpretation, and the interpretations vary with the changing times and the interpreters. Many supreme and lesser courts have repeatedly stated that "pornography" is virtually impossible to define. Recent trends have been to gauge "decency" on local *community standards,* whatever they might be at a given time and place.

The courts have ruled that community standards cannot be decided at a national level. Each of the elements of prurient appeal, patent offensiveness, absence of social value is to be viewed in light of the contemporary moral standards of the community. Possession of obscene material in the privacy of one's home is protected by the First Amendment. It is, however, permissible for the state to restrict access of obscene materials to minors, and the state can adjust to social reality by adopting a definition of "obscenity" which is assessed in terms of the sexual interests of the minor.

> *Article II.* A well regulated Militia, being necessary to the security of a free State, the right of the people to keep and bear Arms, shall not be infringed.

The courts have held that the right to bear arms means that a person has the right to possess firearms and to use them in defense of self or property. The courts have also held that the states may make whatever laws they deem necessary to regulate the possession and carrying of firearms, such as the prohibition against addicts or felons possessing or carrying guns. Carrying certain weapons concealed or mere possession of certain other types of weapons, such as machine guns without specific legal cause or compliance with other regulations, is not unlawful for the various legislative bodies to prescribe or proscribe. When the public safety demands it, the police have a duty to search persons known or suspected of having weapons on their person or in their possession, to confiscate the weapons, and to arrest the persons for violations of the laws.

> *Article III.* No soldier shall, in time of peace, be quartered in any house without the consent of the owner, nor in time of war but in a manner to be prescribed by law.

This article of the Bill of Rights was intended to prohibit the quartering of military troops in private residences, in the manner practiced by the British Army in the American Colonies. It would apply equally to any police agency that would entertain any inclinations of a similar nature.

> *Article IV.* The right of the people to be secure in their persons, houses, papers, and effects, against unreasonable searches and seizures, shall not be violated, and no Warrants shall issue, but upon probable cause, supported by Oath or affirmation, and particularly describing the place to be searched, and the persons or things to be seized.

The article was originally designed as a protection against abusive practices that had been the rule rather than the exception for the British Army and from which the framers of the Bill of Rights sought protection. The purpose for such a rule was explained in 1948 by the Supreme Court in *United States* v. *DiRe,* 332 U.S. 581, 595:

> . . . the forefathers, after consulting the lessons of history, designed our Constitution to place obstacles in the way of a too permeatng police surveillance, which they seemed to think was a greater danger to a free people than the escape of some criminals from punishment.

The provision requiring an affidavit for a search warrant was designed to prevent the practice of police "fishing expeditions."

Most searches conducted by the police are done without warrants, and most are in compliance with the ruling of the Fourth Amendment. Police officers employ a variety of methods in investigating crimes, identifying and arresting the persons responsible, and collecting evidence to assure a prosecution and conviction. If the officers utilize improper methods, there is a danger in losing a case and having evidence excluded as a result. Rules that provide for exclusion of evidence from consideration in court trials is known as the *exclusionary rule;* that is, evidence collected in violation of the Fourth Amendment or other Constitutional provision is excluded.

A key word in the article is "unreasonable," which is sometimes erroneously used synonymously with the word *illegal.* The officer's actions in situations involving searches must be based upon "probable" or "reasonable" cause, and those two words may be used interchangeably. For many years, until 1961 actually, the states each had the complete freedom to make their own rules on search and seizure and were not directly involved with the specific wording of federal rules. Although some states had previously had state supreme court rulings that applied the federal rule as to the reasonableness of searches and seizures, it was not until 1961 when the United States Supreme Court ruled in *Mapp* v. *Ohio,* 367 U.S. 643 that, as a matter of constitutional law, the federal "exclusionary rule" applied to the several states as well as the agencies of the federal government. The states may continue to rule on their own specific cases, but they shall not violate the standards in the Fourth Amendment, so stated the court.

John Edgar Hoover, late Director of the Federal Bureau of Investigation wrote in the *Iowa Law Review* (Winter 1952): "Law enforcement, however, in defeating the criminal, must maintain inviolate the historic liberties of the individual." Judge Lewis, of the Tenth U.S. Circuit Court of Appeals, wrote in *Anspach* v. *United States* 305 R. 2d48 (1958):

> But the prevention and detection of crime is not a polite business and we see no need or justification for reading into the Fourth Amendment a standard

of conduct for law enforcement officials which would leave society at the mercy of those dedicated to the destruction of the very freedoms guaranteed by the Constitution. The "pursuit of happiness" referred to by Justice Brandeis in Olmstead can be destroyed by idealistic theory that shuns the deadly realism of crime.

A police chief wrote this about the police process of arrest and search:

> The importance of arrest, and the search incident thereto, cannot be overemphasized. Arrest affects fundamental individual rights to personal liberty and privacy. The strict and technical laws of arrest and search are an effort to balance the right of society, through government, to protect itself and its members against the right of the individual to life, liberty, and the pursuit of happiness. Because of their importance and complexity, the subjects of arrest, search, and seizure have generated a major training problem. Twenty years ago a police recruit would be told all he needed to know about his arrest powers in a few hours.[3]

> *Article V.* No person shall be held to answer for a capital, or otherwise infamous crime, unless on a presentment or indictment of a Grand Jury, except in cases arising in the land or naval forces, or in the Militia, when in actual service in time of War or public danger; nor shall any person be subject for the same offense to be twice put in jeopardy of life or limb: nor shall be compelled in any criminal case to be a witness against himself, nor be deprived of life, liberty, or property, without due process of law; nor shall private property be taken for public use, without just compensation.

The self-incrimination and "due process" clauses of this article are those that affect the police on a more regular basis than the other clauses. The due process provision is a reference to the normal and legal procedure, which may not be bypassed for any purpose. Federal police agencies were the first to be instructed and required not only to respect an individual's right against self-incrimination, but they were also required to orally admonish him as to his rights against making any statements that could be used against him in a court of law. This federal rule became known as the McNabb-Mallory Rule, based on two cases in 1943 and 1957 respectively.

A series of cases in various states eventually led to what is now known as the Miranda Rule of the U.S. Supreme Court, rendered by that body on June 13, 1966. The rule applies to the admissibility in court of a person's statements made during a custodial police interrogation, which means a questioning session during which the subject being questioned was the suspect of a criminal case and the investigation had focused on him at the time. The Supreme Court ruled that the Fifth and Sixth Amendments shall directly be applied to all the states, and that the police shall comply with the

[3]John P. Howard, "Arrest: An Administrator's View," *Police Work,* April, 1971, p. 13.

rule in the case of all custodial interrogations. The subject must be advised as follows, and he must understand the meaning of what he is being told:

> You have the absolute right to remain silent. Anything you say can, and will, be used against you in court.
>
> You have the right to consult with an attorney, to be represented by an attorney, and to have one present before I ask you any questions.
>
> If you cannot afford an attorney, one will be appointed to represent you before you are questioned, if you desire.

The subject may then waive these rights, and the waiver must be made "voluntarily, knowingly, and intelligently." The Court's rule requires that the officer proceed only after asking the subject: With these rights in mind, are you ready to talk with me about the charges against you? The subject must then reply with an oral affirmative before the officer proceeds. After the interview begins, the subject is given continued protection against himself and any statements he may make by the Court's direction: "If, however, he indicates in any manner and at any state of the process that he wishes to consult with an attorney before speaking there can be no questioning. Likewise, if the individual is alone and indicates in any manner that he does not wish to be interrogated, the police may not question him. The mere fact that he may have answered some questions or volunteered some statements on his own does not deprive him of the right to refrain from answering any further inquiries until he has consulted with an attorney and thereafter consents to be questioned."

The double jeopardy prohibition of the Fifth Amendment is so fundamental to our constitutional heritage that it is considered as incorporated in the due process clause of the Fourteenth Amendment. The basic principle of the double jeopardy ban is that a person who has committed a criminal act can be subjected to only one prosecution or punishment for that act. Accordingly, when a defendant has been prosecuted for a criminal offense and the prosecution has resulted in either a conviction or an acquittal—or the proceeding has reached such a point that a dismissal would be tantamount to an acquittal—any further prosecution of punishment for the same offense is forbidden. The former jeopardy rule applies to all crimes, felonies and misdemeanors alike.

Regarding the grand jury provision, the federal courts require that any federal prosecution for a crime punishable by death or imprisonment in a penitentiary or any other imprisonment at hard labor must be commenced with a grand jury hearing. The courts to date have not extended any federal ruling that states would be bound to the grand jury requirement through the Fourteenth Amendment. Therefore, it is not mandatory in state criminal proceedings.

The due process clause provides assurance that all individuals who come within the jurisdiction of the Constitution and the government shall have the right to equal and correct treatment according to the rules established by law and by the courts in interpreting those laws. "Due process" means that all of the other provisions of the Constitution shall be applied fairly with each person, and they are enforced by this provision and the due process provision of the Fourteenth Amendment.

Under the conditions of the Fifth Amendment Miranda Rule, custodial interrogations, the accused has a right to counsel. Once charges have been filed against the accused, he is entitled to the assistance of counsel at all critical stages of the proceedings. Extending beyond the trial itself, this has been interpreted to include every stage of the proceeding where substantial rights of the accused may be affected. Examples of "critical stages" are (1) a pretrial arraignment, (2) a preliminary hearing, (3) a police lineup after indictment, (4) the entering of a guilty plea at any time, (5) sentencing of the accused, and others, depending on various state statutes and court decisions.

> *Article VI.* In all criminal prosecutions, the accused shall enjoy the right to a speedy and public trial, by an impartial jury of the State and district wherein the crime shall have been committed, which district shall have been previously ascertained by law, and to be informed of the nature and cause of the accusation; to be confronted with the witnesses against him; to have compulsory process for obtaining witnesses in his favor, and to have the Assistance of Counsel for his defence.

The speedy trial provision is met by the police officers' taking the suspect before a magistrate without undue delay and filing charges against him. State law requires that the subject of an arrest be specifically advised of the crime for which he is being charged, except that in some cases this advisement may be waived when it is understood exactly why the arrest is being made, such as when an officer arrests the defendant during the actual commission of a crime or following a pursuit immediately following the act. The witnesses against the defendant are presented in court to give their testimony, and at that time may be cross-examined by the defendant or his attorney.

At the outset of the investigation when an identification may be made by a witness from behind a screen or other device that hides the identity of the witness from the suspect, such a procedure is in the best interest of the safety of the witness and it is not a violation of the defendant's rights under authority of the Sixth Amendment. His attorney may utilize an "early discovery" rule that many states have that allows the defense to demand, and receive, copies of statements made by witnesses in a specific case.

There are times when the identity of confidential informants are the source of information that may lead to the institution of an investigation, and for public safety reasons—such as sustaining the life of the informant—the informant is never identified. In this type of case, however, there must be evidence independent of the informant's information that will stand on its own merits and sustain a conviction of the defendant.

The right to counsel applies only to criminal prosecutions. A witness under subpoena to appear before the grand jury does not have a right to have an attorney present with him, although he may have the attorney standing outside whom he may consult from time to time.

The right to counsel includes the right to select one's own counsel if financially able to do so, the right to have counsel appointed if indigent, and the right to consult with the attorney in private and free from official surveillance. If the accused is indigent, that is, unable to pay for a competent criminal lawyer, the court appoints counsel, and the state pays the fee. According to 18 United States Codes §3006A, indigent defendants are assured the right to counsel and investigative, expert, and other services necessary to an effective defense.

> *Article VIII.* Excessive bail shall not be required, nor excessive fines imposed, nor cruel and unusual punishment inflicted.

Bail has been receiving considerable attention for several decades. Its purpose is to serve as a guarantee that the persons arrested will return to court on the time specified, at which time their bail will be returned to them. What is excessive may depend on the nature of the offense, or it may depend on the amount of bail money the individual can afford to post. When possible, many releases are made with only a signed promise to appear. This is known as an "OR" release, or "own recognizance." When "OR" is denied, and money bond is required, few people are able to produce the required amount of money. Consequently, they go to a bailbondsman, who sells them a bond—an insurance policy—which serves as their collateral to assure the defendant's return to court. Even this can be too expensive for some people, because the bond salesperson collects the premium for the purchase of the bond plus a service charge. "Excessive fines" are as hard to define as would be "excessive bail."

Punishment at one time was by death, branding, public floggings, whipping, and the pillory, to mention a few. Most of that has changed, except that the death penalty is constantly being raised in court as a form of cruel and unusual punishment. Arguments for and against the death penalty are very persuasive and very emotional, each side using the Bible and every other available document to prove their points, often using the same documents, but with different interpretations. What is "excessive" seems to be in the eye of the beholder.

> *Article X.* The powers not delegated to the United States by the Constitution, nor prohibited by it to the States, are reserved to the States respectively, or to the people.

Article Ten provides for the primary police power to be vested in the individual states, which are sovereign in our system of government in the United States.

JUDICIAL REVIEW

The courts have the ultimate authority to interpret laws and their enforcement through their authority to review the actions of both legislature and executive officers—the police—in consideration of the intentions of the Constitution, which is the acknowledged supreme law of the nation. Beyond the authority of the courts, of course, lies the ultimate authority of the people to change the Constitution through the voting process. In reality, the courts serve as the voice and conscience of the people as they see it, which gives them, to put it colloquially, a "mighty big stick." This cudgel is accompanied by the grave responsibility to assure equity and justice.

The effects of judicial review can best be illustrated by a review of court decisions that have directly affected the police and other components of the criminal justice system through changes in their procedures necessitated by those decisions. Court decisions which become standards, or "lighthouses" to aid the police, the prosecutors and defense attorneys, and all the other participants in the system's day-to-day activities in charting their courses of action and avoiding "smashing into the rocks" of unconstitutional behavior are sometimes referred to as "landmark" decisions. Although every individual may have different sets of landmarks, following are some of the cases that have significantly affected criminal justice procedures. They are listed in chronological sequence, and will indicate which constitutional amendments were used as the bases for the decisions by the Courts.

Weeks v. *United States,* 232 U.S. 383 (1914). Rendered inadmissable in federal court any evidence seized by federal agents in violation of search and seizure rules (Fourth Amendment).

Byars v. *United States,* 273 U.S. 28 (1928). Ruled admissible in federal court evidence obtained by state officers as long as it was not obtained in connivance with federal officers. This was sometimes referred to as the "silver platter" doctrine, the federal officers having state officers give them evidence on a silver platter that they could not secure by the same means (Fourth Amendment).

Powell v. *Alabama,* 287 U.S. 45 (1932). A defendent's right to counsel at a trial (Fifth and Sixth Amendments).

Nardone v. *United States,* 308 U.S. 338 (1939). The exclusionary rule extends beyond the unreasonably obtained evidence to the "fruits of the poisoned tree." Such fruits—or products—extend to any information, object, or testimony which was uncovered or obtained, directly or indirectly, through the "tainted" evidence or leads therefrom, and which would not have otherwise been obtained (Fourth Amendment).

McNabb v. *United States,* 318 U.S. 322 (1943). Requires a prompt arraignment and "aims to avoid all the implication of secret interrogations of persons accused of crime." A rule for federal officers (Fifth Amendment).

Wolf v. *Colorado,* 388 U.S. 25 (1949). State courts were not required to exclude unreasonably obtained evidence by any federal constituional rule, the court ruled. The Supreme Court ruled that although the Fourteenth Amendment due process rights assured Fourth Amendment rights to people accused of crimes in the states, the duty of enforcing those rights rested with the states (Fourth Amendment).

Rochin v. *California,* 342 U.S. 165 (1952). Excludes evidence seized by officers whose conduct "shocks the conscience" according to the courts. Reasonableness of the search must be weighed with other factors; in this case a stomach was pumped to obtain swallowed heroin (Fourth Amendment).

Mallory v. *United States,* 499 (1957). Another case like McNabb involving federal agents that required them to arrest on probable cause, to arraign the accused without unnecessary delay, and to interrogate without delay (Fifth Amendment).

Roviaro v. *United States,* 353 U.S. 53 (1957). When the disclosure of an informant's identity becomes essential for a fair trial or is helpful to the defense, the government must disclose the identity of the informer.

Elkins v. *United States,* 364 U.S. 206 (1960). The "silver platter" doctrine Rejected. Evidence collected in violation of Fourth Amendment requirements would be excluded from federal prosecutions regardless of whether such evidence was collected by state or federal police (Fourth Amendment).

Mapp v. *Ohio,* 367 U.S. 643 (1961). Prohibited unconstitutional searches and seizures by state or local officers, similar to the exclusionary rule set in Weeks in 1914. Applied federal rules to state officers (Fourth and Fourteenth Amendments).

Robinson v. *California,* 370 U.S. 660 (1962). Narcotic addiction is an illness not a crime. A state law that imprisons as a criminal a person thus afflicted inflicts a cruel and unusual punishment in violation of the Fourteenth Amendment.

Gideon v. *Wainright,* 372 U.S. 335 (1963). Right to be represented by an attorney and at state expense if the defendent cannot afford one (Sixth Amendment).

Ker v. *California,* 374 U.S. 23 (1964). Held that the federal rule applies to announcing officer's presence prior to breaking to enter for search, except when states recognize certain exceptions. Those exceptions are when there is danger that someone might be killed or injured, or that contraband or other evidence might be destroyed, or there is danger of escape (Fourth Amendment).

Escobedo v. *Illinois,* 378 U.S. 478 (1964). Right to counsel during private interrogation by the police (Sixth Amendment).

Massiah v. *United States,* 377 U.S. 210 (1964). A defendent has a right to an attorney at any time during or before a trial where the counsel's absence might deprive the accused of a fair trial (Fifth and Sixth Amendments).

Miranda v. *Arizona,* 384 U.S. 436 (1966). Established rules for custodial interrogation and the individual's right to counsel during the accusatory stage (Fifth and Sixth Amendments).

Katz v. *United States,* 389 U.S. 347 (1967). Evidence gained through the use of wiretapping—whether trespassory or not—is generally inadmissible. Without prior judicial authorization, wiretapping or electronic eavesdropping without the consent of one party to the conversation is an unreasonable search and seizure (Fourth Amendment).

Gilbert v. *California,* 388 U.S. 263 (1967). Handwriting exemplars may be required of a suspect. They are nontestimonial, identifying physical characteristics outside the protection of the Fifth Amendment.

Gault v. *Arizona,* 387 U.S. 1 (1967). Juvenile has a right to be informed of the specific charge against him, a right to counsel, a privilege not to incriminate himself, and a right to due process including cross-examination and confrontation of the witness (Fifth and Sixth Amendments).

United States v. *Wade,* 388 U.S. 218 (1967). Legal counsel should be available to the accused during a lineup for identification (Sixth Amendment).

Terry v. *Ohio,* 392 U.S. 1 (1968). Reinforces the duty requirement of a police officer to stop and frisk a person for weapons under certain conditions. Distinguishes a "stop" from an "arrest" and a "frisk" from a "search" (Fourth Amendment).

Ginsberg v. *New York,* 390 U.S. 629 (1968). It is constitutionally permissible for states to restrict access of obscene materials to minors, and the state can adjust to social reality by adopting a definition of "obscenity," which is assessed in terms of sexual interests of such minors (First Amendment).

Chimel v. *United States,* 395 U.S. 752 (1970). Limits the extent of a search incidental to an arrest without a search warrant, provides for judicial review prior to searching (Fourth Amendment).

Lego v. *Twomen,* 404 U.S. 477 (1972). The trial judge is the one who determines whether evidence will be excluded because of an unreasonable search. He will make the determination prior to its introduction into evidence, and the admissibility will be based upon the preponderance of evidence as to reasonableness of the search and seizure (Fourth Amendment).

Kirby v. *Illinois,* 404 U.S. 1055 (1972). The right to counsel applies to the accused who has been *formally* charged (such as arrested on a warrant and having a prosecution pending). In the Kirby case, the arraignment or indictment being considered formal charges (Fifth Amendment).

Argersinger v. *Hamlin,* 407 U.S. 25 (1972). No imprisonment may be imposed unless the accused is represented by counsel. This is an extension of *Gideon* v. *Wainwright,* which was a felony case (Sixth Amendment).

Adams v. *Williams,* 407 U.S. 143 (1972). Accepted a police officer's "reasonable cause" as basis for search and arrest. He approached the defendant's car, asked the defendant to open the door. The officer reached inside the car and seized a loaded handgun from the defendant's waistband. The officer had received prior information about the gun from an informant he knew. A subsequent search led to discovery of heroin and other contraband (Fourth Amendment).

Schneckloth v. *Bustamonte,* 412 U.S. 218 (1973). Consent search. The prosecution must show that the consent was voluntary and not the result of coercion or duress, either express or implied. "Voluntariness" is determined by the total set of circumstances. The police are not required to warn a suspect of his right to refuse consent (Fourth Amendment).

United States v. *Robinson,* 414 U.S. 278 (1974). It is reasonable for the police to make a full body search incidental to an arrest, at least when the person arrested is taken into custody (Fourth Amendment).

United States v. *Matlock,* 415 U.S. 164 (1974). Effective consent for a search without a warrant may be given by the accused or by any third party who possesses "common authority or other sufficient relationship" to the premises or effects to be inspected (Fourth Amendment).

Ross v. *Moffitt,* 417 U.S. 600 (1974). Court-appointed counsel on appeal is available at all stages of the appellate process, including petitions for review to the Supreme Court (Sixth Amendment).

Brown v. *Illinois,* 422 U.S. 590 (1975). Proximity of the arrest to recovery of the evidence in point of time, intervening circumstances, such as the Miranda warning, and the purpose and nature of the police misconduct are all relevant factors in determining admissibility of evidence gained (Fourth Amendment).

Faretta v. *California,* 422 U.S. 806 (1975). An accused has a constitutional right to waive counsel and to represent himself in a criminal proceeding (Sixth Amendment).

Michigan v. *Mosley,* 423 U.S. 96 (1975). Mosley was correctly advised of his Miranda rights on two separate occasions about two hours apart. He acknowledged orally and in writing that he had received his Miranda warnings both times. During the second interrogation the officer asked the defendant questions about a homicide unrelated to the robberies about which he was originally questioned. He made incriminating statements and was convicted for first-degree murder. The Court held that the Miranda rule was correctly used and "scrupulously honored." Conviction of the defendant was confirmed (Fifth Amendment).

South Dakota v. *Opperman,* 428 U.S. 364 (1976). Police impounded a car for multiple parking violations. During a routine inventory of the car to provide for security of the car and its contents, police found a quantity of marijuana in the unlocked glove compartment. The search was ruled routine and constitutional (Fourth Amendment).

United States v. *Dinitz,* 424 U.S. 600 (1976). Dinitz was indicted for conspiracy to distribute and distribution of LSD. The jury had been selected and sworn in, and opening statements by counsel had begun. Difficulty with counsel led the defendant to ask for a mistrial, which was granted. In subsequent trial, the defendant petitioned for dismissal because he claimed double jeopardy. The Court ruled that the new trial did not violate the double jeopardy clause of the Fifth Amendment.

Beckwith v. *United States,* 425 U.S. 341 (1976). Two special agents of the Intelligence Division of the Internal Revenue Service questioned Beckwith in his own home after identifying themselves and advising him of his rights against self-incrimination and the nature of their investigation. The defendant made statements and presented records voluntarily and during that time had neither been arrested nor detained against his will. His later conviction was upheld because there was no Miranda violation (Fifth Amendment).

SUMMARY

At no other time in the history of the United States has the Constitution played such a leading role in the process of law enforcement. The police officers walk a thin tightrope while preserving the peace and protecting life and property. They, too, must operate within the law and according to the provisions of the Constitution and the Bill of Rights. They have no time to ponder the finer points of constitutional law, and they must act with speed and decisiveness when the occasion arises. When they effect an arrest of a person or a search of his person or property, they must be acting upon good faith and reasonable cause or by authority of a warrant that must be based upon information from a reliable source and with good cause.

The freedom of man is sacred, but liberty is relative and there are certain obligations to other persons and their liberty as well. Each person must meet these obligations if his own liberty and safety are to be preserved and protected. The police power within the United States that is not specifically delegated to the federal government by the Constitution is inherent within the individual states. They have the right and the duty to legislate for the preservation of peace and protection of the public health, morals, safety, and welfare of the community. The police agencies and their officers are responsible for enforcing the police power but with wisdom and proficiency so as to do the most efficient job within the guidelines established by law and the decisions of the Supreme Court.

EXERCISES AND STUDY QUESTIONS

1. Commit to memory (again) the Preamble to the Constitution.

2. Define "police power."

3. The police are the enforcement arm of which branch of government?

4. Of what significance is the Fourteenth Amendment?

5. What is "due process" and how does it involve a criminal investigation?

6. List and discuss at least three examples of abuse of the right to free speech.

7. Of what significance was *Mapp* v. *Ohio* to local law enforcement agencies?

8. What is the Miranda Rule?

9. What is meant by the term "judicial supremacy"?

10. Which two Amendments to the Constitution are considered as most important in the category of due process?

11. Check the constitution of your state, then list the sections and clauses that are similar to the Bill of Rights.

12. What is double jeopardy, and how is the defendant protected by this rule?

13. Under what conditions, if any, may a person have an attorney during a grand jury hearing?

14. Define "excessive bail," "excessive fines," "excessive punishment."

15. What is a "landmark case," and why does it carry such a designation?

16. What was the "silver platter" doctrine, and what happened to it?

RECOMMENDED SEMESTER/TERM PROJECTS

1. Go through the list of major court decisions listed in this chapter, break them down into categories (search, interrogation, etc.) and then go to the law library and select additional cases in each category. Then prepare a paper showing the evolution of the constitutional limitations on law enforcement during the past two decades. Prepare a few paragraphs commenting on those changes and what effect, if any, they have had on the justice system.

2. Prepare an eight-page paper on police power, its sources, its history, and its present state.

SUGGESTED FOR ADDITIONAL STUDY

FELKENES, GEORGE T., *Constitutional Law for Criminal Justice.* Englewood Cliffs, N.J.: Prentice-Hall, Inc., 1978.

KAMISAR, YALE, WAYNE R. LAFAVE, and JEROLD H. ISRAEL, *Modern Criminal Procedure Cases—Comments—Questions.* St. Paul, Minn.: West Publishing Co., 1974.

LEVY, LEONARD W., *Judicial Review and the Supreme Court.* New York: Harper and Row, Harper Torchbooks, 1967.

LEWIS, PETER W., and KENNETH D. PEOPLES, *Constitutional Rights of the Accused—Cases and Comments.* Philadelphia: W. B. Saunders Company, 1979.

Political Science textbook of your choice.

SKOLNICK, JEROME H., *Justice Without Trial: Law Enforcement in Democratic Society.* New York: John Wiley and Sons, Inc., 1966.

WESTON, PAUL B., and KENNETH M. WELLS, *Criminal Evidence for Police* (2d ed.). Englewood Cliffs, N.J.: Prentice-Hall, Inc., 1976.

WILSON, JAMES Q., *Varieties of Police Behavior, The Management of Law and Order in Eight Communities.* Cambridge: Harvard University Press, 1968.

3

Scope of the Crime Challenge

INTRODUCTION

Why call crime a *challenge?* More appropriate terms, you might argue, might be *scourge* or *plague* or *miasma* or *blight* or—if nothing else—the *crime problem.* But a *challenge?* Probably the most plausible response I can offer to your arguments is that crime has been such an intrinsic part of society that no matter what efforts have been exerted to eradicate it, crime is still here—ubiquitous. Crime is to everyday life what those little stones are to a burlap sack full of pinto beans; there always seems to be an ample amount of each. For that reason, I call crime a challenge!

In this chapter we shall attempt to define crime and criminal law and its origins and developments, we shall review the extent of crime and statistical methods in recording its occurrence, and then discuss the efficacy of crime reporting as it is done at the present time throughout the United States. This will be followed by a discussion of the justice system and its relationship to the crime challenge and alternatives of diversion from the system for those individuals who may be chosen for such efforts at rehabilitation and correction. The objective of this chapter is to cause you to have a clear understanding of the significance and the scope of the crime challenge as perceived by the criminal justice professionals.

ORIGIN OF CRIMINAL LAW

Along with the civilizing of man came the rules of society designed to assure the civilization process. More than four thousand years ago the earliest-recorded information was inscribed on tablets of stone in the days when Hammurabi was ruler of Babylon (about 2100 B.C.). The Codes of Hammurabi expressed an eye-for-an-eye philosophy and provided for retributive justice. These written laws prescribed required behavior and specific punishments for violations of those laws, making the individual responsible for his/her own acts.

In Ancient Egypt, the "seat of wisdom," the death penalty was one of the forms of punishment, but for certain crimes it was often commuted to penal servitude. Punishment was mild, compared to Hammurabi's punishments, which included death for incest, adultery, and theft, and branding the forehead for certain other violations. Egyptian law reflected Egyptian culture at the time. Incest was permitted "because the gods did it." Cleopatra was married to her younger brother Ptolemy XII until his death, then to her still-younger brother Ptolemy XIII prior to her marriage to Marc Antony.

Israel and Mosaic laws incorporated many of the laws of Hammurabi, and Moses also based many of his laws on Egyptian law. He was believed to have been born in Egypt, he was raised and educated in Egypt and lived there until he led his followers out across the desert to Canaan. Some of the highlights of Mosaic law were (1) the laws applied to Israelite and alien equally, (2) polygamy was allowed, (3) slavery was practiced, but every seventh year each slave was given a year of freedom, (4) most sexual law violations were punishable by death, (5) individuals found guilty of crimes of violence were either fined, or they were punished according to the eye-for-an-eye philosophy.

Laws reflected the economic, social, and religious beliefs held by the people at the time and place the laws existed. There is still a direct correlation throughout the world. Laws evolved from religious tenets; customs, mores, and folkways of society; social taboos; prejudices and preconceived attitudes and biases toward people other than those who lobbied for specific laws enforcing their point of view; demands of special interest and pressure groups; and the general needs and wishes of society as perceived by law-making bodies of men and women representing their human constituents. A cursory review of the criminal codes in your own state will reveal a wealth of information about all of those factors in our modern society. A check of the date when a certain crime originated may give the criminal law historian an idea as to the social priorities at that time. In other words, laws—including criminal laws—are the game rules for society.

The legal system in the United States had its roots in England, the home of Common Law. Since the country's first government was under English rule, the English legal system was adopted by the new nation when it emancipated itself from the grips—but not the customs—of the mother country. There are vestiges of Spanish influence in California and French influence in Louisiana, and other influences elsewhere, but the principal foundation of law in the United States is English Common Law. Rather than rely upon unwritten laws, and because of their suspicion of a government ridden with tyrants, the leaders of the new nation decided that all laws should be codified, or written. This assured more continuity, more objectivity, and less likelihood that men could change the laws at their whim and fancy as the winds changed the bends of branches in trees.

The codified law as enacted by legislature is the basic law in the United States, and it is modified and changed by a series of court decisions. The British basic law has been the Common Law, or the decisions of the courts themselves. The laws were made as each case was adjudicated and were court-made laws. When each case came to court, the Common Law was researched for a similar case upon which to base the current situation. If there was no precedent, the case at hand became the precedent for subsequent cases. This was the origin of *stare decisis.*

Specificity is very essential to our legal system. The law must be clearly understood—it must specifically state what it is intended that it state. For example, auto theft involves the taking of an automobile with the *specific intent* to deprive the owner of his property. This "specific intent" part of the law is different from general intent, which is proved by the mere doing of the act forbidden by law, such as failing to stop for a stop sign. "Specific intent," on the other hand, requires proof of a "specific designated state of mind" to violate the law. This is appropriately covered in greater depth in criminal law texts and courses.

The uniformity principle is also very important in our legal system. In theory this principle means that the law is applied to all its violators on an impartial and equal basis. The uniformity principle is, however, applied somewhat at variance with theory, as may be witnessed by the student of jurisprudence or the casual observer.

A criminal law requires or forbids certain behavior, or may provide that careless conduct during what would otherwise be lawful activity if performed with care also falls within the definition of criminal conduct. The law must be enacted by appropriate political authority, such as U.S. Congress, state legislature, county board of supervisors, or city council, must be signed into law by endorsement of the chief executive officer, such as governor or president, and must provide for some sort of punitive sanction for violation. Punishment may be in the form of death, imprisonment, fine, removal from public office, disqualification to hold any office of trust, or a combination of two or more of those sanctions. Above all, the codified law must be clearly written and completely understandable. A law that is vague or uncertain as to its meaning or to what circumstances it would apply or that may be so broad that it covers too many different types of misconduct may be ruled unconstitutional because of its vagueness.

Now for a definition of crime. Edwin H. Sutherland defined it as follows:

> The essential characteristic of crime is that it is behavior which is prohibited by the State as an injury to the State and against which the State may react, at least as a last resort, by punishment. The two abstract criteria generally regarded by legal scholars as necessary elements in a definition of crime are legal description of an act as socially harmful and legal provision of a penalty for the act.[1]

[1]Edwin H. Sutherland, *White Collar Crime* (New York: Holt, Rinehart and Winston, 1949), p. 31.

Criminologists Taft and England succinctly explain their definition of crime in this manner:

> Before any act or omission can be officially labeled a crime, four principles have to be established: (1) that the conduct actually occurred, (2) that the conduct was in violation of the criminal law, (3) that the conduct was committed with intent, and (4) that the alleged violator was capable of the conduct.[2]

The California Penal Code, Section 15, defines crime as follows:

> A crime or public offense is an act committed or omitted in violation of a law forbidding or commanding it, and to which is annexed, upon conviction, either of the following punishments: death; imprisonment; fine; removal from office; or disqualification to hold and enjoy any office of honor, or profit in this state.

The United States is a nation of laws. The entire system is regulated by laws, all of which must be specifically written. A nation that is not ruled by law is one that is ruled by the whim of fallible men, constantly changing with no rhyme or reason depending on the changing moods of the individuals in charge at the moment. Although there are individuals who interpret the laws through their own intellectualizing process, and inequities do occur, the laws of the nation will prevail and be used as guidelines for uniformity and fairness. There is a greater assurance of equal treatment regardless of individual differences, as opposed to chaotic inconsistency. The student errs enormously, however, by seeking to determine what is—and what is not—law by seeking his answers only in the legal code books. The legal code is the basic document and the principal source of the law, but there is another source of the law that cannot be overlooked: the courts.

Although the legislative branch of government is charged with the responsibility of introducing and passing the laws, the final determination of how they shall be applied—if at all—is made by the courts. The law may remain the same as originally written, but it is subject to human interpretation that may change with the general public opinion and the personal philosophies of the judges and Supreme Court Justices. The courts hear the testimony, examine the evidence, then hear the attorneys' arguments, and study the precedents set by the previous cases of similar nature. The process of determining what is law with regard for prior cases with identical sets of circumstances is known as *stare decisis,* or "adhere to the decisions."

It is possible that the courts may rule a law unenforceable because it is not specific enough or it is too vague. Following is an example of a California law that has been the subject of many applications and has been interpreted by some courts as being too vague, therefore unconstitutional:

[2]Donald R. Taft and Ralph W. England, Jr., *Criminology,* 4th ed. (New York: Macmillan Co., 1964), p. 21.

> CPC (California Penal Code) Sec. 650½. Injuring person or property of another. A person who willfully and wrongfully commits any act which seriously injures the person or property of another, or which seriously disturbs or endangers the public peace or health, or which openly outrages public decency, or who willfully and wrongfully, in any manner, verbal or written, uses another's name for accomplishing lewd or licentious purposes, whether such purposes are accomplished or not, or who willfully and wrongfully uses another's name in any manner that will affect, or have a tendency to affect the moral reputation of the person whose name is used, generally, or in the estimation of the person or persons to whom it is so used, or who with intent of accomplishing any lewd or licentious pupose, whether such purpose is accomplished or not, personifies any person other than himself, or who causes or procures any other person or persons to identify him, or to give assurance that he is any other person than himself to aid or assist him to accomplish any lewd or licentious purpose, for which no other punishment is expressly prescribed by this code, is guilty of a misdemeanor. (1921)

The exact origin of criminal laws vary from law to law. There are basically two types of crimes: *mala in se* and *mala prohibita.* The former is interpreted as including those crimes that are "evil in themselves," and the latter is made "evil by law." The *mala in se* crimes are those against the person and certain property offenses that violate the rules of common decency, the various religious tenets, and those that pose a threat to the health and safety of the community. Without risking criticism, we could list the following as *mala in se* crimes: criminal homicide, burglary, theft, armed robbery, child molestation, forcible rape.

In the areas of personal opinions, religious beliefs, and local standards of human conduct, some individuals would automatically include among the *mala in se* crimes the so-called crimes without victims, such as certain types of sexual conduct, use of drugs and alcohol, gambling, prostitution. Others would categorically defend individual rights to participate in all of those activities as a matter of free choice, while still others would select some as evil in themselves and others as evil only because the law says that they are evil.

Mala prohibita crimes are those which are "made evil by law," or not wrongs except that the law says they are wrong. This category of crimes might include such offenses as motor vehicle violations, building code violations, personal sexual conduct between consenting adults in private places, gambling, off-track betting in places where on-track betting is legal, nonpayment of certain taxes, and some types of consumer fraud.

Some criminal laws originated with personal wrongs. Before our modern criminal justice system evolved, acts of personal violence, ravishment, or theft of another person's property were a personal matter and called for the victim or a member of his or her family to seek retribution.

The original theory was "an eye for an eye and a tooth for a tooth" or similar attitude. However, the avenger was not always capable of taking action with the desired results. He sometimes suffered additional injuries of person or loss of property. He was forced to seek aid, sometimes from "vigilante" groups of his peers who organized for their own self-protection. At other times the avenger was obliged to employ professional soldiers of fortune or other professionals to handle his job with dispatch.

The next step in the evolving process was for the people to call upon the government to provide law enforcement and protective services. Today the professional government law enforcement agents are trained and capable, and they investigate the alleged violations, identify and apprehend the offenders, and hail them before the courts for appropriate punitive action.

Retribution through the criminal courts is in the form of fines or imprisonment or both. The fine money goes into the public funds because a violation of criminal law is a wrong against the state or the people as a whole. If the victim wishes to seek personal financial recompense, he must then go to the civil courts and institute a tort action, a personal matter. The goal in a tort action is to receive financial retribution or for the court to order the wrongdoers to perform or to refrain from performing a specific act.

Some criminal laws have been created because of an emotional reaction to indignities foisted upon helpless and unsuspecting victims. Other criminal laws had their origins in the religious and social mores of the community. These offenses are largely those that would be found in the *mala in se* category.

Another category of offenses are those that arose out of a conflict of interest among different special interest groups, or those that are legislated to fulfill a basic need to aid in expediting the smoother functioning of government rules and regulations. These laws most frequently fall into the *mala prohibita* type of offenses.

LAW AS A SOCIAL FORCE

Criminal laws are used as a means of controlling human behavior positively—rather than negatively—by publishing the law and the punishments for violations of the law. Hopefully, such publication will cause a general awareness of the law, and many people will make their own private decisions not to participate in conduct that would be in violation of the laws. Individuals have the freedom to decide whether they will break the rules of society, and many do just that, as they have the same freedom to decide not to break the rules.

Mores, customs, taboos, religious codes, moral and ethical standards, habit, traditions, and everyday behavior are all social forces. Law is another social force. The difference lies in the control of behavior that is contrary to law, and how the violator is dealt with by the government rather than private sources of control.

Peer pressures work on individuals to break the law and other forces are at work among peers to make them want to comply with the law. Sometimes the rewards are greater in the eyes of the offender to commit a crime than the reward would be for not committing the crime. Consider the tremendous pressures at work favoring the use of marihuana and other behavior modification substances, such as drugs and alcohol, certain language styles, manner of dress (or undress), antisocial behavior, and incorrigibility toward parents and other symbols of institutional control, authority figures. Fear of criticism by one's peers may overpower any less personal fear of apprehension and punishment, which may seem more remote and less personal. In fact, there may be a feeling that even though an act is against the law, there will be no punishment or that it will be minimal and far less to fear than ostracism by one's friends. When the controls are removed, the violator literally goes berserk in his or her efforts to yield to peer pressures on all sides and to express emancipation.

The stigmata of being labeled "criminal" or "thief" or "child molester" may cause such trauma for the offender or would-be offender that the mere fear of being found out serves as an effective social control. Fear in itself is a powerful force. On the other hand, the "stigmata" might serve as a badge of skill or courage and be sought by some offenders, such as in some violent street gangs which require initiates to perform some sort of violence, such as assault upon a police officer, in order to prove its accomplishment. The town "bully" doesn't get to enjoy the reputation unless he gets to beat someone senseless once in a while to perpetuate his "social image."

Bloch and Geis discuss this phenomenon in *Man, Crime, and Society.*

> Criminal law is the crucial element in the specification of human behavior. In many ways, individuals learn, though not always in detail, what the law expects of them and what they may and may not do. Recognition of the sanctions contained within the law may affect their behavior and personality in a variety of ways. This does not necessarily indicate, in the classic philosophical view of Thomas Hobbes, that all individuals function because of fear of the law. It does suggest, however, that an awareness of the law provides restraints and incentives to perform in a specified manner, even if, for some reason, the law may be distasteful. How law makes its impact depends upon given individuals and the particular qualities, but that the law operates as a significant social force can hardly be questioned.[3]

[3]Herbert A. Bloch and Gilbert Geis, *Man, Crime, and Society,* 2d ed. (New York: Random House, 1970), pp. 21–22.

The imminence of crime and criminal behavior in the United States or in any other country was explained by Emile Durkheim in his *Rules of Sociological Methods:*

> There is no phenomenon that presents more indisputably all the symptoms of normality, since it appears closely connected with the conditions of all collective life.... What is normal, simply, is the existence of criminality, provided that it attains and does not exceed, for each social type, a certain level, which it is perhaps not impossible to fix in conformity with the preceding rules.... To classify crime among the phenomena of normal sociology ... is to affirm that it is a factor in public health, an integral part of all healthy societies.[4]

Whether to accept or reject Durkheim's point of view is a matter of personal choice. The fact is that his statement has proved to be true at least four thousand years to date, and at the time of this writing there appears to be no spectacular change in sight.

Consider, also, Quinney's statement on the existence of crime in society:

> Crime is such an essential part of society that a society without crime is inconceivable. As long as men make laws, there will be crime. The forms of crime, to be certain, will change as human values change. But as long as men continue to value and preserve, condone and condemn, behavior will be labeled as criminal. And as long as a society includes as one of its cherished values some measure of individual freedom, there will be violations of the criminal law. A crimeless society could only be one that is static and unchanging, one in which persons cease to value and to aspire, and a society more totalitarian in control that we would want to imagine.[5]

IMPLICATIONS OF CRIMINAL STATISTICS

The student, the academician, the police practitioner, and the concerned private citizen are all impressed in some way by statistics on crimes and criminals. Statistical reports are essential to virtually every discussion and study of the problem of crime. Statistical indices reflect trends, identify specific problems, report tabulated facts about crimes and the people who commit them. It is extremely important that any set of statistics, no matter how valid or reliable, be considered with certain reservations. There are wide varieties of policies and practices involved in the input process, and these must all be taken into account when making analyses and comparisons.

One of the most reliable sources of criminal statistics in the United States that deals in nationwide computations and comparisons is the annual publication of the Federal Bureau of Investigation, *The Uniform Crime Re-*

[4]Emile Durkheim, *Rules of Sociological Methods* (Glencoe, Ill.: The Free Press, 1950), p. 68.

[5]Richard Quinney, *The Problem of Crime* (New York: Dodd, Mead, & Co., 1970), p. 202.

ports. Designated in 1929 by the International Association of Chiefs of Police (IACP) as the central clearing house for criminal statistics, the FBI has continuously reported comprehensive statistics of crimes reported to the police, persons arrested for criminal offenses, and a variety of related figures, summaries, analyses, charts, and graphs concerning the incidence of criminal offenses in the United States. The *Reports* also contain some information on the personnel strength of the various police departments and related information concerning their activities.

The law enforcement and investigative agencies reporting represent approximately 98 percent of the total number of agencies in the country.[6] The Bureau provides assistance in the preparation of the reports and the compilation of the statistics to assure maximum accuracy and complete information based on the data available to each agency.

The principal data report in this publication is known as the Crime Index. The Crime Index consists of eight types of offenses, which do not necessarily represent the crimes that one might consider the most serious in the legal or moral sense. The criteria for selecting this list of offenses were their likelihood of being reported to the police and the consistency and accuracy with which they would be reported. The Crime Index represents those crimes that are most likely to be reported to the police. They are: (1) criminal homicide, (2) forcible rape, (3) robbery, (4) aggravated assault, (5) burglary or breaking and entering, (6) theft of property valued $50 and over, (7) auto theft, and (8) arson.

A closer examination of the Crime Index offenses requires some definition of terms, principally because each state and local jurisdictions within each state may have variations in the structure of the laws. For example, theft of property valued over $50 is a felony in some states and a misdemeanor in others. To complicate matters further, the theft laws vary so much that there are some items such as firearms and automobiles that are felonies regardless of their market value. Other items such as fruits and vegetables that may be valued at $50 are the object of grand theft when stolen, while $50 worth of lumber might be considered petty theft, a misdemeanor. The FBI lists are paraphrased here.

Criminal Homicide These are murder and nonnegligent homicides that include willful, unlawful killing of a human as distinguished from negligent causes of death. They exclude accidental or justifiable homicides.

Forcible Rape Forcible rape includes rape by force, assault to rape, and attempted rape. Excluded from this category are those acts classified as rape when the female is under a specific age and the act of sexual intercourse occurs, in this case usually by consent of both participants.

[6]"Crime in the United States 1977," *FBI Uniform Crime Reports,* p. 4.

Robbery Taking of something of value from another person or from the immediate presence of that person through means of force or fear is robbery. A weapon may or may not be used. The element of fear for imminent loss of life or safety must be present.

Aggravated Assault An assault may be classified as aggravated whether or not a weapon is used. This classification of assault may be determined by the very nature of the weapon used, such as a loaded gun or knife capable of causing harm; or the method in which an object not normally considered a weapon is used, such as a chair leg wielded as a club. The assault may also be classified as aggravated by the nature and extent of injury that is inflicted during the assault, such as a blow with a fist to the head of the victim who sustains a fractured skull.

Burglary Burglary generally involves breaking and entering or at least a surreptitious entry by means of a tool or nonauthorized key. But this classification also includes an entry of specified buildings and places without force when, at the moment of entry, the perpetrator entertains the *intent* to steal something or to commit some felony.

Theft, $50 and Over Market value is used to determine which items fall into this category. Excluded from this classification are embezzlement (committed by a trusted relative or employee and not always reported to the police) and theft by means of fraudulent checks and credit cards.

Auto Theft Auto theft includes the temporary or permanent taking of an automobile. Certain unauthorized use of a vehicle in unusual situations may be excluded.

Arson (Added to the Crime Index in January 1979, as the eighth category.) Arson is the willful unlawful burning of real or personal property with malicious intent or intent to defraud an insurer. It does not include unintentional burning or deliberate burning under lawful conditions.

When you examine the *Uniform Crime Reports* for any given year, you will find that offenses are also broken down into Parts I and II. The Part I classification is based on offenses reported to the police. It includes the Crime Index offenses plus the balance of *thefts* including those of items valued at less than $50. The Part II classification, although reported in sequence to Part I and along with the Crime Index, has a distinct difference from the other two. The Crime Index and Part I are computed on the basis of the offenses actually *reported* to the police, whether or not the cases are solved and/or arrests are made. The Part II classification is a compilation of *persons arrested* for the listed offenses. There is not attempt to report those offenses that occur but for which no arrests are made in Part II offenses in the *Uniform Crime Reports.* An increase or decrease in the number of any category of crime in this classification is just a reflection in the change in the number of arrests, nothing more.

The Part II crimes include: forgery and counterfeiting, fraud, embezzlement, stolen property (buying, receiving, and possessing), vandalism, weapons (carrying and possessing), prostitution, commercialized vice, sex offenses, narcotic and drug offenses, gambling, offenses against the family or children, driving while under the influence (alcohol or drugs), liquor law violations, drunkenness, disorderly conduct, vagrancy, other state and local laws not covered elsewhere, and the juvenile detentions (or detention and release) for violation of curfew or loitering and runaway.

Keep in mind the fact that the Part II list in the *Uniform Crime Reports* includes only the number of arrests made, not the number of crimes committed or reported to the police. By reading the list, it becomes apparent that the variables are so numerous that it would be virtually impossible to compile a list of offenses committed or reported in each category, as the *Reports* show in the Crime Index. Embezzlements are not reported for fear that investors in the company might lose confidence in the company, and the offenders are usually trusted members of the company—sometimes high-ranking officers in a corporation—who are allowed to make restitution and not even suffer the loss of their jobs. Vice offenses are seldom reported to the police. Informants and undercover investigations bring many of the offenses to light, and police observation leads to arrest for many others. Assign more or less officers to a vice detail, and the department's vice arrest statistics will change appreciably.

Although various study groups and individuals have made recent proposals, recommending new procedures in reporting, such as questionnaires mailed directly to the people who are expected to accurately report the number of times they have been victimized by crime and whether or not they reported it to the police, or creation of a new agency with some "magic formula" for assuring greater accuracy in reporting than has been our experience to date, there is still no single source of true statistics on crime. All one has to do is to look at the list of offense categories, then do a little soul-searching and self-analysis to determine if we and our own friends, relatives, and neighbors haven't failed to report many criminal offenses within our own private universes.

In a *New York Times* article, "Fuzzy Crime Statistics,"[7] Richard Lyons reported that the FBI's annual report is considerably "distorted by the gross underreporting of crime to the police." Reporting on the survey conducted by the Census Bureau in conjunction with the 1970 census of the United

[7]A *New York Times* article of September 18, 1977, reprinted in *Readings In Criminal Justice 78–79* (Guilford. Conn.: Dushkin Publishing Co., 1978), p. 23.

States for the Justice Department, Lyons stated that the survey estimated "that for each serious criminal act that is reported, two or three others are not, in part because the victims believe that it is futile to file complaints." Lyons also stated that many white-collar crimes are never reported to the police, and "it has been estimated . . . that 90 percent of crimes involving computer manipulations are never reported."[8]

In an attempt to look at both sides of the argument concerning accuracy of police and other criminal justice agency reports, it is necessary to consider the fact that discretionary decisions are made by many individuals within—and outside—the justice system. Many people do not report crimes because of a forgive-and-forget philosophy. Families and neighborhoods are torn apart when criminal complaints are lodged. Some people do not trust the police. Some people lie to the police about crimes that never were committed, but that lead to insurance company reimbursements for losses that are reported as crimes. In order for a crime report to be prepared by the police, all of the evidence and information must be sufficient to establish the elements of the corpus delicti of a crime. A person's statement that he or she was the victim of a crime does not establish as a fact that a crime had actually occurred. Many crimes are not discovered. In some embezzlement cases that I have personally encountered, the method in which the crime was committed was so clever and confusing that evidence could not be collected to prove the offense, much less the guilt of the accused. Unless there is sufficient proof of guilt, prosecutors will decide not to prosecute because they know that it would be impossible to get a conviction in court. Sometimes guilty people are found innocent by juries, probably far more often than innocent people are found guilty in our fallible system of justice.

Following are charts taken from the *Uniform Crime Reports*. Figures 3–1 to 3–7 show crime trends of seven Crime Index offenses—murder (Figure 3–1), rape (Figure 3–2), robbery (Figure 3–3), assault (Figure 3–4), burglary (Figure 3–5), larceny (Figure 3–6), and auto theft (Figure 3–7)—between the census years 1960 to 1970 and the years 1973 through 1977. Overall crime trends are shown for the years 1968 to 1977 (Figures 3–8, 3–9) and for 1973 to 1977 (Figure 3–10).

Because these figures will obviously become more outdated each year (as they are at the time of publication), they are included in the text to show trends, or patterns of change, that you may wish to discuss with your fellow students or instructor. Using this information, you should contact your local police agency and ask to review their most recent statistical reports. By comparing the information you now have at your disposal, you will be able to determine trends for the nation and for your own jurisdiction.

[8]A *New York Times* article of September 18, 1977, reprinted in *Readings In Criminal Justice 78–79* (Guilford, Conn.: Dushkin Publishing Co., 1978), p. 23.

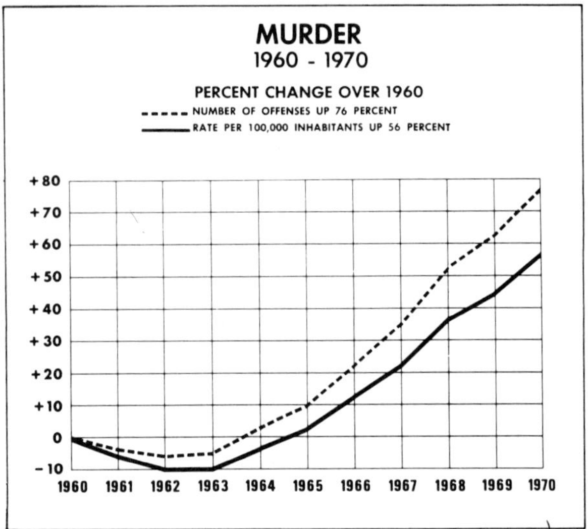

FBI CHART

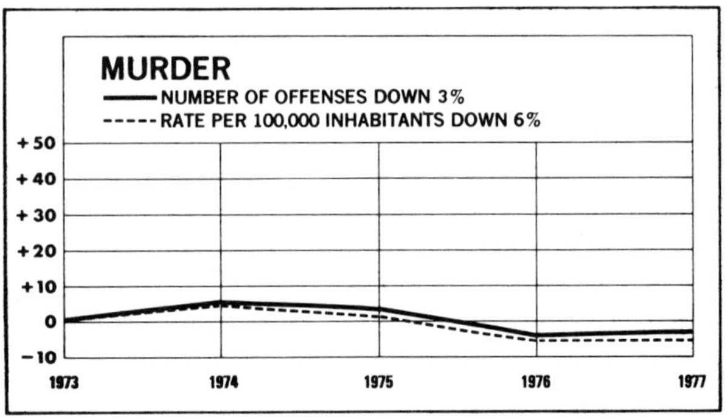

FBI CHART

Figure 3-1 Trends in Crimes of Murder, 1960–1977.

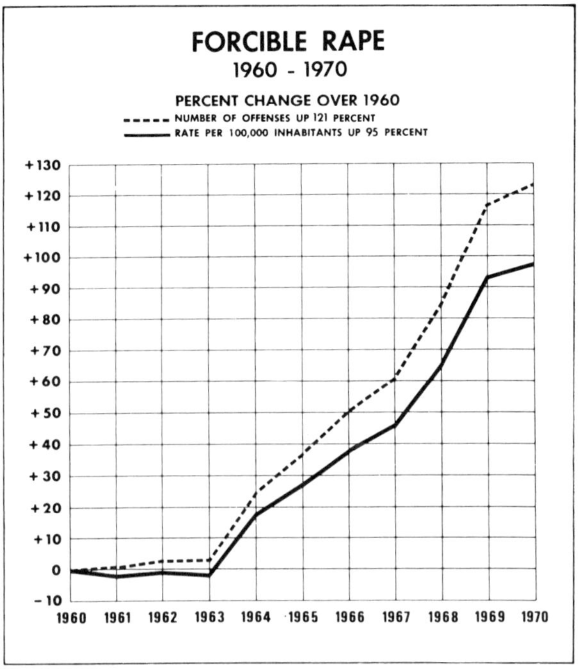

FBI CHART

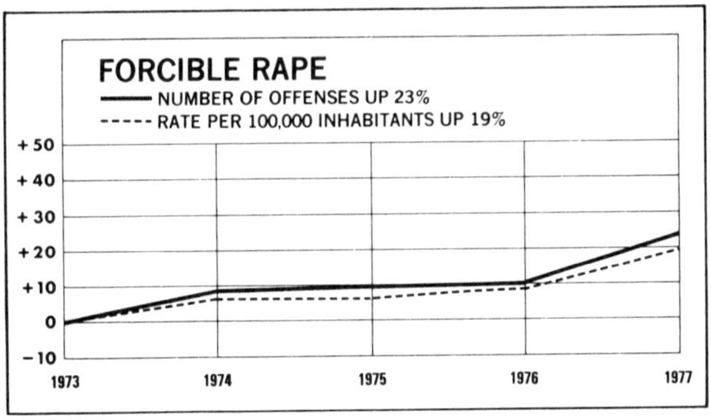

FBI CHART

Figure 3-2 Trends in Crimes of Rape, 1960–1977.

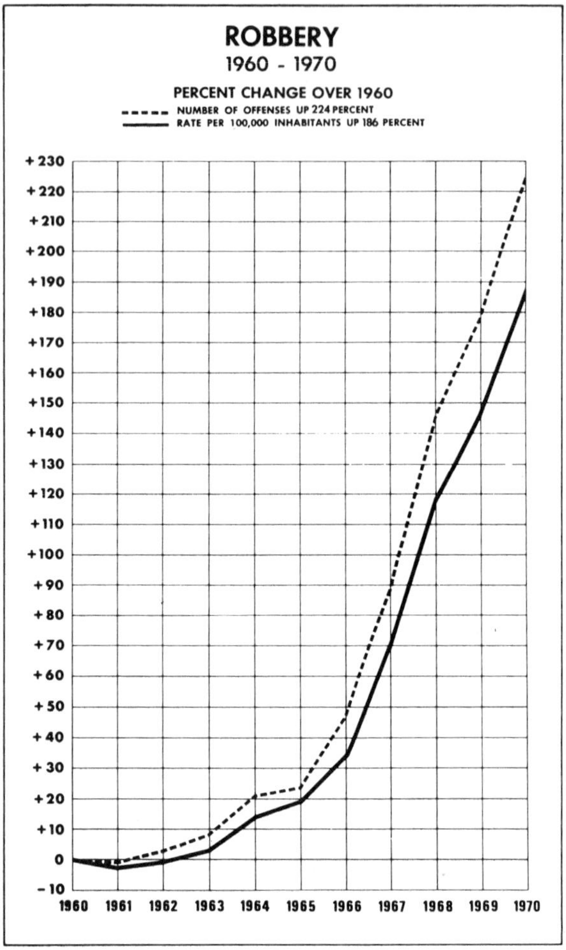

FBI CHART

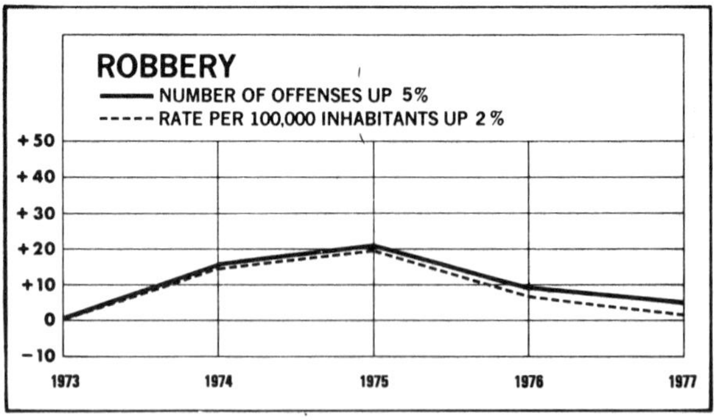

FBI CHART

Figure 3-3 Trends in Crimes of Robbery, 1960–1977.

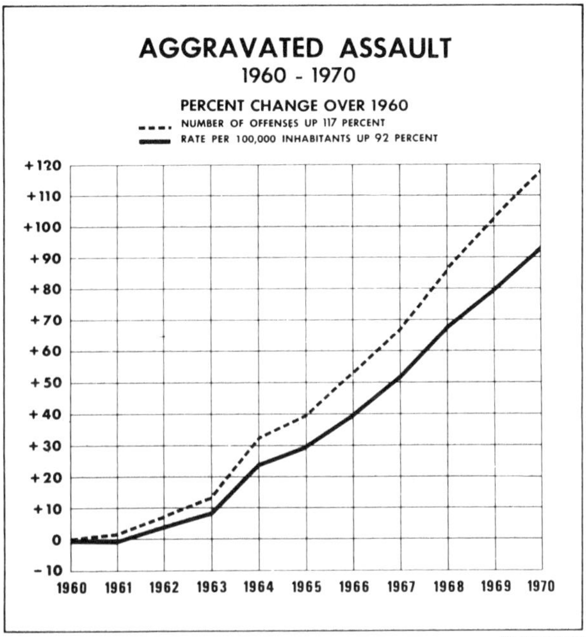

FBI CHART

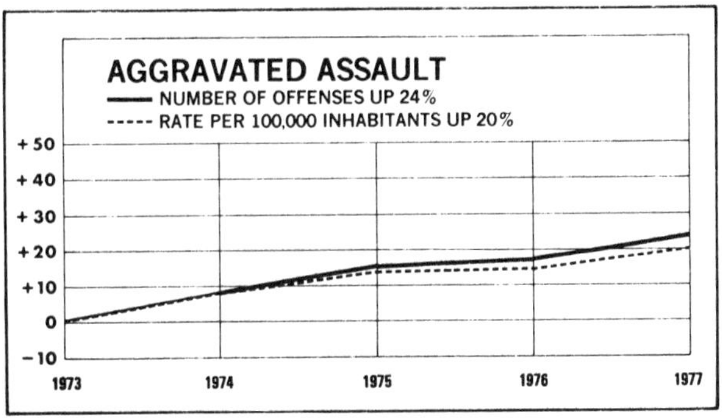

FBI CHART

Figure 3-4 Trends in Crimes of Assault, 1960–1977.

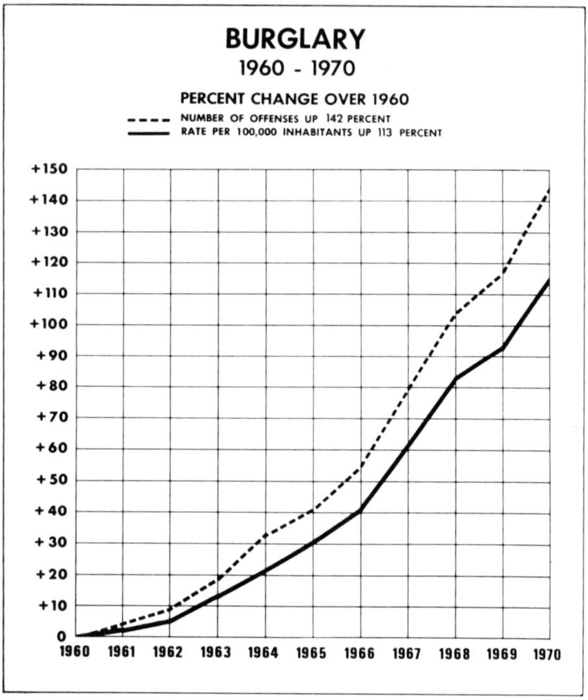

FBI CHART

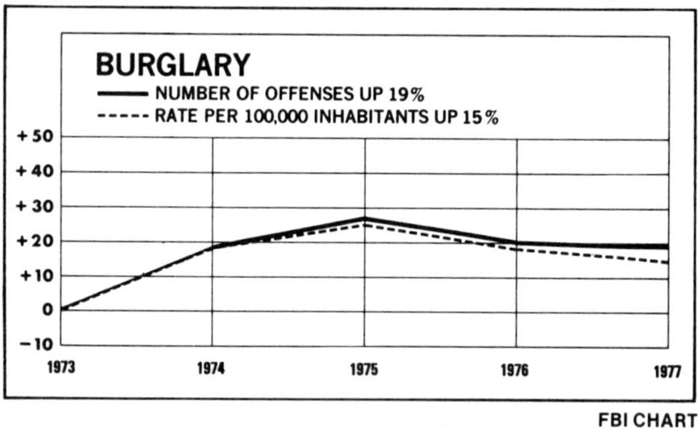

FBI CHART

Figure 3-5 Trends in Crimes of Burglary, 1960–1977.

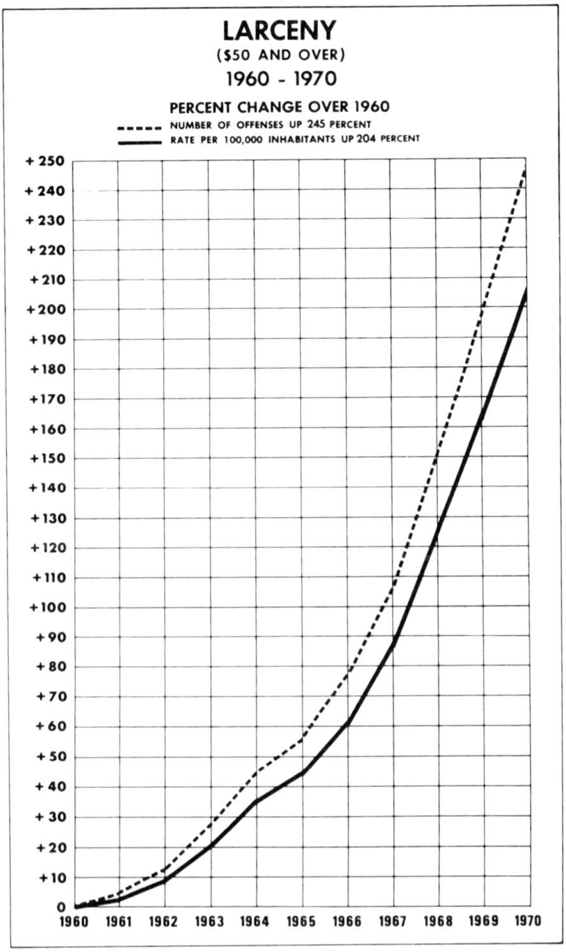

FBI CHART

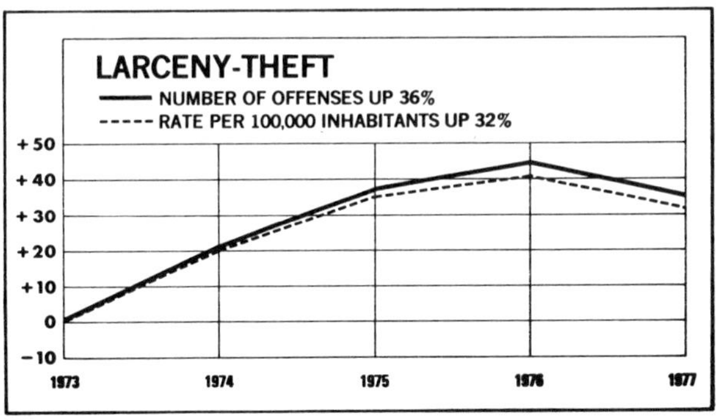

FBI CHART

Figure 3-6 Trends in Crimes of Larceny, 1960–1977.

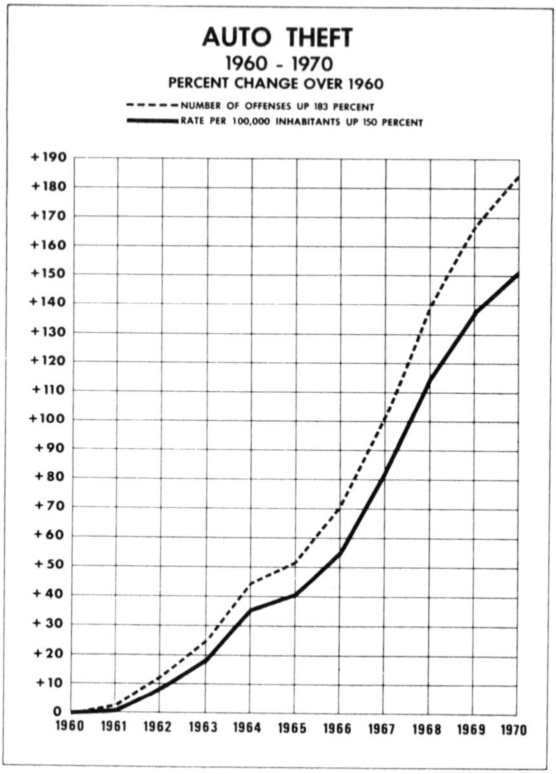

FBI CHART

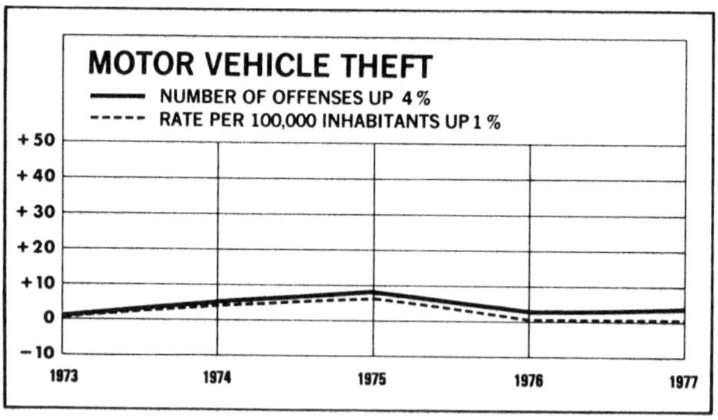

FBI CHART

Figure 3-7 Trends in Crimes of Auto Theft, 1960–1977.

Population [1]	Crime Index total	Violent [2] crime	Property [2] crime	Murder and non-negligent man-slaughter	Forcible rape	Robbery	Aggra-vated assault	Burglary	Larceny-theft	Motor vehicle theft
Number of offenses:										
1968—199,399,000	6,720,200	595,010	6,125,200	13,800	31,670	262,840	286,700	1,858,900	3,482,700	783,600
1969—201,385,000	7,410,900	661,870	6,749,000	14,760	37,170	298,850	311,090	1,981,900	3,888,600	878,500
1970—203,235,298	8,098,000	738,820	7,359,200	16,000	37,990	349,860	334,970	2,205,000	4,225,800	928,400
1971—206,212,000	8,588,200	816,500	7,771,700	17,780	42,260	387,700	368,700	2,399,300	4,424,200	948,200
1972—208,230,000	8,248,800	834,900	7,413,900	18,670	46,850	376,290	393,090	2,375,500	4,151,200	887,200
1973—209,851,000	8,718,100	875,910	7,842,200	19,640	51,400	384,220	420,650	2,565,500	4,347,900	928,800
1974—211,392,000	10,253,400	974,720	9,278,700	20,710	55,400	442,400	456,210	3,039,200	5,262,500	977,100
1975—213,124,000	11,256,600	1,026,280	10,230,300	20,510	56,090	464,970	484,710	3,252,100	5,977,700	1,000,500
1976—214,659,000	11,304,800	986,580	10,318,200	18,780	56,730	420,210	490,850	3,089,800	6,270,800	957,600
1977—216,332,000	10,935,800	1,009,500	9,926,300	19,120	63,020	404,850	522,510	3,052,200	5,905,700	968,400
Rate per 100,000 inhabitants: [3]										
1968	3,370.2	298.4	3,071.8	6.9	15.9	131.8	143.8	932.3	1,746.6	393.0
1969	3,680.0	328.7	3,351.3	7.3	18.5	148.4	154.5	984.1	1,930.9	436.2
1970	3,984.5	363.5	3,621.0	7.9	18.7	172.1	164.8	1,084.9	2,079.3	456.8
1971	4,164.7	396.0	3,768.8	8.6	20.5	188.0	178.8	1,163.5	2,145.5	459.8
1972	3,961.4	401.0	3,560.4	9.0	22.5	180.7	188.8	1,140.8	1,993.6	426.1
1973	4,154.4	417.4	3,737.0	9.4	24.5	183.1	200.5	1,222.5	2,071.9	442.6
1974	4,850.4	461.1	4,389.3	9.8	26.2	209.3	215.8	1,437.7	2,489.5	462.2
1975	5,281.7	481.5	4,800.2	9.6	26.3	218.2	227.4	1,525.9	2,804.8	469.4
1976	5,266.4	459.6	4,806.8	8.8	26.4	195.8	228.7	1,439.4	2,921.3	446.1
1977	5,055.1	466.6	4,588.4	8.8	29.1	187.1	241.5	1,410.9	2,729.9	447.6

[1] Populations are Bureau of the Census provisional estimates as of July 1, except April 1, 1970, census.

[2] Violent crime is offenses of murder, forcible rape, robbery, and aggravated assault. Property crime is offenses of burglary, larceny-theft, and motor vehicle theft.

[3] Crime rates calculated prior to rounding number of offenses.

Figure 3-8 Crime Index, 1968–1977.

National Crime, Rate, and Percent Change

Crime Index offenses	Estimated crime 1977		Percent change over 1976		Percent change over 1973		Percent change over 1968	
	Number	Rate per 100,000 inhabitants	Number	Rate per 100,000 inhabitants	Number	Rate per 100,000 inhabitants	Number	Rate per 100,000 inhabitants
Total	10,935,800	5,055.1	−3.3	−4.0	+25.4	+21.7	+62.7	+50.0
Violent	1,009,500	466.6	+2.3	+1.5	+15.3	+11.8	+69.7	+56.4
Property	9,926,300	4,588.4	−3.8	−4.5	+26.6	+22.8	+62.1	+49.4
Murder	19,120	8.8	+1.8	....	−2.6	−6.4	+38.6	+27.5
Forcible rape	63,020	29.1	+11.1	+10.2	+22.6	+18.8	+99.0	+83.0
Robbery	404,850	187.1	−3.7	−4.4	+5.4	+2.2	+54.0	+42.0
Aggravated assault	522,510	241.5	+6.4	+5.6	+24.2	+20.4	+82.2	+67.9
Burglary	3,052,200	1,410.9	−1.2	−2.0	+19.0	+15.4	+64.2	+51.3
Larceny-theft	5,905,700	2,729.9	−5.8	−6.6	+35.8	+31.8	+69.6	+56.3
Motor vehicle theft	968,400	447.6	+1.1	+.3	+4.3	+1.1	+23.6	+13.9

FBI CHART

Figure 3-9 National Crime, Rate, and Percent Change, 1968–1977.

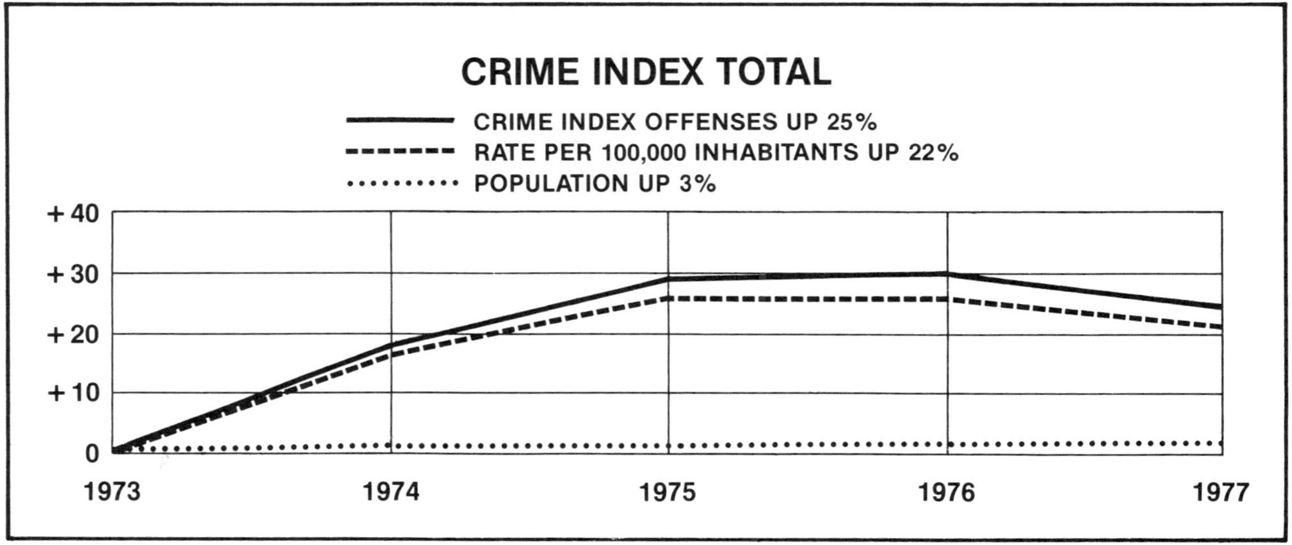

Figure 3-10 Crime Index Total, 1973–1977.

INTEGRITY OF REPORTS

At best, the statistics reflected in the *Uniform Crime Reports* and any other collection of indices represent only those numbers that are reported to the FBI, which acts as the clearing house. The user of the Report is entitled to expect each reporting agency to report with integrity and consistency. However, not all of the crimes committed are reported *to* the police, and there is always the possibility that not all of the known offenses are reported *by* that same police agency. It is pretty much like the situation in which you tell someone to stand at a street corner and report to *you* on how many automobiles pass that corner during a specified time span. The report you receive depends on many variables, and what you receive may be an exact count of the number of automobiles that passed. If you assign the same individual to perform the same task daily and give you a similar report at the end of each period of surveillance, you could reasonably assume that the method of counting and reporting would at least be consistent, and that any gross changes in the statistics would be a reasonably reliable reflection of the actual changes in the traffic flow. Audits are made and a variety of techniques are utilized by the FBI in an advisory capacity, and the agencies themselves are dependent upon the same statistics for a variety of purposes. All of these factors serve to assure the integrity of the report.

What purposes do the Crime Index and various components of the *Uniform Crime Reports* actually serve? They show trends and, sometimes, significant changes in patterns in certain offenses and arrests in specific cities or counties or portions of the country. Increases or decreases in crime occurrences may reflect social changes, variations in criminal activity, and possibly the effectiveness of the police.

Various circumstances in a police department may change substantially and have such a distorting effect on a reporting system that it may be difficult to assess the true situation. For example, a new police chief may drastically change policies and investigative priorities to such an extent that an unusual emphasis on burglaries might lead to a greater number of arrests and more stolen property returned to the victims. Publicity for phenomenal success in the clearance and recovery rate might cause citizen groups to focus on that specific crime, perhaps even to the solicitation of reports to the police. Following his successful operation for a few months, the chief might be alarmed to find that the number of reported burglaries per month is tripled. Does this reflect a greater incidence of crime in our chief's city? Your guess is as valid as mine.

Other variables in the *Uniform Crime Reports* reporting system may be a change in the efficiency of the statistician, a follow-through system to verify that crimes investigated by the officers are reported to the department, an improvement in the system of preparing reports, and the enforcement policies of the department and the individual officers. With all of these variables in mind, it can generally be expected that there is even some constancy to the variables, and the statistics in the *Uniform Crime Reports* may be used with confidence, although not blind faith.

Some observers express more serious concern for the reliability of the *Uniform Crime Reports.* Taft and England list "several reasons for the unreliability of criminal statistics in the United States":

1. Diversity of definitions of the crimes within the fifty states, the federal government, and the District of Columbia.
2. Diversity of sources, consisting of some eight thousand reporting agencies.
3. Undiscovered crime. Exactly how many crimes occur is impossible to determine.
4. Unreported crime, although it has been discovered.
5. Reported crime that is unreported by the police.[9]

Taft and England also observed in their discussion of the *Uniform Crime Reports* that the statistics carry with them no guarantee of accuracy; in fact, the report itself makes that point clear in its introductory remarks. Another admonition to the reader of the Reports is that comparisons of crime rates between cities can be misleading. According to Taft and England, "The configurational nature of criminal activities is not apparent in published statistics (many crimes are committed concurrently, such as assault and robberies, burglaries and thefts that are reported as only one crime)." They also state:

> The real significance of crime in American culture cannot be shown from FBI statistics. Labor racketeering, organized traffic in illicit liquor, prostitution, gambling, narcotics, and stolen goods, and the intricate inroads of crooked commercial and financial practices in legitimate business are far more costly in time, money, and social well-being than the piddling amounts stolen by honest thieves and robbers.[10]

Richard Quinney's opinion of crime reporting and its validity appears in his publication *The Problem of Crime.*

> Any given violation of the criminal law likely carries with it a certain probability that it will come to the attention of law enforcement agencies. The probability that an offense will not be reported or recorded is related to a number of factors: (1) Some offenses are known only to the offender and, thus, are not likely to be reported by the offender. (2) Because of a lack of knowledge of the criminal law, victims and witnesses will not report criminal violations. (3) Witnesses to an offense may not want to report the offense because of inconvenience, embarrassment, fear or lack of interest in law enforcement. (4) The victim or witness may fear the possibility of being implicated in the violation or other violations if investigated. (5) The victim or witness may fear reprisal if the criminal offense is reported. (6) Friends and relatives may try to protect the

[9]Taft and England, *Criminology,* pp. 46–48.

[10]Taft and England, *Criminology,* p. 58.

offender and, therefore, not report the offense. (7) The victim may fear unfavorable publicity and embarrassment. (8) Social values and public opinion do not favor the full enforcement of certain laws. (9) Some criminal offenses because of their nature are not readily visible to the general public or law enforcement agencies. (10) Law enforcement agencies may wish to conceal some criminal offenses.[11]

THE JUSTICE SYSTEM AND ITS RELATIONSHIP TO THE CRIME PROBLEM

The three major components of the system of criminal justice have an extensive repertoire of relationships to the problem of crime in the nation and within the individual jurisdictions of the various agencies. Although they will be discussed in depth in later chapters, perhaps a brief review of the responsibilities of some of those agencies will provide a base from which the study may be carried forward.

Law Enforcement and the Crime Problem

The law enforcement component has a responsibility to make every effort to (1) prevent crime, (2) repress the incidence of criminal activities, (3) identify and apprehend the individuals who violate the laws, and (4) assist in the presentation of testimony and evidence to assure the accused a fair trial with conviction of the guilty as a goal. The activities of the average police officer are by no means limited to these responsibilities, but these are the most closely related to the problem of crime, our topic for this chapter.

Crime prevention involves direct contact with criminal law violators and potential violators, and an attempt to divert them into lawful activities. The likelihood of success in crime prevention is greater with the young child who has not yet developed static behavior patterns or attitudes favorable to criminal activities. Field contacts by the patrol or community relations officer provide many opportunities for the officers to discuss the disadvantages of a life of crime, the likelihood of apprehension, and negative effects of criminal conduct on one's self-image. Because acts committed by juveniles do not constitute criminal acts, dealing positively with juvenile delinquents and near delinquents and diverting them into law-abiding behavior patterns constitute crime prevention.

Repression of crime is accomplished by reducing the opportunity for persons to commit crimes. Aiding private home occupants and businessmen in rendering their residences and places of business burglary and theft resistant is one method of reducing crime opportunities. Vigilant patrol and creation of a feeling of police omnipresence is essential to alter the plans of some persons who are intent upon committing crimes. Field interviews of

[11]Quinney, *The Problem of Crime,* p. 116.

individuals whose presence and activities on the streets indicate to the officer the need to ascertain the lawful nature of their activities are a regular crime repressive police function.

Along with the diligent patrol and frequent contact with the people in his district on a continuous basis to prevent and repress the incidence of crime, a third function must likewise be conscientiously performed: that of identification and apprehension of those individuals who do commit crimes. Exercising his professional prerogatives of using his discretion in making decisions as to priorities and other matters of judgment, the law officer must enforce the law as intended by the legislature. It is the police officer or investigator of other agencies of the law enforcement sector of the criminal justice system who is responsible for introducing the individual into the system once he has been identified as the person responsible for a criminal act. Careful inquiry and skillful collection of evidence often leads to the identification of the persons responsible for a crime. In order that the person be assured of his constitutionally guaranteed rights to a speedy and fair trial, he should be brought before the court and *proven* guilty.

The fourth item listed above—that of assisting the court—is a continuation of the law enforcement or investigative agency responsibility for the arrest. The case is by no means closed until a disposition has been made on the charges. Although the courts component now has the responsibility for processing the case through certain procedural steps, it is still up to the investigating and arresting officers to present their evidence and testimony and to assist the court in assuring the accused a fair trial with the conviction as a goal.

The Courts and the Crime Problem

As the processing component of the system of justice administration, the courts have as their primary objective the fair and objective adjudication of the allegations. In accordance with the Constitution of the United States and the respective states of the nation, along with laws prescribing correct procedure, this component is actually involved much earlier than the time of arrest.

As an officer of the court, the prosecuting attorney advises and assists the law enforcement agency in the investigative process and development of the evidence. He is a police legal advisor in most cases, but in some instances he may actually direct the investigation, such as in major fraud situations involving many local jurisdictions.

In his role as prosecutor, it is the responsibility of the district attorney to present affidavits and witnesses to the judge who sits as a magistrate and makes a determination as to whether there is sufficient cause for the issuance of a search or arrest warrant or a complaint charging an individual with an alleged crime. Because of his unique position as an officer of the court, it is the prosecutor's responsibility to evaluate the case and make his own decision whether to bring the matter before the magistrate in the first place. Once he initiates the action and an individual is to be processed through the courts, the prosecutor assumes the burden of proving guilt of the accused beyond all reasonable doubt. He is also charged with keeping a timetable to assure the accused a speedy trial, the right to be faced by his accuser, and all of the other rights of the accused, who is innocent until he is *proven* guilty.

The court has a responsibility for maintaining schedules that will efficiently keep the cases moving along as required within specific time constraints. The presiding judge must handle the calendar and schedule hearings and trials in the various divisions of the court to assure a minimum delay. He must supervise counsel to the extent that there is no manipulation of the court for an illegal or improper advantage to one side or the other in the adversary system. As a magistrate, the judge determines whether there is sufficient cause for issuance of a warrant, then later in his role as judge, the same man or woman sits on the bench and determines whether the warrant was acted upon within the law and if the evidence or testimony is to be admitted at all.

In 1967 the President's Commission on Law Enforcement and the Administration of Justice reported on its findings during an appraisal of the courts in our nation:

> The Commission has been shocked by what it has seen in some lower courts. It has seen cramped and noisy courtrooms, undignified and perfunctory procedures, and badly trained personnel. It has seen dedicated people who are frustrated by huge caseloads, by the lack of opportunity to examine cases carefully, and by the impossibility of devising constructive solutions to the problems of defendants. It has seen assembly-line justice.[12]

During the past few years, a new professional administrator has emerged on the court scene: the court administrator. Training in the law and court-related functions are part of the administrators' training, but they are also trained to handle the complex matters of budgeting, records-keeping, data-gathering and analysis, fiscal management, collecting and processing fines and other revenues, providing information, and juggling schedules. They manage physical space and facilities and supervise clerks, custodians, maintenance personnel, librarians, and various other staff. This is truly an important position to assure competence in the court's operation, but hardly one that calls for the talents and expertise of a judge.

Reform At the National Conference on Judiciary, March 11, 1971, at Williamsburg, Virginia, Chief Justice Warren Burger stated that the American system of criminal justice

[12]President's Commission on Law Enforcement and the Administration of Justice, *Challenge of Crime In A Free Society* (Washington, D.C.: U.S. Government Printing Office, 1967), p. 128.

in every phase—the police function, the prosecution and defense, the courts and the correctional machinery—is suffering from a severe case of deferred maintenance. By and large, this is true at the state, local and federal levels. The failure of our machinery is now a matter of common knowledge, fully documented by innumerable studies and surveys.

As a consequence of this deferred maintenance we see:

First, that the perpetrators of most criminal acts are not detected, arrested and brought to trial;

Second, those who are apprehended, arrested and charged are not tried promptly because we allow unconscionable delays that pervert both the right of the defendant and the public to a speedy trial of every criminal charge; and

Third, the convicted persons are not punished promptly after conviction because of delay in the appellate process.

Finally, even after the end of litigation, those who are senttenced to confinement are not corrected or rehabilitated, and the majority of them return to commit new crimes. The primary responsibility of judges, of course, is for the operation of the judicial machinery but this does not mean we can ignore the police function of the shortcomings of the correctional systems.[13]

The Bartered Plea The clogged and extremely overburdened courts in our system could be brought to an immediate and dramatic halt if all of the persons charged with any kind of a law violation from a minor traffic violation to the most serious felonies were simply to plead not guilty and ask for a trial. To ask for a jury trial would further compound the impossible situation. The courts place heavy reliance upon the process known as *plea bargaining* which treats conviction and the guilty plea as negotiable items that can be traded off as one would handle merchandise in a flea market. The process has been going on for many years and is as essential to the courts as a steam valve in a pressure cooker. Time and load factors add to the concern of the courts as well as legal time requirements between the various steps in the process of taking a case to court. Unless each case is disposed of in some manner as quickly as possible, a dozen more cases are stacked up in line waiting for a "speedy trial," as provided by the Constitution. There will be more discussion on this controversial but historical process in Chapter 8.

Corrections and the Crime Problem

Once an individual has been found guilty of some criminal offense and is moved on to the next step in the sequence, he enters the correction area of influence. Probation officers are involved in the judicial process and perform presentence investigations along with recommendations to the court as to what they believe will be a more appropriate method for dealing with the punishment and rehabilitation of the persons convicted of crimes. The authority for actually imposing the sentence is that of the judge, but he

[13]From *Addresses and Papers of the National Conference on the Judiciary, March 11-14, 1971 at Williamsburg, Virginia* (Washington, D.C.: Government Printing Office, 1971), pp. 10–11.

strongly weighs the recommendations of the probation officer. Once the judge has prescribed the sentence, the corrections component of the system assumes authority and responsibility.

The model penal code drafted by the American Law Institute has yet to be adopted in its entirety by any state, according to Project Director Charles L. Newman at the Center for Law Enforcement and Corrections at Pennsylvania State University. Sentencing and treatment provisions of that model code include the following:

- To prevent the commission of offenses.
- To promote the correction and rehabilitation of offenders.
- To safeguard offenders against excessive, disproportionate, or arbitrary punishments.
- To give fair warning of the nature of the sentences that may be imposed upon conviction of offense.
- To differentiate among offenders with a view to a just individualization in their treatment.
- To define, coordinate, and harmonize the powers, duties, and functions of the courts and of administrative officers and agencies responsible for dealing with offenders.
- To advance the use of generally accepted scientific methods and knowledge in the sentencing and treatment of offenders.[14]

The process of probation involves casework with individuals who have been determined by the courts as guilty of some criminal act. With the juvenile offender, the language is different because of the difference in juvenile court and probation procedures, but many of the techniques are similar. Essentially, the role of the probation officer is that of a change agent: to work with the offender to effect some change in the offender's habits and attitudes so that there is less likelihood that he will repeat his criminal or asocial activities. The individual is placed at liberty under the supervision of a caseworker, the probation officer.

Parole is quite similar to probation in working style and the objectives are similar. The principal difference is that the individual who is on probation may have served some time in a local or county jail but he has not been incarcerated for extended periods of time, as has the parolee. The process of parole is a conditional release from a correctional institution following a protracted period of imprisonment, from several months to several years. Both probation and parole are alternatives to imprisonment in an institution and the objective is to assist the convicted offender in adjusting to the socialized community life. Failure to successfully adjust to the environment may have been a contributing factor to the individual's commission of his crime, and the caseworker is charged with the responsibility of working with

[14]Center for Law Enforcement and Corrections, *Probation, Parole and Pardons: A Basic Course,* Training Module 6913 (University Park, Pa.: Pennsylvania State University, 1969), p. 9.

the individual to help him learn to cope with community living.

"But does it work?" one may ask. Complete success (whatever that is) is certainly unattainable, but the goal of the caseworker is to strive for maximization of results. Consider this statement in response to that question:

1. In spite of the fact probation and parole services have generally been poorly staffed and supported, about 75% of those placed on probation have not had their probation revoked.
2. In the case of adult parolees, out of 35% to 40% of those who have had their parole revoked, only one third return for the commission of new offenses.
3. According to usual estimates, the revokation rate on juvenile aftercare is somewhat higher than for adult parolees.
4. The above figures should be seen only as indicants of probable success.
5. Probation and parole have not been given a fair trial for the level of professional personnel and support for optimum programming has never been available.[15]

An alternate title for probation and parole may be *community-based treatment.* By using that title, the process may have greater significance, because it involves the offender and his/her socialization and/or reintegration into the community.

Figure 3-11 The Main Gate at the California Institute for Men, Chino.
Courtesy California Department of Corrections.

[15]Center for Law Enforcement and Corrections, *Probation, Parole and Pardon,* p. 13.

Institutional Corrections Most traditional of the institutions are the local city or county jails and the penitentiaries, or prisons. More recently the system has utilized smaller residential units, such as halfway houses, camps, and open units. The institutional directors are equally concerned with the two principal responsibilities of corrections—rehabilitation of the offender and safety to the community—and their responsibilities are multifaceted. The institution must maintain custody and control of the prisoners during their incarceration and must also provide educational, training, and counseling services to make a maximum effort toward their rehabilitation with a goal of a redirected crime-free mode of living.

The jails house a great many people who are innocent. They are being housed pending posting of bail or the final adjudication of their cases in court. Only after they have been proven guilty in court, or they have entered a plea of guilty, can they be considered convicted offenders. Their period of custody lasts from several days to several months, seldom longer than a year except in the case of consecutive sentences.

The residential treatment centers are halfway between the probation mode and that of incarceration. As a condition of probation or parole, depending on the individual's history, the offender is required to live at the center and to participate in the various individualized treatment programs. Such centers, which are located in the heart of the city rather than in some isolated spot miles out of town, serve as a base from which the residents may accomplish their reintegration into the community and at the same time receive the intensive treatment and counseling that may be prescribed in their individual programs.

The purpose for correctional institutions include the following:

1. To seek to limit confinement to persons actually requiring it, for only as long as they require it, and under conditions that are lawful and humane.
2. To afford both the community and the offender temporary and partial respite from each other in order to facilitate resolution of the crisis which led to commitment.
3. To make the confinement experience constructive and relevant to the ultimate goal of reintegrating the offender into the community and of preventing recidivism.
4. To educate the community and its agencies about the problems of reintegrating offenders in order to elicit their collaboration in carrying out specific rehabilitative efforts and in improving conditions which militate against such efforts.
5. To seek continual improvement in the system's capacity to achieve these ends.[16]

[16]Joint Commission on Correctional Manpower and Training, *Manpower and Training in Correctional Institutions* (Washington, D.C.: American Correctional Association, 1969), p. 36.

For the juvenile, generally persons under the age of eighteen, there are principally two basic types of institutions: detention and shelter. The detention facility is for temporary care and custody of a child who has committed a delinquent act in a physically restricting facility pending court disposition or the child's referral to another agency. The second type of juvenile facility is for dependent and neglected children and provides physical restricted custody pending return home or placement for care in another location, such as a foster home. The methods for redirection and reintegration of juveniles place a major emphasis on environmental modification, changes in peer influences, greater involvement with family and community, and individual casework.

The institution serves as a warehouse to store convicted criminals in a location that protects society from those individuals who are housed therein, and it meets the needs of those prescribed punishments that call for isolation from society for specified periods of time. Except for local jails, where little more than short-term physically restricting custody is possible, the longer-term institutions are responsible for reducing crime and delinquency through programs that provide for rehabilitation of the offenders. The task is monumental, and the risks for failure are great, but the most promising method of reducing the rate of recidivism—or repeat offenders—is through aggressive efforts to rehabilitate the offender.

Diversion from the Criminal Justice System Professionals in every component of the system frequently make discretionary decisions to divert the delinquent or criminal law violator away from the formality of the system as an alternative to introducing him to the system by arrest, or they may divert him into some program of treatment in lieu of punishment. The diversion practice takes place frequently with the juvenile offender encountered by the police officer. Estimates have been made that approximately one half of all juveniles who have committed delinquent acts are warned and released without further action. The officer or investigator who chooses to issue a warning instead of making an arrest is employing the diversion alternative.

The prosecutor and defense may stipulate with the consent of the court the provision that the accused person will seek psychiatric or medical help for his problem, which is considered a causative factor for his criminal behavior. The court may initiate the action and suspend or delay a sentence pending the defendant's referral and treatment by a detoxification or narcotics center, or an institution for mentally disordered sex offenders. Sometimes a referral is made by the court to a private organization, such as Alcoholics Anonymous, or to the care of a private physician or some other individual. All of these diversions from the criminal justice system serve to relieve some of the load that burdens the system to the point of almost total breakdown from the tremendous overload.

SUMMARY

This chapter actually consisted of two major parts. The first part addresed the awesome problem of the extent and wide-ranging scope of the occurrence of crime in the United States, beginning with a definition of crime and some of the background of our modern legal system. Law originated from the need of civilized society to have some form of ordered liberty to assure survival. From a matter that required personal retribution for an act of theft or personal violence, the idea that such acts were—in fact—wrongs against the entire society emerged as the prevailing philosophy as it is today. It made more sense to have specially employed policemen, prosecutors, judges, and corrections personnel handle the problems of crime. Along with the refinement of the law as a social force came the need for a more sophisticated system of crime definition and reporting, statistics and record-keeping. Crime Indexes are explained to an appreciable extent in the first part of this chapter.

In the second part of the chapter, we examined the problem of crime and its relationship to the various components of the criminal justice system. Crime prevention and protection of the people are the goals of all components of the system, and each of the many separate agencies within the components have interrelated objectives developed for the purpose of accomplishment of those goals. Law enforcement has prevention and repression of crime, identification and arrest of law violators, and provision of assistance to the courts to assure a fair trial and successful conviction of the guilty as its principal objectives regarding its role in the criminal law enforcement aspects of its responsibilities. The courts and the officers attached to the court as prosecutors, defense attorneys, as well as the judges themselves are pledged to uphold the laws and the constitutions of the federal and state governments. The principal thrust of corrections programs is toward the eventual rehabilitation of criminal law violators. As a system—however loosely affiliated many of these agencies may be—all of the agencies function surprisingly well. Many criticisms have been offered regarding the system, but so many have been supported both financially and politically that as a result, we have witnessed considerable improvement in the system.

EXERCISES AND STUDY QUESTIONS

1. What, specifically, are the elements necessary to classify an act as criminal?

2. How did Taft and England define crime?

3. What is the difference between *mala in se* and *mala ad pı* crimes? Give examples of ten crimes for each category.

4. List and discuss factors that underwrite the credibility of the Uniform Crime Reports, factors that adversely affect their credibility.

5. What is the meaning of *stare decisis?*

6. How would you describe law as a social force if you were asked?

7. What is Durkheim's theory regarding crime? Do you agree?

8. List the seven offenses that comprise the Crime Index. Why were those specific offenses chosen for the Index?

9. List some of the factors that might explain why the Crime Index report may not be completely accurate.

10. What may happen to the crime statistics in a city if there is a change in the public's support and confidence in their police department?

11. List and discuss each of the following:

(a) Law enforcement objectives regarding the crime problems.

(b) The role of the courts in relationship to the number of people who are arrested for criminal law violations and the likelihood that they will repeat their crimes some time in the future.

(c) The role played by probation and parole in behavior modification.

(d) Recent trends in correctional philosophy to reduce crime.

12. What is the bartered plea?

13. What would criminal law enforcement be like in this country if it were not a "nation of laws?"

14. What role does the judge play in the plea-bargaining process?

15. What is the function of the court administrator?

16. From the criminal codes in the state where you live, select at least three laws that are written in such vague and indefinite terms that the Supreme Court might someday rule them unconstitutional.

17. What is the principal source of Mosaic laws?

18. In what way are laws in your state similar to the Common Laws of England?

19. Give examples of laws that originated in (a) religious law, (b) social customs, (c) political pressure, (d) public morality. (List three for each.)

20. What effect does peer pressure have on crime rates, if any?

21. Define criminal homicide.

22. What is a burglary?

23. How does robbery differ from burglary?

23. What is the weakness in a self-reporting victimization survey?

25. Looking at the charts showing crime rates between 1960 and 1977, which of the seven major offenses appears to have climbed most dramatically?

RECOMMENDED SEMESTER/TERM PROJECTS

1. Prepare a paper on one form of diversion that is used in the jurisdiction where you live, such as an alternative to jail for alcoholics, or a drug diversion program. Explain what it is, how an individual is diverted, and explain the process. While preparing your paper, interview prosecutors, a judge, a police officer, individuals who have been diverted, and the people who run the program. Incorporate their views in the paper and your analysis of your findings.

2. With the help of your local police department, prepare a series of charts showing changes during the past five years in the seven Crime Index Offenses. Interview a police chief, a juvenile officer, a detective, a probation officer, and a judge; ascertain their personal views on why the changes, if any, have occurred. Then write your own theory on why the crime picture has changed during the past five years.

SUGGESTED FOR ADDITIONAL STUDY

CHAPPELL, DUNCAN, and JOHN MONAHAN, eds., *Violence and Criminal Justice.* Lexington, Mass.: D.C. Heath and Company, 1975.

GARDINER, JOHN A., and MICHAEL A. MULKEY, eds., *Crime and Criminal Justice: Issues in Public Policy Analysis.* Lexington, Mass.: D.C. Heath and Co., 1975.

MORRIS, NORVAL, and GORDON HAWKINS, *The Honest Politician's Guide To Crime Control.* Chicago: University of Chicago Press, 1969.

SCOTT, JOSEPH E., and SIMON DINITZ, eds., *Criminal Justice Planning.* New York: Praeger Publishers, 1977.

SIMON, RITA JAMES, *Women and Crime.* Lexington, Mass.: D.C. Heath and Co., 1975.

SKOLNICK, JEROME H., MARTIN L. FROST, and JANE L. SCHEIBER, eds., *Crime and Justice In America.* Del Mar, Calif.: Publishers, Inc., 1977.

TAYLOR, IAN, PAUL WALTON, and JOCK YOUNG, *The New Criminology: For a Social Theory of Deviance.* London and Boston: Routledge and Kegan Paul, 1973.

TEPPERMANN, LORNE, *Crime Control. The Urge Toward Authority.* Toronto: McGraw-Hill Ryerson Ltd., 1977.

VETTER, HAROLD J., and IRA J. SILVERMAN, *The Nature of Crime.* Philadelphia: W. B. Saunders Company, 1978.

4

Explanation of Criminal Behavior

INTRODUCTION

Now that you have learned the definition of crime and know something about criminal law and its sources, and you have a reasonable amount of understanding of the scope of the challenge presented by crime, the next step is to explore some of the explanations for criminal behavior. Rather than try to decide when to attach the *criminal* label to the offender, this chapter will be devoted to some of the more popular explanations for the offender's conduct, which is considered criminal.

Depending on your personal bias and interests, you will find explanations for human behavior, including criminal behavior, virtually everywhere. Psychologists, sociologists, biologists, psychiatrists, astrologers, numerologists, human behaviorists, social workers, carpenters, cab drivers, teachers, parents, bartenders, journalists, novelists, television talk-show hosts all have their own theories. Other crime theories are expressed by airline pilots, salespeople, secretaries, and the average persons on the street. Many of their theories are based on scientific knowledge, many are not. Most have some degree of authenticity, whether scholarly or not. In this chapter we shall cover some of the more widely held theories dating from early studies of human behavior to the present.

There is one very important point that we must make at the beginning of this chapter. One chapter of a text on the introduction to the criminal justice system is by no stretch of the imagination an attempt to cover the entire field of criminology. This chapter is merely a survey of several theories so that you may have a greater appreciation for the study of crime and criminal behavior and the various efforts of the criminal justice agencies in coping with this serious challenge. In order to address any problem, the first step is to identify what it is.

After identifying some of the explanations for criminal behavior, the chapter covers some of the more readily identifiable categories of crime and attempts to look at the individuals who might fall into these categories. Crime is a highly personal and individual type of conduct. Therefore, we shall deal only with generalities regarding the categories of genocide, white-collar crime, victimless crime, the career offender, professional criminals, and the incidental, or episodic, violator.

CRIME AS A SOCIAL DYSFUNCTION

The Utopian society, Sir Thomas Moore's ideal state where all is ordered for the best for mankind as a whole and where the evils of society have been eliminated, is impossibly and impractically ideal. Each individual seeks his own Utopia, and one of the many problems confronting him in his quest is that one person's ecstasy is another's agony and his ideals are often in conflict with those of other persons. Life, therefore, is a series of compromises between freedoms and restrictions commingled with the freedoms and restrictions of other individuals in society.

Competition and conflict are intrinsic to a society that is characterized by dynamism, materialism, individualism, fierce loyalty to special interest groups, strong social pressures for prestige and affluence, and differences of opinions and moral standards. Absolute conformity to unrealistic mores of a nonexistent "perfect" society is neither desirable, nor is it possible.

In 1806 Patrick Colquhoun observed in his *Treatise on the Police of the Metropolis* that crime in the London metropolitan area was the result of bad laws, improper police methods, illness, depraved morals, bad education, and criminal habits of the lower class of people."[1]

In early America, Richard Quinney, researcher and professor of criminology, reported:

> American thought is to equate crime with sin, pauperism, and immorality. Even when crime was recognized as a distinct phenomenon, it was usually regarded as an ill that had no place in social life. Crime was one of those conditions that fell with the domain of nineteenth-century reformism.[2]

Criminologists Donald R. Taft and Ralph W. England discuss crime in today's society in their text:

> Both criminal law and crime in the United States express social values, even though not all specific laws are implementations of the mores of the people generally.
>
> Sometimes two sets of values are in conflict; sometimes crime and noncrime are different expressions of the same values. Group loyalty, for example, may be loyalty to a criminal gang or to a community. In American Society, restricted group loyalties are expected and approved. The property owner wishes to keep his property, the thief to take it away; but both value property, both personally seek the prestige which comes from possessing property, and both crave status in their immediate groups. In a society where material success is a major requisite to social status, there will be more crimes against property and more laws for

[1]Patrick Colquhoun, *Treatise on the Police of the Metropolis* (London: J. Mowman, 1806).

[2]Richard Quinney, *The Problem of Crime* (New York: Dodd, Mead, & Co., 1970), p. 50.

the protection of property than in a society where less material basis for status is dominant.[3]

We shall return to the social aspects of crime later when we cover criminal, or social, ecology, the differential association and reference group theories, and other concepts. Whatever its course, one cannot deny that crime certainly is a social problem.

CLASSICAL THEORIES

The Cartesian Dichotomy, a theory advanced by the French philosopher René Descartes (1596–1650), involved the individual's free will in choosing whether to commit crime. Descartes' thesis was that the power of reasoning and free will are divine gifts, setting man apart from all other forms of life. Taft and England had this to say about the theory of Descartes:

> Descartes acknowledged that natural laws governed not only events external to man, but also events occurring within him, that is, his own bodily process of growth, sustenance, and decay. . . . Descartes produced a doctrine which helped shape the eventual reformation of criminal law, provided an important rationalization for punishment, and produced an image of man's mental workings which prevails to this day.[4]

This "free will" philosophy, held by several early criminologists, is frequently called the *Classical School* of criminology. Another scholar who adhered to the Classical School approach was Beccaria.

Cesare Beccaria (1738–1794) based his theory on the belief that a would-be law violator made his decision whether to commit crime or not upon a process of "pain-avoidance" reasoning, making a comparison of the pleasure he would derive from the forbidden act versus the possibility of getting caught and the pain he would suffer if caught and punished. This fear of punishment, Beccaria believed, would discourage the individual and he would choose to obey the law.

In Beccaria's home, Italy, his ideas were not very warmly received. In England the theory "caught on" and for a time the classical theory was most prevalent there. There was no provision in punishments prescribed for crimes committed in error or as a result of extenuating circumstances, such as some degree of culpability on the part of the victim.

In 1765 Beccaria published his *Dei delitti e elle pene,* a treatise on crime and punishment that was translated in 1767.[5] His doctrine represented one of the first iterations of the Classical School on crime cause. Principal points of Beccaria's theory were:

[3]Donald R. Taft and Ralph W. England, Jr., *Criminology,* 4th ed. (New York: Macmillan Co., 1964).

[4]Taft and England, *Criminology,* p. 61.

[5]Quinney, *The Problem of Crime,* p. 46.

1. Commission of crime was a matter of free choice on the part of the wrong-doer.
2. Hedonism exists in that every individual seeks a maximum of pleasure and avoids pain.
3. Punishment for crimes was to satisfy the need for retribution or vengeance but also to serve as a threat of punishment and thus as a deterrent to crimes of a similar nature being planned or considered by others.
4. The laws and their punishments had to be published for uniformity and for their deterrent value.
5. The length of sentences should be fixed by law and should be uniformly applied in accordance with the violations.
6. Children and the insane could not be charged as criminals.

Herbert A. Bloch and Gilbert Geis explained their view of Beccaria's school of thought:

> Permeating this doctrine was the powerful conception that man could determine his own destiny and political future by the controlled use of reason and the accumulation of knowledge based on rational discourse rather than on fear and superstition—a conception nurtured by a line of distinguished philosophers beginning with Thomas Hobbes.[6]

Jeremy Bentham (1742–1832), an English philosopher and jurist, also "engendered the so-called Classical School," according to Taft and England:

> Almost totally divorced from theological dogma, this school maintained (1) that the seriousness of crimes should be measured by their respective social harm rather than by their "sinfulness" or other transcendental qualities and (2) that crime is caused by the *rational* efforts of men to augment their pleasures and to minimize their pains.[7]

Bentham's philosophy was to establish:

> . . . for each crime a punishment whose pains would outweigh any possible pleasure to be gained from them and by assuring the certain and swift administration of justice, rational men, deterred by the realization that a net loss will inevitably result from a criminal act, will refrain from breaking the law.[8]

When reading of the Classical School of thought about criminal behavior and the individual's choice of whether or not to participate, consider the legislators in your own state and their arguments about what should be the punishment for various types of crimes. An emotional plea may be made for very severe punishment, with the proponents insisting that the mere threat of severe punishment and the fear of getting caught would deter many would-be offenders from committing the crimes. Insisting on more positive

[6]Herbert A. Bloch and Gilbert Geis, *Man, Crime, and Society*, 2d ed. (New York: Random House, 1970), p. 85.

[7]Taft and England, *Criminology*, pp. 61–62.

[8]Taft and England, *Criminology*, pp. 61–62.

action by the courts as a signal to other violators of the consequences they will suffer is another "Classical" point of view.

BIOLOGICAL POSITIVISM THEORIES

Born Criminal

Cesare Lombroso (1836–1909) was another early Italian criminologist who focused his attention on the individual when attempting an explanation of crime. His basic premise was that a person was a "born criminal," or a criminal by heredity, a theory of biological positivism.

Lombroso, a medical doctor and professor of legal medicine at the University of Turin, classified criminal inmates by their physical characteristics. According to his theory, there were three basic classes of criminals: born criminals, insane criminals, and criminaloids. The criminal was a degenerate, or defective in some way, an atavistic "throwback" to a more primitive and savage man.[9]

Quinney said of Lombroso and his contemporaries:

> Their approach to the study of crime was positivistic in that they utilize the point of view and methodology of the natural sciences.... While the Classical School emphasized the idea of the choice of right and wrong, the positive school placed the emphasis on the determination of conduct.[10]

Heredity Specific families with extensive criminal histories, such as the "celebrated" Jukes family, were used to illustrate the point. Out of 1200 family members studied by Richard L. Dugdale in 1877, 140 were criminals, 7 of whom were convicted murderers, some 60 were thieves, and the balance were prostitutes. This study shows better than 10 percent criminality in one family.

Although Dugdale, who was an inspector for the New York Prison Association, presented his "evidence" of hereditary degeneracy, he wrote:

> The tendency of heredity is to produce an environment which perpetuates that heredity; thus, the licentious parent makes an example which greatly aids in fixing habits of debauchery of the child. The correction is change of environment.[11]

Heredity should not be ruled out completely by the serious student of crime and its causes. Many distinguished geneticists have made valuable contributions to the study of inherited traits, which indicate that heredity cannot be eliminated as a factor in the influence one's ancestors have on his personal behavior.

[9]Quinney, *The Problem of Crime,* p. 59.

[10]Quinney, *The Problem of Crime,* p. 57.

[11]Richard L. Dugdale, *The Jukes: A Study in Crime, Pauperism, Disease, and Heredity* (New York: G. P. Putnam and Sons, 1877).

contributions to the study of inherited traits, which indicate that heredity cannot be eliminated as a factor in the influence one's ancestors have on his personal behavior.

Phrenology Some attempts have been made to correlate criminality with the configuration of bumps or bone structure of the skull, with physical deformities, ugliness, and a variety of similar single factors. Current literature and news items occasionally refer to studies under way to evaluate social or criminogenic personality changes that accompany corrective plastic surgery. The impact of an individual's new self-image is sometimes dramatic and has ameliorative value.

Physiognomy, or Body Characteristics An early "criminologist," J. Baptiste della Porte (1535–1615) was credited with a study of cadavers of criminals to determine a relationship between body form and types of crime. His theory was that he could recognize a thief by his small ears, bushy eyebrows, small nose, mobile eyes, sharp vision, open and large lips, and long slender fingers. That reads just like the description of a country-western guitar player I know, but the only crime he has committed that I know of is to play off-key once in a while.

Hooten studied approximately 14,000 criminals and over 3,000 noncriminals (most of whom were policemen and prison guards and other people in the justice system).[12] He concluded that criminals are inferior to "civilians" in nearly all of their body measurements, whatever that means. On page 306 of his book, he defined the physical characteristics of the criminal as having low foreheads, characteristic shapes and sizes of noses, compressed faces and narrow jaws, and other anomalies attributed to the criminal.

In 1949 William H. Sheldon published his *Varieties of Delinquent Youth,*[13] in which he used three basic types of body configurations as an explanation of differences in personality and behavior. He classified the "soft and round" body as *endomorphic,* the muscular and angular body as *mesomorphic,* and the thin and gaunt body as *ectomorphic.* He had studied 200 delinquent youths and reported that his study identified the mesomorphic and endomorphic individuals as having stronger tendencies toward delinquency than the ectomorphic youths. He also stated that the potential delinquent could be classified by this method by age six.

Racial Differences

According to Taft and England, "The feeling is widespread among criminologists, race relations experts, Negro leaders, and others that the Negro crime rate is exaggerated because of discriminatory arrest practices on the part of police agencies. Negroes are more liable both to be suspected

[12]Earnest A. Hooten, *Crime and Man.* (Cambridge: Harvard University Press, 1939).

[13]William H. Sheldon, *Varieties of Delinquent Youth* (New York: Harper and Brothers, 1949).

of, and to be arrested for, certain crimes than are whites.''[14] The nonwhite criminal versus the white shows a disproportionate ratio, with the highest rate of arrests per thousand population appearing among the nonwhites. Attempts to show atavistic traits of the nonwhite offender have demonstrated no correlation, which indicates that the higher rate should be attributed to such factors as economic and environmental influences more than any ''throwback to barbarism'' or other expressions of bigotry. The National Advisory Commission on Civil Disorders commented on the statistics that show low-income black areas with ''significantly higher crime rates than low-income white areas.''[15] ''This reflects,'' state Bloch and Geis, ''the high degree of social disorganization in the Negro areas as well as the fact that poor Negroes, as a group, have lower incomes than poor whites, as a group.''

The Report of the National Advisory Commission on Civil Disorders includes the following statement:

> The record before this Commission reveals that the causes of recent racial disorders are imbedded in a massive tangle of issues and circumstances—social, economic, political, and psychological—which arise out of the historical patterns of Negro-white relations in America.
>
> At the base of this mixture are three of the most bitter fronts of white racial attitudes:
>
> Pervasive discrimination and segregation.
>
> Black migration and white exodus.
>
> Black ghettos.[16]

In his book *Man's Most Dangerous Myth,* Ashley Montagu stated that the belief in racial superiority and inferiority is, according to most geneticists, wholly lacking in factual basis.[17]

Many modern theorists have developed their own variations on the biological positivism theme. Terms, such as ''personology,'' and books on how to read human behavior characteristics by studying photographs of individuals, and how to determine body types from the types of crimes they commit have been advanced as scientific theories. Even in your own circle of friends, I am sure you have taken part in a conversation or two in which someone would say ''she sure fooled me, I would never have guessed her capable of such a thing because she looked honest''; or ''I could tell that he was a thief because of the configuration of his eyes and nose.'' How many people do you know that ''look'' honest, or sincere or sinister or friendly?

One serious problem with attempting to explain criminal behavior with the biological positivism theory is that some individuals tend to believe the predictions for their futures, and they feel almost obligated to develop into

[14]Taft and England, *Criminology,* p. 106.

[15]Taft and England, *Criminology,* p. 267.

[16]Report of the National Advisory Commission on Civil Disorders (Washington, D.C.: Government Printing Office, 1968), pp. 9–11.

[17]Ashley Montagu, *Man's Most Dangerous Myth* (New York: Columbia University Press, 1942).

the types of persons they are expected to be. Consider the child who is constantly reminded that he is dumb, that he will never amount to anything, and that he is awkward. He is likely to become dumb and awkward because he is convinced he has no other alternative, a self-fulfilled prophesy. Did you ever hear the old cliche, "You can't teach an old dog new tricks?" How many times have you encountered people who actually believe it. But consider, also, the many who disprove it daily. Consider, if you will, these common stereotypes that become self-fulfilled prophesies for far too many people: (1) She has the temper of a red-head, (2) Indians and alcohol don't mix—they go crazy when they drink, (3) Irish temper, (4) "a loser, just like his father," (5) "the image of her mother," (6) "once a crook, always a crook," and on ad infinitum. It is hard to distinguish which came first, the conduct or the diagnosis.

Chemical Explanations of Crime

The study of chemical imbalance caused by narcotics or drugs and alcohol has led to volumes of reports and findings which can readily be found in any library. There is an unquestionable relationship between those substances and criminal behavior in an indirect manner, such as the motivation for committing crime to have money to support expensive drug habits, and the impairment of judgement and reasoning leading to most traffic fatalities being linked to alcohol ingestion. Whether or not the presence of the chemical in the body can be considered a cause of crime is open for debate. Some studies have been made relative to the presence of positive or or negative ions—phenomena related to atmospheric conditions—and tendencies to commit crime, but no positive findings have been announced. Another study in 1969 by J. I. Rodale reported several cases of asocial behavior in children which showed a correlation between their behavior and the amount of sugar in their blood caused by ingestion of candy used as rewards for good behavior and furnished by parents during their days away from school.[18] The children displayed unusual behavior when they had greater sugar content and showed more acceptable behavior when sugar was withheld from their diet.

Chromosomal Abnormality

During the past several years, particularly late in the 1960s, a theory of chromosomal abnormalities in males guilty of crimes of violence and sex crimes was advanced and given some attention. Called the XYY Syndrome, the theory was based upon the hypothesis that the presence of an extra Y chromosome in the male's cellular structure caused him to be a

[18] I. Rodale, "Does Sugar Make Criminals?" *Prevention,* April, 1969, pp. 107–14.

> super male, with an excess of masculine characteristics and drives, causing aggressiveness, and a stronger tendency to commit crimes of sexual aggression and violence. An Australian murder case in 1968 was alleged by one press release to have been decided on the basis of this chromosomal imbalance, but later it was referred to by the attorney who prosecuted the case as the "myth of Melbourne."[19]

In that case, the phenomenon was mentioned only once and had no significant effect on the decision. In an earlier murder case in France, a convicted murderer's sentence was for seven years instead of the usual fourteen. In that case the XYY syndrome was introduced into the trial, but the decision contained no statement about that factor. What did happen, however, was that this avenue of study pointed the way to further research that may significantly lead to additional explanations of crime from a biological standpoint.[20]

Scientific research has revealed nothing conclusive, to date, to substantiate a direct cause-effect relationship between the extra Y chromosome and criminal behavior.

Climate and Unusual Weather Conditions

The opportunity for more frequent people-to-people contacts, and thus more opportunities for criminal acts, will arise more often in the warmer climates than in the arctic. Unusual "hot spells" are also related to the greater incidence of crimes of violence. However, there are many factors other than heat that are involved, such as more personal interaction among people and more opportunities for conflict, increased leisure time, and greater amounts of alcoholic beverages consumed during the very hot days and nights.

One early theory by Peter Kropotkin was somewhat more complicated but had a more "scientific" flavor. Kropotkin's method was to predict crime by analysis of temperature and humidity:

> By the statistics of previous years one could foretell with astonishing exactness the number of crimes to be committed during the following year in every country in Europe... merely by consulting the thermometer and hygrometer. Take the average temperature of the month and multiply it by seven, then add the average humidity, multiply again by two and you will obtain the number of homicides that are committed during the month.[21]

[19] *Los Angeles Times*, February 3, 1969, Sec. D, p. 3.

[20] A brief reference to this theory appears in *Psychology Today: An Introduction* (Del Mar, Calif.: CRM, Inc., 1970), p. 507. See also National Institute for Mental Health, *Report on the XYY Chromosome Abnormality* (Washington, D.C.: Government Printing Office, 1970), p. 5, in which this statement appeared: "... it seems most important that rather critical legal, social policy and related decisions should not become firm or rigid prior to the development of more adequate and definitive research findings."

[21] Reported by Bernaldo de Quiras, *Modern Theories of Criminology* (Boston: Little, Brown, & Co., 1911), p. 34.

Age and Crime

The national statistics show a direct correlation between youth and crime. It is a young person's folly, so it would seem to the observer of crime statistics. Commission of crime by the young, as shown by the statistics, is not new, and it seems to be related to the physical condition, amount of leisure time, and the economic dependence of the young offender. On a line graph, the crest would appear between eighteen and thirty years with a sharp rise and decline between sixteen and twenty-one. From age thirty, there is a steady decline that increases with advanced age.

Sex Ratios

In the United States women enjoy virtually the same freedom as men, while in other countries there are some women who enjoy no freedom at all. The crime rates for women in the United States are also higher than in other countries. The ratio of women arrested compared to men is about one to five, and the types of crimes they commit have about the same ratio, except for those offenses that are associated with the sex difference.

PSYCHOLOGICAL THEORIES

Crime appears to be directly related to various emotional and physical needs and how one goes about satisfying those needs. Human motivation and learning go hand-in-hand. To some extent, psychological literature indicates agreement that behavior is related to physiological, social, and psychological needs. The individual sets out to meet those needs in whatever manner he has learned, depending on intensity of needs and positive and negative reinforcements along the way.

Based upon Freudian psychoanalytical theory, deviant behavior would be those crimes committed as an expression of basic drives, conflict between the conscience (superego) and human needs; flights from reality; or unconscious efforts to solve emotional problems; to mention a few types of explanation.

Psychologist Henry A. Murray listed twenty basic needs to the individual's personality structure including many of those already listed. His list contains these additional needs:

Achievement. Accomplish something difficult or different.

Aggression. Overcome opposition, punish or revenge an injury.

Counteraction. Overcome a defect or weakness or some difficult obstacle.

Defendance. Vindicate the ego.

Defense. Emulate a model, a modification of mimicry.

Exhibition. Excite, amaze, fascinate, shock, or otherwise make an impression.

Sentience. Seek and enjoy sensuous pleasures.

Succorance. Be supported, protected, or advised.[22]

As reported in *Psychology Today, An Introduction* Abraham Maslow, in *Motivation and Personality,*[23] listed five levels of needs and arranged them in hierarchical order, or a *hierarchy of needs* sequence. His thesis is that the more basic levels of needs must first be satisfied before the individual is able to function effectively to strive toward satisfaction of the next level of needs. From lower to higher categories, Maslow's hierarchy appears in the following sequence:

1. Physiological: thirst, hunger, sex, relaxation, body integrity, air.
2. Safety: orderly, safe, consistent, "just."
3. Love and belongingness: human relationships.
4. Esteem: achievement, competence, independence, freedom, reputation, prestige.
5. Self-actualization: exploitation of talents, capabilities, and potentialities.[24]

As the child matures from childhood to adulthood, he progressively develops his own combination of needs and his own methods for seeking satisfaction of those needs. He learns by doing, by watching others, by studying the methods written and taught by others, and by trial and error. The child learns the many taboos of his own culture that frequently frustrate the drives involved in seeking his goals of satisfaction. The child learns that the pain of punishment may be avoided by minding his parents. As an adult, he learns that sexual satisfaction is sometimes gained by reciprocating for the satisfying experience by assumption of the responsibilities of personal commitment or marriage. He also learns that basic sustenance is achieved with reasonably little effort or conflict, but certain minimum requirements must be met, such as work to earn money to spend.

The individual learns to share, to be patient, and to go about satisfying those needs in an orderly manner in keeping with the customs and mores of the particular society in which he holds membership.

Frustrations are experienced by the individual, and he learns that he will never satisfy all of his needs. What he must learn is self-control and compromise. He learns to work for his money, study for his education, and to respect the rights and property of others if he is to have them respect his rights and property. He learns that some actions are right and other actions are wrong. There are laws, rules, customs, taboos, regulations, bans, and a variety of agents and agencies to enforce them. Through interaction with

[22]Henry A. Murray, *Exploration in Personality* (New York: Oxford University Press, 1938), pp. 158–59.

[23]Abraham Maslow, *Motivation and Personality* (New York: Harper and Row, Publishers, 1954).

[24]*Psychology Today, An Introduction,* pp. 151–52.

others, and with respect to all of these laws and regulations the individual has to obey, the majority of the population somehow manages to develop into law-abiding, socially acceptable members of society. However, many do not seek or attain their goals by lawful means for various reasons.

Coffey and others have reduced deviant behavior to three categories:

1. Deterministic deviance. A person has no control over his behavior and is grossly influenced by external or internal forces.
2. Self-determined deviance. A person has complete control over his behavior.
3. Combination of self-determined and external or internal influences, but exercises a degree of self-control.[25]

The sociopath, or psychopathic personality, is one who is extremely self-centered, impulsive, and aggressive toward society, and who has an attitude of omnipotence. The sociopath lacks a conscience (called the superego by Freud), which reduces his guilt feelings regarding any misconduct because he lacks other feelings that go along with the conscience, including fair-mindedness, empathy, and social sensitivity. Most, or all, of the sociopath's feelings are directed toward others rather than himself. There is an infantile demand for immediate satisfaction of basic drives, with impatience at any delays and intolerance for denial of what he believes that he needs. The sociopath is unable or unwilling to form any affectual bonds with another person and obeys only those rules and laws which he chooses to obey. Not all sociopaths are criminals—nor all criminals sociopaths—but there is a predisposition toward development of delinquent behavior patterns because so many of society's rules are found in the criminal codes.

Low Mentality and Crime

Theories of low mentality and criminal tendencies have been postulated at various times by criminologists. Henry H. Goddard, one of America's distinguished proponents of the psychological school of crime causation, related mental deficiency to crime. In 1914 he estimated that more than 50 percent of all criminals were feebleminded.[26] In a later book, Goddard stated:

> It is no longer to be denied that the greatest single cause of delinquency and crime is low-grade mentality, much of it within the limits of feeblemindedness.[27]

[25]Alan Coffey, Edward Eldefonso, and Walter Hartinger, *An Introduction To the Criminal Justice System and Process* (Englewood Cliffs: Prentice-Hall, 1974), p. 135.

[26]Henry H. Goddard, *Feeblemindedness: Its Causes and Consequences* (New York: Macmillan Co., 1914), p. 37.

[27]Henry H. Goddard, *Human Efficiency and Levels of Intelligence* (Princeton: Princeton University Press, 1920), p. 74.

Although it may be a popular view held by many observers, an experienced police practitioner will discount the theory on the basis of his own investigations. Many crimes are the culmination of well-laid plans by intelligent individuals carried out with extreme cleverness and cunning. Many crimes of embezzlement and "confidence" type situations are sometimes beyond the comprehension and imagination of the average person.

CRIMINAL ECOLOGY

Social ecology has been a topic of serious study by criminologists for many years. Man's environment and the influences it plays on his behavior is considered one of the most significant of the crime cause factors that demands understanding by the professional criminal justice practitioner. Although the methods of statistical computation were undoubtedly crude when compared with our modern data systems, studies of criminal ecology were underway in the early 1800s.

Richard Quinney recounts that foremost among the ecology researchers of the 1830s was Alexander von Oeltingen of Germany, who addressed the problems of crime measurement in his *Moralstatistick.* Adolphe Que'telet studied the social nature of crime as reflected in crime statistics in Belgium. Using maps, A. M. Guerry, who was in charge of judicial statistics for Paris, analyzed crime rates for the various regions of France.

In England there were some studies of the social changes related to the urbanization of that country during the industrial development of the country.[28] Rowson W. Rowson published one study in 1839, *An Inquiry Into the Statistics of Crime in England and Wales.* Other English criminal ecology theorists of about the same era included Joseph Fletcher, Henry Mayhew, John Glyde, and John T. Burt.[29]

Fletcher's theory was that criminals were developed by a process of apprenticeship in certain neighborhoods, prisons, and jails. He opposed the argument that crime was caused by poverty, ignorance, and population density. Mayhew's study involved a comparison of the locations where crimes were committed and the residences of criminals. Glyde studied population density in relationship to crime in Suffolk. In 1863, Burt suggested that criminals came from criminal classes that already existed.

In his excellent book, Quinney observed:

> The writers of this period, 1860 to 1885, viewed crime as a product of "disharmony" in the operation of social forces, "constituents," or institutions of society.... In their explanation of crime in terms of social conditions, most of the writers assumed that the operation of any one factor could only partially

[28]Quinney, *The Problem of Crime,* p. 47.
[29]Quinney, *The Problem of Crime,* p. 48.

> explain the phenomenon of crime. While they pointed to associations, they believed that a multiplicity of social causes operated to produce crime. Of the many factors considered, most popular in the explanation of crime were drinking, lack of trade education, desire for luxuries, poverty, oblivion of religious and moral principles, idleness, abnormal family relations, bad company, and, in general, civilizations.[30]

In the United States it became particularly evident in some of the larger cities that there were certain neighborhoods or larger parts of the city that had more crime and spawned a disproportionate percentage of delinquents and criminal law violators.

Throughout the United States, particularly in the urban areas where an individual may get lost from the prying eyes of caring relatives or curious neighbors, criminal law violators are found among the social derelicts, the dropouts, bohemians, hippies, hoboes, vagrants, bums, winos, and various other subcultures that abound in the low-rent neighborhoods. Although certain neighborhoods may not have spawned or nourished such social dropouts or nonconformists, the neighborhoods nevertheless serve as their haven because they are less apt to be rejected or ejected.

The Committee for Economic Development made the following statements regarding the ecology of crime:

> The highest crime rates, five to ten times those for rural areas, are found in the congested centers of great cities, in association with a long list of other social ills. Housing there is generally substandard, often unfit for habitation; unemployment is endemic, especially among the young; health and sanitation services are weak; many of the public schools are demoralized, with heavy drop-out rates; and deep poverty is pervasive.
>
> Relatively high rates of juvenile delinquency have occurred consistently over a long period of time in central city slum areas, regardless of their social and ethnic constituencies. Delinquent behavior is often considered "normal" and socially acceptable there, while non-delinquent behavior may seem abnormal. Many parents strive to overcome these influences, but family and social sanctions are ineffective against peer-group support for unlawful conduct. Spontaneous criminality and easy recruitment by organized syndicates frequently result.[31]

One of the pioneers in the study of criminal ecology in America was Clifford K. Shaw. The object of his study was the city of Chicago, Illinois. Actually, Shaw and his colleagues conducted a number of studies that were reported in detail in a series of publications.[32]

[30]Quinney, *The Problem of Crime,* p. 48.

[31]Research and Police Committee of the Committee for Economic Development, *Reducing Crime and Assuring Justice* (New York: Committee for Economic Development, 1972).

[32]Clifford K. Shaw, *Delinquency Areas,* 1927; *The Jock-Roller,* 1930; *Natural History of a Delinquent Career,* 1931; *Brothers in Crime,* 1938; *Juvenile Delinquency and Urban Areas,* 1942 (Chicago: University of Chicago Press).

Shaw's long-term study involved his use of pin maps. He located on the maps the residences of approximately 56,000 delinquent children and adults of both sexes.

The studies by Shaw and others showed that certain neighborhoods housed disproportionate percentages of delinquent children and criminal adults. Those neighborhoods were characterized by disorganization and congestion and "anomie," which may be most succintly defined as a state of normlessness, and a lack of regulatory controls.

The neighborhoods were in the center of town, adjacent to industry and commerce. During the Industrial Revolution and the accompanying mass migration to the cities, the people who worked in the factories had to live nearby. The factories depended upon centralized steam power and transportation, and the result was an industrial community of low-priced housing for the laborers. The residential zone immediately adjacent to the factories served as a transition zone. As each new migrant group moved into the city, they resided in the area called Zone I in Shaw's study (a series of concentric circles starting at Zone I and numbered progressively higher as the zones moved out). As the people became more successful, they moved to better neighborhoods, then the next migrants moved in.

Shaw's study, covering a period of over twenty years, showed a succession of several minority groups: Swedish, Syrian, German, Polish, Irish, Jewish, Italian, and Negro. Other studies showed similar trends with New York's most recent immigration of Puerto Ricans. In each of these decadent neighborhoods, a delinquent subculture was developed and has been perpetuated throughout the years by the current residents. There has been a succession of conflicts between the cultures of the newcomers and the dominant groups already in residence. The newcomers have never been welcome, but the "street culture" has continued to be perpetuated and passed on from group to group although there is conflict between the groups.[33]

As they reported in one book, Shaw and McKay concerned themselves with broken homes as an adjunct to the other factors they studied, and found that only 42.5 percent of the delinquent children were from broken homes. They interpreted their findings as meaning that broken homes were *not* the principal cause of juvenile delinquency.[34]

Taft and England expanded on Shaw's identification of the "criminal zones" and listed seven types of neighborhoods "that are significant for their influence on delinquency." Their list includes (paraphrased):

1. A poverty area with fairly normal family organization.
2. The slum, which involves poverty as well as anomie and a heterogeneous population.

[33]See Taft and England, *Criminology,* p. 156; and Quinney, *The Problem of Crime,* p. 82.

[34]C. R. Shaw and H. D. McKay, *Juvenile Delinquency in Urban Areas* (Chicago: University of Chicago Press, 1942), p. 55.

3. An interstitial area similar to the slum and shut off from conventional society by some physical or social barrier and involving conflicts of culture in this sort of no man's land.
4. A rooming-house area characterized by impersonal relations.
5. The ghetto, an area occupied by a single minority group.
6. A vice area, a police-protected area where prostitution and gambling go on without intervention by the police.
7. A deteriorated rural area that serves as a hideout or rest area for city gangsters in this type of ghost town.[35]

When considering juvenile delinquency and its causes, the Gluecks suggest that some consideration be given to recreation, or lack of it.[36] They found that delinquents are more outgoing and active than nondelinquents, and recreational diversion is at least one variable in juvenile deviance. This underlines studies that show delinquent children seek exciting diversions which take them to dark streets and vacant lots and places that pique their curiosity and appeal to their search for adventure. Their delinquent acts become their recreation.

Crime continues to be explained in terms of social ecology. In September 1970, a report on the training needs of the New York City Police Department explained it thusly:

> With the increasing growth of the suburbs, the central cities have suffered a retardation of population growth. As has well been documented, this demographic shift has left areas of blight and decay in the central cities and has accelerated the social deteriorations in areas of the central cities occupied by minority groups. Projected patterns of growth suggest, in the case of the New York metropolitan region, that these trends will continue. In net, there is rapid growth for the region and slow growth for the central city.[37]

As is the case in the study of crime theory, certain factors must be borne in mind that will temper any overconfidence that the student may invest in such a theory. About the ecological theory, Taft and England observe:

> Delinquent acts of little children may occur near their homes, and in that case their correlation in space may conceivably have some significance for causation. But adult professional crime in these days of easy transportation will occur whenever opportunity for profitable activity is the greatest, which may be hundreds of miles away from the criminals' homes. Hence maps of the home addresses of adult criminals at the time of their acts need not even suggest possible causal influences.

[35]Taft and England, *Criminology,* pp 165–168.

[36]Sheldon Glueck and Eleanor Glueck, *Unravelling Juvenile Delinquency* (New York: Commonwealth Fund, 1950), p. 102.

[37] National Institute of Law Enforcement & Criminal Justice, *Police Training and Performance Study,* PR70-4 (Washington, D.C.: Government Printing Office, 1970), p. 2.

> All such studies are in serious difficulties.... What we really need to locate is not necessarily the current residence of a criminal but the location of the causes of his criminal patterns of behavior.[38]

The Ecological Theory and Gangs

Alienated individuals find each other while searching for their own identities, and they tend to set their own norms. Alienation and deviant behavior may include conduct that is classified as criminal behavior. The adolescent may reach a point where he must "devalue" his parents (in order to improve his self-image), according to Hahn. Such devaluation is accomplished "frequently by open criticism of the parents personally, intellectually, and culturally."[39] During this period in the youth's development, there is a search for models and heroes to worship and to emulate. Eventually, as the process of maturation continues, the individual develops a more tolerant and realistic attitude toward his parents. The process reminds me of something that has been attributed to Mark Twain (paraphrased): "When I was a kid of seventeen I thought my father was the dumbest man in the whole world; then when I was twenty-one, I was amazed at how much the old man had learned in four years." Perhaps the alienation may be attributed, in part, to the process of "desanctifying" parents while suffering the trauma of discovering that they are only human, while at the same time the adolescent is searching for his own identity among his personal strengths and weaknesses.

Sometimes the adolescent discovers that there is an entire different universe outside the walls of his own safe home and the "hothouse" environment with a television set his only contact with the real world. This phenomenon sometimes occurs when the pampered and carefully protected middle-class child alienates himself and becomes a member of the street culture. Concept of universe is illustrated by the overheard conversation between two fish: "What do you mean, there is no God? Who do you think changes the water every day?" According to Cohen, juvenile gang members who seek each other through their common alienation from their parents and other reference groups set their own norms. This serves four important functions for them:

> First, gang members can explore the extent to which each is willing to go in accepting and implementing alternative rules. Second, they can explore the extent to which they can rely on each other for support. Third, each member has an opportunity to test the degree to which his techniques for neutralizing the influences of law-abiding society are successful and accepted by others.

[38]Taft and England, *Criminology,* pp. 153–54.

[39]Paul H. Hah, *The Juvenile Offender and the Law* (Cincinnati: W. H. Anderson, 1971), p. 67.

Fourth, the gang can try out various courses of delinquent actions and judge the commitment that each member of the gang is willing to make of each type of action or specialty.[40]

MULTIPLE FACTOR THEORIES

In 1925 Cyril Burt concluded

> Crime is assignable to no single universal source, nor yet to two or three: it springs from a wide variety, and usually from a multiplicity, of alternative and converging influences.[41]

John L. Gillin wrote in 1926 in the way of a social-psychological explanation:

> Hence there is a conspiracy of conditions which account for his becoming a criminal—conditions in his own constitutional make-up, in his early development, in his lack of training, in his poverty, and in the surrounding social atmosphere, including habits, customs, ideals, beliefs, and practices. The social conditions around him set the stage on which each of these factors plays its part and release in his conduct the good or evil in his nature. Thus, is the criminal made.[42]

Theory of Differential Association

The late Edwin H. Sutherland postulated his genetic explanation of crime, commonly known as his differential association theory and discussed in depth in *Principles of Criminology.*[43] The theory involves environmental influences, ecology, psychological considerations, and sociological principles. The principal premise of the theory is that criminal behavior is learned through interaction with others by means of the same mechanisms that are involved in any other learning process. In capsulated form, the explanation is summed up:

> The specific direction of motives and drives is learned from definitions of the legal codes as favorable or unfavorable.... Differential associations may vary in frequency, duration, priority, and intensity...and a person becomes

[40] Albert K. Cohen, *Delinquent Boys: The Culture of the Gang* (Glencoe, Ill.: The Free Press, 1955), pp. 60–61.

[41] Cyril Burt, *The Young Delinquent* (New York: D. Appleton), p. 3.

[42] John L. Gillin, *Criminology and Penology* (New York: The Century Company, 1926), pp. 250–51.

[43] E. H. Sutherland and D. R. Cressey, *Principles of Criminology,* 9th ed. (Philadelphia: J. B. Lippincott Co., 1974), pp. 75-91. The theory first appeared in Sutherland's 3rd edition in 1939, pp. 5-7. Cressey has since updated his own views on this theory but has left it intact so that students may continue to use it as a point of discussion on crime cause theories. His most recent edition includes an in-depth evaluation of his own on the theory.

delinquent because of an excess of definitions favorable to violation of law over definitions unfavorable to violation of law.

Learning crime in the same manner as learning in general prompts reflection on the process of learning itself. Consider the explanation of this process by John Dollard and Neal E. Miller:

> Four factors are exceedingly important in learning. These are: drive, cue, response, and reinforcement. The drive impels responses which are actually channelized by cues from other stimuli not strong enough to act as drives but more specifically distinctive than the drive. If the first response is not rewarded, this creates a dilemma in which the extinction of successive non-reinforced responses leads to so-called random behavior. If some one response is followed by reinforcement, the connection between the stimulus pattern and this response is strengthened, so that the next time the same drive and other cues are present this response is more likely to occur. Since reinforcements presumably produce their effect by reducing the strength of the drive stimulus, events cannot be rewarding in the absence of the appropriate drive. After the drive has been satiated by sufficient reward, the tendency to make the rewarded response is weakened so that other responses occur until the drive reappears.[44]

REFERENCE GROUP THEORY

Dr. Martin R. Haskell, criminologist at California State University, Long Beach, introduced a sociopsychological explanation of crime that he calls the reference group theory. He offers six propositions as an explanation of his theory:

1. The family is the first personal reference group of the child.
2. The family is a normative reference group. (The norm conforms to the larger society.)
3. Prior to his participation in a delinquent act, the delinquent boy adopts a street group as a personal reference group.
4. The street group that becomes the personal reference group of the lower class boy in New York has a delinquent subculture.
5. A boy for whom the street group is a personal reference group is likely, in the dynamic assessment preceding a delinquent act, to decide in favor of the delinquent act.
6. The individual tends, as a member of a personal reference group, to impart into its context attitudes and ways of behaving that he is currently holding in sociogroup life.[45]

[44]John Dollard and Neal E. Miller, *Personality and Psychotherapy—An Analysis in Terms of Learning, Thinking, and Culture* (New York: McGraw-Hill Book Co., Inc., 1950), p. 47.

[45]M. R. Haskell, "Toward a Reference Group Theory," *Social Problems,* Winter, 1960–61.

Composition of the Population

Age, race, and sex ratios in a community are directly related to crime rates. A homogeneous community of longstanding stability will have less conflict than the dynamic community with a wide variety of racial, ethnic, and cultural differences. The younger population will have had less time to attain the stability level of the older members of the community.

Relationship of the Police to the Community

The method of selection and retention of the police officers has a direct relationship to the image of the entire department and the attitudes of both the citizenry and the police officers themselves. The number of policemen per thousand population has a direct bearing upon the effectiveness of the police. Enforcement policies as articulated by the chief have a similar impact on the community.

Commissioner Patrick V. Murphy of the New York City Police Department stated in 1970:

> The police service relies on the theory that we are essentially an honest and peaceful society, and that most people voluntarily comply with the law. The presumption that we are a peace-loving people may be a fallacy.[46]

Although taken out of context of the entire speech, the rhetoric reflects the question asked repeatedly by many administrators: How are we to address the increasingly difficult challenge of the mushrooming crime problem? If we are not to presume the majority of the people we serve to be peaceful and law-abiding, then are the police to become an army of occupation? Within the framework of our present existence, there must be a considerable amount of mutual trust and respect.

Social Attitudes

Contempt or disregard for the law has been a trend in many communities: One has only to read a newspaper to see that flagrant acts of criminal behavior occur under the guise of so-called peaceful demonstrations or similar affairs. A vocal minority is involved in such lawlessness, but they are capable of being a troublesome minority. The general attitude of the community will be reflected in the actions of the juries and the courts in such cases when arrests are made. "Moral holidays" occur when certain acts that would otherwise be considered crimes are sometimes allowed to occur because of the "temper of the crowd" or the spirit of the occasion. Halloween

[46]From a speech in December 1970, as reported in the *Los Angeles Times,* December 13, 1970, *Sec.* H, p. 1.

has been regarded by many people as a moral holiday when certain minor acts of vandalism may be considered "in the spirit of the day."

Bookies and operators of houses of prostitution may earn hundreds of dollars a day, and sometimes considerably more, but they may receive suspended sentences or be required to pay small fines when found guilty of their crimes. The action is explained by a statement such as "they didn't hurt anyone," or "their victims were just as guilty as they were," or "it's only a minor crime." All of these factors are directly related to the incidence rates of all crimes in any given community. The community with a consensus that indicates a desire for a corruption-free government will reflect that attitude in the people who hold office in that community.

Culture and Subculture

Within every predominant culture there are many subcultures. Not all subcultures are any more of a threat to the total society's norms than perhaps influencing a change in eating habits, or different forms of entertainment or games to play which are characteristic of certain subcultures. There is the subculture of the underworld, however, which does pose a threat to society. In his discussion of gang behavior, Cohen explains the variance with the broad culture's norms, which may also be characteristic of certain other subcultures that are at odds with society in general. A subculture is a group at variance with the broad culture's patterns, mores, and traditional ideas. According to Cohen's theory, the variance of the gang's subculture is in part attributed to the "significantly different social worlds" between middle-class children and working class children as they grow up. As the working class child experiences frustration in achieving culturally desirable goals, the readily available alternatives emerge. Such alternatives may include deviant and criminal behavior. There is a struggle between a means and an end, a struggle for wealth. If they cannot acquire it by legitimate means, then they go for the alternatives.[47]

Economic and Social Crises

Personal acquisition of property and vigorous business practices perpetuate an attitude of competition. Personal prestige is gauged by many people on the basis of personal wealth. Some people cannot acquire such wealth by legal means, and will cheat, steal, and amass great fortunes in other unethical and illegal ways. White-collar criminals use their businesses and professions as a means to acquire wealth by criminal means, and the professional and career criminals make a business or profession out of crime.

[47]Cohen, *Delinquent Boys: The Culture of the Gang,* p. 25.

Many criminals in all three categories of crime—white-collar, professional, and career—have been eulogized. Witness the influence of peddlers and politicians who have been staunchly defended in spite of their flagrant criminal acts and hailed as heroes.

Contrary to what one might believe would occur during an economic depression, the rates of property crimes do not rise. Instead, they go down. One reason for this downward trend may be that there is a less significant difference between the relative wealth of the classes. In times of affluence, the gap is greater, and the crime rates go up.

There is a correlation between the economic stature of the arrested criminal and his crimes; although, the fact that he is impoverished is not a sure predictor that the poor man will commit crimes. Most criminologists theorize that the correlation is more likely to be the result of the living patterns of the poor and their environment of frequent contacts with the delinquent subculture that exists in impoverished areas.

Commissioner Murphy, in the same speech referred to earlier in this chapter, stated:

> George Bernard Shaw once wrote that security cannot exist where the danger of poverty hangs over everyone's head. Poverty degrades the poor and infects with its degradation the whole neighborhood in which they live. And whatever can degrade a neighborhood can degrade an entire civilization. In this context, poverty is a burden not only on the poor but also on every intermediate level of our social and economic structure.

The Social Science Research Council published a large number of studies concerning crime and the problems of poverty and unemployment during the Great Depression of 1930–35. Taft and England summarized those findings:

1. Neither American, English, nor European research has shown any clear relationship between depression and crime generally.
2. Evidence of relationship between nonviolent crime and depression is wholly inconsistent.
3. Many studies have shown that robbery and other property crimes with violence do increase when there is a large amount of unemployment.
4. Some studies have shown crimes against morals to decrease.
5. There is no evidence that crimes against the person generally increase.
6. Recent studies have tended to show that crime has generally increased in good times.
7. ...it is not an immediate decline in accustomed material well-being but a continuance of, or change in *relative* well-being, which is frustrating and sometimes results in criminal reactions.[48]

[48]Taft and England, *Criminology,* p. 24.

Discussing those studies and the findings, Taft and England stated that a tentative general conclusion concerning business depression and crime may be stated as follows: "Very serious threat of starvation probably will drive most men to petty crime, but, at least where there is reasonable provision of relief, this does not occur."[49]

Mobility

The basic family group is not static in most of the growing urban communities and no longer serves as the primary reference group for many individuals. Mass communication and transportation have caused the individual to become a part of the larger society in general instead of his own family and neighborhood. He seeks entertainment, employment, and recreation wherever he chooses, and he may move away from home with no provocation. He may move to a city where he is comparatively free from the social and ethical pressures imposed by his peers and those who have exercised authority over him. Community responsibility is lacking in the transient. Although he may not become a criminal, the transient has no social ostracism to face if he does.

Effect of Labeling

When does one become a "criminal," or a "juvenile delinquent?" When he or she commits a crime or delinquent act? No. The person is considered innocent of any criminal act until proven in court to be guilty. Actually, then, "criminal" and "delinquent," to mention just a few of many labels, are attached only after a finding or plea of guilty. Once assigned the label, the culprit becomes one of those "bad people"—a "crook," "thief," "punk," "burglar," "rapist," "child molester," and so forth. Many theorists believe that attachment of the label has a negative effect on the individual so labeled, and that from that time on there is a danger that the individual will begin performing as expected. Once typecast, as certain actors in make-believe theatre are, it is even difficult in that world to get anyone to see them as anything other than a "heavy," a "nice guy," a "villain," or a "hero." In the real world, breaking the cast and making others see the "former criminal" as anything else but "criminal" is nigh impossible.

Carey addresses the problem thusly:

> The impact on the labeled person is generally negative. If we are talking about someone defined as a delinquent, the end product would be a boy declared

[49]Taft and England, *Criminology*, p. 25.

> a ward of the juvenile court and adjudged to be delinquent by peers, school, family, and finally, by himself. The process creates expectations that the person will persist in violating, thus leading to a self-fulfilling prophesy. The delinquent's life chances are also affected, his opportunities are restricted. This may lead to further elaboration of the delinquent role as an attack on, or defense against the labelers. This phenomenon is called "secondary deviation." In short, the major consequence of labeling for the labeled is to speed him along on a delinquent and criminal career.[50]

In *Crime and Justice—American Style,* Schrag identified and defined nine steps in the labeling process, as he saw it:

1. No act is intrinsically criminal, but is made so by law.
2. Criminal definitions are enforced in the interest of powerful groups by their representatives, including the police.
3. A person does not become a criminal by violating the law, but by the labeling process by which authorities confer the status upon him.
4. Dichotomizing people into criminal and noncriminal categories is contrary to common sense and empirical evidence.
5. Only a few persons are caught in violation of the law, while many may be equally guilty.
6. While the sanctions used in law enforcement are directed against the total person and not only the criminal act, the severity and consequences of the penalties vary according to the characteristics of the offender.
7. Criminal sanctions also vary according to other characteristics of the offender, such as minority groups, transients, the poorly educated, residents of deteriorated urban areas, and other factors.
8. Criminal justice is based on a stereotyped concept of the criminal as a willful wrongdoer, who is morally bad and deserves condemnation.
9. Once labeled as a criminal, it is difficult for an offender to "live down" the label and restore himself to a respected status in the community.[51]

TYPES OF CRIMINAL BEHAVIOR

When one studies crime, its causes, effects, and all of the many related aspects, it is also necessary to study the types of criminal law violator. The most distinctive method used to study the criminal is to study him as an entity unto himself, an individual who commits an act or is guilty of an omission that is defined in the legal codes as a criminal offense. This individualistic approach is not invalid, but for the busy police science student and police practitioner this method is too time-consuming. A less exacting but still valid method for studying the criminal is by category. When using

[50] James T. Carey, *Introduction to Criminology* (Englewood Cliffs: Prentice-Hall, 1978), p. 119.

[51] Clarance Schrag, *Crime and Justice—American Style* (Washington, D.C.: Government Printing Office, 1971), pp 81–112.

this method, however, one must not lose sight of the fact that the subcategories vary with personal differences.

For the sake of discussion in class in somewhat of an organized fashion, we shall group criminal offenders into four categories: (1) incidental offenders, (2) exceptional offenders, (3) career criminals, and (4) professional criminals. Then, we shall take a look at four distinctively different types of crime, which we have categorized here as (1) white-collar, (2) organized, (3) victimless, and (4) genocide. Certain types of offenders and their offenses defy classification and justifiably should not necessarily be reduced to labels, as discussed earlier in this chapter, but these categories merely serve as landmarks in your study itinerary.

Incidental

Most of the three precent or so of the American population convicted of criminal law violations fall within this category. For this person, his or her crime is an episodic occurrence, and has no pattern of preparation, continued violation, or perhaps not even another violation during a lifetime. The incidental offender has been arrested as a juvenile or adult for the first time, perhaps a second or third widely separated in time and space, and in all probability the nature of violation—if more than one—will be different from the last, or the next.

Traffic law violations usually fall into this category. Crimes of opportunity or chance are usually incidental, such as an impulsive shoplifting incident, a sudden assault in response to an insult or misinterpreted gesture, petty theft from an automobile, a crime of opportunty such as embezzlement by a trusted employee who sees a chance to pay off a hounding creditor, even a murder which is committed under circumstances which seem to the offender at the time his own interpretation of the only way to solve the problem caused by his love for his wife and another woman.

The seriousness of the crime is not criteria for categorization as an incidental offender. Rather, it is the thing that one might do as a single episode in his lifetime, then probably never repeat. Consider the following as examples of incidental offenders:

1. On the way home from a school dance, the young man has just taken his girlfriend home on the last bus. He is four miles from home and there are no more buses running until seven in the morning. He has to get some rest before going to class in the morning. As he is walking, he sees a bicycle parked in front of a house. He takes the bicycle, rides it to a spot within two blocks from his home, then abandons it and walks the rest of the way home.
2. In a nightclub, a rowdy and uncouth man is making very descriptive comments about the physical attributes of another man's ladyfriend, being

careful not to leave out any of the more bawdy terms used to describe a woman's body. Then he reaches toward her as if to goad the boyfriend into getting angry. The lady's escort, believing that her honor was in need of defending, uses one karate chop and downs the rowdy.

3. In a fit of anger at a driver, screaming insults and making gestures to her from his car in the outside lane on the freeway, a young lady suddenly speeds up and rams the man's car broadside, causing him to run off the road and strike three pedestrians before coming to rest alongside a telephone pole.

All these and millions more offenses like them could easily be considered single episodes, and the offenders "incidental."

The incidental offender is one who may commit his crime without premeditation or design prior to the act, but because of the circumstances as they occur at the time, all of the elements of the crime are present and the violator becomes another statistic. Because of the larger number of episodic or incidental offenders, they give the police the greatest problems. They often commit one offense and never repeat. Many of them do not develop patterns that lead to their identification, and they are not discovered. When they are apprehended, their cases are appropriately adjudicated. Unless they develop asocial or criminal behavior patterns, they are seldom heard from again, but there are thousands more who take their places on the court calendars and "police blotters." Their offenses are unpredictable and there seems to be little the police can do to prevent them except by maintaining a constant and vigilant patrol.

Exceptional Offenders

Unique because of the unusual nature of their crime or some unusual personal characteristic, exceptional offenders may actually be exempt from criminal prosecution. There are certain categories of persons who are incapable of forming intent, such as mentally ill or lack of mentality; others are too young, such as juveniles; and still others may be considered operating under mental disorders, as with some sexual offenders, or under the influence of narcotics or dangerous drugs. Habitual offenders of the narcotics and drug laws, and alcoholics may be listed in the category of exceptional offenders because of mind-impairing influences from external sources.

Child molesters, or paedophiliacs, or other abnormal sexual preferences, such as the necrophiliac, who prefers his sexual partners to be dead, fall into this special category. Crimes against nature or assaults committed with wanton disregard for the victims are usually committed by unusual or exceptional offenders. In many cases, offenders who fall into this category are diverted into treatment programs rather than sent through the motions of prosecution and conviction, only to go through the jail or prison system and return to society with the same abnormal problems they had before they went in. How to process them presents a tremendous series of problems for the professionals in the justice system, because they do not respond to traditional methods of punishment and attempts at rehabilitation.

Career Offenders (Recidivists)

The career offender is a failure. He spends a lifetime in and out of custody. Although the offender who falls into this category may be difficult to distinguish from the professional offender, specialists do make the distinction on the basis of individual personalities of the violators and on their level of skills rather than their crimes.

Crime is a way of life to the offender in this category, and it usually starts at a very early age. Exactly where and when he was indoctrinated into a life of crime varies, but it is usually during adolescence. The "street culture" or "delinquent subculture" is part of the child's environment, and if the child's activities and attitudes are not directed toward lawful and socially accepted activities and attitudes, his life of crime usually begins.

The career offender is in the lower levels of the criminal class structure. He is a misfit in the law-abiding community. He develops and maintains social and "business" relationships that help him eke out a living in his own parasitic way and that protect him from discovery and apprehension as long as possible.

If he were to be identified by his crime specialty, the career offender is usually found in the category of "property" offenders. Because he is not willing or able to consistently make a living by lawful means, he must make a profit out of his crimes. The individual who commits murder for a living may be classified in this category, but he is not likely to continue such employment for as long a period of time as other criminals because of his particular specialty. The career offender is usually a burglar, a robber, a petty thief, a dealer in stolen cars, or a check passer. Whatever his crime, the career offender is a specialist and his arrest record will generally reflect a series of similar offenses.

Professional Offender

There are a few factors that distinguish the professional from the career criminal, the most significant of which is the comparable degrees of success. The career criminal's record usually shows a long series of arrests and delinquency since childhood; the professional criminal's record is free from such a pattern. Any arrest record that he may have will show comparatively lower frequency and—in all probability—a lower percentage of convictions for those arrests. The professional can be so classified on the basis of his comparative proficiency and success. Like the true professional he is, the professional offender has a high opinion of himself and his skills, and will strive to work only with other professionals. He may express his feelings that suckers are made to be "taken," that he only preys on those who need to be taken advantage of, sort of a modern Robin Hood.

The professional criminal does not consider himself a criminal, and he is not likely to associate with other persons who are criminals. He is an assimilationist, blending himself into the total community in a respectable middle-class environment, and his friends and associates are respectable citizens, frequently leaders in business and government.

A police officer may refer to a frequently arrested shoplifter, pick-pocket, or burglar as a professional thief. Actually, it may be largely a matter of semantics to attempt to distinguish between the two, but for the sake of keeping the two classes apart in this chapter, I suggest that you consider the professional as one who is more apt to commit the more sophisticated crimes of theft by fraud, embezzlement, and confidence games, and such burglaries as those involving the "cracking" of safes and high-value losses that require skill and planning. The professional is more difficult to identify as a criminal because he is usually prepared to register surprise or indignation when found out and will make apologies or restitution because of "this terrible mistake." He may have influential friends who make excuses for him and whom he uses—probably without their awareness of the fact that they are being used—to get him out of his troubles. The professional criminal is also prepared for his defense, and it is not unusual for him to buy witnesses and to be represented by high-priced attorneys.

White-Collar Offender

As a contrast to the professional criminal, who makes a business out of his crimes, the white-collar criminal makes a crime out of his business. This category includes the businessman and professional who violate the criminal statutes during the normal course of their business. Crimes by employees committed against their employers may be regarded by some experts as white-collar crime, such as the bank official who is finally indicted for embezzlement of hundreds of thousands of dollars of the bank's money over a period of several years.

White-collar crimes as referred to in this chapter include such offenses as price-fixing by so-called "competing" corporations, making false statements in income tax claims, fraudulent advertising schemes, selling food supplement and vitamin pills or energy potions that do not do what they are purported to do for the body. Other white-collar crimes include adding water to frozen food products, false labeling and packaging by butchers and grocers, and many fraudulent practices carried on by virtually every type of business and profession in existence. Some lending institutions manage to collect more than the legal interest rate; some attorneys charge for investigative services that are never performed; some doctors charge their patients for drugs that are not actually administered; and some politicians keep their well-oiled machines running on their constituents' gasoline. Most of these crimes are not detected, and relatively little punitive action is taken.

The nation's newspapers constantly contain almost unbelievable stories of massive criminal violations by corporations, except, perhaps, those of the newspaper's advertisers. Michael Hirsh wrote *The Sins of Sears Are Not News In Chicago.*[52] His was a story about a 1974 charge by the Chicago regional office of the Federal Trade Commission that Sears, Roebuck, and Company had been systematically engaging in bait-and-switch selling tactics —that is, advertising merchandise at low prices to get customers into the store, then making the advertised merchandise unattractive or unavailable while selling the customer on a higher-priced item after he had been "baited" into the store. The matter was given virtually no news media coverage, and absolutely no coverage by Chicago television stations. Not limited to Sears, many advertising claims by manufacturers not only use bait-and-switch tactics, but just simply make false claims.

During the Watergate investigations, revelations were made about Gulf Oil's $12 million in political contributions made between 1960 and 1973 both in the United States and abroad. Other admissions included American Airlines' report to the Watergate Special Prosecution Force on July 6, 1973, that they had made a $55,000 contribution from corporate funds to President Nixon's reelection campaign. By mid-1976 more than 150 corporations had admitted making illegal contributions at home and abroad. Domestic contributions made by Ashland Oil, Firestone Tire and Rubber Company, Minnesota Mining and Manufacturing Company (3M), Northrup Corporation, and Phillips Petroleum Company included payments made to forty-five members of Congress. Questionable payments were made abroad by Exxon Corporation ($56 million in Italy), Lockheed Aircraft Corporation ($22 million, $12.5 million of which was made in Japan, causing quite a stir there when it was brought to light), American Home Products Corporation, Merck and Company, United Brands Company, and Levi Strauss and Company.

How is it that in this society the white-collar criminals can get away with their offenses, sometimes flaunting violations with what appears to be absolute impunity, and get fat off the naiveté of the public? To put this problem in its true perspective, it is first essential to point out that the number of observers who would ask this question are obviously in the minority. It is simply a matter of fact that a generally accepted attitude with regard to white-collar crimes is one of detached passivity. The phrase *caveat emptor*

[52]Originally appeared in *Columbia Journalism Review,* reprinted in *Crime and Justice In America,* Ed. Jerome Skolnick, Martin Forst, and Jane Scheiber (Del Mar, Calif.: Publisher's Inc.) pp. 51–53.

(translated as "let the buyer beware") has been applied in the attitudes of many agencies, including the courts, toward the victims of white-collar crimes. Although they are in the statutes as crimes, the white-collar crimes are not prosecuted or otherwise handled in the same manner as those of burglars and robbers.

Although there have been some notable exceptions, the president of a law-breaking corporation is not likely to be sent to jail for a violation of the Sherman Antitrust Act. Many studies have been made of this subject, and the consensus of the criminologists who have studied white-collar crime is that a preponderance of the larger corporations in the United States in nearly every category, including banking, manufacturing, mining, securities, mercantile, and numerous others have not only been guilty of criminal offenses and sustained little or no punitive action, but they have been constant repeaters over a period of several years.

In their revealing article written for a newspaper course book of readings, Ralph Nader and Mark Green wrote in "Crime In the Suites":

> When judges were asked "Why do so few convicted Sherman Act violators ever serve jail sentences?" in a recent questionnaire sent by the writers to all district court judges, some of the typical replies were: "recidivism is unlikely," "violators are not hardened criminals," "defendants are victims of economic forces," and "not clear in corporate case that guilty ones are in court."[53]

White-collar criminality is deleterious for the entire community. It enriches the pocketbooks of the people who commit the offenses, but common knowledge throughout the community that such a situation exists and that the violator is not impugned or punished in any manner because of his political or monetary power or because of a lack of sufficient evidence to prove the offense or for any other reason causes the people in the community to develop their own standards and ethical values accordingly. The "guy who cheats a little bit" is really not too bad when he has the biggest house, the biggest cars, the most money, and the greatest social prestige in town. The white-collar law violator, people rationalize, is not *really* committing a *serious* crime. Nobody is getting hurt. The man is a good citizen otherwise and, therefore, is not a criminal but a shrewd businessman. Other side effects of "turning the other way" when it comes to white-collar crimes are that it reduces respect for the law ("laws are only for fools" or "laws are made to be broken") and for the entire system of the administration of justice.

One example of the general attitude of the lawmakers toward one type of white-collar crime is the Sherman Antitrust Act. Offenders may reap

[53]Ralph Nader and Mark Green, "Crime In the Suites," *Crime and Justice In America, A Course By Newspaper Reader,* ed. Jerome H. Skolnick, Martin L. Forst, and Jane L. Scheiber (Del Mar, Calif.: Publisher's Inc. 1977), p. 32.

millions of dollars in profits while their punishment—if handled as a crime —is merely for a misdemeanor. Three methods for enforcement of that particular law are (1) criminal prosecution (the last resort although the first alternative), (2) cease and desist orders by the courts upon appeal by the U.S. Attorney General or a state district attorney, or (3) the victims may sue in civil court for damages. Although the offense is a criminal matter, it is most frequently handled as a tort with no penal sanctions involved.

Nader and Green recounted the following information.

> Since 1890, there have been a total of 461 individual defendants *sentenced* to prison. Most were labor racketeers or individuals who mixed violence with a labor or management scheme. In almost all cases, the sentences were immediately suspended. In the more than 80 year history of the Sherman Act, there have been only *three* occasions when businessmen have actually gone to jail for a criminal violation.
>
> ...From 1890 to 1955 the Sherman Act fine was $5,000 per violation. Both are insignificant, dwarfed by the $49 million average net income for each of the top 500 industrial firms in 1969. Moreover, the actual fines levied are usually far below the maximum possible. Between 1946 and 1953, for example, the average Sherman Act fine was $2,600. Despite the tenfold increase in possible penalties in 1955, between 1955 and 1956 corporate fines averaged only $13,420 and individual fines $3,365....Lee Loevinger, former antitrust division chief, has described GE's $437,500 total fine in the electrical cases (1961 price-fixing conspiracy) as "no more severe than a $3 ticket for overtime parking for a man with a $15,000 income." While some court-imposed fines achieve cooperation and others seek deterrence, antitrust fines do neither.[54]

Organized Crime

Prostitution, gambling, illicit liquor production and distribution, and narcotics trafficking are all "big money" to the underworld. Whenever any of these enterprises extends beyond a "single agent" opereation, it takes on the characteristics of organization. But it may not be as simple as it appears. Organized crime has its tentacles sunken deeply into virtually every type of criminal operation in the United States. It uses many legitimate businesses as a "cover" to explain the wealth of the organized crime operators and their presence in locations where they can get "a piece of the action" in vice operations.

In *Police Administration,* Wilson and McLaren define organized crime as

> the combination of two or more persons for the purpose of establishing, in a geographic area, a monopoly or virtual monopoly in a criminal activity of a

[54]Nader and Green, "Crime in the Streets," *Crime and Justice in America,* pp. 32–33.

> type that provides a continuing financial profit, using gangster techniques and corruption to accomplish their aim.[55]

Contrary to what might be popular belief concerning the types of criminal activity organized crime encompasses, their enterprises extend far beyond the vices. Major predatory crimes which are operated and/or supported by syndicates and cartels of criminal operators include robberies, pickpocketing, car thefts, extortion, major shoplifting operations, burglary, confidence games, abortions, pornography, baby adoption rackets, dishonest carnival gambling, and receiving and transferring stolen goods. A lucrative "scam," or illegal operation, that has been implemented by some organized crime syndicates has been the "bankruptcy scam." It goes as follows: (1) Form a new corporation, (2) open a new bank account with a large sum of money, (3) establish credit, (4) open store and warehouse, (5) make small purchases and pay promptly to establish credit, (6) make large purchases on credit and delay payment, (7) sell or conceal merchandise, (8) conceal income from sales, (9) sell excess merchandise at drastically reduced prices, (10) conceal all proceeds and assets, (11) file bankruptcy, (12) form new corporation and begin again.

In the summer of 1963 a small unobtrusive-looking man of Sicilian descent made a television debut. His name was Joseph Valachi. His act was neither music nor sleight of hand; it was more of a monologue. The storyteller's tale was an awesome one that he presented before the television audience via a U.S. Senate subcommittee hearing. It was all about the machinations of an evil subculture in the United States and other countries that he called "Cosa Nostra," or "our thing," more commonly known as the Mafia.

The Mafia had its early beginning in 1282 in Sicily, when the townspeople of Palermo formed a vigilante group that roamed the countryside killing French soldiers to avenge the rape-slaying of a young bride. The cry of the people was *Morte alla Francia Italia Anela* or "MAFIA," which translated means "Death to the French is Italy's cry." Since that time the Mafia has continued to exist under a variety of conditions. For hundreds of years the predatory band of renegades consisted of heroes to the people of Sicility in the form of an "underground," who harassed the French oppressors. As it exists now, the organization was formed in the eighteenth century as an underground organization to combat the French oppression of the Sicilian people. The Mafia very effectively plundered, robbed, and kidnapped for ransom, and the movement's members and leaders were respected by the citizens as the Robin Hoods of Sicily. After the island was unified as a part of Italy, there was no longer a need for the Mafia underground and they

[55] O. W. Wilson and R. L. McLaren, *Police Administration,* 4th ed. (New York: McGraw-Hill Book Co., Inc., 1977), p. 385.

were out of a job. But the band of pirates on the highways and the mountains continued to operate. Their method was the same, but their victims became their own countrymen. The champions became, as a result of political transformation, an organization of notorious criminals.

Many distinguished experts on organized crime in the United States have known of the Mafia in the United States and of its insidious purpose. It was first exposed in this country by New Orleans' chief of police, David Hennesey, in 1890, and it is still in existence. Joseph Valachi's testimony concerning the existence of the Mafia, or Cosa Nostra, as he called it, was not as spectacular in its content as it was in its character. The revelation by Valachi was a breach of the code of silence, or "Omerta," by one of the organization's own members.

Although the details of an organization can be carefully laid out in orderly fashion, and committee reports and documents prepared by eminent specialists can provide incontrovertible proof that organized crime exists, the direct testimony of one of the co-conspirators had a greater impact and was a more convincing type of proof. Whatever Mr. Valachi's accomplishments may have been in his lifetime, they were eclipsed by his testimony about the Cosa Nostra. It was a most dramatically convincing vehicle, one that provided the millions of television viewers a glimpse at the true story of the Mafia and organized crime.

Dr. Donald R. Cressey wrote the following introduction to the consultant paper he presented to the President's Crime Commission that succinctly outlines the problem of organized crime in the United States:

> In the United States, criminals have managed to organize a nation-wide illicit cartel and confederation. This organization is dedicated to amassing millions of dollars from usury and the illicit sale of lottery tickets, chances on the outcome of horse races and atheltic events, and the same on manipulation of sexual intercourse, narcotics, and liquor. Its presence in our society is morally reprehensible because any citizen purchasing illicit goods and services from organized criminals contributes to an underground culture of fraud, corruption, violence, and murder. Nevertheless, criminal organizations dealing only in illicit goods and services are no great threat to the nation. The danger of organized crime arises because the vast profits acquired from the sale of illicit goods and services are being invested in licit enterprises, in both the business sphere and the governmental sphere. It is when criminal syndicates start to undermine basic economic and political traditions and institutions that the real trouble begins. And the real trouble has begun in the United States.[56]

Organized crime has a bureaucratic structure, and in many respects is similar to a large corporation with a franchise system. Two significant dif-

[56]Donald R. Cressey, *The Functions and Structure of Criminal Syndicates,* consultant paper to the Task Force on Organized Crime (Washington, D.C.: Government Printing Office, 1967), p. 25.

ferences are the types of businesses involved and the manner in which the business is conducted and the company rules enforced. There is considerable involvement of organized crime in legitimate business, but its principal moneymaking ventures are gambling, narcotics, prostitution, business and labor racketeering, boxing, bootlegging of liquor, and murder. In each of the major metropolitan areas where organized crime flourishes, there is a leader who rules by force and fear. There are no formal organizational manuals or charts, but the members know what areas "belong" to whom and which of the many operators is in charge. The organization is secret, and the secrets are carefully guarded, with death a punishment for their revelation.

A capsule look at organized crime may provide some insight into the scope of the problem. Heroin traffic is estimated to cost users in the United States more than $300 million each year. "Lucky" Luciano is alleged to have made a profit of approximately $10 million per year from prostitution and narcotics smuggling prior to his imprisonment and eventual deportation to Italy, from which he continued to operate as a worldwide Mafia leader. Al Capone, a small-time procurer from New York, moved to Chicago and failed to gain admittance into the Mafia but did manage to muscle his way to the top of an organization that yielded for him an annual estimated income of $20 million. In the ten years from 1920 to 1930, one estimate of Capone's earnings showed that he had amassed at least $25 million from gambling, $10 million from prostitution, $10 million in narcotics, and $50 million from the illicit liquor and beer industry that thrived during prohibition.

In 1950 Malcolm Johnson wrote of "scarface Al Capone":

> Of all the gangsters who flourished during prohibition, none attained such power and wealth as Scarface Al Capone. This deceptively mild-looking little man with soft brown eyes migrated from Brooklyn to build an empire of crime in Chicago with influential underworld connections throughout the country. It was one of the ironies of the times that Capone enjoyed complete immunity from the law for the reign of terror he invoked. He was never brought to trial for any of his major crimes including the numerable murders committed by his paid gunmen on orders from himself. When the law finally nailed Capone it was for income-tax evasion. He was convicted in 1931, served seven years in prison, then retired to a life of luxury in Florida until his death, of paresis, in January, 1947. Capone's gang lieutenants carried on his organization, which is still active in Chicago.[57]

The Eighteenth Amendment to the U.S. Constitution provided fertile ground for organized crime and its principals. Prohibition was an attempt to change human behavior by legislation, and the people who wished to

[57]Quoted by Gus Tyler, *Organized Crime In America* (University of Michigan Press, Ann Arbor Paperback, 1967).

partake of alcoholic beverages were forced to violate the law to satisfy their wants. Organized crime readily, willingly, and capably provided for the needs of those people who were willing to violate the law to avoid changing their behavior patterns. Organized crime thrived because of the need for a powerful organization that could sustain such an illicit operation in defiance of the law. Organized crime exists when the following factors are present: (1) There is a need for a product or service by a large number of people; (2) society is failing to provide such a product or service by lawful means; and (3) there is an organized group ready and willing to provide the product or service.

There have been many investigating teams and committees established and sustained for the purpose of studying the problem of organized crime. Local, regional, and nationwide intelligence units investigate and disseminate to other agencies information concerning organized crime and the many people who comprise its ranks. Varying degrees of success are met in combating organized crime, but it continues to thrive in our society.

During an extensive Senate investigation in 1951, Senator Estes Kefauver and his committee in their *Third Interim Report* reported to an apathetic nation:

> There is a sinister criminal organization known as the Mafia operating throughout the country with ties in other nations, in the opinion of the committee. The Mafia is the direct descendant of a criminal organization of the same name originating in the island of Sicily. In this country, the Mafia has also been known as the Black Hand and the Unione Siciliano. The membership of the Mafia today is not confined to persons of Sicilian origin. The Mafia is a loose-knit organization specializing in the sale and distribution of narcotics, the conduct of various gambling enterprises, prostitution, and other rackets based on extortion and violence. The Mafia is the binder which ties together the two major criminal syndicates as well as numerous other criminal groups throughout the country.[58]
>
> The power of the Mafia is based on a ruthless enforcement of its edicts and its own law of vengeance, to which have been creditably attributed literally hundreds of murders throughout the country.

In their final report, the committee concluded:

> The most shocking revelations of the testimony before the committee is the extent of official corruption and connivance in facilitating, and promoting organized crime. Nevertheless, it should not be assumed that our revelations cast doubt as to the integrity of the great preponderance of law enforcement and other officials. On the contrary, our findings and conclusions relate only to a small but disturbing minority of such officials. The committee found evidence

[58]Senate Special Committee to Investigate Organized Crime in Interstate Commerce, *Third Interim Report* (Washington, D.C.: Government Printing Office, 1951).

of corruption and connivance at all levels of government—Federal, State, and local. . . . The evidence of corruption and connivance with government officials on the state and local levels with organized crime is present in four different forms:

1. Direct bribe of protection payments (juice) are made to law enforcement officials, so that they will not interfere with specific criminal activities.
2. Political influence and pressure of important officials or political leaders is used to protect criminal activities or further the interests of criminal gangs.
3. Law enforcement officials are found in possession of unusual and unexplained wealth.
4. Law enforcement officials participate directly in the business of organized crime.[59]

Why does our society allow organized crime in all of its ugliness and with its Saroyan-like characters with the "funny" monickers (Bugsy, Scarface, Two Fingers, Fats, Ducks, Lucky, Trigger, Little Augy, Big John) to continue to thrive like a leech sucking the life blood from a society that cannot spare the blood? It is apparently accepted in a society as a "not-so-ugly" and "not-so-unwanted" syndicated service that has permanently ingratiated itself to a large enough segment of society that it is a necessary part of society—necessary, that is, to those who avail themselves of the goods and services that organized crime provides for them.

Concerning organized crime and politics, Block and Geis explained it as follows:

> Two basic items help to explain the role of organized crime in electoral affairs. First, running for political office is expensive, and a candidate must usually either have personal wealth or secure contributions for his campaign from groups or individuals who have such wealth. Second, groups or individuals who contribute money to political funds usually do so with the understanding, implicit or explicit, that they will later be granted certain benefits, such as being left alone. Money is rarely given for pure altruistic reasons, such as a desire for better government.[60]

The organized crime leaders do not resemble the "common criminal." Cressey explained the difference between the "common" criminal and the organized crime principal for the President's Crime Commission Task Force on Organized Crime:

> The basic distinction between ordinary criminals and organized criminals in the United States turns on the fact that the ordinary criminal is wholly pred-

[59]Senate Special Committee to Investigate Organized Crime in Interstate Commerce (Washington, D.C.: Government Printing Office, 1951).

[60]Block, and Geis, *Man, Crime, and Society,* p. 195.

atory, while the man participating in crime on a rational, systematic basis offers a return to the respectable members of society. If all burglars were miraculously abolished, they would be missed by only a few persons to whose income of employment they contribute directly—burglary insurance companies, manufacturers of locks and other security devices, police, prison personnel, and a few others. But if the confederation of men employed in illicit businesses were suddenly abolished, it would be sorely missed because it performs services for which there is a great public demand. The organized criminal, by definition, occupies a position in a social system, an "organization," which has been rationally designed to maximize profits by performing illegal services and providing legally forbidden products demanded by the members of the broader society in which he lives. Just as society has made a place for the confederation by demanding illicit gambling, alcohol and narcotics, usurious loans, prostitution, and cheap supply of labor, the confederation makes places, in an integrated set of positions, for the use of skills in a wide variety of specialists.[61]

Congressional Record, Tuesday, March 11, 1969:

U.S. Senator John McClellan, Chairman of the Subcommittee on Criminal Laws and Procedures in a speech before the U.S. Senate stated:

"Legitimate business is another area into which organized crime has begun most recently and widely to extend its influence. In most cities, it now dominates the fields of juke box and vending machine distribution. Laundry services, liquor and beer distribution, nightclubs, food wholesaling, record manufacturing, the garment industry, and a host of other legitimate lines of endeavor have been invaded and taken over. The Special Senate Committee to Investigate Organized Crime in Interstate Commerce, under the leadership of Senator Estes Kefauver, noted in 1952 that the following industries had been invaded: advertising, amusement, appliances, automobile, baking, ballrooms, bowling alleys, banking, basketball, boxing, cigarette distribution, coal, communications, construction, drug stores, electrical equipment, florists, food, football, garment, gas, hotels, import-export, insurance, jukebox, laundry, liquor, loan, news services, newspapers, oil, paper products, radio, real estate, restaurants, scrap shipping, steel surplus, television, theaters, and transportation."[62]

"Victimless Crimes"

During recent years, considerable discussion and legislative debates have taken place involving crime categories that have been called "crimes without victims," or "victimless crimes." Although laws may be enacted and enforced for what the courts have described as essential for the public health, welfare, and morals, among other considerations, some individuals

[61]Cressey, *Criminal Syndicates,* p. 29.

[62]John McClellan in a speech given before the U.S. Senate, March 11, 1969, as reported in the Congressional Record, CXU, No. 43, p. 3.

have assumed the posture that there are certain activities that involve personal habits and private morals. In line with the personal nature of the acts involved, the argument usually evolves around the question as to whether personal choice of consenting adults in their own privacy should be free from legal restraints or whether there should be laws in existence.

The criminal statutes that are usually discussed in this "victimless crime" category usually include prostitution, homosexual and other sexual practices generally described as perverse, obscenity in publication and in exhibitions, gambling, and the abuse of narcotics and dangerous drugs. Depending on the speaker, this list may vary somewhat, but they usually involve a question of private versus public morals. Two of the many views expressed are presented here for your consideration with a view to your own exploration and evaluation.

An American Bar Association committee report presented one view:

> The burdens imposed on the criminal justice system by overcriminalization must be significantly reduced and, where possible, eliminated completely.
>
> - Legislative reform commissions should be established to consider repeal of laws which define victimless conduct as criminal and which divert the resources needed by the criminal justice system to combat urban crimes.
> - Repeal of such laws should be given top priority by the nation's legislatures.
> - Where appropriate, repeal of laws governing victimless crimes should be accompanied by a strengthening of social agencies most qualified to provide necessary services to those whose conduct is now controlled only by criminal law.[63]

Former Los Angeles police chief, Edward M. Davis, had this to say about the matter:

> There have been demands that these so-called "victimless" crimes be legitimized by legislation. This course of action, it is argued, would enable the police to deploy manpower against seemingly more serious crimes—those involving complaining victims. Assertedly, this re-allocation of police resources would result in reduced levels of crime. Supporters of this concept maintain that these offenses should be accepted as manifestations of an enlightened public morality, and that police control must be viewed as an unwarranted abridgement of individual freedoms. However, such a point of view displays a dangerous naivete which does not consider the pernicious nature of "victimless crimes."
>
> ...Crimes of the "victimless" character attack the individuality which is so highly valued by Americans for they have an eroding effect upon our principles and values, and particularly of those persons directly involved.[64]

[63] ABA, *New Perspectives on Urban Crime,* p. 1.

[64] Edward M. Davis, "Victimless Crimes—The Case for Continued Enforcement, *Journal of Police Science and Administration,* I, No. 1, March, 1973, p. 11.

Genocide

Genocide, or destruction of—in whole or in part—any national, ethnic, racial, or religious social group, is one of the most serious of all crimes. Although probably the most dramatic and most highly publicized act of massive genocide was committed under the direction of Adolph Hitler in the 1940s, we have seen evidence of it at various times and places continuously since the beginning of recorded history. On December 9, 1948, the General Assembly of the United Nations approved the Convention on the Prevention and Punishment of the Crime of Genocide. It became law in 1951 and was signed by more than sixty nations. As defined by that law, the following acts constitute the crime of genocide:

1. Killing members of the group.
2. Causing serious bodily or mental harm to members of the group.
3. Deliberately inflicting on the group conditions of life calculated to bring about its partial or total physical destruction.
4. Imposing measures that intend to prevent births in the group.
5. Forcible transferring children of the group to another group.

SUMMARY

In this chapter we have explored, although somewhat cursorily, many of the explanations of the causes and effects of crime, several categories of criminal offenses and the people who commit them, and a discussion of some of the problems that face the criminal justice system in our modern society. Crimes and the people who commit them should not be classified or graded as one labels fruits or vegetables for canning and the market. Although paragraph headings and names we have attached to some of the subjects covered in this chapter for the sake of discussion may encourage such categorization, may we hasten to add that the study of criminology is not an exact science, but a searching inquiry into the vagaries of man and his environment.

EXERCISES AND STUDY QUESTIONS

1. In what ways may human needs be used to explain the causes of crime?
2. What is the "Cartesian Dichotomy?"
3. What is Hedonism and what type crime might a Hedonist commit?
4. What was Maslow's hierarchy of needs, and how does it relate to the study of crime causes?
5. How would Freud explain deviant behavior if he were here today?
6. Describe Beccaria's "pain avoidance" theory.

7. What are psychological needs? physical needs? social needs?

8. Describe a sociopath. If you have ever known one, how does that person compare to the description in the text?

9. Who was Lombroso, and what did he have to say about the criminal characteristics in individuals?

10. What is "biological positivism?"

11. How did Sheldon explain the endomorphic, ectomorphic, and mesomorphic body shapes and their relationship to crime?

12. Describe the phenomenon known as the "Myth of Melbourne" and the current position on crime cause as related to the XYY syndrome.

13. List and discuss at least three current theories on crime cause that you did not find in this text.

14. In his Chicago study, what did Shaw show with his pin maps?

15. Shaw's study involved many minority groups. Of those listed, which one demonstrated the greatest propensity for criminal behavior?

16. Define "social ecology."

17. Explain in a few words why the adolescent would seek membership in a gang.

18. Describe Sutherland's theory of differential association.

19. How does Haskell's theory concerning reference groups differ from Sutherland's theory of differential association?

20. Does the text offer any proof that crimes of violence increase during a full moon?

21. What are the dangers attendant to giving an offender a label?

22. Describe the incidental offender and give an example of three types of crime one might commit.

23. What is your opinion about the relationship between poverty and criminal behavior?

24. What is an exceptional offender? Give two examples of the types of crime that are likely to be committed by this individual.

25. Distinguish a career offender from a professional offender as described in this chapter, and give two examples for types of crimes likely to be committed by each.

26. What is a recidivist, and what can be done to prevent one from being classified as one?

27. What types of criminal behavior are most frequently associated with the phenomenon known as organized crime?

28. Give at least three examples of white-collar crimes you have read about, particularly during the last three months.

29. What is a bankruptcy scam, and how does it work?

30. Define "genocide."

31. What is a "victimless crime?" Give an example of one.

RECOMMENDED SEMESTER/TERM PROJECTS

1. Write a one-paragraph statement concerning your definition of a victimless crime, and write a position paper on whether or not you believe such crimes should be "decriminalized."

2. Prepare a list of types of conduct for which you cannot find a criminal law, and state why each one should be made a crime. Then, go through the criminal code for the state where you live and list those offenses you believe should be taken off the books, giving your reason why each one should be "decriminalized."

SUGGESTED FOR ADDITIONAL STUDY

BLOCH, HERBERT A., AND GILBERT GEIS, *Man, Crime, and Society* (2d ed.). New York: Random House, 1970.

CAREY, JAMES F., *Introduction to Criminology.* Englewood Cliffs: Prentice-Hall, 1978.

COHEN, BRUCE J., ed., *Crime In America: Perspectives On Criminal and Delinquent Behavior* (2nd ed.). Itasca, Ill.: F. E. Peacock Publishers, Inc., 1977.

CRESSEY, DONALD R., *Theft of the Nation: The Structure and Operations of Organized Crime in America.* New York: Harper & Row, Publishers, 1960.

FOX, VERNON, *Introduction To Criminology.* Englewood Cliffs, N.J.: Prentice-Hall, Inc., 1976.

HAHN, PAUL H., *The Juvenile Offender and the Law.* Cincinnati: W. H. Anderson Co., 1971.

KEFAUVER, ESTES, *Crime in America.* New York: Doubleday and Company, Inc., 1951.

President's Commission on Law Enforcement and Administration of Justice, *Task Force Report: Organized Crime.* Washington, D.C.: Government Printing Office, 1967.

______, *Psychology Today, An Introduction.* Del Mar, Calif.: CRM, Inc., 1970.

QUINNEY, RICHARD, *The Problem of Crime.* New York: Dodd, Mead, & Co., 1970. See also his update of this same title written with John Wildeman, published by Harper & Row, Publishers, 1977.

SANDHU, HARJIT S., *Juvenile Delinquency: Cause, Control, and Prevention.* New York: McGraw-Hill, Inc., 1977.

SCHAFER, STEPHEN, *Introduction To Criminology.* Reston, Va.: Reston Publishing Co., 1978.

SHAW, C. R., and H. D. MCKAY, *Juvenile Delinquency In Urban Areas.* Chicago: University of Chicago Press, 1942.

SKOLNICK, JEROME H., MARTIN L. FORST, and JANE L. SCHEIBER, eds., *Crime and Justice In America. A Course by Newspaper Reader.* Del Mar, Calif.: Publishers, Inc., 1977.

SUTHERLAND, EDWIN H., and DONALD R. CRESSEY, *Principles of Criminology* (9th ed.). Philadelphia: J. B. Lippincott Company, 1974.

TAFT, DONALD R., and RALPH W. ENGLAND, JR., *Criminology* (4th ed.). New York: Macmillan Co., 1964.

TAYLOR, IAN, PAUL WALTON, and JOCK YOUNG, *The New Criminology: for a Social Theory of Deviance.* London: Routledge and Kegan Paul, Ltd., 1973.

VETTER, HAROLD J., and IRA J. SILVERMAN, *The Nature of Crime.* Philadelphia: W. B. Saunders Company, 1978.

5

Evolution of the System of Criminal Justice

INTRODUCTION

Probably one of the best places to start when studying the criminal justice system of the present is to look at its origins. The justice system is rich in history and inseparable from the society which it serves. Modern criminal justice has its roots implanted among the roots of modern civilization. Some of the earliest methods and agencies have survived the test of time and are stronger than ever today.

Capital punishment, although rarely performed today, was common four thousand years ago. The shire-reeve of merry olde England is now the County Sheriff, the town marshal of 1655 has been replaced by the chief of police and the municipal court marshal. The grand jury and the jury trial originated in 1166. The state-supported public defender appeared on the scene in 1913. Probation started with a little old shoemaker named Augustus in 1841, and the juvenile court made its debut in 1899. Although imprisonment for wrong-doing began long before 1790, it wasn't until that year when the predecessor of today's American prisons began.

In this chapter we shall explore ancient history law enforcement, including the philosophies of Plato, Hammurabi, Draco, Justinian; then go into the more recent English criminal justice system, which provided the foundation for our own system in the United States. The constitutional safeguards written into the first ten amendments—the Bill of Rights—were guaranteed as a result of pressures brought about by the people who had suffered at the hands of an unfair central English government and a tyrant-king.

The chapter is rounded out with a survey of the development of the U.S. Judicial and Corrections systems. Although the former has its roots in England as does law enforcement, the latter is more indigenous to the eastern United States, with some influences from other countries. For example, probation was developed in Boston, based upon conditional release concepts from Anglo-Saxon times; the Quakers of Pennsylvania were quite influential in development of modern prison systems; parole came from the Irish and English, but was improved upon in the United States.

DEVELOPMENT OF LAW ENFORCEMENT

The history of civilization reflects a parallel history of various forms of social controls, laws and regulations, and some type of enforcement body to carry out the will of those who govern as the enforcement arm of the executive authority of the government, as prescribed by the laws promulgated by the legislature, and as interpreted by the judicial body within the governmental structure. The mode of law enforcement has depended largely upon the type of government in existence, ranging along the entire spectrum of political and philosophical thought.

Law enforcement in the United States is generally modeled after the English system of law enforcement, as is the court system and some of the correctional concepts in current practice. But law enforcement did not originate in England. Historical data record that laws and law enforcement existed in ancient Egypt, Rome, China, Greece, and all of the civilizations that have been documented by recorded data.

ANCIENT HISTORY

Some historians have written that there were laws and some sort of police enforcement as long ago as 4000 B.C. in China and Egypt. It is only logical to assume this if there was any form of civilization. The first permanent record of any sort concerning law enforcement to which we can refer with any authority are the Codes of Hammurabi, the Babylonian ruler who lived about 2000 B.C. His codes were inscribed on stones of black diorite, found by modern archaeologists, and are still legible. They prescribe and proscribe rules of conduct and provide for specific methods of punishment for the violators. They have been called one of the greatest contributions to mankind. The 4,000 lines of script, broken down into 282 clauses, included three essential parts, in addition to the death penalty as punishment for most of the crimes: (1) the concept of "if a freeman destroys the eye of another, his eye shall be destroyed," and "if anyone breaks a freeman's bone, his bone shall be broken," (2) the sanctity of an oath before God, and (3) the requirement of written evidence in all legal matters.

In Ancient Greece, the board of Ephors was comprised of five elected citizens of Sparta. This all-powerful board served as executive, judicial, and legislative officials of government. This body existed from about 800 B.C. until about A.D. 200, except for a short time when it was abolished circa 227 B.C. The Ephors provided a form of civilian control over the dual kingship of Sparta, and whenever there was a dispute between the two kings, the ephors made the vote that broke the tie. They possessed the highest executive power in the country, and there were no controls over their personal conduct except the influence and authority of the other members. An ephor presided over the Senate and Assembly, carried out its decrees, supervised education, levied fines, inflicted other forms of punishment, arrested and tried other ephori for suspected transgressions, and performed all other types of regulation. This type of law enforcement naturally spawned the corrupt enforcer and enriched the greedy because there was no control over them by the people, except to vote against them at election time, if they dared.

In 620 B.C. Draco was appointed thesmothete (lawgiver extraordinary). He consolidated and tightened up the laws for the city-states of Greece, prescribing death as punishment for most crimes, including theft. The term "Draconian" is a synonym for harshness, as is the word "Spartan." Solon became the ruler of Athens about 594 B.C. He lessened the harsh punishments, eliminating the death penalty for all crimes except murder. He prescribed fines for rape and seduction, and legalized prostitution. Solon is known as one of the seven sages of Ancient Greece, and his name is a synonym for "wise rule."

Plato, originally named Aristocles (427?–347 B.C.), was a Greek philosopher who developed the idea that justice was the central force of morality that inspires men to do what is right. He categorized crimes according to time of day and seriousness and prescribed punishment in degrees to match the degree of crime. His student, Aristotle (384–322 B.C.), another philosopher who was also teacher to Alexander the Great, authored the Constitution of Athens in his *Politics.* He defined law as an agreement between people to do justice to each other. He addressed the difference between rule of law and rule of men and stated that rule of law should prevail.

In 451 and again in 450 B.C. two groups of magistrates known as decemvirs were appointed in Rome to draw up a code of laws, known as the Twelve Tables. They still exist as the basis for modern Roman law, and much of our civil law in such matters as ownership, inheritance, torts, and judicial process. The use of courts and judges to settle disputes began in Rome. About two hundred years later, or about 250 B.C. the rights of habeas corpus and appeal were added to the Roman Laws.

The most significant contribution to law by Rome was in the Emperor Justinian's (A.D. 483–565) *Corpus Juris Civilis,* or *Body of Civil Law.* Three Roman rules that are intrinsic to the United States' system of laws include the right of the accused to face his accuser, the right to be considered innocent until proven guilty, and the right to a fair trial. In A.D. 785 Charlemagne enacted his Capitularies (bodies of laws), in order to assure uniformity throughout the Roman Empire. The laws involved crimes, weights and measures, tolls, commerce, and emergency measures for dealing with famine and pestilence. The Constitutio Criminalis Carolina, enacted during the reign of Charles V in A.D. 1532, regulated the standing and oath of magistrates, the character of witnesses, penalties for crimes, and circumstances when torture was permissible.

The first recorded police agency in Egypt was created about 1400 B.C. when the pharaoh Amenhotep set up custom houses and a marine patrol to guard against smuggling. In France marshals were appointed by the King to serve as the police for the nation. In A.D. 875 a body of armed and trained men was created, and called the maré chausée. During the reign of Francis I (1494–1547) a military force of mounted archers was formed to protect the highways. This force was the predecessor to the police of today in France, the gendarmerie.

THE ENGLISH BACKGROUND OF OUR U.S. POLICE SYSTEM

The police role as we know it in the United States is to serve as the enforcement arm of the executive branch of government. The powers and limitations are established by law and are generally limited to the protection of life and property and the enforcement of written laws only. The judging and punishing of offenders is the responsibility of other branches of our government. Although the origins of the many peoples in this country are in almost every part of the world, the U.S. police system is principally based upon the English system. Federal, state, and local law enforcement agencies operate independently within their own spheres of jurisdiction without any semblance of hierarchy. As we discuss the historical evolution of English law enforcement, the similarities will be readily apparent.

Anglo-Saxon Period

During the latter part of the Anglo-Saxon period in the ninth century, King Alfred established what was to be one of the most significant police roles in English history. Recognizing the need for stricter adherence to the rules of society by the people, Alfred established a "tithing system" in each county, or "shire." The chief judicial and law enforcement officer in each shire was the "shire-reeve," an appointee of the crown. In the language of the Saxons, the reeve had been known as the *gerefa.* This individual was the local government, representing the state in all matters of nationwide or local importance. He served at the pleasure of the king, and his tenure was dependent upon order within his own jurisdiction as well as profits to the king.

Law enforcement under the broad, general control of the shire-reeve was accomplished by means of the tithing system. Each head of a household would be responsible for his own family's conduct, as well as that of the other tithings, or members within his group of ten families. These ten families would be under the direction of one of their number designated as chief tithingman. The philosophy of this method was to make neighbors responsible for each other, compelling them to bring the wrongdoer to trial or else suffer the consequences themselves. It was an honor system on a national scale. The tithings were grouped into larger units known as "hundreds"; the hundreds in the shire, or county, comprised the major structure of the political organization within the shire. All able-bodied men in the shires were usually armed, and were always ready to form the *posse comitatus,* or "power of the county," wherever and whenever the "hue and cry" was sounded by the shire-reeve or one of his lieutenants—the chief tithingman—announcing that a wrongful act had been committed by someone within the shire. The shire-reeve and his posse would seek out the violator and bring him to trial and punishment. Everyone within this system was involved in the enforcement of the laws and edicts of the land under the guidance of the shire-reeve.

Norman Period

The Norman king, William I (the Conqueror, 1027–1087), kept the tithing and shire system during his reign, but reinforced its strength by giving the shire-reeve a military rank in addition to his already powerful civil position. He was usually selected from the landlord baronage, and the position was frequently passed along from father to son for several generations. The shire-reeve served at the pleasure—or displeasure—of the king and usually retained a firm grip on that office as long as he was instrumental in gaining a profit or advantage for the crown.

The prototype of our American county sheriff maintained his role as chief law enforcement officer in the shire for several hundred years. Sometime early in the Norman period (1066–1285) the *Comes Stabuli* (constable) appeared on the scene. Constables were hired on a full-time basis to aid the shire-reeve in carrying out his duties, thereby giving some continuity to the task of law enforcement. The *Comes Stabuli* were not much unlike the modern American town constable or chief of police.

In 1072, the *Vicecomes,* or traveling (circuit court) judges, were introduced to the English scene, and the law enforcement powers of the sheriff and constables were separated from their judicial powers.

Prior to the year 1166, there were many different types of private policemen hired by the citizens and merchants to protect their persons, their homes, and their shops. The shire-reeves and the assistants, the *Comes Stabuli,* were more concerned with the more important matters of the crown, such as land and tax problems, and crimes against the populace as a whole rather than crimes against individual victims, such as burglary or assault. But during the year of 1166—a significant one for the history of law enforcement—King Henry II (the Law-Giver) issued his *Legas Henrici,* which made criminal law enforcement a public matter. He separated offenses into felonies and misdemeanors by defining the felonies and leaving all other offenses in the category of misdemeanors. His decree stated: "There will be certain offenses against the King's peace, arson, robbery, murder, false coinage, and crimes of violence. These we deem to be felonious." His justices toured the countryside, administering a strengthened criminal law system. In 1811 Henry II's Assize of Arms established a national guard.

The Magna Carta was signed under protest by King John in 1215 at Runnymeade and was an agreement that the people would be provided "due process of the laws," protecting the individual against unnecessary infringement upon his rights and liberty by the crown. Governmental organization was changed so that there was more local control with a separation of state and local governments. Article 13 of Magna Carta stated in part, "... the city of London shall have all its ancient liberties and free customs... and all other cities and villages shall have their liberties and customs." Another article in that document concerned due process, and read: "No freeman shall be taken or imprisoned or disposed or outlawed or banished or in any way destroyed except by the legal judgement of his peers or the laws of the land."

Perhaps the greatest feature of the Magna Carta was that it became a symbol of the supremacy of the Constitution over the king. One of the most significant contributions of the Magna Carta is that it showed the viability of opposition to excessive use of royal power.

Westminster Period

In Westminster, then capital of England, King Edward I established a curfew in 1285 by ordering that the city's gates be closed so that the undesirables would be locked out of the city at nighttime, and the residents and other occupants be locked in. In order to enforce the curfew, a night watch was created. The night watchmen were called bailiffs. Their duties included guarding the gates to the city between sunset and sunrise, checking on the security of all places within the city, and keeping track of all "persons and lodgers." Members of the night watch were selected from the ranks of able-bodied men in the community on a compulsory basis and were paid for their services. They carried lanterns and staffs while on patrol and were virtually ineffective, according to historians. One branch of the night watch of that time was the *Police Desmour,* charged with the responsibility of regulating streetwalkers and prostitutes and keeping them in their designated areas.

In his Edict of Winchester in 1285, Edward charged local property owners, in groups of one hundred each, with responsibility for keeping the peace in their respective districts. Thus, the tithing system was reinforced by this edict. The edict laid down the principle of local rather than central government responsibility for law enforcement.[1] Penalties were imposed on those who protected or concealed criminals, and established a Watch and Ward system of patrol for protection.

It was not until about the fourteenth century that policemen were actually trained for their jobs. The office of justice of the peace was created to replace the shire-reeve, and to more efficiently handle the duties of his office. Each shire, or county, was provided three or four men "learned in the law" with full authority to "pursue, arrest, chastise, and imprison." They were assisted by the constables, who had previously been under the control of the shire-reeves. The justice of the peace retained his role of policeman and judge for about seventy-five years, when the office evolved into a strictly judicial role.

In 1487 Henry VII (1457–1509) established the Court of the Star Chamber as a judicial instrument under which alleged criminal offenders were charged, tried, and sentenced without any right to present evidence or testimony on their own behalf. During the reign of Elizabeth I, from 1533 to 1603, the Court of the Star Chamber was not used. Charles I, who reigned from 1625 to 1649, revived the Star Chamber, although Parliament declared in a Petition of Right in 1628 that no one should be imprisoned without due process, as provided by the Magna Carta. Charles continued to use it for another twenty years, when he finally abolished it in 1648. For his transgressions and abuse of the people, Charles was defeated in Civil War in 1649, captured, tried, convicted, and beheaded.

Watch and Ward Period

Between the years 1500 and 1800 several different police systems were inaugurated in England. There were basically three new systems: the merchant police or Ward and Watch, the parochial police, and the military police. The merchant police were private watchmen employed by the bankers and merchants to protect their property. They guarded the places at nighttime and also worked as private detectives for the purpose of locating and recovering stolen goods. One of those detective forces was the Bow Street Runners, a colorful cutthroat group of bounty hunters for criminals and their booty. They carried on their operations initially for Magistrates John and Henry Fielding.[2]

Sir Henry Fielding, author and jurist wrote in 1751, three years following

[1]Donald R. Taft and Ralph W. England, Jr., *Criminology*, 4th ed. (New York: Macmillan Co., 1964), p. 319.

[2]Henry Goddard, *Memories of a Bow Street Runner* (New York: William Morrow, 1957).

his appointment as magistrate for Middlesex and Westminster: (1) Policing was a municipal function, (2) men recruited for policing should be well paid, (3) a mobile patrol was needed to police the highways, (4) runners were needed to get to the scene of the crime quickly, and (5) a separate police court should be established.[3]

The second type of police force to appear during that period was the parochial police, who were employed by the religious parishioners for the protection of their members and their property. The third police force was the government-operated military police under the direction of the provost marshal and the crown.

In 1655 Oliver Cromwell divided England and Wales into twelve police, or military, precincts. He placed a marshal in charge of each precinct and maintained control of the people by means of this system during his reign. The rule was military and the law was Martial Rule, which superseded all forms of local government control. The Magna Carta and the Bill of Rights were disregarded under the guise of military expediency.

Following Cromwell's death in 1658, and the short stay in office by his son, Richard, Charles II—son of Charles I—took the throne. Charles II vowed to honor the Magna Carta and Petition of Rights. In 1679, Parliament enacted the Habeas Corpus Act. Under that Act, the accused must be brought before a magistrate, evidence presented, and an explanation given of why he was being held. Following the flight of James II, William of Orange was offered the crown in 1689 with the provision that he would honor the English Bill of Rights.

By 1792 the population of London had grown to nearly 1 million. In that year the Middlesex Justices Act provided for a police force of only 126 constables, which was hardly conducive to crime control. Regarding that era, Taft and England reported:

> The inadequacy of so small a number in London . . . (of one million people) . . . soon became evident. Crime and disorder went unchecked, the latter becoming particularly threatening after the turn of the nineteenth century, when riots against the corn laws and against machines put the English government in fear for its very existence.[4]

Modern Period

In 1829, Sir Robert Peel, British Home Secretary during the Prime Ministry of the Duke of Wellington (later Prime Minister himself from 1834 to 1835 and 1841 to 1846) proposed the Metropolitan Police Act, also known

[3]Fielding, Henry, *An Enquiry Into the Cause of the Late Increase In Robberies* (England, circa 1751).

[4]Taft and England, *Criminology,* p. 320.

as An Act for Improving the Police In and Near the Metropolis. In 1817, as Secretary for Ireland, Peel had established the Irish Constabulary. His bill called for a centrally controlled police force for the Greater London Metropolitan area. He based his conclusions as to the need for a new police system upon a study completed by Dr. Patrick Colquhoun. The various police agencies, both public and private, were ineffective. Peel labeled the Ward and Watch the "shiver and shake watch." He stated that the men comprising the watch spent half the night shaking from the cold and the other half shaking from fear. Sir Robert's bill was passed, and the entire world watched the creation of one of the first truly professional police agencies. The police departments in the United States were patterned after the London Metropolitan Police, as we shall see in this and succeeding chapters in this book.

Sir Robert first divided the London Metropolitan area (not the City of London, which is a small and separate entity) into sectors, or districts, and replaced the existing police systems with his new organization, one sector at a time. He personally interviewed and selected all candidates for the new department, and out of 12,000 who applied, he put together a force of 3,314 men. Tenure was dependent upon the ability and production of the men, and candidates served a probationary period. Turnover during the first few years of operation was enormous, and Sir Robert stated: "The securing and training of proper persons is at the root of efficiency." By 1835 the entire department was organized and operational, with headquarters at Scotland Yard. The exact origin of the name Scotland Yard is subject to debate, but the ancient buildings and grounds bore the name until 1890, when the department moved to New Scotland Yard.

The force was organized along military lines, although their uniforms were nonmilitary in appearance and they were allowed to carry only truncheons, or short nightsticks. Police agencies have since been considered paramilitary in nature. Numbered police badges were issued to identify the men as individuals as well as officers of the law. The salaries of these new officers were dependent upon their effectiveness in reducing crime, and they were assigned to shifts that rotated around the clock. The reporting system was improved so as to provide statistics on the crime picture in the area as well as to provide modus operandi information to assist in the identification and apprehension of offenders. A detective bureau was established for the purpose of conducting investigations under circumstances in which the appearance of the uniform would hinder investigation.

Twelve principles of modern law enforcement emerged at the time of the Peelian Reform and the establishment of the new London Metropolitan Police Department. As you read them here, compare them to the requirements of law enforcement today in the United States nearly a century and a half later.

Principles of the Peelian Reform

1. The police must be stable, efficient, and organized along military lines.
2. The police must be under government control.
3. The absence of crime will best prove the efficiency of the police.
4. The distribution of crime news is essential.
5. The deployment of police strength, both by time and area, is essential.
6. No quality is more indispensable to a policeman than a perfect command of temper. A quiet, determined manner has more effect than violent action.
7. Good appearance commands respect.
8. The selection and training of proper persons are at the root of efficient law enforcement.
9. Public security demands that every police officer be given an identifying number.
10. Police headquarters should be centrally located and easily accessible to the people.
11. Policemen should be hired on a probationary basis before permanent assignment.
12. Police crime records are necessary to the best distribution of police strength.[4]

We have devoted a great deal of space to the English police system because it is apparent that the American system developed along the same general lines in techniques and traditions. The various law enforcement officers who appeared in England have their American equivalents, as we will see in subsequent chapters. These include the modern American sheriff, marshal, constable, justice of the peace, jury, grand jury, and the many other police officials who comprise the American law enforcement segment of the criminal justice system.

THE EVOLUTION OF LAW ENFORCEMENT IN THE UNITED STATES

Early Law Enforcement In 1833, the City of New York was so impressed with the efficiency of the Metropolitan Police Department in London that a delegation was sent to that city to study the department with a view toward adopting some of their ideas. The result was the formation of the New York City Police Department in 1844 along the general lines of Scotland Yard. The department in New York was the first of its kind in the United States, followed by Boston in 1850, Chicago in 1851, Cincinnati in 1852, Philadelphia in 1855, Baltimore in 1857, and Detroit in 1865. Others throughout the country followed suit rapidly in the years that followed. The major difference between the two systems is the form of control. The American police forces are comparatively free from any federal or central control; each autonomous community is responsible for the establishment, maintenance, and administration of its own police department.

But let's go back to the earlier beginnings of law enforcement in the United States. When the settlers came to this country, they brought with them their various traditions and customs. As a body, the new residents of this country were suspicious and contemptuous of a strong central government; local autonomy was fiercely defended. The law enforcement bodies were no exception in this trend toward local control. Although the systems of the Old and New World were similar, the controls were diametrically opposed. The control of the local police in most European countries was by strong central governments. The English customs had the greatest amount of influence on our police systems, so the offices of the shire-reeve and constable in England became the sheriff and constable in the populated areas of this country, and the U.S. marshal was the law enforcement officer in the territories and unpopulated areas. The local sheriffs and constables were elected for short terms by the people whom they served instead of being appointed by any central authority. This was, of course, after the settlers had emancipated themselves from English rule and formed an independent government.

New England became a land of settlements and villages centering around industry and commerce. The municipal type of government was formed, and the municipal police officer—the constable or "watch and ward" type of patrolman—was elected into office. In the South, agricultural and rural, the county form of government and the county sheriff were adopted as most suitable to fill the needs of the people.

It appears that when the first counties were established in Virginia in 1634, the office of *sheriff* was introduced to the United States. Maryland followed, and in both states the sheriff was delegated the same powers of the office held in England.[5]

Many other types of law enforcement were tried in various parts of the New World. These various systems were usually holdovers from the native countries of the residents of the different communities. For example, in New Amsterdam, later New York, the police patrol officers of the night watch for many years were called the "rattle watch" because they carried with them larger versions of the rattles now used as party toys with which to warn would-be offenders of their presence. Boston had an organized night watch as early as 1636, whose purpose it was to patrol the streets to combat larceny. Philadelphia had a similar night watch, and other cities of any size had some semblance of night patrols. Most of them were vigilante, or volunteer, groups that poorly supplemented the sheriffs and constables and their few assistants.

A day watch, organized to combat crime when the night watch was not operating, was created about 1800 in New York. This was the first daytime,

[5]Larry A. Giddings, Mark Furstenberg, and Henry J. Noble, *Manual on Training for Sheriffs,* LEAA Grant No. 268 (Washington, D.C.: Government Printing Office, 1968), p. viii.

paid police force to appear in America, and the two separate watches—night and day—continued to operate independently for many years. Other communities followed the lead of New York by hiring fulltime, paid policemen, but there is no record of there ever having been a round-the-clock police force in the United States until 1844, when New York City combined the day and night watches into a single police force fashioned after the London Metropolitan Police Department. Boston followed in 1850, and the modern noncivilian police force as we know it today made its appearance on the American scene. It is interesting to note that it was not until the year 1855 that the police were allowed to wear uniforms. Prior to that time, it was considered un-American for civilian police officers to wear any clothing that would give them a military or "uncivilian" appearance.

Figure 5-1 The signal bell was used by many police departments to summon their officers to headquarters.
Courtesy Police Department, Lawton, Oklahoma.

The people in Chicago were confronted by "policemen" with a very definite military appearance; law enforcement duties were performed by soldiers from Fort Dearborn until about 1851, at which time the city's population had reached 100,000.[6]

Since 1844 the police service in the United States has remained pretty much the same in some respects and has changed drastically in other respects. Let's take a look at some of the landmarks in the progress of law enforcement

[6]Taft and England, *Criminology,* p. 320.

in the cities and counties of the United States. Many systems that originated many years ago appealed to the residents and became so much a part of the communities that they are still in existence today throughout the country.

Sheriff and Constable The sheriff and constable are constitutionally elected officers and are usually designated as the chief law enforcement officers in their respective areas of jurisdiction. The sheriff is generally the title assigned to the officer for the county, and the constable is usually responsible for a smaller area, such as an unincorporated township. Their terms of office are usually for two to four years, and in many states they cannot succeed themselves in office. The philosophy behind this law is that within a short period of time in office an individual cannot gain too much control over the people who elect him. The office of constable is slowly fading into oblivion, but the sheriff is pretty well ensconced in county government in many parts of the country with little likelihood that he will disappear from the scene for many years to come. We will discuss the duties of the office of sheriff later in this book, but a cursory glance at the comparative roles of the sheriff of the past and present will show that there is actually little difference.

Police Chief Election of municipal chiefs of police was quite common when local departments were first established. Public suspicion of government officials was prevalent, based upon actual experience with the corrupt officials who served for life at the pleasure of the king. Short terms assured the people that their police administrators were new to the job and would not have time to become corrupt or too powerful in office. This system was found to be an illusory concept, however. Not only were the chiefs not able to gain control of the community, but they hardly had sufficient time to gain control of their own officers or to acquire sufficient experience to perform their jobs efficiently. Their terms were so short that they did not give up their civilian occupations while in office. The artisans, shopkeepers, and businessmen had their futures to consider, so they were policemen on a part-time basis only and seldom devoted their full energies and resources to the important task of running a police department.

Because of this lack of professionalism that resulted in election of politicians as police administrators, the trend has been for many years to permanent appointments of administrators qualified by experience and ability instead of by popularity at the polls. Tenure is based upon continued good performance and substantial results in the reduction of crimes and traffic collisions, and clearance of crimes. The elected police chief system remains in only a few cities.

Police Administration In the mid-1800s, administrative police boards were established. The chief of police was a professional and retained his job on a continuous basis, but the theory of the board system was to maintain civilian control over the police department to assure responsiveness to community needs. The boards were composed of judges, mayors, and private citizens, and the police chiefs served at their pleasure. This system lasted many years, but it was found that there were many major disadvantages, including the prevalence of political corruption. At best the board members often proved themselves bungling, inexperienced, meddling amateurs.

The next step in the evolution of police administration was state control of the local agencies. This system was a reaction to the politically corrupt local boards, and the theory was that the new system would be free from local partisanship and that the citizens throughout the state would be assured of adequate and uniform law enforcement. After all, they argued, the state laws were promulgated for the entire state, and the state could best determine how those laws should be enforced. Except for several cities that still operate within the framework of this type of administration, most states and cities found that this system was not the answer to the problem. Control reverted to the local governments. The reasons for failure were that the laws were *not* uniformly applied. They were completely disregarded in some areas and overenforced in others. Fiscal support and police protection in some sections of the state were disproportionate. There was too much absentee administration and a lack of responsiveness to local demands and needs.

The next system of police administration to appear was the commission government charter. The elected commissioners were charged with operating various branches of city government, and the public safety commission (police, fire, and sometimes health and sanitation departments) was one of those commissions. This system was found inadequate as was the administrative police board comprised of amateurs. It, too, is on the decline.

The mayor-council and council-city manager types of municipal government are now more prevalent and efficient as local systems. The former type of government is quite efficient when the mayor is a fulltime official and a capable administrator. The latter type assures more continuity in the business administration and executive control of the overall operations because a professional nonpolitical administrator is managing the affairs of the community. Under either system, the chief of police is usually selected on the basis of education, experience, and demonstrated ability, and he continues to serve as administrator of the police department as long as he continues to perform the job efficiently and effectively.

DEVELOPMENT OF THE JUDICIAL SYSTEM

Lower Courts The judicial system in the United States operated on a very localized level for many years, and much of the system that migrated with the people from England still remains quite similar in many respects to today's small-unit court—the justice of the peace and his justice court.

According to a 1971 report of the Advisory Commission on Intergovernmental Relations:

> In the colonial period, the lower courts were justice of the peace courts. By the 19th century, there was an increasing tendency to replace the JPs with magistrates or local inferior courts with somewhat increased or specialized jurisdiction. In some cases, the county courts were given jurisdiction concurrent with the justices of the peace.[7]

Although the report states that many jurisdictions abandoned the justice of the peace, that report indicates that in 1971 only seventeen states had abolished the justice court statewide, and that at least four more had replaced that court in selected cities. More than half of the states apparently have justice courts to this date, a court that originated in fourteenth-century England.

Jury The jury by the peers of the accused, or persons selected from the same community occupied by the accused, and the grand jury originated in the year 1166 during the reign of King Henry of England. The jury heard testimony and passed judgment on guilt or innocence. The grand jury was charged with the responsibility to make inquisitions into facts of crime and render *Vere Dictums,* or verdicts, which were called indictments. The modern grand jury is utilized today in various ways. Some states utilize the grand jury for all felony prosecutions,[8] which is a duplication of the process of pretrial investigative procedures and parallels or duplicates the process of initiating felony prosecutions in the municipal court by means of a preliminary hearing. Current recommendations are that the grand jury be either discontinued entirely or that it be used at the discretion of the prosecutor as a means of expediting a case by avoiding the delays of court and the extension of information secrecy until the actual time of the trial in the higher court.[9]

Federal Courts The system of federal courts was established by the Judiciary Act of 1789, which also established the office of the Attorney General and the federal marshal, who serves as the court bailiff for the thirteen federal districts.[10]

Contemporary Court Systems The court systems in existence today are little different in basic structure from the times when they were established in their respective states by constitutional proclamation. The court of last

[7]Advisory Commission on Intergovernmental Relations, *State-Local Relations in the Criminal Justice System* (Washington, D.C.: Government Printing Office, 1971), p. 89.

[8]Advisory Commission, *State-Local Relations in the Criminal Justice System,* p. 51.

[9]The grand jury proceedings are secret, which means that the identity of witnesses and disclosure of evidence may be held in confidence during continued investigations that may involve a series of indictments.

[10]Rita W. Cooly, "The Office of the U.S. Marshal," *Western Political Quarterly,* XII, No. 1, Part 1, March, 1959, pp. 123–40.

resort, or the highest appeal court, is the state supreme court. The next level of court is the intermediate appellate court, which exists in approximately one-half of the states, and which hears appeals from the trial courts. The third level court is the court of original or general jurisdiction, which usually hears criminal felonies and civil cases of greater significance (usually determined by the amount of money sought as reparation), with the designation superior court, and with countywide jurisdiction. The fourth level consists of the courts of limited jurisdiction, which handle misdemeanors, most traffic cases, small claims, police courts, and civil cases of lesser significance. These lower courts are found in the smallest subdivision within the state, and usually serve court districts of rural areas and/or one or more smaller cities. In some states the size of the court district has determined which court is to be installed, such as in California where the justice court serves a district with a population less than 40,000 and the municipal court serves a district with a population of 40,000 or more.

The historical development of the state has a bearing on the courts as well as the evolution of law enforcement. For example, California as a Province still felt the Mexican influence. According to Elizabeth Pedrotti, "There were the *avuntamientos* (town councils), the *alcaldes* (magistrates or mayors), the *jucces de paz* (justices of the peace), the *regidores* (councilmen) and the *sindicas* (clerks)."[11]

Pedrotti quotes Paul Mason in his *Constitutional History of California:*

> The judicial system provided for the provinces of Mexico corresponds very closely with the present judicial system of California; the tribunal and courts of *segunda instancia* correspond with our supreme and appellate courts; the courts of *primera instancia,* with our superior courts; the *alcaldes* courts, with our municipal courts and the justices' courts with our own justice courts. The judicial system adopted by the first constitution was the system already established under the laws of Mexico.[12]

Juvenile Court The first juvenile court in the world was established in Illinois in 1899. According to Saleem A. Shah:

> When Illinois established the first juvenile court in the world in 1899, expectations for its performance were high. It gave to juvenile delinquency a status of something less than crime. Youthful deviance defined as delinquency was to be treated correctively, not by punishment.[13]

Jeffrey E. Glen and J. Robert Weber reported that the court was to deal with children who had violated the criminal law, or children who had been brought to the attention of the court as neglected, homeless, or otherwise

[11]Elizabeth Pedrotti, *The California Court System* (Sacramento, Calif.: State Printing Office, 1967), p. 1.

[12]Paul Mason, *Constitutional History of California,* n.d., n.p.

[13]Edwin M. Lemert, *Instead of Court/Diversion in Juvenile Justice* (Washington, D.C.: Government Printing Office, 1971), from the introduction by Saleem A. Shah of the National Institute of Mental Health, p. iii.

disreputable.[14] They reported that by the 1920s virtually every state in the United States had passed some special legal provisions for delinquent and neglected youth. There were benefits from the change.

> In removing children from the jurisdiction of the criminal court by establishing the juvenile court the intent was to do away with both the punitive philosophy of the criminal court as well as the method of trial and punishment. A new philosophy was developed. The child was regarded as immature and thus not wholly responsible for his acts. The child was entitled to protection, rehabilitation, or retraining. The juvenile court was to act as a wise parent who would plan for the total welfare of the child rather than punish the child for a specific act.[15]

In 1938 the federal government passed a Juvenile Court Act, which provided for handling juvenile federal law offenders in special juvenile courts, and by 1945 every state in the union had enacted legislation providing for such courts.[16] The courts have not necessarily been totally separate from the regular court system, however. Glen and Weber report:

> At the outset of the juvenile court movement, the "court" itself was conceived of as nothing more than a different set of procedures for dealing with youths. Thus, there were no "juvenile courts" as separate judicial entities.
>
> In recent years, several alternative schemes for juvenile court organization have been tried. Some states, such as Connecticut and Utah, have established statewide juvenile courts, with their own judiciary, completely separate from the civil and criminal courts of the State. Other states, including California, Washington, and Ohio, have established separate divisions of their highest courts of general trial jurisdiction to deal solely with juvenile cases.[17]

DEVELOPMENT OF THE CORRECTIONAL SYSTEM

Traditional methods of punishment for many centuries were capital punishment, physical torture, and banishment. Such methods were decisive and permanent; the punishment of death served the needs of the group by eliminating the wrongdoer and satisfying a desire for revenge. Torture was an extension of the eye-for-an-eye philosophy, and included such things as crucifixion, exile into starvation, maiming, drawing and quartering, branding, dragging through the streets, and cutting off or out the offending part. Methods of taking the offenders' lives were demonstrative and served as a public spectacle to deter others from committing similar crimes. Stoning,

[14]Jeffery E. Glen and J. Robert Weber, *The Juvenile Court—A Status Report,* Department of Health, Education and Welfare Publication No. (HSM) 72-9115 (Washington, D.C.: Government Printing Office, 1972), p. 1.

[15]Glen and Weber, *The Juvenile Court—A Status Report,* p. 2.

[16]Lemert, *Instead of Court/Diversion in Juvenile Justice,* p. iii.

[17]Glen and Weber, *The Juvenile Court—A Status Report,* p. 3.

hanging, beheading, poisoning, and being thrown from a convenient cliff constituted the different types of capital punishment.

During the eighteenth and nineteenth centuries, although still emphasizing corporal punishment, torture and banishment, the penal system was making some subtle changes. According to one source, the Quakers in 1682 "initiated a century and a half of experimentation with new penal concepts."[18] A long list of capital crimes were abolished, and the various types of torture were replaced by imprisonment at hard labor. The prisoners were intended to reflect in solitude as repentance.

During the time of reformation, penologists began to recognize criminals as persons who had committed crime as a matter of free will because it gave them pleasure or profit. The correctional tool of imprisonment was implemented to penalize lawbreakers to the extent that the pleasure or profit gained by commission of the crime was negated by the punishment. The Walnut Street Jail was opened in Philadelphis in 1790 by a Quaker organization under the leadership of Dr. Benjamin Rush.[19] Harry E. Barnes and Negley E. K. Teeters reported that although the place was merely a converted jail, it was, in practice, a penitentiary for the Commonwealth of Pennsylvania and received commitments from throughout the state. A block of small cells was constructed with a small exercise yard attached. The prisoners were placed in solitary confinement where they were forced to meditate and serve penitence.[20]

Known as the Auburn Plan, the silent system or congregate system was established in 1815 at the New York State Prison at Auburn. Prisoners worked together in the same room, instead of in their individual cells, which had been built too small for inmates to use certain types of vocational training equipment, such as spinning wheels. Inmates were forced to move in a lockstep whenever they moved in a group from one place to another, and they were not allowed to talk to one another, which made supervision easier.[21]

The Walnut Street Jail was succeeded by two penitentiaries, which opened in 1826 and 1829 at Pittsburgh and Philadelphia, respectively. The segregation of inmates was rigidly maintained. This prison system was known as the Pennsylvania System. This particular system has more or less faded into the past in the United States. The Auburn System has been extensively copied and is very much in evidence today.[22]

[18]Center for Law Enforcement and Corrections, *Jails and Prisons.* Training Module 6908 (University Park, Pa.: Pennsylvania State University, 1969), p. 3.

[19]Center for Law Enforcement and Corrections, *Jails and Prisons,* p. 4.

[20]Harry E. Barnes and Negley E. K. Teeters, *New Horizons in Criminology,* 2d ed. (Englewood Cliffs, N.J.: Prentice-Hall, Inc., 1972), p. 12.

[21]Louis P. Carney, *Introduction To Correctional Science,* 2d ed. (New York: McGraw-Hill Co., 1979), pp. 78–79.

Probation

The practice of conditional release on the individual's own recognizance and the suspended sentence originated in Anglo-Saxon times and was brought to the colonies as a part of the common law that was later codified in the United States.[23] Probation as practiced today, which involves a period of supervised freedom during which time the probationer is expected to develop acceptable life style and behavior patterns and to divert his energy and desires from criminal activities, originated in Boston in 1841. John Augustus, a local craftsman, volunteered his services to the court to screen and place in the community those children that were considered worth the risk, then provided some supervision while they were out on probation.[24] That same source reports that this voluntary probation service was given official recognition in 1869, when the state of Massachusetts assigned a state agent to the Board of Charities in Boston, who attended court hearings, made arrangements for placement of juveniles on probation to friends of the court.[25]

The first law that made probation a legal service was passed in Boston in 1878. At first the probation officer was appointed by the mayor, then this responsibility was later passed on to the courts. By the late 1890s a statewide probation system had been adopted in the state of Massachusetts. Since that time probation has extended throughout the United States, including juvenile probation (about 1900), and federal probation, which was established in 1925.[26]

Parole

Although involving casework and other techniques quite similar to those of probation, parole has been separate and distinct in origin and development. The program involves "aftercare" type casework with convicted offenders following a period of imprisonment, and the principal thrust of parole is reintegration and socialization. Parole and pardon are related in some respects. They both follow a period of imprisonment. The pardon was a form of executive clemency action in which the individual was granted a pardon on condition that he be transferred to the colonies or to some place in bondage to work out an indebtedness to the crown or to some other per-

[22] Vernon Fox, *Introduction to Corrections,* 2d ed. (Englewood Cliffs, N.J.: Prentice-Hall, Inc., 1977), p. 12.

[23] Center for Law Enforcement and Corrections, *Probation and Parole,* Training Module 6907 (University Park, Pa.: Pennsylvania State University, 1969), p. 2.

[24] Center for Law Enforcement and Corrections, *Probation, Parole, and Pardons: A Basic Course,* Training Module 6913 (University Park, Pa.: Pennsylvania State University, 1969), p. 8.

[25] Center for Law Enforcement and Corrections, *Probation, Parole, and Pardons,* p. 8.

[26] Center for Law Enforcement and Corrections, *Probation, Parole, and Pardons,* p. 8.

son. A pardon may have involved a reduction in sentence in return for some favor or for good conduct. Parole was structured as a conditional release from imprisonment. The individual was provided the opportunity to "make it" on the outside under supervision prior to being released completely on his own at the conclusion of the prescribed time for him to be under the control of the corrections agency.

Indentured service was a form of conditional release, or parole, which originated in England in 1717. The prisoner was purchased from the Crown and was taken to the colonies for a prescribed period of mandatory service. Another form of parole was a conditional release from prison for certain reasons such as good behavior known as the *ticket of leave.* Used in England and Australia in the eighteenth century, the leave was granted to persons who were allowed to seek employment in certain districts under specified conditions. "Until 1811 tickets of leave were freely given to prisoners for good conduct, meritorious service, or the purpose of marriage."[27]

The indeterminate sentence and an early form of parole appeared in 1837. It was known as the Mark System, or the Irish System. Created in England and adopted in Ireland, the conditions were these: (1) Imprisonment was with training and employment, (2) employment was on public works, and (3) eventual release from prison was made conditional on good behavior and monthly reports.[28] The first working system of parole is attributed to Alexander Maconochie in the penal colony on Norfolk Island in New South Wales in 1840.

The Elmira Reformatory Plan of 1876 featured the indeterminate sentence and parole concepts, as reported by the Center for Law Enforcement and Corrections.[29] Education in Elmira was compulsory, prisoners were granted privileges on the basis of capacity and behavior, and they were selected for parole according to the following provisions: (1) required to maintain a good record for one year, (2) had to submit suitable plans for employment, (3) required to report to guardian upon release and the first day of each month, and (4) the guardian submitted regular reports on the inmate's progress to the Elmira Reformatory.

SUMMARY

The history of the system of administration of justice is quite extensive, and this chapter is in no way intended to detract from some serious in-depth study of the matter. In this chapter we have merely touched upon some of the highlights in history. We have missed in our discussions more than we

[27]Center for Law Enforcement and Corrections, *Probation, Parole, and Pardons,* p. 7.

[28]Center for Law Enforcement and Corrections, *Probation, Parole, and Pardons,* pp. 8–10.

[29]Center for Law Enforcement and Corrections, *Probation, Parole, and Pardons,* pp. 7–8.

have included, obviously, and the serious student interested in the historical progress of the justice system should continue to research the subject. Law enforcement had its origins in symphony with the development of civilizations, and there has yet to be any evidence to the contrary. The courts and the police—law enforcement—in the United States are principally based upon English Common Law that later migrated to the colonies with the people, and which have evolved into a somewhat sophisticated series of agencies with similar and interrelated responsibilities. Corrections systems have had more recent beginnings, or so the historical chronologue has indicated. Actually, modern corrections—or penology as it was called for some time—has developed principally during the last century.

EXERCISES AND STUDY QUESTIONS

1. Where did the eye-for-an-eye philosophy of punishment come from?

2. The term "solon" is often used for legislators. What is the origin of the word?

3. Who defined law as an agreement between people to do justice to each other?

4. According to the text, what was Hammurabi's contribution to the criminal justice system?

5. What relationship do the Twelve Tables, drawn up in Rome in 450 B.C., have with our modern law in the United States?

6. Study the tithing system in England established by King Alfred, then compare it to the type of organization prescribed for Moses by his father-in-law, Jethro in EXOD. 18:13-27.

7. What country had the greatest influence on the criminal justice system in the United States?

8. What are the similarities and differences between the shire-reeve of early England and the sheriff in the county where you live?

9. What is "hue and cry" and how does it work?

10. At what time in history were felonies and misdemeanors first broken down into these categories?

11. What was Magna Carta, and of what significance is it in history?

12. What was the purpose for curfew when it was established, and how does it compare with curfew as we know it today?

13. What was Sir Robert Peel's great contribution to modern law enforcement?

14. Where was the Star Chamber? What was its purpose?

15. Discuss the principles of the Peelian Reform; explain how each of the principles relates to modern law enforcement in your state.

16. What was the purpose of the English Habeas Corpus Act?

17. Who was Patrick Colquhoun, and what was his contribution to the criminal justice system?

18. What is the major difference between the municipal police forces and the local police units in England, if any?

19. Which city was the first in the United States to model its police force after the London Metropolitan Police?

20. What influences did the "old world" have on the types of policing that were adopted at various places in this country?

21. In what major U.S. city did the Army provide police services for a few years?

22. Today, what is the most common method for selection of a chief of police?

23. What type of courts were the lower courts in the U.S. in Colonial times?

24. Describe the origin and function of the grand jury.

25. What is a Vere Dictum?

26. What is the court of last resort in your state?

27. In which court in your state are felonies tried? Misdemeanors?

28. When and where was the first juvenile court established?

29. What is the Auburn plan?

30. What was John Augustus' contribution to the justice system?

31. What did the Quakers contribute to the penal system?

32. Where did probation start?

33. When and where did parole begin?

34. What was indentured service, and when did it begin?

RECOMMENDED SEMESTER/TERM PROJECTS

1. Select one of the three components of the criminal justice system—law enforcement, courts, or corrections—and write a detailed history of that component for a specified period of time. For example: Law Enforcement in the United States between 1930 and 1950; From Depression to Prosperity.

2. Write a history on one of the various court or police processes described in this chapter, such as habeas corpus, or right to be confronted by one's accuser, or the parole process.

SUGGESTED FOR ADDITIONAL STUDY

GIDDINGS, LARRY A., MARK FURSTENBERG, and HENRY J. NOBLE, *Manual on Training for Sheriffs,* LEAA Grant No. 268. Washington, D.C.: Government Printing Office, 1968.

GODDARD, HENRY, *Memories of a Bow Street Runner.* New York: William Morrow, 1957.

GURR, TED ROBERT, *Rogues, Rebels, and Reformers, A Political History of Urban Crime and Conflict.* Beverly Hills: Sage Publications, Inc., 1976.

KILLINGER, GEORGE G., and PAUL F. CROMWELL, JR., *Penology: The Evolution of Corrections on America.* St. Paul: West Publishing Co., 1973.

PRINGLE, PATRICK, *Hue and Cry: The Story of Henry and John Fielding and Their Bow Street Runners.* New York: William Morrow, 1955.

TAFT, DONALD R., and RALPH W. ENGLAND, JR., *Criminology* (4th ed.). New York: The Macmillan Co., 1964.

6

The Police

INTRODUCTION

The police component of the criminal justice system serves as the enforcement arm of the executive branch of government. There are police agencies for all levels of government—federal, state, and local—that may be included in the category of law enforcement, or investigative or regulatory, usually referred to as police agencies. In this chapter we shall expolore the police agencies, their interrelationships, and their basic functions. The objective of this chapter is to bring about a greater knowledge of the respective roles and responsibilities of these many thousands of agencies utilized by city, county, state, and federal governments.

THE POLICE CONGLOMERATE

Each type of police agency had its own separate origin. The municipal police departments and the sheriffs' departments are the basic police agencies in the United States government system. Those agencies are responsible for the fundamental obligation of maintaining peace and enforcing laws throughout the nation in their respective jurisdictions.

At state government levels, there are many police agencies that have been created to meet specific needs, but not to have the broad general powers of the local police forces. Yet, their jurisdictions are statewide geographically and for the purpose of enforcing those specific sets of laws they are held responsible for, as opposed to the city or county boundaries which serve as geographical restrictions on the police activities of the local police.

Federal police agencies, similar to state police in many respects, have specific limitations on the laws which they investigate and enforce, but their geographical jurisdiction spans the entire United States, the high seas, and throughout the world in certain cases involving affairs and/or citizens of the United States.

From time to time, different legislative bodies have created the need for new police agencies by making new sets of laws. Although existing agencies might have been able to take on the extra work load, perhaps the highly specialized nature of the laws make it more desirable to create a new agency. For example, licensing and regulation of establishments selling alcoholic beverages led to creation of liquor control boards or departments of alcoholic beverage control in each of the states. Automobile and driver licensing, and regulation of auto dealers and related auto industries brought about the need for each state to have its own department of motor vehicles. Because of the highly specialized needs of those agencies to have their own investigative and enforcement units, came the advent of police agents employed for those specialized functions.

Literally hundreds of specialized enforcement bureaus and departments have sprouted up through the past several decades like toadstools following a warm spring rain: highway patrols, secret service, drug enforcement bureaus, military police, consumer fraud enforcement, professional and vocational standards, fish and game, harbors and navigation, border patrol, coast guard, labor law enforcement, and on ad infinitum.

Some police agencies may be created as a result of special interests, and constituents are convinced that delegation of such important responsibilities to any other police agency would be catastrophic. Some specialized agencies have been formed because of real or imagined distrust of existing agencies. Suddenly a new police agency appears on the scene. Except for the local city and county police agencies, the majority of police forces, particularly federal and state forces, are of relatively recent origin. The first state police agency —the Texas Rangers—was not created until 1835. The first federal police agency was the Postal Inspection Service, which was founded in 1775. The Secret Service followed in 1865.

When studying the police system, consider first the various local police forces, each responsible for policing its own respective political subdivision of the state: the cities protected by the city police, and the unincorporated and rural areas policed by the constable, the marshal, or the sheriff. Each jurisdiction could be related to the other jurisdictions as interlocking pieces in a jigsaw puzzle. The many state and federal agencies have similar jurisdictional relationships with the emphasis placed on division of responsibility as opposed to geographic allocation of jurisdictional boundaries. There are overlapping pieces in the system's jigsaw puzzle, however, and there are jurisdictional disputes and conflicts. The conflicts are probably more evident in the federal jurisdictions because they all have no geographic boundaries within the United States, whereas the local departments are separated by city limits and county lines.

There is considerable overlapping of federal police and investigative responsibilities, and also to a lesser extent of state agencies. Rivalry, distrust, and intrigue have been the products of jurisdictional conflicts, although the trend during recent years has been toward a greater amount of cooperation and more professional attitudes. Three alternatives to the existing interforce conflicts of federal agencies with overlapping jurisdictions have been advanced by observers of the problem. One alternative is to retain all of the existing agencies, but to redefine their respective jurisdictions systematically to assure a minimum of conflict. The second alternative is to establish a central bureau by consolidating all of the existing agencies. The third alternative is to retain the present system, or "nonsystem," and to establish an interdepartmental committee as a single coordinator to direct the efforts of the many agencies with a minimum of duplication and conflict. Similar proposals could be applied to the many agencies of the states.

At the local levels, there should be no displacement of the existing arrangement of having police departments in each separate political subdivision that are directly accountable to the people of that jurisdiction. The first proposal of the preceding three that were presented with respect to the federal agencies—retention of the existing agency but redefining the jurisdiction—already applies to local police agencies. The second proposal—consolidation of all agencies—is not practicable nor desirable at the local police level. The third proposal—that of coordination of several agencies—is feasible. Coordination of such operations as records keeping, training, laboratory, and similar functions placed at strategically located positions in the state and operated jointly by the many contributing and participating agencies would result in a greater amount of uniformity in procedures, greater efficiency, and would assist the progress of police service toward eventual professionalization.

There are nearly one-half million officers and agents working for approximately forty thousand separate agencies in the United States with law enforcement and/or investigative responsibility. Such a nonsystem of cooperating agencies has room for improvement, but a great deal of credit must be accorded to the many thousands who perform their duties as capably as they do. Such is the police nonsystem.

Another type of police agency that should be included in a discussion of the police system is the private police segment, which comprises approximately one-half mission employees, equal to that of the government-operated police in the United States. Private police forces are generally formed by large corporations because of their need for more concentrated protective services than can be provided by the government police. Many private police agencies are very capable and efficient. An example of a very organized and efficient private police force is the railroad police of the United States and Canada, the largest privately supported police agency in the world. The force is composed of several thousand agents stationed throughout the two countries, supported by approximately four hundred separate railroads.

Many other very efficient private police agencies exist to perform all types of protective and investigative duties. As a matter of fact, industrial policing is a highly specialized police function that requires a great variety of skills. There are other organizations, however, that have been composed of hoodlums and troublemakers. A vivid example of such a force was the

Coal and Iron Police in Pennsylvania, created by several mine operators for the purpose of forcibly breaking up labor strikes. That particular organization was outlawed by the Pennsylvania State Legislature in 1835.

LOCAL POLICE AGENCIES

The Municipal Police Department

The entire police and policing picture centers around the city or township police department. They are charged with crime prevention and repression, traffic law enforcement, protective patrol services, arbitration in neighborhood and family disputes, apprehension and arrest (or citation or warning) of criminal law violators, and recovery of stolen property. The local police officers also perform a multitude of nonenforcement tasks, such as providing information and assistance to visitors and tourists, as well as residents, vehicular and pedestrian traffic control, safety education, crowd control at sporting events and other public gatherings, and the general task of maintaining order and peace in their respective jurisdictions.

The city police departments comprise a large portion of the more than forty thousand law enforcement agencies that employ nearly one-half million men and women in the United States to provide for the protection, comfort, assistance, and maintenance of a moral conscience for the nearly 200 million people in their jurisdictions. The organization of the municipal police department will be outlined in the next chapter. The local agencies—although not specifically mentioned in those chapters—include the municipal police departments, town constabulary, township and borough police, and county law enforcement agencies.

The federal and state law enforcement and investigative agencies have limitations on their scope of authority, which usually restrict their officers and agents to the investigation and enforcement of only those laws and other matters that specifically relate to their specialties. The municipal police department is charged with the responsibility for taking an active part in both investigation and enforcement of federal and state laws as well as the ordinances of their own specific political subdivisions. The extent to which they become involved varies with the nature of the offenses and their working relationship with the various other agencies.

City police officers may arrest a common thief and uncover a cache of smuggled tax-unpaid liquor and a kilo (roughly two pounds as packaged by smugglers) of marijuana. The jurisdictions involved in these violations include the local department, of course, but also a few other agencies. The Bureau of Alcohol and Tobacco Tax Division of the Treasury Department is responsible for "bootleg" alcoholic beverages, and the Bureau of Customs also has a jurisdictional interest in the liquor if it came across a border. The illegal narcotics in such a case may involve still additional agencies. The Bureau of Customs would have a legal interest because of the smuggling violation, although there is no legal means for the smugglers to possess the marijuana because it has been outlawed in the United States since 1937. In addition to the local police department's legal interest in effecting the arrest for the state law violations for possession of the illicit drugs, the state agents would be concerned because of the significance of the drug's presence and the statewide narcotics problem, and the federal agents would be concerned because of the violation of a tax law involving marijuana and also the nationwide implications of smuggling the drug. The agency that would handle the case initially would be the local police department.

In the hypothetical case at hand, the local department would take custody of the evidence and properly preserve it for later presentation in court, the concerned agencies would be notified, and the appropriate reports prepared and disseminated. The suspect would be interviewed by representatives of all involved agencies and follow-up investigations initiated as a result of those interviews. But what of the initial arrest and prosecution? The local agency would, in all probability, be the one that would make the formal charges for the state violations of theft and unlawful possession of marijuana. Any additional charges would be initiated by the agencies having specific jurisdiction, and separate trials for those offenses would be held later.

In some situations there are offenses that are subject to concurrent jurisdiction, such as bank robbery, interstate transportation of a stolen vehicle, taking a kidnapped victim across state lines, and hundreds of others. Those offenses are likewise investigated and enforced by agents of more than one agency. They cooperate effectively to their mutual advantage. The prosecution is usually at the initiative of the agency in whose jurisdiction the original violation occurred, and the products of the efforts of the other agencies are added to the weight of the prosecution.

The County Sheriff

In the majority of counties in the United States, the sheriff is the principal law enforcement officer with his jurisdiction primarily limited to the unincorporated areas of that county. In his duties as officer of the court and in the execution of his nonenforcement duties, his jurisdiction includes the entire county. In the state of Louisiana the political subdivision in which the sheriff performs his duties is called the parish, but in nearly all other respects his roles are the same.

The sheriff fills his office by popular election in nearly all jurisdictions of the United States, and his term of office is for two, three, or four years. Rotation of the office is almost universal because legislation either limits the tenure of most sheriffs to a single term or a limited number of terms. The theory behind such a limitation on tenure is to prevent the man in office from acquiring too much power while holding that office, an atavistic attitude of early Americans who suspected the motives of anyone in public offices.

Throughout the United States the multifaceted responsibilities and duties of the sheriff vary from state to state and from county to county within the individual states. In virtually all areas of the United States, the sheriff is responsible for carrying out all orders—including serving papers and writs—plus all the other functions required of him and his deputies as bailiff of the Superior Court. The sheriff is also keeper of the county jail and all presentenced and postsentenced prisoners.

In the counties of some states, the sheriff and his or her deputies are responsible for traffic enforcement and accident investigation on the streets and highways in their jurisdiction, which is the unincorporated (not within city limits of the several cities in the county) area of the county. In states where there is a highway patrol with statewide jurisdiction, the sheriff handles the traffic function only within those cities where the sheriff is contracted by the city to operate as a city police department; then in the unincorporated areas of the county, the highway patrol handles traffic matters.

The sheriff is often combined with the office of some other county official, such as the coroner. In some states, where consolidation of agencies has been found economically advantageous, the sheriff may also direct the offices and activities of the marshal and constable, which are similar to those of the sheriff in all respects in the lesser courts.

In parts of the South and Southwest, the sheriff serves as tax collector and as public administrator for the property of persons who die intestate. In the state of California, the county is the principal political subdivision of the state and the sheriff is the principal law enforcement official in each county. He is so designated because he maintains the county jail, serves as bailiff to the superior court, and in times of an insurrection or major disaster involving more than one city and parts of the county, he may act as the coordinator of all of the concerned police agencies as designated in mutual aid agreements between the various communities. There is no hierarchy of command in this arrangement (except during special emergencies and by prior agreement), and during normal times and conditions, the various law enforcement agencies are completely autonomous and are under the direction of their respective chiefs of police, with absolutely no accountability-responsibility relationship with the sheriff.

The sheriff and his deputies have a variety of duties, some of which are listed as follows:

1. Execute civil and criminal processes throughout the county, including various writs of execution and attachment and warrants of arrest.
2. Keep the county jail and its prisoners.

3. Keep the peace in the unincorporated areas of the county. In order that he may accomplish this objective, the sheriff and his deputies may take whatever preventive and enforcement action that he deems necessary, including arresting and taking before the magistrate people who have committed or have attempted to commit public offenses.
4. Attend superior court and obey and carry out all lawful orders of the court, and also act as court crier and bailiff.
5. Attend all meetings of the Board of Supervisors (the governing body of each county government in California, the same as city councils govern city government) to preserve order and serve notices, subpoenas, or other processes directed by the board.
6. Investigate public offenses that have been committed and cause those who have been identified as violators of the law to be prosecuted.

The sheriff is the county officer who is charged with the authority to command as many able-bodied male inhabitants of the county to assist him in carrying out his duty to preserve the peace and to maintain order. This power is called the "power of the county," or *posse comitatus.* In some jurisdictions, the sheriff may also fill the role and the office of marshal, as described in the next paragraph.

The Marshal

The role of the marshal as an officer of the court is similar to that of the sheriff, except that he is the bailiff and agent of the municipal court, while the sheriff serves the superior court. The marshal serves writs, subpoenas, and other papers issued by the court, and escorts prisoners from the jail or holding cells in the courthouse to and from the courts he serves for trials and hearings. The marshal protects the municipal court judge and the people in the court.

The marshal is elected in some jurisdictions and appointed in others. Except where the marshal's office is incorporated by the local jurisdiction to include the duties of the chief of police as town marshal, his duties are usually restricted to those enumerated in this paragraph. It is no small task, but it is comparatively limited in scope.

The Constable

The constable is recognized by the constitutions in approximately twenty states, particularly in New England, the South, and the West. Selection of the constable is usually by popular election. He serves a township, and his duties are primarily to maintain the peace and serve processes for the local justice court. He may also serve as a tax collector or poundmaster, and whatever other duties as may be described by the government in his own state and county. Constables collect fees and mileages for execution of arrest warrants, and transportation of prisoners. In some jurisdictions, the constable may be under the direction of the sheriff.

Miscellaneous Local Police Forces

At various times in history, and for various purposes, different types of policing organizations have been formed. Some of those organizations were formed for specific purposes and then disbanded when the need no longer continued to exist; some of the organizations continue to exist at the present time.

Vigilante committees have been formed at various locations, usually at times when the residents found that the local police were ineffective either because they were overwhelmed by the incidence of crime, or they were inefficient. Cattle rustling in the West during the 1800s was a sizeable problem that the people attempted to solve by rule of the vigilante, organizing their search and arrest parties, taking the law into their own hands, independent of the law officers of the day. They chased down, apprehended, and sometimes even tried and executed the offenders on the spot.

During the late 1920s, prior to the FBI involvement in protection of banks against bank robbery and other crimes, a bankers' vigilante group was formed in the Midwest for the purpose of apprehending bank robbers. Law enforcement today calls for greater efficiency than can be accomplished by a vigilante group, and without proper guidance and training, an organization of this type could promote anarchy. Although the police departments do everything they can to discourage the formation of vigilante groups—sometimes mobilizing and training large auxiliary police units to serve in lieu of such a citizens' police unit, some urban neighborhoods have experienced so many robberies and street crimes that vigilante groups of men and women patrolling the streets in private cars with citizen band radios have popped up from time to time in such cities as New York and Washington, D.C.

Park police have been created by some of the larger cities to provide protection and informational services to the visitors to their parks. Parkway police may be found on the parkways and boulevards in some states and have the specific purpose of guarding public buildings or monuments.

Examples of two local police forces that serve local needs but which were developed for special purposes include the New York City Housing Authority and New York City Transit Authority Police Departments. The Housing Police patrol the grounds, cellars, roofs, stairwells, and elevators of the public housing projects. The Transit Authority, including 483 subway stations,[1] provides police services on the public transportation vehicles and terminals throughout the city.

[1]James S. Kakalik and Sorrel Wildhorn, *Special Purpose Public Police* (Washington, D.C.: Government Printing Office, 1971), pp. 14–15.

Reserves Developed during times of extreme emergency, particularly during and following the World War II years of the early and midforties, the auxiliary or reserve police forces appeared on the American scene. When adequately trained and equipped, these men and women serve as the extra strength that is so direly needed at certain times of disaster or other emergency but which is otherwise unavailable. Selected from the community, some reserves are young potentials for the regular service who are screened for full-time service through assessment of their performance while on duty. Other reserves are gainfully occupied in other professions or businesses and choose the police reserves as a form of community service, often performing as officers with full peace officer authority. Under normal circumstances the reserves accompany fulltime officers as the second officer in a patrol car, sometimes working solo or in pairs in units by themselves, and public relations officers, community service agents in such units as crime prevention teams, radio dispatchers, complaint desk officers, and in practically every other activity within the department, including administrative and supervisory duties.

The Coroner

With a background similar to the history of the sheriff, the coroner comes to modern enforcement from ancient times. Today he is an officer of the county and may be found in virtually all parts of the country either as coroner or medical examiner. The coroner's ancestor was called the coronator, and he represented the King of England at public hearings. In the United States, his principal jurisdiction involves the determination of causes of death and care and custody of the remains and personal effects of deceased persons.

The office of coroner or medical examiner may be combined with that of sheriff, tax collector, public administrator, or any other public office that may be combined with his office by law. The coroner is a county officer, and in California he fills the office of the sheriff when it is left vacant. The coroner need not be a medical doctor or have any legal knowledge to be elected, but the coroner in some jurisdictions has been replaced by a medical examiner who is a doctor, and in many others the people have elected doctors to the office.

The coroner is required by law to investigate and sign the death certificate in all of the following circumstances in California according to the Government Code, Sections 27491.1:

> . . . all violent, sudden or unusual deaths; unattended deaths; deaths wherein the deceased has not been attended by a physician in the ten days before death; deaths related to or following known or suspected self-induced or criminal abortion; known or suspected homicide, suicide, or accidental poisoning;

> deaths known or suspected as resulting in whole or in part from or related to accident or injury either old or recent; deaths due to drowning, fire, hanging, gunshot, stabbing, cutting, exposure, starvation, alcoholism, drug addiction, strangulation, or aspiration; death in whole or in part occasioned by criminal means; deaths associated with a known or alleged rape or crime against nature; deaths in prison or while under sentence; deaths known or suspected as due to contagious disease and constituting a public hazard; deaths under such circumstances as to afford a reasonable ground to suspect that the death was caused by the criminal act of another, or any deaths reported by physicians having knowledge of death for inquiry by the coroner.

The coroner may examine the body at the place of death and take custody of the remains for the purpose of identification or determination of the cause of death and may exhume a body, cause a post-mortem examination or autopsy to be made, or hold an inquest to inquire into the cause of death. After determining the cause of death, the coroner signs the death certificate. If an inquest jury finds that the death was caused as a result of a criminal act of another person, he shall properly notify the appropriate law enforcement agency, and the prosecuting attorney in accordance with state law. In cases when the identity of the killer is known and he is not in custody, the coroner may issue a warrant of arrest. Although the laws of the state may provide for this option, the practice is not common. The matter of prosecution is left to the prosecuting attorney, who submits the allegations to the magistrate, who issues a warrant of arrest.

The purpose of an inquest is to determine cause of death and the relevant facts attendant to the death. When the inquest jury finds that a death was the result of criminal action of another, the police and prosecuting attorney have—in all likelihood—already been intensively involved in the investigation. The coroner lends his resources and expertise to assure a competent prosecution. The observer should be careful not to confuse a coroner's inquest with a criminal trial.

STATE POLICE AGENCIES

State Justice Department

The attorney general is the chief law officer and ministerial officer of the state court system, the chief counsel in all litigation involving the state, and the chief administrative officer of the state justice department. The attorney general prepares and disseminates opinions relating to the interpretations by his office of the criminal law, and in the absence of written or case law, the attorney general's opinion has the same force and effect as law.

In addition to providing assistance in the investigation and prosecution of criminal cases in the state, the attorney general represents the state on appeals from the lower courts to the appellate jurisdictions at state and

Figure 6-1 State police officers perform a variety of functions: top, in undercover narcotics investigations; middle, traffic enforcement; and bottom, giving roadside assistance.
Courtesy Kentucky State Police.

federal levels, and his office processes extradition and interstate rendition proceedings for persons who have fled from the state—or have left the state—to avoid prosecution.

Some states have agencies under the supervision of the attorney general and the justice department that are created for the primary purpose of assisting local law enforcement agencies in the state in the (1) identifcation of criminals, (2) control and supervision of certain types of offenders, (3) location of missing persons, and (4) technical and scientific analysis of evidence.

State laws usually require that chiefs of police, sheriffs, and other law enforcement agencies forward daily the fingerprints and other arrest data to the state agency responsible for maintenance of records and statistics. The data required usually includes copies of investigation reports on felonies of all types, sex offenses, narcotics and dangerous drug violations, and certain cases of statewide significance, along with a detailed description of stolen property. It is the responsibility of this agency, which is usually a part of the attorney general's office, to coordinate and correlate this information, to attempt to identify the responsible criminals by their modus operandi (method of operation), and to promptly forward to the contributing agency any information that may assist it in identifying and apprehending the responsible parties.

A bureau of statistics may be a part of the justice department or similar state agency. If such a state agency exists, its general responsibilities should include the compilation and analysis of information relating to criminal activity in the state, crime trends, achievement of law enforcement, and the results of prosecution. The data is often correlated with that of the statistics section of the FBI for the compilation of the Uniform Crime Reports.

The "State Police" Department

At the state government level in the police ''nonsytem'' most law enforcement and investigation agencies are specialized in nature. Their jurisdictions vary with their specific functions, but they usually have statewide authority to perform those police duties—however limited in scope they may be. Highway patrols, for example, uniformly enforce state traffic laws on the highways, and alcoholic beverage control agents enforce licensing and other liquor laws in the entire state.

Each state is different from all the others with respect to its state police agencies, depending upon its history and evolution of policing needs. Starting with the Texas Rangers in 1835 and continuing to the present, new agencies are being formed and old agencies reorganized to meet the changing requirements of the evolving community. Massachusetts employed state constables in 1865 for the purpose of suppressing commercialized vice. The Pennsylvania State Police and the Arizona Rangers were created in 1901, and New Mexico founded its state police in 1905.

Connecticut organized a state police agency in 1903 with a primary objective of investigating and suppressing commercialized liquor and gambling violations. They now examine operators' license applicants and are involved in arson investigations. The Pennsylvania, New York, West Virginia, and New Jersey state police also double as fire, fish, and game wardens. The New York state police officers serve as court officers for justices of the peace on Indian reservations.

California's state police are limited in jurisdiction to state buildings and grounds throughout the state, including the state college and university campuses. Although their uniforms and badges are identical and their paychecks originate from the State, each of the many police agencies for the various state colleges and universities functions as a separate entity. Another separate agency, the California Highway Patrol, has statewide jurisdiction on the state's highways for traffic enforcement, accident investigation, and related responsibilities.

In addition to the state police, there are many other investigative and law enforcement agencies, each with a specific agency or bureau to which it reports and a specific list of laws and rules with which it is to be concerned.

There is no uniformity in state police and investigative agencies, but there is some similarity. With that premise in mind, let's look at some of those agencies.

State Adjutant General

The National Guard and Air National Guard, or State Military Department, provide a military force with dual federal and state status, and they are available to both the federal government and the state in the event of a national or state emergency. Their organizations are set up in accordance with the laws of the states and the regulations of the Army and Air Force. The governor is the commander-in-chief. Under his direction, and in his name, the adjutant general is the chief-of-staff and commander of all state military forces.

Military control is the initial force of government and the ultimate power of government. It is defined as the "initial force" because it overcame the enemy and established the government in the beginning. It is the "ultimate force" in that the state militia is the governing authority when all other powers are ineffective to protect the state against invasion, insurrection, disaster, or unlawful disturbances.

Some form of military control is a traditional and obviously essential part of every government. Under normal conditions this control is exercised by the local law enforcement agencies and the control is basically exerted in subtle form by the presence of the officers throughout the community, who take whatever enforcement action is necessary as the need arises. When the military force in the form of the police is ineffective, it becomes necessary to invoke the more powerful force of the government, the National Guard.

The problem of when to call upon the services of the National Guard is serious, and the responsibility for making the decision should not be underestimated in a free country such as the United States. The entire judicial system is suspended under martial rule. The habeas corpus and due process provisions of the Constitution and the Bill of Rights are suspended. Martial rule is proclaimed by the governor, and it is in existence only when the state militia supersedes one or more local police agencies by his proclamation. It is a form of executive control that arises in self-defense of the state. There must be a very real need for such martial rule before the governor may proclaim its existence. Its objective is to preserve the public safety and good order of the community. The governor has the responsibility and authority to determine the need for martial rule and to suspend it at the earliest possible moment when its need no longer exists.

Under all but exceptional circumstances, the state militia will act "in aid of the civil authority." While acting in such a capacity, the militia's aid to local law enforcement agencies is limited. There is no suspension of local control or any of the judicial or legal processes. Objectives and missions are assigned by the local civil authority, and the military power shall be subordinate to civil authority. When the local executive officer of the city or county where the problem occurs requests the governor to declare martial rule, the governor then evaluates the situation and the request and makes the decision of whether to activate the martial rule. The manner used to quell the disturbance then becomes a military objective, which is handled as an army would capture a building or an area held by the enemy. The local police act in aid of the military force during martial rule.

Once the problem is solved, and the riot or insurrection is put down, the martial rule is discontinued and local rule restored. The decision whether to declare martial rule is a grave one, as the local police will have to live with the problems that follow, including destruction of property, loss of lives, and the animosities that arise during the riots, the name-calling, and recriminations.

The greatest difference between martial rule and civil rule is in the arrest and detention process. Ringleaders of a mob may be detained without formal booking procedures and held throughout the entire disturbance, then later released without trial. Such a detention is considered *preventive* and not *punitive.* In some cases when the military assists local police and when martial rule has not been proclaimed but when the public safety demands that such processes as preventive custody be used, the courts have ruled that such action was necessary and have refused writs of habeas corpus and denied claims of false imprisonment. In such cases the condition is defined as "preventive" or "qualified" martial rule.

The governor activates the militia, as mentioned earlier, and, if necessary, declares martial rule whenever the need for such action is called to his attention in any acceptable manner. Normal channels usually provide for such notifications to be made by the chief executive officer of any city or county, any justice of the state supreme court, judge of the superior court, or any sheriff. The request shows cause for action and a statement to the effect that the civil power is not sufficient to cope with the problem. Some states provide that martial rule may be utilized in any situation of great need, except when any such condition results from a labor controversy.

Highway Patrol

Highway patrol organizations are charged with the enforcement of state traffic laws and all laws governing the operation of vehicles on the public highways throughout the state. They may be a separate entity, as in California, or a part of the state police, as in Pennsylvania and elsewhere. The primary purpose for these organizations is to provide for the safety of all motorists. Although a state highway patrol usually has principal enforcement jurisdiction on the highways in the unincorporated areas of the state, some states provide that the highway patrol officers have full peace officer authority, and they may enforce traffic laws upon any public highway in the state. In times of civil disturbance or disaster, it is the responsibility of the highway patrol to keep traffic lanes moving and open.

Because of the large area to be covered, the state highway patrol is divided into geographical districts, with a ranking staff officer in charge of each district. The districts may be further divided into squads or other smaller units, depending on the needs of the agency and the size of the state. Enforcement activities are accomplished by patrol officers in uniform and distinctively marked patrol cars and motorcycles to perform the following functions:

1. Enforce the laws regulating the use of vehicles.
2. Maintain preventive patrols on the highways.
3. Regulate traffic movements and relieve congestion.
4. Investigate traffic accidents.
5. Make surveys and studies of accidents and enforcement practices for the purpose of improving traffic safety.

Some state highway patrol organizations maintain a traffic safety section that coordinates traffic safety programs throughout the state to assure uniformity in adherence to the many traffic laws. They assist all organizations, both public and private, in planning and operating effective safety programs. They assist local agencies by providing intensive enforcement training for traffic personnel. Auto theft records may be maintained more efficiently by a state agency such as a highway patrol because of their statewide jurisdiction, and they may provide laboratory and investigative personnel to assist local agencies in the investigation of hit-and-run cases and auto theft.

In addition to those functions listed in the preceding paragraphs, some highway patrol agencies coordinate the activity of and maintain records on commercial vehicle enforcement, maintain public scales on the highways, inspect all school buses, and investigate accidents involving school buses throughout the state. Licensing or registration of official smog control devices or headlights, or other safety equipment installation, and inspection stations may also be functions of the state highway patrol, as they are in California.

Department of Motor Vehicles

A state motor vehicle department is a service agency that has three major functions:

1. Registration of motor vehicles, collection of fees, and maintaining registration records.
2. Licensing drivers, collecting fees, and maintaining files on licenses.
3. Administration of financial responsibility laws.

Investigators assigned to this type of agency are involved in investigation of thefts and unlawful transfer of ownership of vehicles. Other investigators will include cases of altered license plates; forged or counterfeit auto registration certificates or drivers' licenses, and a variety of suspected law violations by auto dealerships and auto wreckers.

State Bureau of Narcotics

State narcotics agents are responsible for the investigation and enforcement of violations of the state narcotics laws. Their involvement with the lone users of narcotics and the peddlers of the drugs on the streets is usually through their cooperation with the many local law enforcement agencies and their vice officers. They are principally engaged in the investigation of alleged infractions of the law by persons who are in lawful possession of the drugs but may unlawfully or negligently dispense them. They investigate pharmacies, hospitals, and the offices of doctors, dentists, and veterinary surgeons for illegal sale and use of narcotics. State narcotics agents also seek out manufacturers and distributors of illicit drugs and generally enforce the legitimate use and dispensation of the drugs. This bureau is also responsible for the seizure of vehicles used in narcotic traffic and the abatement of properties used for the purpose of housing traffickers and users of drugs. This latter process involves a civil action against the owner of the property, which results in actual closure of the building sometimes for as long as a year. The threat of such action is usually sufficient warning to cause the owner of the property to exert influence on the tenants to cease their unlawful activities or face eviction.

Alcoholic Beverage Control

The state department of alcoholic beverage control in many states has licensing authority concerning the manufacture, importation, and sale of intoxicating liquors. The agency has statewide jurisdiction over the administration and enforcement of the state alcoholic beverage control laws that provide for the licensing and regulation of the alcoholic beverage industry in the state. In some states such an agency may also be given the responsibility to assess and collect excise taxes on the manufacture, importation, and sale of alcoholic beverages. The latter responsibility, however, may be handled by a taxing agency instead of by the department of alcoholic beverage control.

The agents assigned to control state liquor laws are primarily involved in the investigation of applicants for licenses to sell alcoholic beverages and to report on the moral character and fitness of the applicants and the suitability of the premises where the sales are to be conducted.

Violations of the laws that are most frequently encountered by the investigators of an agency of this type are sales to minors, consumption and possession by minors, sales after hours, conduct of the premises as disorderly houses, sales to obviously intoxicated persons, and failure to "fair trade" or post prices. Investigators of the alcoholic beverage control are peace officers in most states, and they have the authority to make arrests at any place in the state. They confiscate evidence, prepare reports, and testify in court in the prosecution of criminal law violators. Because all dealers in alcoholic beverages are licensees, the department handles many disciplinary matters of licensees administratively. Punishment may consist of a written notice to comply with the regulations or a permanent or temporary suspension of the license and forfeiture of the license fees.

Fish and Game Wardens

Game wardens enforce and prevent violations of laws and other regulations that relate to the conservation and protection of fish and wildlife. The duties of a warden include effecting arrests and issuing citations and warnings to the violators. They investigate wildlife crop damage complaints, advise landowners on the control of wildlife, and issue kill permits. Other duties include the feeding of game birds and animals during unusual weather conditions, assisting in the planning of controlled hunts, and operating checking stations in controlled hunting areas. The Department of Fish and Game and its agents are responsible for assisting in safety programs for hunters and fishermen, for securing assistance from various organizations in planting of fish and rescue operations, and generally assisting in the maintenance of hunting and fishing areas in the state to assure both wildlife conservation and perpetuation of the outdoor sports.

Labor Law Enforcement

The division of labor law enforcement of a state's department of industrial relations or similar agency is particularly responsible for enforcing regulations assuring ideal working conditions for the workers in the state. The laws enforced by such an agency include those that relate to the payment of wages, employment of women and children, private employment agencies, ventilation and sanitary conditions of places of employment, weekly day of rest, hours of work, and general conditions of work. Agents assigned to a labor law enforcement division or bureau are responsible for the additional duties of assuring compliance with the law in labor disputes, investigating industrial accidents and industrial safety, and maintaining labor statistics.

State Fire Marshal

The state fire marshal is a peace officer in most states. He has the primary responsibility of preventing fires by performing the following functions:

1. Elimination of fire hazards on state-owned and tax-deeded property.
2. Establishment and enforcement of fire and panic safety regulations in all state institutions.
3. Investigation of fires vaulting from crime or where crime has been committed in connection with any fire.
4. The development of uniform fire and panic safety regulations and the enforcement of such regulations in areas outside of corporate cities and fire protection districts.
5. Administration of a continuous educational fire prevention program.
6. Aid and assistance to local fire officials in the enforcement of fire safety laws, ordinances, and regulations.
7. The establishment of minimum safety requirements governing the manufacture and sale of flammable clothing, the operation of circuses and tent shows, and the flame-retardant treatment of drapes and curtains used in schools or places of public assemblage.
8. Regulation of fire safety in the dry cleaning industry.
9. Regulation of the sale, discharge, and public display of fireworks.
10. Issuance of fire clearances to private institutions such as sanitariums licensed by the State Department of Mental Hygiene, Social Welfare, or Public Health.
11. The approval of fire safety plans of new institutions or additions to existing institutions before they are constructed.

Horse-Racing Board

In states where there is parimutuel betting, the horse-racing board or a similar agency administers laws governing horse racing and supervises the conduct of racing at all race tracks in the state. It allots dates for racing, supervises parimutuel betting, and licenses associations conducting the meetings and persons connected with the meetings.

Investigators assigned to the horse-racing enforcement agency are responsible for routine enforcement of the horse-racing laws and rules, and for inspectional duties around the tracks. They watch for violations in the stable area, such as tampering with the horses, or the presence of unauthorized and unlicensed persons. In the public areas, such as the grandstand and the clubhouses, the investigators look for and take appropriate action against (consisting of arrest or ejection) bookmakers, pickpockets, and other undesirables. Away from the tracks the investigators check out rumors and information concerning "fixes" of races; they search for lost parimutuel tickets and investigate license applicants and the various people who frequent the race tracks.

"Generalist" Agencies

Various licensing commissions and boards, usually at the state level, establish and administer the many laws related to their respective professions and services. The board members are usually appointed from the ranks of their own professions and serve for specific periods of time. They act to maintain ethical standards of their professions. They employ staffs of investigators, or they may make use of an investigative "pool" that provides investigators when the need arises. Investigation is the primary role of the agents assigned, but they may be designated as peace officers for specific law enforcement responsibilities. Just a few of the boards and commissions involved with this type of investigative responsibility are insurance agents, investment specialists, real estate brokers, chiropractors, medical doctors, pharmacists, dentists, athletes, accountants, engineers, beauticians, private detectives, funeral directors, nurses, social workers, and barbers.

Disaster Services

Disasters acts enacted during World War II and the years following provided legislation for the provision of mutual aid among the various political subdivisions in times of major disasters and civil disturbances. According to the laws of many states, the mutual aid is voluntary when the emergency is not extreme and mandatory when the emergency is extreme. When he determines the need for assistance in accordance with this act, the chief of police or sheriff may request assistance under these conditions:

natural disaster, riot, or similar occurrence that taxes the capabilities of the police agency beyond its ability to effectively handle the situation. Mutual aid is voluntary under most conditions but mandatory during times of extreme emergency.

The State Disaster Office is usually responsible for the following:

1. Development and maintenance of the master emergency plans and programs of the state.
2. Recommendation for assignment by the Governor of appropriate emergency roles to the other agencies of state government and to the local governments.
3. Provision of assistance to agencies and local governments of the state in planning, programming, organizing, equipping, and training for necessary emergency organizations.
4. Coordination between federal, state, and local agencies of emergency plans.
5. Assistance for all agencies and local governments in obtaining federal funds and equipment to implement approved emergency plans and programs.
6. Coordination of planning activities pertaining to past attack management of resources and economic stabilization functions that might have to be performed by state agencies due to disruption of normal procedure on a national basis.

FEDERAL POLICE AND INVESTIGATIVE AGENCIES

The federal government has no single law enforcement or investigative agency that has unlimited jurisdiction. As pointed out in the first part of this chapter, the various city and county police agencies are responsible for enforcement of the basic state and local laws that provide for the public health, safety, and morals. The federal agencies have been created for the purpose of investigating and/or enforcing specific laws and to cope with specific problems that extend beyond the jurisdictional boundaries of state and local forces. One agency was created to protect the currency (Secret Service) and another for the purpose of enforcing federal tax regulations (Alcohol, Tobacco, and Firearms Division of the Treasury Department). These are just two of the many agencies. In the next few pages let us look at some of the police and investigative agencies of the federal government. When reading of these agencies, keep in mind the fact that there is no rank order, no hierarchy of command or responsibility. Each operates within its own sphere of responsibility and authority and reports to a specific department or bureau to which it is responsible.

Department of the Treasury

The Secret Service The Secret Service has been in continuous service since July 5, 1865.

> It was currency counterfeiting problems during the Civil War that established a need for a law enforcement branch of the U.S. Treasury Department.

> Shortly after onset of the war it was estimated that about one-third of the currency then in circulation was counterfeit.... The unit was instructed to launch war on counterfeiters and restore the public's confidence in the nation's currency.[2]

It took the new unit five years to round up a substantial number of the counterfeiters, reduce the amount of counterfeit currency in circulation, and establish the integrity of the "greenback."

In 1894 a small detail of the Secret Service provided some protection on a part-time basis to President Cleveland following threats to his life. It was not until after the assassination of President McKinley in 1901 that Congress officially extended the duties of the Secret Service to full-time protection of the president. In 1913 protection extended to the president-elect, in 1917 to the president's immediate family, in 1951 to the vice-president. Following the assassination of President Kennedy in 1963, protection extended to his widow and children. White House detail has primary responsibility for those protection services.

The Internal Revenue Service The intelligence unit of the Internal Revenue Service is concerned with the enforcement of laws concerning internal revenue and income taxes. It is authorized to examine bank accounts, and inquire into income matters and business transactions. The Alcohol, Tobacco, and Firearms Division has primary responsibility for the tax law enforcement relative to alcoholic beverage production and certain weapons. The enforcement agents of this unit enforce the National Firearms Act, which regulates the possession of automatic weapons and defines certain firearms that are illegal to possess.

The Bureau of Customs Customs agents are responsible for enforcement of the laws involving illegal importing and exporting, customs, and navigation. Customs enforcement men and women guard baggage enclosures, ships, motor vehicles, aircraft, railroad cars, and patrol docks and airfields. They prevent unlawful loading or unloading or delivery of merchandise, smuggling, or other acts against the laws of the United States. Customs agents assess and collect duties and taxes on imported merchandise. The bureau is decentralized and most of its personnel are stationed throughout the country, principally at the 289 ports of entry.

Department of Justice

The Attorney General The U.S. Attorney General is the chief law enforcement officer of the federal government, and his office is responsible for criminal prosecution of all violators of federal laws throughout the

[2] "A Salute to the U.S. Secret Service," *Police Chief,* XXXII, No. 9, September, 1965, pp. 8–9.

country. The Justice Department, under the direction of the Attorney General, has several primary operating units with responsibility for the investigation and enforcement of certain federal laws including the Immigration and Naturalization Service, the Federal Bureau of Investigation, and the Drug Enforcement Administration.

Federal Drug Enforcement Administration Narcotics agents have principal jurisdiction over enforcement of federal laws regulating the legal traffic in narcotics in the United States and in monitoring such traffic at both international and national levels. The Federal Drug Enforcement Administration is responsible for enforcing the federal laws regulating the production, sale, and transportation of narcotic drugs. The agents of this bureau work very closely with state and local law enforcement agents because of the need to work as a team to cope with the problems of the unbelievably efficient underworld organization of narcotics traffickers, which nets fantastic profits throughout the world. They work both undercover assignments to identify and prosecute the criminal drug trafficker and routine inspection assignments to assure adherence to the legal narcotics and drug traffic. Two of their objectives are to reach the highest level of sources of supply and to apprehend the greatest quantity of illicit drugs before they reach the street.[3] Formerly a part of the Treasury Department, this agency now operates under the jurisdiction of the Attorney General in the Department of Justice.

The Federal Bureau of Investigation The Federal Bureau of Investigation of the Department of Justice is not a police agency but an investigative agency with jurisdiction over all matters in which the United States is or may be a party in interest.

The FBI has broad investigative jurisdiction encompassing all federal law violations but limits its scope to about 160 federal laws, including all of those federal statutes not specifically assigned to another agency. Among those matters that are within the primary jurisdiction of the FBI to which its investigators direct the major portion of their attention are the following: administrative investigations, admiralty matters, antitrust laws, civil rights violations, Atomic Energy Act investigations, bankruptcy violations, bribery, copyright violations, crimes on the high seas involving U.S. vessels, crimes on Indian or government reservations, espionage, Federal Kidnapping Act, Federal Reserve Bank Act, frauds against the government, illegal wearing of service uniforms, interstate transportation of stolen vehicles or stolen property, killing and assaulting federal officers, location of escaped federal prisoners, mail fraud, National Bankruptcy Act, passports and visas, patent violations, robbery and burglary of National FDIC-insured and Federal Reserve System banks, unlawful flight to avoid prosecution or confinement, White Slave Traffic, and others. The principal investigative responsibility

[3]Kakalik and Wildhorn, *Special Purpose Public Police,* p. 7.

for protection of the national security has been placed in the hands of the FBI.

In addition to the investigative functions of the agents of the Federal Bureau of Investigation, that agency provides assistance to local law enforcement agencies with training of its officers at the National Academy and maintains a criminal laboratory that is available for assistance in local investigative matters. Since 1930 the FBI has been the central clearing house for the most complete files on fingerprint and arrest files, and the agency serves the majority of all the country's law enforcement agencies by maintaining criminal statistics and by disseminating the information on a regular basis in its Uniform Crime Reports.

Immigration and Naturalization Service This branch of the Justice Department was created by authority of an immigration law of 1891 (26 Stat. 1085) and enforces and investigates laws related to the admission, exclusion, and deportation of aliens, as well as the naturalization of aliens lawfully residing in the United States. Its border patrol covers the borders and points of entry into the United States to prevent the illegal entry of aliens. The Immigration and Naturalization Service supervises the naturalization of aliens in the courts, provides textbooks and assists in the education of aliens seeking naturalization, and registers all aliens in the United States.

U.S. Marshal The marshals are assigned directly to the Attorney General's office and perform general federal law enforcement activities, with duties and responsibilities similar to those of the county sheriff. Major duties consist of serving processes, making arrests, attending court, seizing property, conducting sales to satisfy liens, transporting prisoners, acting as bailiffs in the federal court, and generally functioning as federal enforcement officers.

Department of Transportation

The Coast Guard, formerly a branch of the Treasury Department in peacetime and an arm of the Navy during time of war, is the seagoing law enforcement arm of the Department of Transportation. The Coast Guard, which changed to its current name in 1915, was previously the *Revenue Cutter Service.* Duties of the Coast Guard include patrolling the coast lines of the United States to prevent smuggling of contraband and aliens, enforcing laws related to navigable waters, maintaining port security, providing sea rescue services, and the preservation of fish, animals, and birds along the coasts and islands.

The Office of Civil Aviation Security was established in 1971, in part as as response to a tremendous need for coordinated enforcement and protective services to the aviation transportation industry attributed to the phenomenal increase in the rate of hijackings. Augmented by officers of the several agencies of the Treasury, Justice, Defense, and State Departments, this agency has primary responsibility for civil aviation security, cargo security, and program development.[4]

Postal Inspection Service

The "silent investigators," or postal investigators have been in business in an almost anonymous role (hence, the silent investigators title) since 1775 when Postmaster General Benjamin Franklin appointed a man named Goddard to the position of surveyor. In 1801 the position title was changed to "special agent," and in 1880 the change was to "inspector."[5]

Postal inspectors are concerned with two types of investigations: (1) criminal investigations relating to the postal service and (2) service investigations concerning the protection of postal revenues, the economic operation of the postal service, and conformity to the laws and regulations of the services.

Criminal laws involving the postal inspectors are covered in Title 18 and Title 39 of the U.S. Code. Those laws involve mail-conducted lotteries, obstruction of correspondence, theft of mail, frauds through the mails, burglary or robbery, and use of the mail to distribute obscene and crime-inciting material.

Other Federal Police Agencies

The State Department Office of Security is another of several agencies that investigates the backgrounds of critical personnel. Its principal duty is to investigate visa and passport applications.

Under the Department of Defense, the military services operate both criminal investigative and intelligence units. In the Air Force, the Office of Special Investigations (OSI) handles both types of investigative and enforcement duties.

The Department of Interior has four units charged with the investigation and enforcement of federal laws. The Fish and Wildlife Service enforces the laws involving migratory game birds, fish and wildlife restoration acts, and international agreements on interstate transportation of wildlife. The Bureau of Indian Affairs maintains order and suppresses illegal liquor and drug traffic on Indian reservations. The Bureau of Mines investigates and enforces regulations concerning mine accidents, explosions, and fires. The National

[4]Richard G. Kleindienst, *Attorney General's First Annual Report: Federal Law Enforcement and Criminal Justice Assistance Activities* (Washington, D.C.: Government Printing Office, 1972), pp. 7, 423.

[5]Arthur S. Aubrey, Jr., "United States Postal Inspection Service," *Police,* XIII, No. 2, November-December, 1968.

Park Service maintains a staff of National Park Rangers, who perform police services in the national parks throughout the country.

The Department of Agriculture enforces more than fifty laws that protect the farmers and consumers. This agency is also responsible for national standards in weights and measures in cooperation with the local and various state agencies.

The Department of Health, Education and Welfare is involved in police type enforcement work in the areas of purity and standards of food, drugs, cosmetics, and standard labeling laws.

Within the Department of Labor is the Bureau of Labor Standards. This bureau was established in 1934 to promote industrial safety and health. Responsibilities include the development of standards in the field of labor legislation and labor law administration, and working with the various other agencies involved in implementing international labor standards.

The U.S. Forest Service and its Rangers are principally concerned with fire prevention and control problems and management of recreation areas. Their law enforcement activities involve theft or damage to trees, setting fires, and failure to have spark arresters on motor vehicles.

Independent Agencies with Federal Jurisdiction

In addition to those agencies that are directly related to the executive arms of government, there have been numerous quasi-government agencies that operate with the full force and effect of law enforcement agencies, except that they enforce most of their rules by means of administrative actions. A representative sampling of those agencies includes the following:

1. The National Transportation Safety Board investigates all civil aircraft accidents and regulates civilian air traffic.
2. The Civil Service Commission has an investigative division that performs the following functions:
   - **(a)** National agency checks, inquiries, and personnel investigations for nonsensitive positions.
   - **(b)** Thorough investigations beyond the scope of (a.) for sensitive positions.
   - **(c)** Investigations on matters relating to the enforcement of civil service laws and rules.
   - **(d)** Qualification investigations of applicants for high-level administrative and professional positions with the agencies of the federal government.
3. The Federal Communications Commission regulates interstate commerce by means of the many communications media. Their personnel are responsible for enforcement of the Communications Act, which provides for licensing and regulating of operators and broadcasting stations. In cooperation with an international committee, the FCC designates frequencies to various applicants and works to assure maximum compatibility among the many licensees.

4. The Federal Trade Commission is responsible for looking into—and taking appropriate action when necessary—incidents of unfair competition and deceptive and monopolistic practices in interstate commerce.
5. The Securities and Exchange Commission prosecutes malpractice cases in securities and financial markets.
6. The Interstate Commerce Commission regulates common carriers in interstate commerce and is also involved in the investigation of railroad accidents.

Military Police and Investigative Agencies

Within the jurisdiction of the military services and the Uniform Code of Military Justice are several enforcement and investigative agencies that function similarly to their civilian counterparts. Those agencies include the military police of the several services and the Armed Services Police, which is a consolidated agency of the several services in certain metropolitan areas in which there is a concentration of military installations and personnel. Each service has a criminal investigation division that concerns itself with investigations of crimes and other violations of the Uniform Code of Military Justice and related matters that involve the military services and the military personnel and civilians who are affected by the code.

Operating along somewhat different avenues of investigation, generally with low visibility and dependent on informants and observations of certain individuals and their associates, are the intelligence or counter-intelligence units. These units are concerned with subversive activities, sabotage, treason, disaffection, and other matters of a sensitive nature that affect the services. These agencies include the Office of Special Investigations (OSI) of the Air Force, Office of Naval Intelligence (ONI), and the Counter-Intelligence Corps (CIC) of the Army.

Central Intelligence Agency

Interest in this agency of the federal government is often quite high because of the glamour attributed to it by news publicity at various times of international crisis. Actually, it is a correlative function as far as the criminal justice system is concerned. The Central Intelligence Agency is not an enforcement or investigative agency.

INTERNATIONAL COOPERATION OF POLICE AGENCIES

Reference is frequently made in popular television and motion pictures to some form of super agency of several governments that may operate under the director of some international organization. Actually such an organization does exist, but on a different scale and at a lower key. Such an organization is the Interpol, or the International Criminal Police Organization.

In an interesting article Arnold Sogalyn explained the mission and function of Interpol.[6] Interpol is a truly international agency employing the manpower and resources of approximately 111 countries located throughout the world. Operating through the Secretariat at Paris, this organization can exchange information and assistance on criminal matters such as drug traffic, smuggling, or theft operations without having to negotiate through diplomatic channels for each new situation.

Originally represented by the FBI from 1939 to 1950, membership by the United States for many years following that decade was on an informal basis with the Bureau of Narcotics, the Bureau of Customs, and the Secret Service. In 1958 Congress amended the Enchling Act to permit the Attorney General to designate the Treasury Department as the U.S. representative to Interpol. Since 1958 the United States has continued its membership in the organization through the Treasury Department's Office of Law Enforcement Coordinator in Washington, D.C.[7]

PRIVATE POLICE AND INVESTIGATIVE AGENCIES

In the United States in the year 1975 more than 1 million people were employed in either the public or private sectors of security services. One out of every 250 persons in the entire population of the nation was employed as a policeman, investigator, guard, watchman, or some other capacity in security involving an expenditure of more than $40 per capita for those services.[8] While we have for so many years addressed ourselves to a study of the government-based security services within the criminal justice system, an equally large number of people and types of operations have been developing almost without attention or recognition—into a massive network of private police systems. James Kakalik's and Sorrel Wildhorn's excellent report on private police in the United States was funded by an LEAA grant to study the scope and impact of the private police, and should be the subject of intensive study during the next few years just as the study of the public police has been during the preceding generation. According to Kakalik and Wildhorn, the principal agencies such as Burns, Pinkerton's, and the Railway Police provided most of the professional investigative services in the United States until about 1924.[9]

The private police are employed to protect private interests and supplement—rather than compete with—the protective and enforcement activities

[6]Arnold Sogalyn, "The Role of Interpol in Law Enforcement," *Police Chief*, XXXII, No. 12, December, 1965; pp. 57–59.

[7]Sogalyn, "The Role of Interpol in Law Enforcement," pp. 57–59.

[8]Private Security Task Force Report: *Private Security Standards and Goals* (Cincinnati: W. H. Anderson Publishing Co., 1977), p. 1.

[9]Kakalik and Wildhorn, *Private Police in the United States*, pp. 17–18.

of the public police. With powers of inquiry and arrest the same as that of any other citizen (which, incidentally, is not substantially different than the powers of the public police), the private police perform either on a contract or in-house basis the following functions:

1. Information gathering (e.g., preemployment checks, insurance or credit application checks, insurance claim investigations, antipilferage undercover work in retail and industrial establishments, criminal investigations, martial investigations).
2. Maintaining order on, and proper access to, private property (e.g., guarding sporting events, recreational events).
3. Protection of persons and property by preventing and detecting crime, reducing losses to crime, and/or apprehending suspected criminals (e.g., guarding homes and commercial, institutional, and industrial establishments, antishoplifting activities in retail establishments, armored transport of valuables, alarm systems, surveillance systems, locks, and mobile patrolling).[10]

The effectiveness of the private police depends to a great extent on their role perception: how the private police themselves see their roles and how the public perceives them. About this problem, Kakalik and Wildhorn made the following observations:

> There are two polar views of private security. One holds that private security services (provided by high-quality personnel and equipment) effectively complement the public police by providing security and other related services in areas and situations where the public police do not—either because the public police are not given adequate resources or because they are legally constrained from doing so. This view also holds that current controls and regulation are adequate, since private police seldom abuse their powers. The other view holds that the private security "industry" feeds on fear and provides ineffective security services by untrained, low-quality personnel who are a potential danger to the public and who, in fact, abuse their limited powers. This view also holds that current controls on, and regulation of, private police are inadequate.[11]

This assessment of the effectiveness of private police prompted the following statements:

> Perhaps the relative lack of information on effectiveness stems from the greatly increased demand for contract security services over the past decade, the limited supply of such services, the fact that purchases of such services are, for various reasons, often interested in obtaining low-cost, rather than high-quality, service, and the fact that such effectiveness evaluations would require extensive and costly data collection.
>
> ... It must be remembered that there are two dimensions to effectiveness, or benefits. First, there are the objective, or measurable, benefits; for example,

[10]Kakalik and Wildhorn, *Private Police in the United States,* p. 24.

[11]Kakalik and Wildhorn, *Private Police in the United States,* p. 1.

> the reduction in losses to crime effected by a specific security program, or the number of burglars caught after, as compared to before, a particular alarm system was installed. The other dimension is the user's or purchasers' *perceptions* about benefits. A homeowner may feel more secure when he contracts with a central alarm services firm, even though there might be few objective benefits. On balance, it must be concluded that users perceive the benefits of private security as being worth the cost since private services are increasingly in demand.[12]

Special needs of private sectors of the community require the services of private police patrols and investigation agencies. During the professional growth and development of the governmental agencies, their private counterparts have kept pace in many respects. Representing private individuals and corporations, these private operators serve in a wide variety of roles as representatives of those who employ them.

Concentrated patrol of special areas, such as private islands or residential complexes is accomplished by private guards. Popular motion picture and television representations of the types of duties performed by these individuals is based on some fact. Internal investigations of officers and employees of corporations from banks to service station chains, from warehouse to factories are not quite so glamourous, but they do consume considerable time of private investigators. Another principal type of work conducted by these men and women is industrial espionage, which has all of the flavor of international espionage, but involves substantial fortunes instead of domestic security. Patents and formulas on toys, soaps, tools, automobiles, and virtually every type of competitive industry are extremely valuable and the subject of considerable concern to their owners or custodians.

SUMMARY

In spite of, or because of, the various divisions of authority and responsibility, law enforcement and criminal investigations on a nationwide, statewide, or local level somehow manage to maintain the peace and protect the lives and property of a large percentage of the population. Proponents for centralization of power may profess that efficiency would be increased by arguing that not only would the best of talents throughout the country be pooled and harnessed but the various agencies would be more inclined to work toward common objectives with consistent policies. Proponents for decentralization of power and perpetuation of the system as it is now, with the various agencies each striving to accomplish its own objectives—which may or may not be similar to another agency—agree that this "local rule" philosophy is the answer to maximum police efficiency.

Actually, it appears that local autonomy has many distinct advantages. One of those advantages is that the local police chief, who lives in or near

[12]Kakalik and Wildhorn, *Private Police in the United States,* p. 25.

the city where his department operates, is responsive to the needs of his own community and is directly aware of the community standards in moral and social behavior and knows his jurisdiction intimately.

Both concepts have value. Local direction of daily police operations is more directly relevant to the specific needs of the community. However, coordination of information systems, communications, training, laboratories, research, and many specialized services may be accomplished more efficiently by a central agency.

During the lifetime of the reader, "revolutionary change" has been commonplace in many facets of law enforcement and so has the lack of change in yet other facets.

The existing police system has been analyzed, discussed, evaluated, compared, studied, and inspected from within and from without. No doubt, changes will be made. At the present time the trend appears to be toward pooling of resources and facilities in information and communications systems, training programs, laboratory services, intelligence operations, and research projects. Additionally, there is some pooling of the traditional field operations by either a "joint powers" consortium or by consolidation of several agencies into one.

In this chapter we have examined the many agencies of the law enforcement component of the criminal justice system, from the local to the state and federal police departments and investigative agencies, with a recap on the private segment of the system that has previously received little attention. The private agencies are commercial profit-based service organizations designed and operated to provide specific services in the interest of those who contract their services for a fee. The public agencies are government-based agencies that provide either general or specific services in the interest of the government-defined needs of the public, and the fees are derived from taxes.

The local police departments of municipalities and the county sheriffs of the many counties and parishes throughout the country provide the basic police functions essential to the maintenance of the society of ordered liberty in this representative republic. The special purpose agencies that operate within the smaller governmental subdivisions include such units as housing authority or transit authority police who provide patrol and protective services in specific locations and on district-owned vehicles. Other local officers include the marshal and constable, who perform court-related functions in the lower courts just as the sheriff performs in the superior court in the county. The coroner has certain police responsibilities, but is principally concerned with death investigations and certain matters related to personal effects and estates of the deceased and the appropriate disposition of the remains. He does have the ultimate authority in the determination of cause of death, but usually conducts his investigations in cooperation with the county prosecutor and the police departments, who have the investigative personnel and extensive resources at their disposal to perform most effectively.

At the state level—although the term "level" should not be interpreted to imply that there is any hierarchical scale of authority-responsibility relationships—the police and investigative agencies are involved in matters of general or specific interest but with a statewide jurisdiction. The highway patrol, for example, patrols the highways and enforces traffic regulations throughout the state, but does so within city limits by invitation from the cities and in agreement with the local departments. State licensing and regulating agencies are concerned with minimum standards, ethics, and occupation-oriented laws. For example, the Department of Motor Vehicles is responsible for the licensing of motor vehicles, vehicle operators, salesmen, agencies, and administrative matters involving the automobile industry.

The federal law enforcement and investigative agencies are principally concerned with the police power of the federal government. National and international matters of significance consume the time and energies of the agencies of the federal government, such as the U.S. Marshal, the Federal Bureau of Investigation, Secret Service, Postal Inspection Service, and a long list of special needs agencies. The federal agencies have jurisdiction throughout the United States and its protectorates, and, in many cases throughout the world in matters involving the United States. Their work in the jurisdictions of other agencies involves considerable cooperation and coordinated efforts of the many agencies involved. There are many investigations that involve overlapping, or concurrent, jurisdiction. Each agency concerns itself with those matters falling within its respective jurisdiction and the efforts and the results are—hopefully—the product of a cooperative relationship. There are problems, of course, but in such a vast system involving hundreds of thousands of individuals there is a surprising degree of efficiency and effectiveness.

EXERCISES AND STUDY QUESTIONS

1. What is the exact relationship of the Federal Bureau of Investigation to the police department in the city where you live?

2. List the state police and investigative agencies operated within your state.

3. What is the largest private police agency in the United States, according to the text?

4. What were the three alternate ideas that have been suggested to relieve or reduce interforce conflicts of the several federal agencies with overlapping jurisdiction?

5. What is your opinion of the autonomy of local departments with law enforcement responsibilities—should there be more or less autonomy?

6. Give at least three examples of hypothetical cases involving concurrent jurisdiction.

7. Discuss the condition known as "martial rule" and its relationship with local law enforcement agencies in the jurisdiction where it is in effect.

8. In which matters are the duties and responsibilities the same for the sheriff, the marshal, and the constable?

9. List at least four occasions when the coroner is responsible for the investigation of death.

10. If you had a case for the state fire marshal, how would you go about making contact with him?

11. Under what branch of government is the Coast Guard assigned, and what are its basic responsibilities?

12. Describe the functions of the DEA, and explain how it would operate in cooperation with your local police department in a case of concurrent interest and jurisdiction.

13. Is there a supervisor-subordinate relationship between the sheriff and local police chiefs?

14. Have you read about any vigilante groups that have been created as a result of a local need in your state? If so, what were the circumstances?

15. Is there a reserve police force in the city where you live? If so, how are the reserve officers utilized?

16. In the event the coroner determines at an inquest that a named individual was criminally responsible for another's death, what would be the next thing that he would do?

17. What problems could arise following martial rule?

18. List and explain at least three state police agencies that were not covered in this chapter.

19. What is the function of the Federal Aviation Authority?

20. In your state, what is the function of the alcoholic beverage control agency of the state?

RECOMMENDED SEMESTER/TERM PROJECTS

1. Visit or write to a federal or state law enforcement or investigative agency. Interview as many people as you can and find out as much as you can about that agency. Describe the objectives of the agency, the legal jurisdiction, and the duty requirements of the people who work for the agency.

2. Prepare a proposal for the consolidation of criminal justice agencies with similar responsibilities at the federal or state or local level. Show how the agencies can be consolidated, what would be the advantages as opposed to the disadvantages, and compare your proposal to the type of consolidation that has occurred in certain locations in the country, such as the Miami-Dade area of Florida and Clark County, Nevada.

SUGGESTED FOR ADDITIONAL STUDY

BENT, ALAN EDWARD, *The Politics of Law Enforcement.* Lexington, Mass.: D. C. Heath and Company, 1974.

GOLDSMITH, JACK, and SHARON S. GOLDSMITH, eds., *The Police Community.* Pacific Palisades, Calif.: Palisades Publishers, 1974.

GROSSMAN, BRIAN A., *Police Command. Decisions and Discretion.* Toronto: Macmillan Company of Canada, Ltd., 1975.

MORE, HARRY W., JR., ed., *The American Police: Text and Readings.* St. Paul: West Publishing Co., 1976.

SMITH, BRUCE, *Police Systems in the United States* (2d ed.). New York: Harper and Brothers, 1960.

7

Basic Police Operations

INTRODUCTION

Although this text is designed to introduce you to the entire criminal justice system, and certainly not just the police component, it may seem somewhat incongruous to devote a chapter to the police organization and not separate chapters of a similar nature to the working parts of the other components of the courts and corrections. The reason is simply that, when one encounters the police on a daily basis, there appears to the observer to be a clearer distinction of functions than there is with other agencies. Also, the police are the most visible from the outside looking in. Basic structures of agencies of the other components will be covered in the other chapters, although not in as much depth.

In this chapter we shall discuss the basic objectives of the typical local police department, then briefly examine each of the many sections or units of that department organized for the purpose of accomplishing those objectives. The objective of this chapter is to prepare the reader/student so that he/she may diagram the basic police department and explain the primary functions of each of the subunits described in this chapter.

THE POLICE MISSION

The basic responsibility—the police mission—of the police component of the criminal justice system is to protect and serve the people. The agencies responsible for the fundamental accomplishment of that mission are the many thousands of local police organizations: the city police and the county sheriffs' departments. All other agencies are special purpose units. The local agencies have responsibility and authority to assure the public safety, health, welfare, morality, and general prosperity of those they serve.

Although their general structure will remain somewhat the same, each organization has its own distinctive characteristics. Variations in organization depend on differences in the organization's (1) purpose, (2) methods to be used, (3) functions to be performed, (4) people to be served, (5) time of day and day of week, (6) geographical area, plus (7) any special needs that are unique to the one organization.

The purpose of the police agency include its goals and objectives. The goals of the typical department include the following:

- Assurance for the people that they may live in a society of ordered liberty with a minimum of governmental influence and with a delicate balance of rights and responsibilities.
- Protection of life and property through continuous, vigilant patrol and preventive maintenance activities.
- Fair and impartial enforcement of the laws.
- Prevention of criminal and asocial behavior through public information and personal contacts with would-be violators and their victims.
- Crime repression through an attempt to develop a feeling of ever-presence of the police without a threatening over-presence.
- Return to rightful owners property that has been stolen, lost, or embezzled.
- Aiding in the prosecution and fair adjudication of cases involving people accused of crime through identification and apprehension, presenting evidence, and giving accurate testimony.

For the Sheriff's department add:

- Serve as bailiff to the superior court and others, if duties include those of the marshal and constable, following the orders of the judge and handling required processes.
- Management of the county jail and pretrial and posttrial prisoners.
- Perform the duties of such other offices as are delegated by law, such as coroner, tax collector, public administrator, or other.

Although each police department should identify its own objectives, most of them will include those listed in Chapter 1:

- Police ever-presence.
- Benevolent services.
- Crisis intervention.
- Assure peaceful assemblage.
- Investigate crimes and arrest offenders.
- Enforce all laws.
- Investigate traffic collisions and enforce traffic laws.
- Investigate license law violations.
- Direct pedestrian and vehicular traffic.
- Crime prevention, repression, and preventive maintenance.
- Investigate complaints and handle calls for service.
- Vice control.
- Juvenile delinquency prevention and control.
- Community interaction.
- Property and evidence storage.
- Reports and records and provide appropriate information.

THE ORGANIZATIONAL PLAN

The police organization should be divided into subunits dependent upon the same criteria listed as those required to distinguish from one type organization to the other. (1) *Purpose.* The purposes of the department are varied and numerous. Dividing the agency by purpose would lead to the development of the following subdivisions: traffic enforcement and accident investigating, juvenile delinquency prevention, follow-up investigation, records-keeping and public information, business office, vice control and enforcement. (2) *Methods.* Separating the functions by method would separate the patrolling function from the follow-up investigation unit and the adult investigation function from the juvenile unit because methods would vary. Vice investigations are conducted in a different manner than burglary investigations. (3) *Functions.* Dividing the organization by function leads to placement of some individual in charge with both accountability and responsibility, and would include separations of almost all the various tasks within the department. Then, tasks would be grouped so that major work units were developed. (4) *People to be served.* Juveniles are handled differently than adults; the probation officers and juvenile court are different people than the prosecuting attorney and adult court, and the laws differ. Attitudes may be different, as well as enforcement philosophies. (5) *Time* and (6) *area* are factors in the division of the patrol—and others also—unit to be divided into "watches," or shifts, to serve the different times of day and into districts or substations to handle the geographic divisions.

When the police chief or sheriff proceeds to break down his agency into working units, there are a few basic principles of organization that must be taken into account: (1) Specify goals and objectives (which we covered earlier), (2) develop an organizational plan (which we are doing now), (3) organize according to the plan, (4) prescribe relationships, (5) minimize dual accountability, (6) limit the scope of supervision, (7) integrate and coordinate the functional units, (8) staff the organization for maximum effectiveness, and (9) develop methods for control.

When the chief first begins his plan, he breaks down the various units or subunits into distinguishable categories. His outline may resemble Figure 7-1.

By designating each unit separately in such a diagram, the chief is identifying each as a separate entity with its own set of goals and objectives as well as distinctive procedures, which may be different from the other units. He is also delineating areas of responsibility because ultimately a single individual must be held accountable to the chief for the successful operation of that unit.

Although two or more units may be under the direction of—and the responsibility of—only one person, each unit must have a specific designated person who is accountable to the chief for the unit; this is step one: identify functional units.

The second step in organizational planning is to show relationships. Although staffing may not be done until later, it will be necessary for the chief to know the people he will be assigning to these various positions because unique talents, strengths, and interests will certainly influence unit designations and relationships.

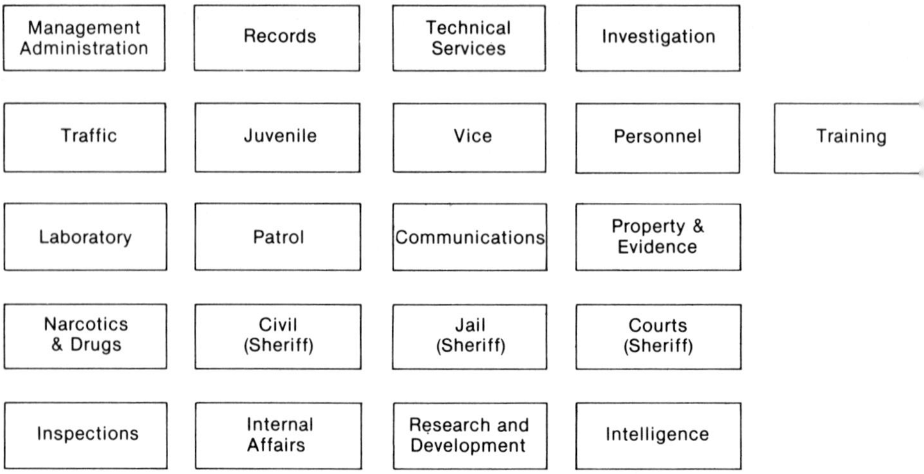

Figure 7-1

To show groupings and hierarchies of responsibility-accountability, the unit boxes are placed above, below, or in line with one another. (Refer to Figure 7-2.) Units that are subordinate to another will be placed underneath the higher-ranking unit. Units that are equal to one another may also be placed below others on the chart, but the solid lines going to the higher unit will show which are subordinate to which, and which are equal.

Both diagrams showing traffic division relationships are similar in that they show three subunits as part of, or subordinate to, the major traffic unit. Therefore, in addition to relative locations on the chart, it is possible to show relationships by the manner in which the connecting lines are drawn. In both illustrations, the three subunits are separately in line with the major division. Lines show channels of communication within an organization as

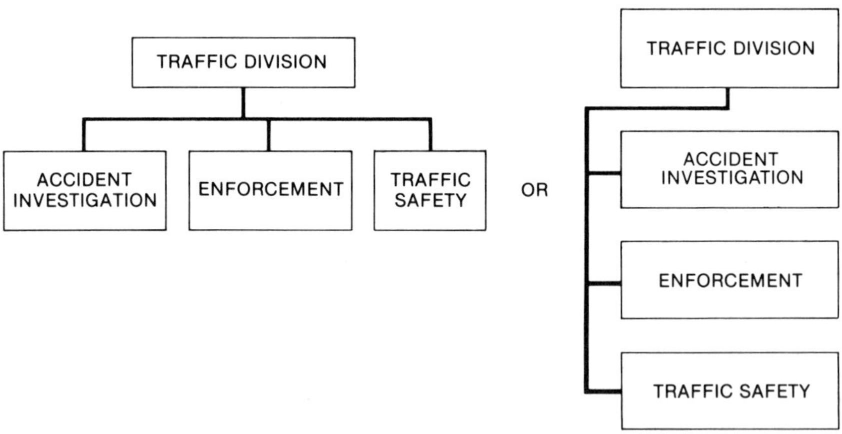

Figure 7-2

well as the hierarchy. The lines of communication are similar to telephone or power or water lines showing flow and accessibility. In both of the charts, the individual in charge of each of the subunits is equal in authority and possibly equal in rank (although there are exceptions) to each other, and each of the other three reports directly to the individual in charge of the major unit. In case of any dispute between two or three of the subordinate leaders, the higher ranking officer would break the tie.

The charts in Figure 7-3 show groupings. The absence of lines in the first chart makes it impossible to determine the exact lines of authority-accountability, although their relative positions would at least indicate that under the chief of police there appears to be three major units—line, staff, and auxiliary—each one headed by a superior officer, and a fourth unit—the intelligence unit—set off to the side. This configuration indicates three major division directors reporting directly to the chief, plus the intelligence unit also reporting to the chief. Because of its placement on the chart, it would appear that the intelligence unit would be handled by a supervisor or a police officer of lesser rank than the other three unit commanders.

In the second chart of Figure 7-3, the lines make more readily apparent who is responsible to whom. Each of the five major divisions is headed by a commanding officer or director, each of the five possibly of equal rank, and their subunits and their hierarchy and accountability clearly delineated.

Step three in the organizational plan is to staff the organization. Except when the organization is brand new and all the employees are just beginning to work at the same time as the chief, the chief will have to make his assignment choices based on personnel available, along with their existing strengths and areas of expertise. The ranks of officers—captains, lieutenants, sergeants, detectives, officers—will also limit the alternatives the chief may have to choose from.

Step four is to implement and coordinate the plan. The police chief prepares a plan that will assure the organization's accomplishments of the objectives it has set up for itself, assuring the greatest amount of efficiency and effectiveness, yet still allowing for necessary flexibility to compensate for shifts in priorities and other needs based on changing circumstances in weather, climate, people, and all the other variables that affect the police problems. The categories of responsibility are identified and grouped according to organizational needs. For example, a major consideration would be in dividing those functions that require officers working in uniform, such as patrol and traffic from those that require nonuniform, or "plain-clothes" officers, such as detective and juvenile.

This is obviously an oversimplification of what sometimes poses a complex problem. For the purpose of this expository text, however, there is no need to go into detail. Of primary concern is the size and population of the jurisdiction to be served and the available number of personnel that may be employed. From that point, the priorities in objectives are established,

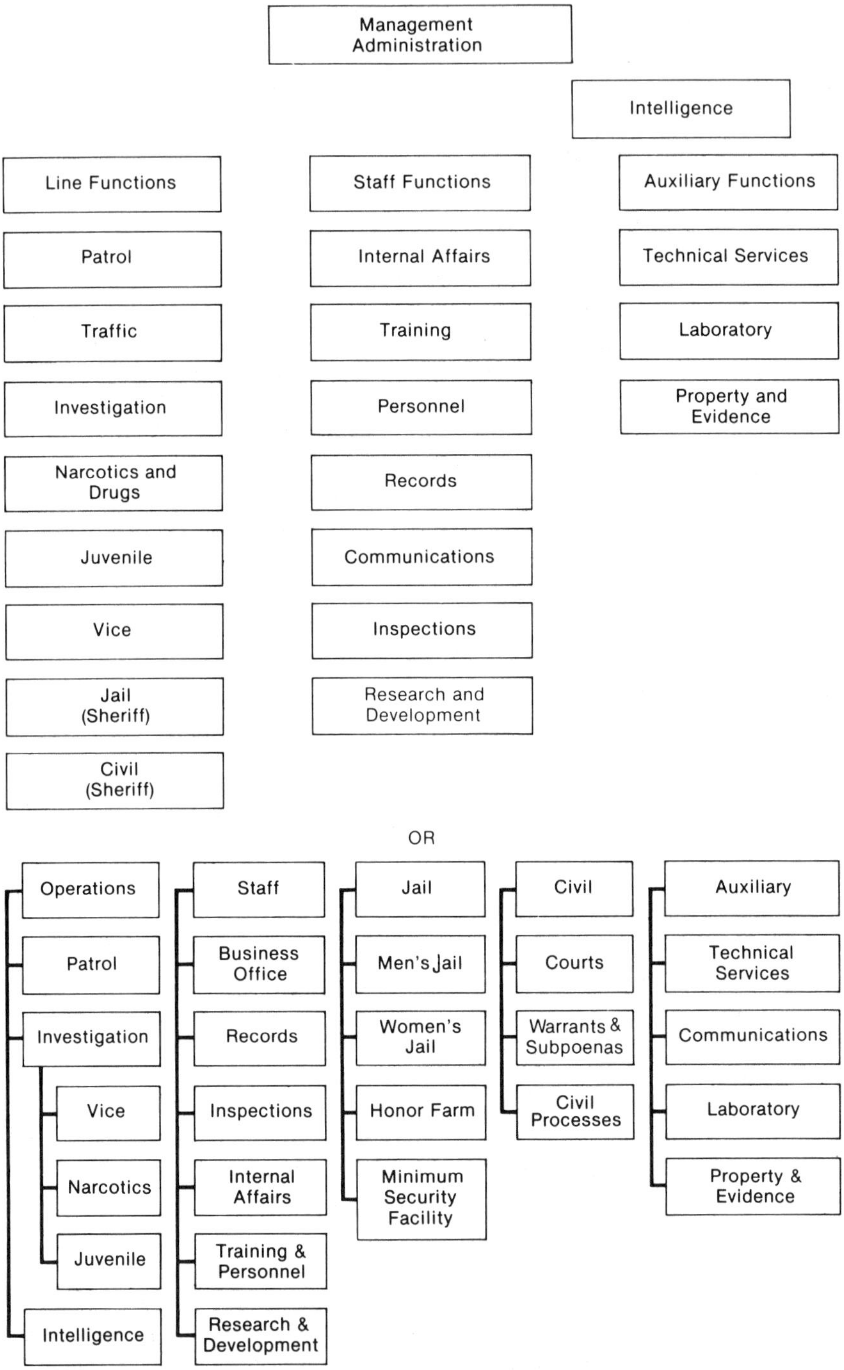
Management Administration
Intelligence
Line Functions
Patrol
Traffic
Investigation
Narcotics and Drugs
Juvenile
Vice
Jail (Sheriff)
Civil (Sheriff)
Staff Functions
Internal Affairs
Training
Personnel
Records
Communications
Inspections
Research and Development
Auxiliary Functions
Technical Services
Laboratory
Property and Evidence
OR
Operations
Patrol
Investigation
Vice
Narcotics
Juvenile
Intelligence
Staff
Business Office
Records
Inspections
Internal Affairs
Training & Personnel
Research & Development
Jail
Men's Jail
Women's Jail
Honor Farm
Minimum Security Facility
Civil
Courts
Warrants & Subpoenas
Civil Processes
Auxiliary
Technical Services
Communications
Laboratory
Property & Evidence

Figure 7-3

units and their responsibilities grouped so that they can be adequately supervised, a hierarchy established, people assigned, leaders identified and designated, relationships prescribed in a chart or table of organization, and the organization put into service.

Military ranks are frequently used for supervisory and command-level positions, such as corporal, sergeant, lieutenant, captain, major, and colonel. The top-ranking officer is either the Chief or Sheriff, but may be designated as Administrator, Superintendent, or Director, with his or her assistants designated as assistant- or vice- whatever the chief executive is called. Inspectors and commanders may be somewhere in the higher-level positions, although in some departments the title "inspector" is used instead of "detective." The operating-level personnel will be designated the same as other civilian positions for clerical and other office help, plus such designations as policeman or police officer, detective, investigator, agent, or officer.

After the organization has been separated into divisions, or groupings, with supervisors designated, the superstructure is drawn to show responsibility-accountability relationships within the hierarchy of the organization. Utilizing the basic principles of organization already discussed and many others that will not be covered in this text, the administrator goes to work, keeping in mind the necessity to clearly define responsibility and authority relationships. He must recognize the fact that every supervisor or administrator can supervise only so many people (exactly how many depends on a number of variables, such as how well trained they are, what their functions are, and other considerations) and acknowledge one inviolable principle that every individual should have only one direct-line supervisor. A police or sheriff's department might have a table of organization like that in Figure 7-4. Any titles and unit designations will fit.

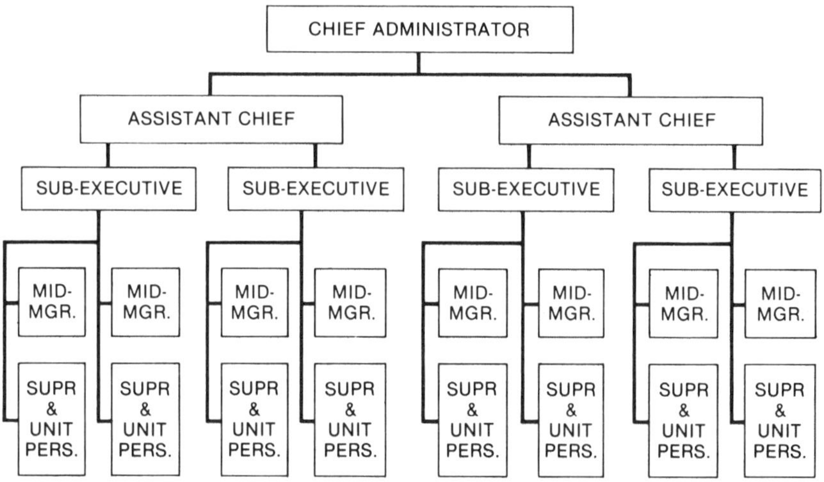

Figure 7-4

FUNCTIONAL RESPONSIBILITIES

Some of the basic functional units within the organization of the local law enforcement agency include those that follow:

Uniformed Patrol

In the very small department, the uniformed patrol is the only unit in the department, including the chief or the sheriff. In any size department, the patrol unit is the primary operating unit of the city or municipal police department and usually comprises one-third to one-half of the entire work force. The sheriff's department is distinctively different at this point. Because the sheriff is also the keeper of the county jail and bailiff for the superior court, the patrol unit (and other units as well) is one of the *three* major units in the department. The size of the patrol unit will be in direct relationship to the area and population of the county not otherwise served by all the municipal police departments in the same county.

In highly urbanized areas the sheriff could have only a very small patrol force in relationship to much larger jail and bailiff (sometimes referred to as the civil division) operations. In the rural county with few incorporated cities, the sheriff's patrol unit could be from two to ten times as large as all other units in the department.

In the municipal police department, the patrol unit is the operational division that performs all of the basic police services as the spinal column serves as the support for the human body. All other services are supplemental to patrol. Proof of that fact is illustrated when one takes a look at the many very small police departments throughout the country. The patrol unit may be the only one that is actually in existence, with officers devoting part of their time to other functions, such as traffic, juvenile, detective, communications, or vice. As a matter of fact, although the appearance of an officer in a working assignment out of uniform usually leads one to believe that he is something other than a patrol officer, it is not unusual for officers of the patrol unit to divest themselves of their readily identifiable uniforms from time to time to perform some type of work that calls for a less conspicuous appearance. Though still a patrol officer, that individual will appear to be working as a detective.

The patrol unit is primarily responsible for maintenance of the peace and protection of the lives and property in the jurisdiction. The police department's objectives are also those of the patrol unit, but this function has particular responsibility for (1) patrol and observation, determining what is "normal" and dealing with the "abnormal" as it arises, (2) miscellaneous benevolent services, such as giving aid and assisting in rescues, (3) responding to miscellaneous requests for police assistance, (4) investigating complaints of criminal and antisocial behavior, (5) investigations of persons and situations that call for law enforcement and preventive action, (6) preliminary investigation of crimes and accidents, (7) collection and preservation of evidence and returning lost and stolen property to its owners, (8) apprehension of traffic and criminal law violators, (9) presenting evidence and testimony in court, and (10) preparation of reports.

The patrol unit provides continuous, round-the-clock, round-the-calendar service in uniform and in distinctively marked cars and other vehicles. They are in constant contact with each other and the patrol units of other departments in neighboring jurisdictions as well as throughout the country. Whenever anything calling for police action occurs within their jurisdiction, and when they discover the need, or their services are requested, the patrol unit is usually the first to respond. Because of their constant presence on duty and on the streets, they are often the city government's direct contact with the people. For many, the only visible representatives of the city or county government are the police, to whom people express their displeasures and direct their requests for action regarding many of the government's problems. In that sense, the police are—through their patrol units—the public relations representatives for the governments which employ them.

Vehicular and Pedestrian Traffic Control

The municipal police, and the sheriff in counties where traffic is included in his responsibilities, are responsible for the flow of pedestrian and vehicular traffic free of congestion and collisons. (In cities where the sheriff's department acts as a municipal police department by contract with the city government, the sheriff performs the same as the municipal police.) Even though officers assigned to other units throughout the department may also be responsible for traffic control and/or collisions investigation, it is usually the commanding officer of the traffic unit who has the responsibility for guiding the department's overall traffic activity in accordance with department and the traffic court's philosophies and policies.

The traffic specialists assigned to the traffic unit are principally concerned with the following responsibilities: (1) directing the flow of vehicular and pedestrian traffic; (2) preventing injuries and property damage through traffic engineering, education, and enforcement; (3) investigating traffic collisions and finding means to identifying and reducing the causes of collisions; (4) apprehending and aiding in the prosecution of traffic law violators; (5) establishing and carrying out selective enforcement practices, citing offenders on the basis of collision cause, location, and time of day, and disseminating appropriate information to the public in order to attempt to secure voluntary compliance; (6) regulating parking requirements and removing abandoned and disabled vehicles from the public streets; (7) enforcing regulations concerning special vehicles and drivers, such as ambulances, buses, and taxis; (8) handling traffic safety education; and (9) coordinating the department's traffic responsibilities in cooperation with other agencies in the city, state, and federal governments with related responsibilities.

Depending on the miles of roadway and special characteristics of the streets and roads to be covered, the agency utilizes a variety of vehicles. The motorcycle, although the most expensive in terms of manpower and rider safety, is still the basic traffic enforcement vehicle in most urban jurisdictions. It is maneuverable in all kinds of traffic where other vehicles cannot move in heavy traffic. Other vehicles include the helicopter, automobile, and other vehicles designed for special purposes. The helicopter has been found most useful, as has the fixed-wing airplane in overall traffic coordination, identification of problem areas, pursuits, rescue, and general enforcement.

Criminal Investigation

Depending on the extent to which the patrol unit in the department handles the initial phases of an investigation, if at all, the investigation unit performs the following functions: (1) interviews victims, witnesses, and suspects in crimes and other incidents that fall within the responsibility of the unit; (2) examines crime scenes and collects evidence; (3) searches for, and identifies individuals suspected of criminal conduct; (4) develops informants and sources of information; (5) recovers stolen and embezzled property; (6) develops and disseminates information to patrol officers and the public in techniques of crime prevention; (7) secures complaints and warrants of arrest and makes arrests; (8) assists the prosecuting attorney in courtroom presentation of assigned criminal cases; (9) and prepares investigative and statistical reports.

Investigators are assigned to specialize in specific types of cases, such as burglary, robbery, thefts, check offenses, or general categories of crimes against persons and crimes against property. In some departments, they are assigned to handle all follow-up investigations within an assigned geographic area. Some officers look upon an assignment to the investigation unit as a temporary training assignment, while others seek permanent assignments and develop a high degree of specialization in their assigned areas.

Many criminal violators have a tendency to repeat their crimes more than once, often living a lifetime of alternatively committing their crimes, getting caught and spending time in jails and prisons, then back through the cycle all over again. Investigators learn to identify the criminals through their behavior patterns, such as a particular method used to gain entry into a house, unique types of tools, the words used when a victim is confronted, or similarities in time of day when or type of establishment where victimization occurs. The investigator learns to identify suspects by their habits or behavior patterns, known as their modus operandi.

Some investigations involve the use of several of the sciences, such as chemistry, fabric analysis, comparisons of tools and their marks through the use of microscopes, and miscellaneous instruments in exploratory investigative research. Scientists who have training and education in biological or chemical science or some other scientific discipline are known as criminalists. Investigators work with these specialists, constantly trying new techniques in identifying suspects, and some investigators develop their own unique talents in criminalistic techniques.

Juvenile Unit

The ages of the clients determine this specialized unit, victims and suspects being juveniles and often affected by laws quite different than the criminal codes. Court philosophies may differ from the adult criminal courts and the juvenile courts, which, in many states, are actually divisions of civil courts, and the laws provide for different methods of processing, holding, adjudicating, and punishing and/or rehabilitating juveniles. The juvenile unit of the police department is responsible for the administration of the department and for prescribing the policies and philosophies of all of the officers with respect to juvenile matters in harmony with the policies of the juvenile court and other juvenile officials in other agencies.

The juvenile unit may be separate from the investigation unit or may be a part of it, with specialists assigned to cases involving juveniles as suspects or victims. Assigned officers may be selected because of particular talents or interests in dealing with young people and often undergo specialized training. Techniques of criminal investigation may be similar, but practices, such as questioning children, may call for special talents, depending on the department's attitude toward that type of specialization.

Officers assigned to the juvenile unit are often additionally assigned to participate in youth activities in the community, crime prevention programs in cooperation with social service agencies, and in various delinquency prevention programs. Their duties may include visiting places of recreation and congregation of juveniles and attempting to identify predelinquent behavior with the purpose of diverting them into socially and legally acceptable behavior patterns.

Vice Detail

The vice crimes include many law violations that are considered by some advocates for change as "crimes without victims," such as gambling, prostitution, some sex offenses, liquor law violations, and other types of behavior. The opposing viewpoint is that so-called crimes without victims do have victims in the children and families of the individuals involved in activities, even though they themselves do not believe that what they are doing is improper. As far as the police department is concerned, if the laws are on the books and the assignments are made to officers to enforce those laws, or if the violations are discovered by the officers, then it is not left to the discretion of the officers to completely ignore the violations. Ultimate actions by the courts and intermediate decisions by prosecutors and administrators toward specific types of violations will, of course, affect the discretionary decisions made by the operational officers.

Development and utilization of informants, and "cops-and-robbers" games of playing hide-and-seek with vice-law violators are sometimes the order of the day because so many of the participants live an almost Saroyan-like existence, only in real life situations in which such tremendous amounts of money are involved that lives are in jeopardy. Punishment for violation of a confidence among vice operators could very well be death. Also because of the tremendous profits involved, many vice activities are either directly or indirectly enmeshed with organized crime and criminal syndicates. Working a case up to a point where an officer has sufficient evidence to go for a complaint and hope for a conviction may involve endless hours or leads that go nowhere and having to work through informers and undercover operators who may or may not be trusted, and then only under very closely defined circumstances.

Narcotics and Dangerous Drugs

This unit may be a part of the vice unit, but during the past two decades has grown so highly specialized that consolidation occurs only in the smaller departments. Explaining the types of investigations and the methods used would be in virtually the same language as the preceding paragraphs on the vice detail. The difference in assignments is in the clientele and the nature of the violations. Intrigue and drama may be more imagined than real, but the glamour attached to the assignment may lead to development of a sort of mystique surrounding the activities of this unit. The work is quite monotonous, actually, because there is so much waiting between the exciting times. Because of the complexity of the methods used to build a case, the laws of search, seizure, entrapment, evidence, and arrest, and the confusion that often occurs during the height of an arrest, the challenge is great, and officers who work this detail develop great skills in those areas.

Intelligence

This unit may work directly for the chief administrator, because many of the investigations involve allegations of criminal and police collusion or police misconduct. Large-scale vice operations cannot go on without some sort of protection or nonaction on the part of some official and a reasonably large segment of the community. Because of that fact, intelligence investigations often reveal connections between the underworld and politicians and/or public officials. Most of the work performed by the intelligence unit is collecting and filing information and keeping the chief administrator informed on all facets of an investigation at all times. The principal objective of this unit is to keep criminal organizations from operating in the jurisdiction and to maintain the integrity of the department.

Internal Affairs Unit

The internal affairs unit may be the same as the intelligence unit, or they may be separate. If they are, then the responsibility for department integrity is delegated to the internal affairs unit.

Auxiliary, Administrative, and Support Units

Although they are of lesser importance to the overall effectiveness of the police department, the units that would fall within this category will not be covered in this chapter. They include those functions that would not be considered as basic operating units, such as the business office, records, property and evidence, laboratory, communications, budget control, personnel, training, community relations, research, and many others.

Jail Unit

The sheriff is responsible for maintenance of the county jail and its occupants. In highly urbanized areas where there is very little unincorporated land in the county, the sheriff may have most or all of his deputies assigned to this division and the courts. Supervision problems present themselves in both areas of supervisor-subordinate relationships and jailor-inmate settings.

Considering the reality that everyone is innocent until proven guilty in court, a large share of the jail occupants are innocent people and unruly innocent people pose serious problems. Sentenced prisoners must be segregated according to sex, age, felons and misdemeanants, sexually promiscuous persons, experienced from the uninitiated, and those who misbehave from those who conduct themselves according to the rules of the jail. Maintenance of the jail also involves transporting prisoners to and from jail, the hospital, dentist, state and federal prisons, other jails, police, and sheriffs' headquarters, as well as housing, feeding, and providing recreational activities.

The jail unit may manage other facilities in addition to the main jail, such as jail wards in hospitals, honor farms, and other minimum-security facilities and housing units.

Civil Unit

In addition to serving as bailiff in the court, the sheriff must provide deputies to protect the judge and the courthouse, and to take action outside the courtroom throughout the county, serving subpoenas, writs, and a vast assortment of other papers. The supervisor of this unit must serve as liaison between his own sheriff and the many judges in the superior court who occupy the county courts.

SUMMARY

In this chapter, we have covered the basic operating units of the typical police department or sheriff's department and their objectives. Although there are basic principles of organization, and broad, general policies are prescribed by law and by other bodies of individuals, the chief and sheriff are ultimately responsible for their stated goals and objectives. For that reason, the actual organizational plan and making it work are the chief executive's responsibility.

EXERCISES AND STUDY QUESTIONS

1. What is the basic operating unit of the police department?

2. What two basic units does a sheriff's department have that a municipal police department will not have?

3. Where there is a state highway patrol, what unit will the municipal police department have that a sheriff's department will not have?

4. List and discuss the ten basic goals of a police department that appear in this chapter, plus any that the author overlooked.

5. List at least five objectives of a police department that are listed in this chapter.

6. List at least five additional objectives of a police department that do not appear in this chapter.

7. For what reason do you believe police departments use military ranks and titles?

8. What are three primary functions of patrol?

9. List three of the primary functions of traffic.

10. List and discuss the relationship between the patrol unit and investigation.

11. What is *modus operandi*?

12. Why is it necessary that the department have a juvenile unit?

13. Why is working a vice detail so difficult?

14. Why would a department separate its vice and narcotics units?

15. If there is a separate intelligence unit and a separate internal affairs unit, which one would be concerned with department integrity?

RECOMMENDED SEMESTER/TERM PROJECTS

1. Visit a local police or sheriff's department and get a copy of their table of organization. Interview as many people as necessary so that you might complete the project. Then, prepare a paper in form similar to this chapter, explaining all of the functioning units of that department and their relationships.

2. Make a list of all of the administrative, line, and staff functions within a police agency and prepare a set of objectives for each unit.

SUGGESTED FOR ADDITIONAL STUDY

ADAMS, THOMAS F., GERALD BUCK, and DON HALLSTROM, *Criminal Justice Organization and Management.* Pacific Palisades: Goodyear Publishing Co., 1974.

LYNCH, RONALD G., *The Police Manager.* Boston: Holbrook Press, 1975.

SHANAHAN, DONALD T., *Patrol Administration: Management By Objectives.* Boston: Holbrook Press, 1975.

WESTON, PAUL B., *The Police Traffic Control Function* (3rd ed.). Springfield, Ill.: Charles C. Thomas, Publisher, 1975.

WHISENAND, PAUL M., and R. FRED FERGUSON, *The Managing of Police Organizations.* Englewood Cliffs, N.J.: Prentice-Hall, Inc., 1973.

WILSON, O. W., and ROY CLINTON MCLAREN, *Police Administration* (4th ed.). New York: McGraw-Hill Company, 1977.

8

The Courts

INTRODUCTION

Essentially a descendant of the English court system as are so many other institutions of the American Criminal Justice System, the basic structure and functions of the courts in this country have changed very little since Colonial days. There are actually fifty-one court systems in the country: the federal courts and the court systems of each of the fifty states. Authorized by their respective constitutions, the courts comprise the third branch of government designed to provide a balance of power in our government structure.

In this chapter we shall look at the courts systems; their relationships to the other components of the criminal justice system; and court-related agencies, such as the grand jury, the coroner, and quasi-judicial boards. We shall also trail through the courts both a felony and a misdemeanor case, beginning with the arrest by the police and following through the trial to the point where the sentence is prescribed by the judge.

COURTS—THE "PROCESS" PHASE OF CRIMINAL JUSTICE

The courts component of the criminal justice system is the "process" part of what we present in this text as a three-part system. The police comprise the "input" part, courts are the processing component, and "output" includes the corrections subunits of probation, parole, and the institutions.

Representatives of the police, or "input" phase, make the initial decision of whether to introduce individuals to the system through arrests and summonses. Based upon facts discovered during their investigations, they make the decision to proceed with criminal charges. The next step is for the police to present the case to the prosecuting attorney, the first step in the "process" phase. It is here, in the office of the people's prosecutor (usually called the district attorney or state's attorney), that the hard decisions are made of whether to proceed with the charges originally presented by the police, to file an alternative charge, or not to file at all. Once the decision is made to proceed, the matter then goes to the court.

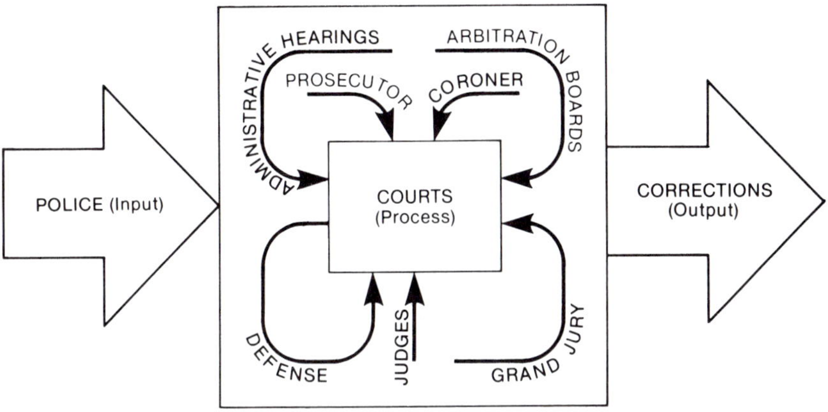

Figure 8-1

THE COURTS AND THEIR RELATIONSHIP TO THE POLICE AND CORRECTIONS

The American system of jurisprudence is based upon codified laws. There are criminal codes covering literally thousands of acts (or nonacts) of human behavior that legislators have defined as criminal law violations. New laws are added with fervent zeal to maintain a peaceful ordered liberty, and existing laws are reviewed and changed from time to time. Sometimes old and unused laws are retired, or "decriminalized." The legislature provides the tools for the police to work with and the legal restrictions on how the correctional process should work. But the key to the system's success or failure lies in how the courts interpret the laws, process the accused, and provide for correction of the convicted offenders.

Three major premises comprise the doctrine of *judical review,* which some writers refer to as "judicial supremacy." Those premises are that (1) the courts may make the final determination as to what is law and what is not; (2) the courts may require—through legal means at their disposal—adherence to lawful conduct by the administrative branch of government; and (3) the courts may invalidate a legislative action on the basis of unconstitutionality. This doctrine refers to the Supreme Court, but the general principle is carried down to the lowest court at state level. A state legislature may enact a law that a city council heartily endorses and that reflects the attitude of the community. As a result of such endorsement, the city administrator may convey the message to the police chief, who orders his officers to enforce the law "to the letter." When a defendant appears in court, a "not-guilty" decision or a suspended sentence may reflect an attitude on the part of the court that the law is either unfair or unjust. The defendant might be found guilty and sentenced, then appeal to a higher court, and on up through the various higher courts to the state or even the U.S. Supreme Court. The Supreme Court might then decide that the law is unconstitutional and, therefore, invalid. This does not mean that the law was *illegal* because it was promulgated by legal process and it is *legal.* All of the subsequent police and court action was likewise legal, but once the decision is rendered by the Supreme Court, the law is no longer enforceable.

Judicial review takes on forms other than after-the-fact review. For example, when a police officer develops leads that cause him to believe a warrant for a search or an arrest should be issued, he takes the matter before a judge, who is sitting as a magistrate rather than in a judging role at the time, for review of the facts and examination of witnesses who testify and sign an affidavit to the facts they present as justification for the search and/or arrest. The magistrate issues the warrant only if he or she is convinced that there exists substantial cause for the search or arrest, or both.

Judicial discretion is practiced by a lower court judge when hearing testimony and examining evidence to determine that a crime was, in fact, committed, and if the accused should be held to answer to the charges—or *bound over*—in the higher court where the trial is to be held. During the trial, the judge has the authority to exclude evidence on the basis of unconstitutional behavior of the police in collecting and presenting such evidence. The judge may even declare a mistrial and dismiss the charges on Constitutional grounds.

The corrections component of the system is directly related to the authority of the court. Probation officers in many jurisdictions serve under direction and at the pleasure of the local courts. Conditions of probation may be standardized, but they are articulated by the judge who grants probation in lieu of all or part of the incarceration in jail or prison. Although sentencing laws may restrict the latitude within which a judge may function, the judge decides whether to sentence an individual to concurrent or consecutive terms in prison. Three concurrent terms of five years each would mean that the convicted person would serve only five years, less time off for good behavior, while three consecutive terms of five years each would mean that the individual would spend fifteen years less "good-time" off. A substantial difference, obviously.

THE FEDERAL COURT SYSTEM

Federal Courts

In the federal system of justice administration, there is a complete system of courts to serve the various needs created by the Constitution and various acts of the legislative and the executive branches of government. For the military service and adjudication of the Uniform Code of Military

Justice, there is the system of Courts Martial, and the Military Court of Appeals. There are various special purpose courts in addition to the Military Courts, including the Court of Systems and Patent Appeals, the Court of Claims, and Customs Court. At the trial level, ninety-three district courts are located throughout the country. Appeals from the district courts are remanded to the appellate courts for the resolution of issues of procedure and constitutionality.

The Supreme Court

State sovereignty is great according to the U.S. system of government as it was intended by its founders, and with respect to that sovereignty the final arbiter in a case or controversy in any state is that state's supreme court. Only under certain circumstances shall the case be studied and decided by the U.S. Supreme Court, and the primary qualifications must be that there is a diversity of citizenship of two or more states, or there must be a federal question involved.

Although the Supreme Court is involved in a few administrative and supervisory functions as head of the federal judicial system, the principal role of the court is to decide cases. "Original" cases may be taken directly to the Supreme Court, and this is the type of case that usually involves issues to test or challenge the constitutionality of a rule or law. The second type of case decided by the Supreme Court is the appeal from the lower federal or state courts. These cases involve the same type as those that are listed above, as well as suits to enforce laws or treaties of the United States, cases involving diversity of citizenship, and suits to enforce the U.S. Constitution.

The Supreme Court of the United States consists of a chief justice and eight associate justices. They are appointed by the President with the advice and consent of the Senate, and they hold office for life during their good behavior. There can be no question as to the tremendous influence that the Supreme Court has upon not only the judicial system and law enforcement but upon the entire populace of the nation. Not only must the members of the court be great jurists, but they must be master statesmen as well. The Constitution is the supreme law of the land, and the Supreme Court serves to interpret and perpetuate its principles.

THE STATE COURT SYSTEM

Justice Courts

The justice court, which is still very much in evidence, is a vestige of colonial days, and usually serves the smaller and less populous judicial districts. A rural and small-town or village court, the justice court has limited jurisdiction in criminal matters. It is restricted to misdemeanors of lesser

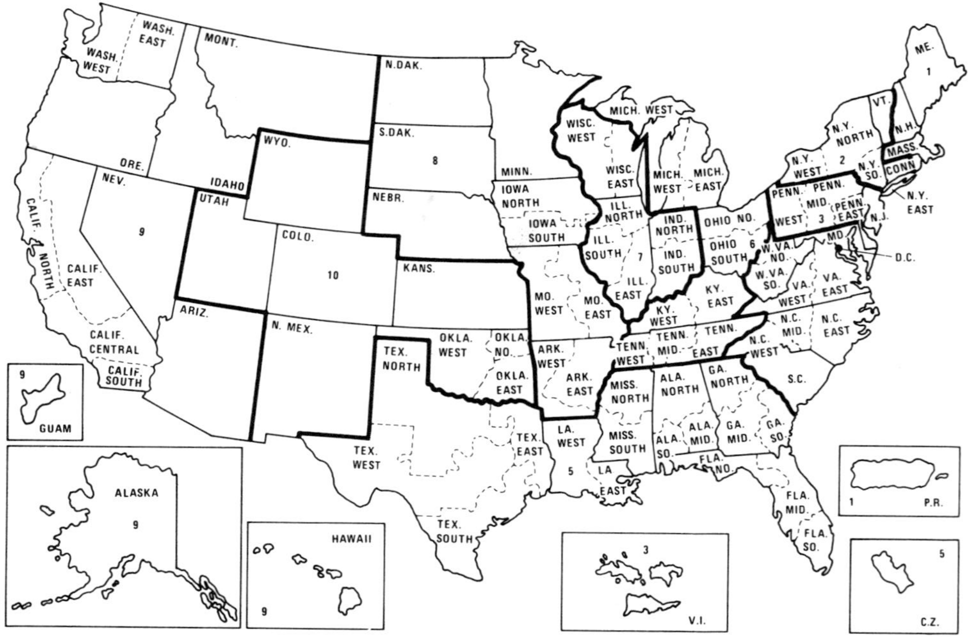

Figure 8-2 The United States Courts of Appeals and the United States District Courts. The numerals indicate the various courts of appeals and the heavy lines represent the jurisdictional boundaries of each circuit. The broken lines represent jurisdictional boundaries of district courts in states having more than one district.

Source. The United States Courts, Their Jurisdiction and Work, *Committee on the Judiciary of the House of Representatives, Washington, U.S. Government Printing Office, 1975, p. 6.*

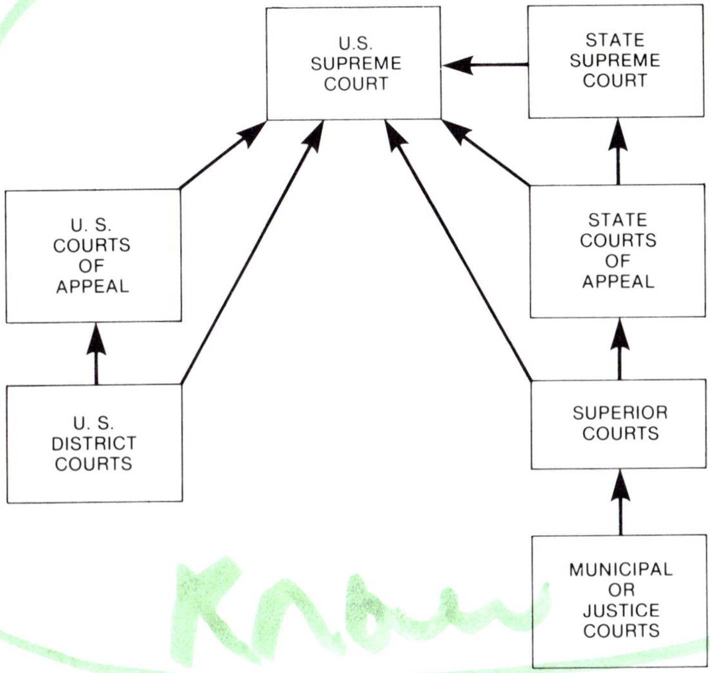

significance and handles only minor civil cases. The functions of the small claims court, a do-it-yourself court, which is concerned only with a maximum of $500 or $1000 and where attorneys are excluded, may be assigned to the justice court as it is to the larger municipal court. The justice of the peace in this court may not have any legal experience, as is the case in some states, and may perform his/her services while operating some other business at the same time. The bailiff for the justice court is the constable, who keeps peace in the courtroom, serves subpoenas and writs, and generally carries out the directions of the court. The justice court, other courts that deal with misdemeanors and other minor offenses, and the less significant civil cases, regardless of what name they go by, and the municipal court are often referred to as "inferior courts," as opposed to the "superior" superior court. The designation is based upon the fact that they are characterized by certain features that are less in stature than the superior court, such as (1) the judge may not be required to be an attorney, as is the case with some justices of the peace; (2) the judge's pay scale is lower; (3) verbatim transcripts of trials are not prepared; (4) appeals usually go to a higher court within the county, such as superior court, instead of an appellate court; and (5) the facilities are not usually as well appointed. Another feature, of course, is that these courts handle only "inferior" types of cases.

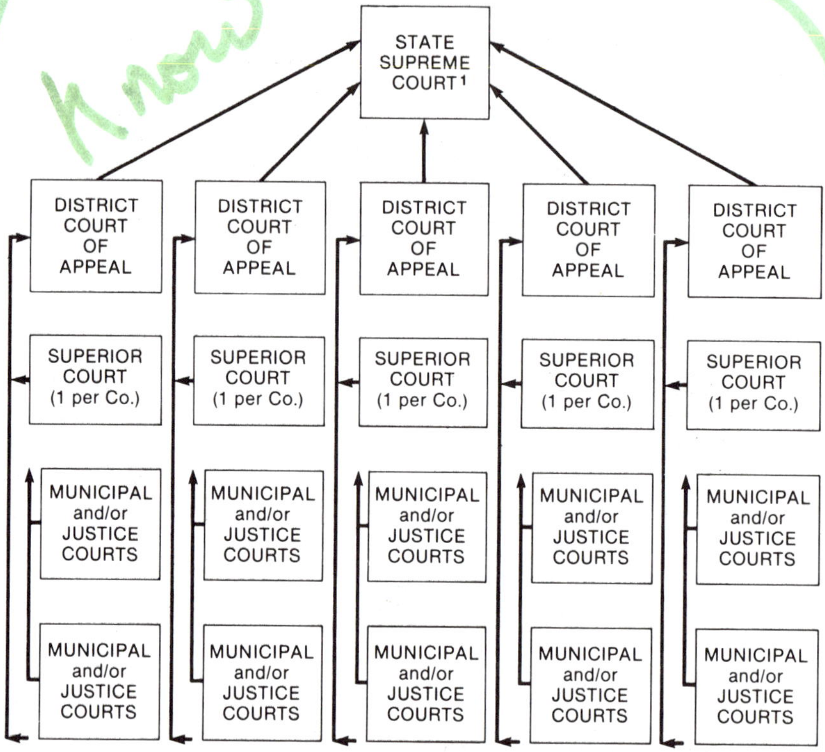

Figure 8-4 State Court System. Supreme court consists of a chief justice and a number of associate justices (six associates in California). Jurisdiction is statewide. District courts of appeal have geographic jurisdictions, each covering a proportionate share of the state, handling appeals from the several superior courts. Municipal and/or justice courts, also referred to as inferior courts, number from one to several dozens in each county, the county being subdivided into municipal court districts. Appeals from the lower courts, which usually do not keep verbatim transcripts of trials, are heard by superior court. Except in specified cases, and within prescribed limitations, the state supreme court is usually the court of last resort within each state.

Municipal Courts

This court may be called the mayor's court, the police court, or by some other name that designates it as one of the trial courts where the greatest volume of cases are tried in civil and criminal matters. The municipal court may serve one city or several. It usually consists of a court district that

[1]In New York, the supreme court would appear on this chart in place of superior court, and the court of appeal is the highest court in that state. Other states vary depending on their respective laws and constitutions.

is one of several within a county and that serves a population greater than that of the justice court. In states that have no justice courts, the municipal court has replaced it. Jurisdiction involves civil cases in which the claimant seeks damages amounting to $5,000 or some similar amount determined by law as the maximum, with higher amounts referred to the superior court. Misdemeanors committed within the municipal court's jurisdiction are tried in this court, and preliminary hearings for felonies may be held in the municipal court to determine if there is sufficient proof that a crime has been committed and that there is reason to believe that the accused should be held to answer to the charges in superior court.

The municipal court judge sits as a magistrate with a related, but separate, role than performed as a judge. In his role as magistrate, the judge is acting upon information and belief at the time of issuance of a warrant. He/she later examines the evidence in a judicial role and admits its introduction if it has been collected in accordance with the law and Constitution. The municipal court judge may hear pleas for dismissal on the grounds that the evidence that is about to be introduced was collected in violation of some provision of the Constitution, or through some error in procedure. The trial or hearing is held at that point; then the judge examines the evidence on a *motion to suppress evidence* and determines whether to allow the evidence or testimony to be used in the trial. Evidence that is excluded may not be considered either by the judge or the jury when determining guilt of the accused. The judge has the authority to dismiss the charges and order the release of the accused, or may order the jury to find the accused not guilty because of the absence of sufficient legal basis to sustain the charge, or may actually reduce the charge of a felony to a misdemeanor before the trial. The judge may do this on his or her own volition or upon the motion of counsel. The prosecuting attorney may have reconsidered and determined that the case should be pursued as a misdemeanor, or the proposal may be the result of plea bargaining.

The preliminary hearing that is held by the municipal court for the purpose of hearing testimony and examining evidence to make a determination as to whether the accused should be *bound over* to answer the felony charges in superior court leads to the judge's instructions to the prosecuting attorney to file an *information* in that court that initiates the felony trial. In some cases, an alternative method is used for bringing the case to the higher court. That alternative is known as the *indictment,* which emanates from the grand jury. In such a case, the prosecuting attorney may choose to avoid the open court preliminary hearing in favor of the secrecy of the grand jury proceedings, where the hearings held in secret sessions may lead to secret indictments of perhaps a number of persons accused of related crimes.

In misdemeanor cases, the municipal court judge may sentence the accused to jail and/or probation and/or a fine. Although the term of probation is not considered as punishment, violation of that probation may well lead to a period of incarceration for the violation. In a felony case, the judge may receive a guilty plea but must *certify* the plea to the superior court along with the case, where the superior court judge will pronounce the sentence.

The bailiff for the municipal court is the marshal, whose duties and responsibilities to the court are similar to those of the constable to the justice court.

Superior Court

There is usually only one superior court per county, although there may be literally hundreds of divisions of that court as there are divisions of the municipal court. Jurisdiction of the superior court includes (1) juvenile court, a separate civil division of the court that directs the county's juvenile justice network, including guidance and direction of the juvenile probation efforts; (2) all felony trials and related hearings; (3) certain "high misdemeanors" in some states; (4) civil suits involving reparation for an amount larger than that allowed in the municipal court; (5) court of equity, in which an order to "right a wrong or injustice" is sought rather than money damages; (6) probate court, which is involved in the states and related matters of the deceased; (7) appeals from the lower courts on matters of judicial error or constitutional issues; (8) courts of conciliation or divorce; (9) writs of habeas corpus and other types of legal actions involving property and debts; (10) reciprocal enforcement of family support laws in cooperation with other states; and (11) sanity and alcoholic commitment hearings.

Superior court judges recommend candidates for the grand jury each year, select and supervise the county probation officer, sit as an appellate court in issues appealed from justice or municipal courts, and perform a variety of other court-related services including the performance of marriages, issuance of warrants, and issuance of writs and similar court orders.

The sheriff and his/her deputies serve as bailiffs to the superior court. Besides serving writs and subpoenas, the sheriff may provide protection for the judges of the courts and building security, and perform any other services required by the court.

The District Courts of Appeal

The appellate courts meet at various locations in the state. In some jurisdictions the appellate court operates on a circuit court basis and convenes for a few months in each of two or three different locations. Each appellate division serves a specified portion of the state and its various trial courts. The division is comprised of three judges who sit and decide on issues as a group, but more often they review cases on an individual basis, meet frequently and discuss their cases, and then either concur with the judge who is writing the decision, or they dissent. The majority view is the binding one, as it is with the supreme court, which consists of several justices.

Dean Charles W. Joiner, of the Wayne State University Law School, described the function of the appellate courts in a presentation at Williamsburg:

> 1. In the individual case, an appellate court corrects the mistakes made at the lower level so as to prevent miscarriages of justice between the litigants. This action also tends to provide an effective way of encouraging modesty among the trial judges which is important to creating confidence in the system.
> 2. In the larger sense, the appellate court, by its opinions, tends to teach other judges, lawyers, and all citizens something about the law, what premises are acceptable, what interpretations are proper. In a sense, the litigation of some individuals has a larger public purpose, particularly at the appellate level. Private litigation provides the vehicle for development and direction of growth in the law, for unifying different interpretations, etc.[2]

The appellate court in some states is a part of the supreme court, which is the court of last resort. In other states, there is a separation of responsibility with the intermediate courts and the supreme court having authority to review different cases. Depending on the volume of the cases that go up from the trial courts, the state may create whatever system that best suits its needs, which might include assigning commissioners or trial judges on a temporary basis to assist with the work load.[3]

Jurisdiction of the appellate court extends to case review that may be a court-determined, or legally prescribed right to review, and to other cases that the appellate court reviews at its discretion upon petition for such review. The effect of the appeal may be a reversal, which puts the litigants back at their original starting point, or the case may be returned to the trial court to correct earlier errors that had been made during the trial, or a new trial may be ordered.

State Supreme Court

The court of last resort in the state, the supreme court, is the highest appeals court to which most cases may be taken from the trial courts or the intermediate appeals court. Exceptions, of course, involve issues of the U.S. Constitution and other matters that are clearly within the purview of the U.S. Supreme Court. With great respect for the sovereignty of the states,

[2]Charles W. Joiner, "The Function of the Appellate System," from *Addresses and Papers of the National Conference on the Judiciary, March 11–14, 1971 at Williamsburg, Virginia* (Washington, D.C.: Government Printing Office, 1971), pp. 97–102.

[3]Joiner, "The Function of the Appellate System," pp. 99–104.

the rights of the state supreme courts are recognized and enforced. The chief justice and the justices of the supreme court hear cases on appeal or by their direction in matters described briefly in Chapter One of this text: equity, probate, capital convictions, writs, applicants to the state bar, and numerous other issues involving interpretations of laws and the constitution of the state.

The cases appealed to the supreme court are decided upon and disposed of in the same manner as are those that are handled by the appellate courts. In states where there is no intermediate court of appeal, the supreme court handles all appeals from the lower trial courts.

In a state having a unified court system, that is, one that has been reorganized throughout the state into a true state system of courts under coordinated leadership, the chief justice must have the proper administrative structure and tools, according to Chief Justice Edward E. Pringle of Colorado. These tools include:

1. Reorganized and unified court structure, with elimination of overlapping jurisdiction and integration of minor courts.
2. Constitutional authority and responsibility vested in him for administration of the judicial system (including assignment of judges) and administration of rules (both procedural and administrative), and, incidentally, that authority must include the power to designate chief or presiding judges in the various judicial districts or circuits and the power to delegate to these judges degrees of authority to administer those districts or circuits.
3. Some form of judicial selection and tenure other than partisan elections and based on merit, and including a removal commission.
4. Constitutional provision for a state judicial administrator or administrative director responsible to and appointed by the chief justice or supreme court, with the administrator having a staff of professional assistants in several disciplines, in addition to adequate clerical support.
5. State funding administered by the judicial branch, under the authority of the chief justice, including budget preparation and submission thereof directly to the legislature.
6. Separate judicial personnel system administered by the judicial branch covering all court personnel—including probation, if possible, and providing for salaries, appointment, removal, etc.[4]

The Grand Jury

The grand jury is a body of citizens chosen for a specified period of time (usually one year) to audit the various offices of government and to conduct investigations of public offenses committed or subject to trial in its

[4]Edward E. Pringle, "The Role of the State Chief Justice," from *Addresses and Papers of the Natonal Conference on the Judiciary, March 11–14, 1971 at Williamsburg, Virginia* (Washington, D.C.: Government Printing Office, 1971), pp. 82–83.

county of jurisdiction. The grand jury's origin is in England, when it was instituted in 1215 with the Magna Carta. The original principal purpose of the grand jury was to protect the people against the tyranny of their own government. This has been extended considerably to include the examination of evidence and witnesses to determine whether a person should be held to answer for a felony, which is an alternative to the municipal court preliminary hearing in some states, but which is routine in all felony cases in other states. Other functions of the grand jury include visiting and inspecting all branches of government, such as county hospitals and jails, coroner's offices, the courts, and various other government operations to perform in an audit capacity. The jury recommends corrective action in such cases that require structural or procedural changes in government operations: In criminal matters, the jury issues a true bill, which is an order to the prosecutor to file an indictment in the superior court charging the accused with a specific crime. A federal grand jury operates similarly with the federal courts.

Although utilization of the grand jury for all felony prosecutions would be an unwieldy and virtually impossible process in some jurisdictions, there are advantages to the grand jury *indictment* over the *information,* which the prosecutor files at the direction of the lower court after the preliminary hearing. Two advantages of the grand jury proceeding are confidentiality

Figure 8-5 Simulation of the Grand Jury Examining a witness.
Courtesy Grand Jury, County of Sacramento.

and objectivity. The objectivity of the prosecuting attorney is essential to all cases, and there is little problem in most cases. But, consider the situation when a public official, a police officer, or some other person who may be in a close working relationship with the district attorney is suspected of or has been accused of a crime. Regardless of the action taken by the prosecutor, there will be many people who will believe that he acted in deference to that relationship. By taking the matter to the grand jury, the prosecutor is passing on the responsibility to that body, and any decisions will be those of the grand jury.

The secrecy of a grand jury indictment is in sharp contrast to the open court procedure of a preliminary hearing in municipal court. In the first place, members of the grand jury are sworn to secrecy, which means that all matters that come before that body for inquiry or investigation are kept confidential. Attendance at the meetings is by invitation only and attorneys are not allowed to accompany their clients who are subpoenaed before the grand jury. A witness may give information and present evidence to the jurors, who continue with the inquiry until they have satisfied their need for a complete investigation, which may include many people participating in various activities over a long period of time. While the investigation is going on, the grand jury may be making determinations that certain individuals should be held to answer for specific crimes, then at the conclusion of the investigation a series of secret indictments are issued by the jury.

An example of how a grand jury may be utilized for the greatest advantage might be found in a typical "buy program," or an extended narcotics investigation. The typical arrest for possession of narcotics or dangerous drugs leads to a preliminary hearing, at which time the evidence is produced, the witnesses examined, the legality of the evidence challenged by the defense and established by the prosecution. Then the magistrate directs the district attorney to present an information to the superior court for the trial. Using this procedure, there is little likelihood of doing much about the problem of narcotics traffic in the area. The "grand jury method" would be for the officer to make contact with the user of narcotics in some undercover role as another person who "makes the scene." Through a period of contacts and various associations with several users, the undercover agent is able to gain an introduction to a peddler. Still in his undercover role, he makes a purchase. Armed with the evidence, the officer goes to the prosecutor and they present the case before the grand jury, which may also include several separate indictments against persons for possession of drugs with whom the officer has associated during the investigation. The grand jury votes for indictments, but they do so in secrecy. The case continues, however, because the dealers and users are not aware of the investigation.

The undercover officer goes back to the scene of his earlier investigative activity and continues to make purchases and continues to go before the grand jury and present the evidence that leads to more secret indictments. As the officer gets better known in his assumed undercover role, the dealers who are unable to supply his growing demands for narcotics introduce the officer (who is not known to them as anything but a user or dealer who has a great demand and who is—to them—a good customer) to suppliers higher in the system of narcotics dealers. The officer continues to build cases, and the grand jury continues to vote for indictments. Finally, when the officer can no longer continue the investigation with safety or further yield to the investigation, the prosecutor secures warrants for several people who are to be charged with the various narcotics violations, and then arrests are made simultaneously throughout the area. By using this method of investigation, and with the aid of the secret grand jury proceedings, the police are able to more effectively address the narcotics problem because they have been able to identify the higher-level suppliers instead of just arresting the users. This type of investigative strategy, with the cooperation and assistance of the prosecutor, the grand jury, and many assisting agencies, is also effective in organized crime activities and other crimes such as prostitution, gambling, and dealing in stolen property.

Disadvantages of the grand jury have been pointed out by various study groups and commissions. Following is an excerpt from one such report that points up some of the reasons why use of the grand jury for indictments be abandoned:

> Those states still requiring indictments to be returned only by grand juries should eliminate that rule. Grand juries should focus attention upon special situations, such as those involving official corruption.
>
> Many of the 50 states have eliminated the rigid requirements that grand juries must hand down all indictments for serious offenses. There is a growing consensus that this is archaic. Grand juries place heavy burdens on the prosecution and create long delays in resolution of criminal charges. The composition of grand jury panels is also subject to challenge. States now using other arrangements show no signs of return to the former practice, nor of any resulting denial of substantive justice. Professional, tenured, and properly supervised prosecution would make the rigid grand jury requirement obsolete. Prosecutors could then be trusted to bring cases before the courts without delay, upon presentation of information.[5]

PROSECUTION AND THE DEFENSE

Presentation of cases in a court involves the adversary system. In a noncriminal—or civil—case, the *plaintiff* and the *respondent,* or *defendant,*

[5]Committee for Economic Development, *Reducing Crime and Assuring Justice: A Statement on National Policy,* prepared by the Research and Policy Committee (New York: Committee for Economic Development, 1972), p. 27.

both enter the trial at an even point, with an equal advantage. The *litigants* each present their case by introducing evidence and testimony. The case is weighed by the judge or jury on its merits, which consists principally of the evidence presented. Whichever side in the case has the *preponderance* of weight in favor of his side of the case will win the lawsuit. The process involves a balancing of the scales with each side having an equal weight at the outset of the case.

In a criminal trial, the issue is much different. The accused is presumed to be innocent, or the preponderance of the case is immediately in his favor. In accordance with the American system of criminal law, the accused stands innocent until *proven* guilty. The burden of proving the accused guilty of the crime rests on the prosecutor. The defense at no time has to prove innocence. As a matter of fact, and procedure, the defendant shall be considered innocent at all times until he is proven guity *beyond all reasonable doubt* in the judgment of the judge or—in a jury trial—the jury. "Beyond all reasonable doubt" does not mean absolute certainty, but the courts have held that there must be a moral certainty that the accused did commit the crime.

Prosecuting Attorney

For the federal government the prosecutor is known as the U.S. Attorney, for the state he is the attorney general, for the trial courts the prosecutor is the district attorney. The district attorney usually prosecutes misdemeanors and felonies in the courts. The lower trial courts may use corporation counsels or city attorneys to prosecute misdemeanors. In civil cases the attorney general, county attorney, city attorney, or corporation counsel will represent the government. There are variations throughout the country, but one will usually find the DA as the prosecutor of most criminal trials.

An elected official and officer of the court, the district attorney represents the people of the state as the victim of the crime committed in the state (a crime being a *public* offense). The prosecuting attorney is generally responsible for determining—upon examination of reports and other inquiries he deems appropriate—whether or not to seek a complaint charging an individual with a crime and what charge will be filed against that person. In addition to the assessment of the crime by the prosecuting attorney and his decision to prosecute or not, the grand jury is used extensively as a body to hear testimony and examine evidence presented by the district attorney to determine whether or not a prosecution will be pursued by way of an indictment.

The district attorney is the legal advisor to the county grand jury. Other responsibilities include the initiation of proceedings against inebriates, the mentally ill, narcotics addicts, and nonsupport of minor children cases. Many district attorneys employ their own staffs of investigators.

One may ask why there is an entirely different staff of investigators for the prosecuting attorney when the police agency with primary jurisdiction conducts the investigation that leads to the arrest. Although there may be a problem caused by an incomplete investigation by the police detective, this is actually a secondary purpose for the district attorney investigator. The emphasis is different once the case is on its way through the courts, and the DA's investigator works as the attorney's field man, who assists the DA in lining up witnesses and evidence, handling last minute details, and conducting background data for the trial that may not have a direct bearing on the evidential value of a bit of evidence but is critical to the case in a variety of other ways. The investigator serves as an assistant to the prosecutor during the trial while the police detective is busy attending to dozens of other cases. In some jurisdictions it is not unusual for a prosecuting attorney to operate his own intelligence unit in cooperation with other local agencies to combat organized crime, which is directly related to so many of his other prosecutions.

In a criminal case, the procedure usually begins with the field police officer, who is the first on the scene of the crime. Either he makes an arrest at the scene or following a pursuit, or he carries the investigation through as far as he can, gathering and preserving the evidence, taking statements from the victims and witnesses, and preparing his reports. He may or may not identify the culprit at that phase of his investigation. In most cases he does not identify his suspect at that time. The follow-up investigator, usually an officer assigned to a "plainclothes" or detective detail, is responsible for continuing with the investigation. At some point in the investigation the case reaches the stage when the investigator must seek a complaint and a warrant that will lead to the arrest of the person responsible for the crime. As soon as the investigator has compiled sufficient evidence to prove that a crime has been committed, and he has built up sufficient proof that a specific individual should be held to answer to the charges, the investigating officer presents the case to the district attorney or one of his deputies, who are also attorneys and serve in the same capacity as he.

The prosecutor is responsible, as an officer of the court, to inquire into the officer's investigation sufficiently to convince him that the facts are as the officer has presented them in his reports and discussions. This should in no way be misunderstood to infer that the prosecutor is determining guilt, as that is strictly the prerogative of the court, but he must be reasonably convinced that the individual to be charged is guilty in his mind so that he will proceed with his part of the series of events. The district attorney makes a determination at this point whether to proceed with the prosecution.

If he makes the decision to prosecute, he next approaches the judge, who is functioning as a magistrate. The prosecutor files a complaint with the magistrate. The magistrate reviews the information presented on the complaint. The information is very minimal, just enough to convince the magistrate that a crime has been committed and that the district attorney has sufficient cause to charge the individual he has named as the accused. It is important to continue with the notion that at this time the accused is still innocent, because he has yet to appear in court to be proven guilty. The magistrate is not passing judgment on the accused, only on the merits of the case. If he agrees with the prosecutor, whose responsibility to the court as one of its officers is recognized by the magistrate, he then issues a warrant for the arrest of the suspect, who must be brought to the court to answer the charges.

After the arrest, the accused selects an attorney to represent him, or the court assigns an attorney to him. Throughout the process at every step along the way, the district attorney represents the people and the defendant has his attorney to protect his interests. The district attorney may meet and confer with the accused and his attorney and recommend that the accused plead guilty of the charges to avoid prolongation of the process. The accused must be proven guilty if he chooses—on advice of his counsel—to proceed with the trial, but he may waive that right to the trial by entering a plea. He may agree to plead guilty to a lesser charge, which may be negotiated with the combined consent of the prosecutor, the defense, and the judge. This process is known as *plea bargaining,* which is utilized by the prosecutor with the approval of the courts to speed up the processing of so many cases in a busy court.

In court, the prosecutor presents evidence and witnesses who give testimony to substantiate the charges earlier developed during the investigation and as briefly recounted in the complaint. The defense cross-examines, which is usualy a device to raise questions of doubt as to the validity or veracity of the evidence or testimony and to make points supporting innocence of the accused. In a misdemeanor case, the trial is held in the lower trial court and the prosecutor presents the case in that court. If the charge is a felony, this first court appearance is not a trial at all, but what is known as the *preliminary hearing.* In a preliminary, the judge sits as a magistrate and determines only if proof has been presented by the prosecutor that a crime has been committed and if there is sufficient information to instruct the prosecutor to file an information in superior court charging the accused with the offense charged in the complaint.

During the trial, a judge presides over the proceedings. If a jury has been chosen and is sitting as a part of the trial, the jury is responsible for making a value judgment on guilt beyond a reasonable doubt based upon their unanimous assessment of the evidence and information presented by the prosecutor. The judge determines whether each item of evidence shall be introduced, and he serves as the legal arbiter; in other words, the judge determines legality, while the jury determines fact. In the absence of the jury, the judge decides both legality and fact and it is he who declares guilt. In the absence of a guilty finding, the accused goes free, still an innocent person.

Defense Attorney

Every person accused of a crime shall have legal representation. This is a provision of the Sixth Amendment to the U.S. Constitution. The accused shall have a fair trial, and he has the right to "due process," which essentially means that his trial shall be in accordance with established procedures. This is a provision of the Fifth Amendment to the U.S. Constitution. Without competent legal representation an accused individual who is innocent may be denied the rights assured him by the Constitution. The courts recognize this as a possibility, therefore they assign counsel to the accused when he has not chosen one himself, and such assignment may be made even over his objections. In the event that the accused wishes to represent himself without counsel, the court very carefully examines the matter and renders its legal decision on whether the accused is competent to represent himself. Only then does it allow for the matter to proceed.

Throughout the process, beginning when the accused and his attorney first meet, the attorney as an officer of the court and also as the legal representative of the accused is obliged to advise his client on the points of law and proceedings throughout the entire process. His role is to assure his client of a fair and impartial handling of his case from beginning to end. You may ask the question, "What if the defense attorney knows that his client is guilty, should he still serve as his attorney?" The answer is a qualified yes. Qualified for this reason: Although the attorney is convinced of his client's guilt perhaps by that person's own admission, he has yet to be proven guilty. Certainly, the accused must be represented by competent attorneys, whether they committed the alleged crimes or not. With his knowledge of the facts as presented to him by his client, his responsibility to the court as an officer of that court as a skilled attorney, is to advise his client in the best interest of justice and of his client. Such advice may well be that the accused should agree to a negotiated plea for a lesser charge offered by the district attorney, or a recommendation that he plead guilty to the charges.

The attorney must maintain the confidence of his client and cannot disclose information given to him in confidence in this attorney-client relationship. For example: An individual commits an aggravated assault and contacts his attorney. There is an understanding that the attorney-client relationship exists because the culprit asks for advice and the attorney agrees to hear him out and advise him. After hearing the details, the attorney tells his client to give himself up to the police and plead guilty. Not accepting this advice, the client dismisses the attorney and goes to another one who advises him to do nothing and to keep his mouth shut. Although the relationship is severed, and there is even some doubt as to whether a true client relationship was established—there was certainly none of the usual rapport—there is no doubt that the dismissed attorney cannot disclose the information without violating his code of ethics as an attorney. The defense attorney must staunchly defend his clients, even the "guilty ones." A mistrial may be declared if at any time during the proceedings it becomes evident that either the prosecution or the defense is not adequately representing a client.

There are many defendants who cannot afford what might be considered a "good attorney." Upon certification that the defendant is indigent and cannot afford to pay an attorney, the court will provide one at the state's expense. As an officer of the court, an attorney may be assigned to handle the defense except when it would interfere with the other demands of his responsibilities to his clients and the court. In a great many jurisdictions the county position of public defender has been created. This officer is responsible to the indigent accused, to defend him and to assure him of his constitutional guarantee to a competent defense. Although not a new office, the tax-supported defense attorney has taken on new meaning and emphasis to assure the accused of every possible means of well-qualified legal representation.

TRACKING THE CRIMINAL TRIAL PROCESS

Although there are many similarities in procedure with both felony and misdemeanor violations, different courts are involved—in some cases more than one court is involved in the same case—and the actors and possible results of the trial are different. Because of the differences, each category—felony and misdemeanor—will be tracked separately. Although many felony arrests lead to eventual misdemeanor prosecutions, they are originally treated as felonies. It is usually somewhere along the way, at one of the steps in the process, that a decision is made to drop the felony charges and refile the case as a misdemeanor.

The Misdemeanor

The Offense If observed or discovered, the crime is then considered by one or more persons in view of the circumstances and a decision is made of whether to report it to the police. Many crimes are not discovered or recognized as crimes, and many types of behavior may be interpreted by the uninitiated as criminal when not actually violations of the law or not capable of being proven.

Police Intervention The investigating officer may be a victim or witness but in most criminal offenses is not and must rely upon evidence and statements of others in order to make a decision regarding the course of action that he or she will take. The officer's discretionary powers then determine the next step. The officer may determine that there was no crime, or that there was a crime but that there would be no further action necessary, or that there was a crime but further investigation or "cooling off" by the victim and/or witness would be best before proceeding, or that he will arrest the violator, if available for arrest.

Arrest If a person who observed the offense being committed in his presence makes the arrest, and if the officer appraises the situation and determines that there is sufficient cause for the arrest, the officer will accept the arrestee—or the arrest may be made while in the officer's presence after his or her arrival, in which case the officer will also accept the arrestee. The officer is not required to continue with the arrest unless there is, in his opinion, sufficient cause for the arrest. If the officer was present when the violation occurred, then the officer makes a personal decision of whether to arrest at the time or to postpone the arrest until later, at which time a complaint and warrant will be necessary.

Diversion There are certain types of crimes and individuals that may call for some type of corrective action to prevent or reduce the likelihood of repetition. As a part of the authority of the police, the prosecutor, and the courts to proceed with criminal charges, there is also the authority to use discretion and decide not to proceed. One type of discretionary alternative is *diversion,* which may include an agreement not to file criminal charges providing the accused agrees to go through a voluntary detoxification program for drug or alcohol addicts; another would be to submit to a civil court process and be committed to psychiatric treatment or counseling.

Although diversion from criminal conviction and a possible term of imprisonment in a correctional institution may seem appealing, particularly to the individual who is about to be convicted, the "break" they are about to receive may not be so great after all. A civil commitment may be for a period of time until the patient is "cured," which may be for a considerably longer period of time than if the person were convicted and sentenced to serve a specific number of days or months. This is another argument for a more uniform application in diversionary alternatives.

Citation or Jail In some jurisdictions, and in many misdemeanor violations, the officer may collect evidence and testimony, then issue a citation to the offender in lieu of taking the arrestee to jail for booking. While the offender is being cited by the officer, he is under arrest. Then, when he signs a promise to appear, which is on the citation form, the offender is—in effect—being released on his promise to appear in court to answer to the charges, a form of bail. The other method for the officer to consummate the arrest, the more traditional one, is to take the arrestee to the local jail, where he is searched for weapons, is fingerprinted and photgraphed, and held until he is either released on bail or goes to his first appearance in court.

Pretrial Custody A 1977 study suggested three things that could be done to contain the pretrial jail population:

1. Optimum use of summons, citation, pretrial release, and diversion.
2. Prompt decisions on pretrial release (reduce from three days to one day as the maximum time one is held).
3. Expedite processing cases against persons not diverted or given pretrial releases.[6]

Issuing a summons or citation in lieu of arrest would completely eliminate the jailing process altogether prior to trial. Many programs increasing the number of pretrial releases without bail have been inaugurated throughout the country with what the reports indicate as successful. Prompt decisions on pretrial releases may require a greater preponderance of evidence prior to arrest, or more sophisticated processing procedures and records-keeping functions coupled with greater speed in the decision-making process, perhaps reprioritizing personnel assignments. The third item on the list, that of expediting the process, might be enhanced by streamlining what might be an outmoded and cumbersome process, and developing guidelines to aid in the decision-making process.

Bail When the offender signs a promise to appear in court on the prescribed date, he is actually offering his promise to appear as his bail. When the person goes to jail, money or a bond may be required as bail, or a signed promise to appear may be accepted. This "bail without money" is known as "OR," or "own recognizance." Whatever form of bail the accused offers, its purpose is to assure the person's appearance in court to answer to the charges. A bail bond is an insurance policy, used in place of money.

Complaint and Warrant The officer prepares an investigative report, and processes the evidence. The report is either sent or personally delivered to the prosecuting attorney, who examines the information presented and makes a determination as to what charge, if any, will be filed against the suspect. The prosecutor may agree with the officer and decide to charge the same offense for which the arrest was made, a more appropriate charge, or none at all. If the suspect is in custody and the prosecutor decides that no charge will be filed, a release form is sent to the jail and the prisoner released with a notification that no charges will be filed. In some jurisdictions, the arrested person is asked to sign a waiver which acknowledges that the officer had probable cause for the arrest when it was made, but now, on examination of the case further, no charges would be filed. This is a form of protection against spurious false-arrest charges. A false arrest would not be related to what the prosecutor decided to do about pursuing the case; a false arrest is one that is made with malice and without reasonable cause existing at the time of the arrest. The prosecutor prepares a complaint if the decision is to proceed with the case. The prosecutor takes the complaint, which includes

[6]John J. Galvin, Project Director, et al., *Instead of Jail: Pre-and Post-Trial Alternatives to Jail Incarceration,* Vol. V (Washington, D.C.: National Institute of Law Enforcement and Criminal Justice, October, 1977) pp. 6–7.

an affidavit signed by the arresting officer or other person alleging the facts of the crime. The judge, sitting as a magistrate, reviews the complaint and affidavit and issues the warrant on the basis of the information presented. The judge may decide not to issue a warrant, but seldom contradicts the prosecutor at this stage of the case.

If the arrest had not been made at the time of the crime occurrence, the warrant is sent to the police in whose jurisdiction the crime was committed, and that department takes whatever action is necessary to make the arrest. Warrant files in every major police and sheriff's department are usually filled to capacity waiting to be served on violators to be arrested, probably most of them for traffic violations and failure to appear in court for traffic or criminal charges. If the arrest had been made earlier, then the warrant is sent to the jail to verify the charges against the person arrested.

Arraignment This is the first appearance of the accused person in the criminal offense. If the person had been held in jail awaiting the arraignment, the law requires an early date for the arraignment, while those released pending court action may have a few days longer daily. The purpose of the arraignment is to advise the accused of the charges, which may have been amended or changed since the arrest, to advise the accused of his or her constitutional rights relative to the charges and the process, to assure representation by counsel—appointing one if the accused is indigent (cannot pay for an attorney), setting or changing bail or making arrangements for "OR," and setting a date for the trial. If the accused has legal representation and wishes to plead guilty, a guilty plea will be accepted.

Pretrial Motions Usually limited to felony cases, this is the time prior to the trial when the attorney for the accused files for discovery of information held by the prosecution, moves for dismissal of the charges for lack of insufficiency of evidence, moves for certain evidence to be quashed or set aside, and may make a motion of some other type, such as mental condition of the accused not being ready for a trial, or perhaps some recommendation for diversion of the accused into some sort of narcotics or alcoholic rehabilitation program instead of progressing with the prosecution.

Trial The jury is selected—if jury trial—to serve as a trier of fact, while the judge rules on matters of law. If the case is heard without a jury, known as a court trial, the judge is both trier of fact and law. Prosecution and defense make their opening statements, usually laying out the case as they intend to present their respective sides. The prosecution then puts on its case, being required to prove guilt beyond a reasonable doubt. The defense then has the opportunity to move for dismissal or for a directed verdict of not guilty. The defense then puts on its defense, which is designed to attack, or draw away from, the sufficiency of the prosecution. The accused does not have to prove innocence, just raise sufficient doubts, and then the prosecution has to overcome those doubts. The prosecution follows with a rebuttal, and the defense then may move again for a dismissal. Closing arguments are offered by the prosecution, the defense, and the prosecution again. The judge instructs the jury on points of law and options they have, plus whatever other legal advice that is required. The jury deliberates and comes back with a verdict.

The Felony

The Offense The private person may arrest someone for committing a felony, even though the person who committed it did so out of the immediate presence of the person making the arrest. This is different from the misdemeanor, which requires actual perception by one or more of the senses that amounts to physical presence. The private person cannot arrest for suspicion, but the peace officer may arrest without a warrant for a crime that may or may not have been committed, and the arrest may be of a person who may or may not have actually committed it. This is known as a suspicion arrest, and most felony arrests are made on suspicion without an arrest warrant.

Police Intervention The nature of the crime being a felony, there seems to be greater likelihood that the police will take some more positive action than they would in misdemeanor cases. Also, it is not as essential that the police have private persons willing to sign complaints and to make "private persons' arrests." Police latitude is greater in felony cases.

Arrest Usually made without a warrant, the arrest may be made even though the investigation has just begun. The officer may arrest on multiple charges that may later be dropped because they are all related to the same series of acts. The prosecutor will later decide on sufficiency of evidence and appropriate charges to file.

Jail and Bail Citations are not issued for felonies. The accused is taken to jail and taken through the booking process. Bail may be cash or bond or "OR."

Complaint and Warrant This phase of the process is identical to the misdemeanor process. There may be more changes in charges filed versus "arrested for" because of sufficiency of evidence, availability of witnesses, and greater pressures to "plea bargain" for lower charges, reduction of felonies to misdemeanors, reduced number of offenses charged, or a plea of guilty in exchange for assurance of less punishment, possibly a trade of release for information against a codefendant or more serious violator.

Arraignment The first arraignment is held in the lower court, the municipal court, even though the trial will be held later in superior court. This is the same as with the misdemeanor, and again, changes may be made that will be proposed to the court at this time.

Plea Bargaining At this point, it is perhaps appropriate to discuss the commonly used expedient in the court, but highly controversial topic: the *bargained plea. Plea bargaining* and *bartered plea* are commonly used to describe the procedure whereby the accused is allowed to plead guilty to a lesser charge than originally filed, such as pleading guilty to misdemeanor assault instead of felonious assault. An individual may be charged with only one crime instead of two or more in exchange for a "bartered" plea of guilty to the one crime charged. Sometimes a plea is bargained for an alternate charge, such as reckless driving instead of driving under the influence of alcohol or a drug, or disturbing the peace instead of indecent exposure. The benefits are immediately recognizable.

The ABA's Special Committee on Crime Prevention and Control made this observation on the bartered plea:

> Guilty pleas serve as the safety valve which enables many overburdened courts to hold their own against the flood tide of cases confronting them. The high incidence of pleas to a lesser charge is disturbing, however. Too often it represents a beleaguered court's willingness to be more lenient than it would ordinarily be solely to save court time—a practice known in court parlance as "giving away the court house for the sake of the calendar."
>
> ...The problem is that the fundamental goal of dispensing justice fairly and evenly through the judicial process is jeopardized when increasing numbers of guilty pleas become essential for the courts to avert paralysis and collapse.[7]

Many times, the process allows the attorneys—with the judge's approval—to barter for a more equitable disposition than would have originally been acquired. Consider the following circumstances which might justify plea bargaining:

1. *"Suspicion" arrests.* A great many, probably more than half, arrests are made for felony violations without a warrant and based on information the investigating officer has at the time of the arrest. The arrest is made, then the investigation continues. Then witnesses disappear and certain bits of evidence originally believed to be significant lose their validity after closer examination. All that can be proven in court would be a lesser and less involved crime. The defendant pleads "not guilty." Knowing that the prosecution will be too difficult—maybe impossible—to prove, the prosecuting attorney agrees to reducing the charges in trade for a "guilty" plea.

2. *"Stacked charges."* When conducting initial investigations and making on-the-spot arrests based on the information and circumstances at the moment, it is not uncommon for the arresting officer(s) to review the circumstances, then review the criminal codes, and charge the arrestee with every one of the crimes that the person had committed. For example, the

[7]American Bar Association Special Committee on Crime Prevention and Control, *New Perspectives on Urban Crime* (Chicago: American Bar Association, 1972), p. 69.

police stop a car that is not registered to the driver. They check and find that the car had been stolen. While searching the suspect, the officers find an opened container of alcoholic beverage, some citizens band radio gear that the suspect cannot explain, a revolver under the back seat, and the suspect had also violated a series of three traffic laws before the officers stopped him. Being conscientious officers, they book the suspect for (a) suspicion of stealing the car, (b) possession of an open container of alcoholic beverage, (c) suspicion of receiving stolen property (the CB items), (d) carrying concealed weapon, (e) suspicion of armed robbery (possibly used the revolver in a robbery, and he happens to resemble a wanted robbery suspect). The officers then give the suspect a traffic citation for the driving violations, which he puts into his pocket.

After the arrest, the follow-up officers carry through with the investigation and find that they can only prove (a), (b), and the traffic violations. The owner of the car claims ownership of the revolver, and the officers cannot locate an owner of the CB gear who would go into court and testify that the property was his and had been stolen. Knowing that the stolen car violation would yield an acceptable sentence, the prosecutor drops the alcoholic beverage violation and goes to court. The circumstances of the car theft may show that the suspect had driven it only five miles, that he was known by the victim (owner of the car), and that it was apparently only a "joy-riding" episode. When it finally gets to court, the prosecutor and defense agree that the charge will be reduced to a misdemeanor "joy-riding" offense, and that the defendant will plead guilty. The officers were correct in the action they took, but as the case unfolded, so did the complexion of the case. What would you have done if you were the (a) officers or (b) the prosecutor?

3. *Multiple arrests.* An officer stops a carload of young men and women and discovers that the car has been stolen and that the glove compartment contains a quantity of narcotics. Since there are five people in the car, the officer arrests all five for (a) stealing the car and (b) possession of narcotics. The officer books all suspects into the county jail. Follow-up investigation leads to the discovery that a witness saw only one person—the driver—steal the car. Also, since the officers did not see any of the car's occupants actually holding, or in possession of, the narcotic substance, the prosecutor who reviewed the case with the follow-up investigators anticipated that it would be virtually impossible for him to get a conviction of anyone for possession except, perhaps, the driver. Consequently, of the five individuals originally arrested, charges are filed on only one person. Prior to the trial, it would not be unusual for a trade to be made to drop the narcotics charge in exchange for a guilty plea to the grand theft, auto.

4. *Improper arrests, or arrests based upon faulty information or unacceptable evidence.* No one is perfect, including police officers. Even honest errors can cause a great deal of grief for everyone concerned in such an

unfortunate event when the wrong person is arrested or the right person is charged with the wrong crime. Plea bargaining makes allowances for such errors.

5. *Witness difficulties.* Since few trials are held immediately following arrests, witnesses die or forget, or change their minds about what their testimony should be. Sometimes a witness, because of prior criminal record or other problem with reputation for not telling the truth, cannot be used by the prosecution. Many witnesses want to be charitable and want to "forgive and/or forget." What happens to the witnesses that the prosecutor was planning to use will determine how much can be proven in court. Rather than lose the case entirely, the prosecutor may move for a reduction in the charge.

6. *Communications problems.* If, for some reason—probably poor communications—witnesses, victims, defendants, attorneys cannot get everything together for a trial, a bargained plea to a lesser charge may be more beneficial and economically feasible to the alternative of putting on a case that will result in mistrial or a finding of "not guilty."

7. *Attorneys' judgment.* Either while acting alone or in concert with another prosecutor or even the defense attorney, the prosecuting attorney reviews the case, plans his strategy, and considers possible outcomes. He may decide that there is a greater chance of getting a conviction for a lesser offense. He works out a compromise solution with the defense and saves the cost of a trial.

Throughout this discussion, no mention was made about the leniency or harshness of judges. Although the judge must approve the bargained plea and give it his official approbation, he is not usually involved in the bargaining sessions. He merely acts on what is proposed to him. The key individual in the plea-bargaining process is the prosecuting attorney, whose personal and political motives play a part in the process of deciding whether or not to prosecute and, if so, for what charge.

> The responsibility of the judge and the other officers of the court—both prosecution and defense—is to make judicious use of the device as a means of expediting the process truly "in the interest of justice" and in accordance with the laws. They must constantly guard against the bartered plea being used by unscrupulous persons to manipulate the system and render it ineffective. Above all, particular emphasis must be made on the importance of eliciting guilty pleas only from those who are—in fact—guilty. If the courts are so overburdened that innocent persons find it more to their advantage to plead guilty and to get their time in jail awaiting trial declared by the judge to be their punishment, while the innocent persons who hold out for a trial languish in jail for greater periods of time, then the ends of justice have certainly not been met.

One type of offender who is finding it difficult to negotiate for reduced charges is the career criminal. Jeffrey Perlman of the *Los Angeles Times* reported on such a program, which has been operating with federal funds granted through the Law Enforcement Assistance Administration in twelve California counties (including the county where I live and work) and twenty other jurisdictions throughout the United States. Perlman stated:

> Special prosecution teams, working with one-third of the normal case load, zero in on defendants with long criminal records of victimizing large numbers of citizens.
>
> With virtually no plea bargaining and with more attention to preparing evidence, conviction rates have gone up and, in some areas where studies have been made, crime rates have gone down.[8]

Obviously directed toward the relatively few individuals who commit the majority of crimes, the program is directed at isolating those individuals from the society they plunder for greater lengths of time, thereby appreciably reducing the crime rate. The same report stated that only 49 convicted robbers in this Career Criminal Prosecution program had been responsible for 10,505 felonies—about 214 per robber.

Preliminary Hearing Held in municipal court, the purpose of the preliminary is to have the prosecution prove the elements of the crime, and to produce sufficient evidence and testimony to convince the judge that the accused should be held to answer to the charges in superior court. It is not necessary to prove guilt, just to convince the judge that the charges are not false or fabricated or insufficient. In the preliminary hearing the judge does not determine guilt, nor is he/she going to be the judge who later must make that judgement.

Motions to quash, suppress evidence, and dismiss occur. As a matter of fact, it is not unusual at all for the preliminary to be recessed for a time so that a motion to suppress evidence may be given a hearing. The judge then hears testimony surrounding the manner in which the evidence was collected and rules on whether or not it was collected and introduced within constitutional boundaries. If so, the judge directs the preliminary to continue without that evidence losing its value. If the evidence is excluded, then it cannot be used in the preliminary or in any subsequent trials. Once the judge determines that all requirements are met, the judge will direct the prosecutor to file an information in the superior court and prosecute it as a felony. At this stage, plea bargaining or a decision of the prosecutor may cause a change in the charges, and the accused will then either be charged with a felony in superior court as directed by the judge, or be scheduled for a misdemeanor trial in municipal court.

Grand Jury If the prosecutor chooses not to go through the preliminary-hearing process in a felony, as explained in the discussion of the grand jury in this chapter, the matter is brought before the grand jury. If the jurors

[8]Los Angeles Times, April 1, 1979, Part X, p. 1.

determine that there is sufficient proof that a crime was committed and if they believe the accused should be held to answer, then the grand jury instructs the prosecutor to file an indictment in superior court. The grand jury takes the place of the preliminary hearing.

Motions At this point, the defense has an opportunity to attack sufficiency of the evidence again (or for the first time if the case went through the grand jury, because counsel is not present and often the accused does not know that he is to be charged until after the grand jury files the indictment). Other motions listed previously may also be entered and acted upon by the court.

Arraignment This arraignment is made in superior court. It is similar to the arraignment held in municipal court, except that the charges and other information may have changed in the interim.

Discovery and other motions regarding evidence revealed as a result of the discovery may be part of the pretrial routine to save time in the actual trial, and to allow more time for adjustments in charges and for more plea bargaining, if necessary.

Trial The felony trial is similar to the misdemeanor trial, except that it is held in superior court and verbatim transcripts are made of the entire trial. In the preliminary hearing for felony trials, verbatim transcripts are also taken, because the preliminary hearing—although held in a municipal court—is an integral part of the felony process.

THE JURY TRIAL

The accused has a Constitutional right to a jury trial. As a matter of routine, and also as a simple matter of logistics, it is virtually impossible for every criminal trial to be attended by a jury. In the majority of cases, therefore, we see the encouragement of—and the practice of—trials without a jury. (In some jurisdictions a jury trial is not available in cases which do not call for jail time as punishment.)

Such a trial is called a *court* trial, and the judge functions in the dual role of judge and jury.

Jurors are selected usually by a lottery system from the county's rolls of registered voters, assumed to be the peers of the accused, who is likely to be a resident of the same county occupied by the jurors. Various methods are used to summon the jury and to provide for their service, but once empaneled to sit as a jury in a criminal trial they function as the judges of fact in the case. While the judge determines which evidence and witnesses will be authorized for presentation during the trial in accordance with the rules of procedure and evidence and serves as the arbiter on the law, the jury determines the truth and weight of the evidence and then passes judgment on the guilt of the accused.

Juries usually consist of twelve members, except when waived in accordance with accepted practice, or in some jurisdictions where a jury of a lesser amount of jurors has been established by law. They hear testimony and examine evidence, receive instructions from the judge as to the legal considerations as to their role during the trial, and form opinions about the guilt or innocence of the accused. At the conclusion of the trial, the judge instructs them as to their role in the matter, and provides them guidelines to follow when arriving at their conclusions. The jurors then retire to their chambers where they meet as a committee to discuss and to vote on the issues. In a criminal trial, the jury must vote unanimously for a guilty verdict. They may decide that there is no justification for a guilty verdict, or they may become hopelessly deadlocked over the issues. In the third instance, the judge may declare a mistrial, which would necessitate a new trial at the initiation of the prosecutor again. In the absence of a finding of guilt, the jurors vote for a not-guilty plea. The jury advises the judge that they find the accused guilty or not guilty, at which time the judge assumes his role in the case to proceed with sentencing or to order the release of the accused.

CORONER'S INQUEST

Although not a court, the coroner's inquest has a quasi-judicial appearance in procedure and outcome. The coroner is charged with the responsibility for determining the cause of death under a list of many different conditions, including deaths occurring during surgery, death occurring under suspicious circumstances, death of a person who had not had the attention of a physician for a specified period of time, and many other occasions. There are certain situations when the cause of death may be obvious, but the circumstances surrounding the death may be open to question. An example of a death might be a self-defense situation between an occupant of a house or operator of a business who kills a burglar during the commission of what appears to be a crime, but there is some question as to whether the death was necessary under the circumstances as they appeared to the officer at the time he arrived on the scene some few minutes after the occurrence.

The investigating officer would take the statements of the witnesses and gather the evidence that may or may not substantiate the statements of the person who claimed the need to kill his assailant in self-defense. The coroner's responsibility is to determine cause of death, and the police responsibility is to investigate the case from a criminal prosecution standpoint. In addition to performing an autopsy and establishing the time of death, the type of wound and weapon used, the coroner may determine that further inquiry is necessary. Sitting in his role as hearing officer, the coroner may impanel a jury from available adults he is able to summon to the place of hearing, which may be a room in the funeral home or an available courtroom or other public place. The coroner subpoenas witnesses and they are sworn in to testify to their observations and the role they played in the investigation. Witnesses may include the individual whose actions caused the death, the officers on the scene, and any other witnesses the coroner may choose to testify including the doctor who performed the autopsy. At the conclusion of the hearing, the jury makes a determination as to cause of death. The decision may be "accidental" or "caused by the criminal act of another," or "by negligence," or other decisions.

In the event the coroner's inquest yields a conclusion that the death was a criminal act of someone, the coroner recommends to the prosecutor that some criminal action and/or further investigation should follow. The prosecution, of course, is the prerogative of the district attorney and the recommendation of the coroner is just that: a recommendation. Inquests are not held on a regular basis, nor are they automatic in all suspicious deaths. Neither are autopsies held in all cases. The coroner has the authority to make his decisions about how to pursue his inquiry, although he may act at the request or recommendation of the prosecutor, or perhaps at the insistence of the survivors when they may raise questions that the coroner believes should be asked during a formal inquiry.

ADMINISTRATIVE HEARINGS

Various governmental bodies have the authority to subpoena witnesses and to conduct such inquiries that are necessary to their operations. City councils, county boards of supervisors, personnel commissions, licensing boards, school boards, human relations commissions, and numerous other agencies hold hearings and make administrative decisions that have binding effect on the individuals who are the subjects of their inquiries.

For example, a school teacher may be charged with some type of administrative violation that may or may not concurrently be a criminal matter. The administrative hearing is held independent of any other issue and has no direct relationship to any other action. The board may sit as a body and swear in witnesses, hear testimony, and conduct its inquiry with the chairman or president of the board presiding in his quasi-judicial role, or the board may appoint an attorney to sit as the hearing officer to preside at the hearing and to present to them a summary of the hearing and his recommendations. In either case, the board makes the final determination as to the fate of the accused teacher and it may vote to suspend or to withdraw his credentials or license. The result is that this professional individual has been denied, by board action, the right to practice his profession anywhere in the state.

ARBITRATION BOARDS

Arbitration boards have been established to relieve the burden on the courts in personal injury cases involving competing insurance claims resulting from traffic collisions or industrial accidents. Labor-management relations have been handled by arbitration boards as well. The result in these various types of quasi-judicial hearings has been a reduction of the burden on the courts and a considerable speeding-up of the litigation, which previously would have taken several years in some cases had it gone to the courts for disposition. Arbitration board hearings are usually held in conference rooms of one or both of the attorneys involved, or in some other neutral area, usually not a courtroom.

PRESENTENCE INVESTIGATION

Following the guilty verdict and preceding the judges imposition of the sentence, the judge may order a presentence investigation to be conducted by the probation officer. The defendant may demand immediate sentencing, and he will if he believes that it will be to his advantage that he do so, but most defendants welcome the investigation. The purpose of the presentence investigation is to inquire into the background and the personal life of the defendant, his work and personal history, his integration in the community, and the various factors that will provide the judge with the insight to use his wisdom in imposing the sentence that the judge deems most appropriate for the offense, the temper of the community, whatever other pressures play on his conscience, and that he believes will be most appropriate to lead to the eventual rehabilitation and reintegration of the defendant.

THE SENTENCE

Although there are a few mandatory sentences in certain types of offenses, the judge has a wide range of discretion within which he may operate when imposing sentence. There are maximum fines and terms of imprisonment in the county or city jail in misdemeanor cases, and prison sentences for felony convictions may be somewhat static. The judge may suspend sentence altogether, or he may sentence the defendant who has been found guilty of a felony to a long period of probation with a short term in jail as a condition of that probation. The judge may sentence the defendant to a definite period of time in the penitentiary, or prison, or he may preside in a state that provides for indeterminate sentences. In that case, the judge merely remands the convicted defendant to prison "for the term prescribed by law," which may consist of a minimum and a maximum term with the exact amount of time to be established by a state board of corrections. Whatever the sentence is to be, the judge relies with some confidence upon the findings of the probation officer during his presentence investigation and his recommendations regarding the sentence.

The Determinate Sentence

First introduced in California in 1917, the indeterminate sentence went into the past with the Determinate Sentencing Act of September 20, 1976. After about two years of hot debates and what seemed certain loss in committees and shelves, the state legislature finally succeeded in changing to a determinate-sentencing procedure. Several court cases led to the eventual success of this new law, particularly the Rodriguez case (14C. 3d 639), in which the California Supreme Court found that twenty-two years of imprisonment for nonviolent fondling of a six-year-old child, even under a life sentence, was unconstitutionally excessive. The sentence had been changed more than once by the Adult Authority. The court held that the Adult Authority could adjust a sentence upward once the sentence had been set. The court also held that a prisoner could not be held for an excessive time "solely because he was not competent to take care of himself in the free society" once the sentence was fixed. In the Stanley Case (54 C.A. 3d 1030, 1976) the California Appellate Court held that fixing sentences and parole dates should take into account such matters as acceptable in-prison conduct, reclamation potential, postrelease social safety, premonitions of danger not revealed by overt behavior ("gut feeling"), nature of the present offense, and prior criminal history.

Legislators and penal system experts had—at various times—been at odds with the philosophy of the Adult Authority's practice of waiting for well into a prisoner's sentence before fixing actual sentence expiration and parole eligibility. The argument was that the prisoner should have his sentence fixed early so as to have a date to expect his sentence to end.

Determinate sentencing gives very little recognition to any "rehabilitative" factor, which is debatable whether prisons rehabilitate, and places greater emphasis on the culpability of the offender for his crime, the seriousness of the offense, and past criminal record.

The result of the determinate sentencing law in California is that terms will be fixed by judges within very narrow ranges of time set out by statute, rather than being fixed at whatever time an administrative board chooses to fix the time within a very wide range of time (example: one to fourteen years, five to twenty years, and other spans of time). Such sentences set by the judge may be mitigated or aggravated, depending on such facts as no prior record or extensive record, by use of weapons or use of violence, or for causing an excessive amount of property loss. Judges still retain the discretion to sentence concurrently or consecutively. Within the institution, sentences may be reduced by one third for "good time" and participation in prison programs, which may be rehabilitative in nature. Sentences also carry a parole period of not more than a year following time in prison. Prisoners sentenced to life imprisonment may still be subjected to some indeterminate time and their parole may be increased for a period up to three years, to be determined at the discretion of a newly established administrative board.

COURT REFORM

In a call for reform and a review of the existing procedures in courts that involve interminable delays, Chief Justice Burger of the U.S. Supreme Court stated:

> Someone must remind the bar and the public of the enormous cost of a trial. Reliable estimates have been made indicating that the cost is in the neighborhood of $250 per working hour in some courts, not including plant and equipment cost—or lawyers.[9]

Edward Bennett Williams, Chairman of the American Bar Association Committee on Crime Prevention, stated the following:

> I submit the time has come to take a long agonizing look at our criminal courts. The criminal courts of troubled urban America are failing wretchedly. Like scarecrows put in the fields to frighten the birds of lawlessness, tattered and unmasked from neglect, frightening to no one, they have become roosting places for the crows. To the innocent, to the victims of crime, to the witnesses of crime, to the illiterate, the uneducated, and the poor, many of our big city criminal courts are a sham and a broken promise.[10]

In his presentation, Mr. Williams presented specific proposals for change in the urban criminal justice system with an emphasis on the courts component. Those proposals included the following:

1. Recognize mandatory use of the grand jury as outmoded and no longer necessary.
2. Use the bail system with more imagination. Money bail for the poor is meaningless. Bail can be used as a means to enforce drug-free periods by lifting bail in cases of drug abuse.
3. At arraignment judges should make liberal use of the discovery procedure (allowing the defendant to have access to evidence and testimony that will be used against him in a trial) so that more persons will enter pleas.

[9] "Justice in the States," from *Addresses and Papers of the National Conference On the Judiciary, March 11–14, 1971 at Williamsburg, Virginia* (Washington, D.C.: Government Printing Office, 1971), p. 16.

[10] Edward Bennett Williams, Chairman of American Bar Association Committee on Crime Prevention, "Crime, Punishment, Violence: The Crisis in Law Enforcement," from *Addresses and Papers of the National Conference on the Judiciary, March 11–14, 1971 at Williamsburg, Virginia* (Washington, D.C.: Government Printing Office, 1971), pp. 36–37.

4. Dispense with the written motions, provide for oral motions ten days after the arraignment, and provide that the case may be set no later than sixty days from the time the case is instituted.
5. Modernize the preparation of transcripts through computerization.
6. Take no more than one day in jury selection.
7. The trial judge should order a background report on each defendant at the time the case gets into the court. In the event the defendant is found guilty, sentencing can be handled immediately without delay.
8. The case should be set for appeal immediately after sentencing, and there should be a ten-day maximum for filing the record with the appellate court.
9. Argue cases without the now-required briefs.
10. The appellate process should be unsigned, short, and concise.[11]

In the Bar Association's report on the Committee on Crime Prevention several months later, that committee presented their list of recommendations for improvement of the court process, which included those presented at Williamsburg in 1971, as well as the following:

1. Transfer nonserious offenses, such as traffic and housing code violations, to specialized bodies, and transfer to nonjudicial bodies certain types of conduct that "harm no one other than those involved." (The list included public drunkenness, narcotics addiction, vagrancy, and deviant sexual behavior).
2. Divert some cases before trial into a period of probation without conviction, which would involve prosecutorial discretion.
3. Provide more funds to probation officers to "permit careful screening of defendants to determine those meriting pretrial release, to provide close supervision for those who are released, and to assure the early preparation of preventive reports."
4. "Computers should be utilized to assist the court in scheduling, doing routine paperwork, avoiding conflicts, equalizing work loads, analyzing backlogs, and providing various types of judicial statistics needed for effective court operation and planning."
5. Cut down on the "intervals between the time when a defendant is arrested or charged and the time his trial commences. . . ."
6. Provide trained court administrators to provide specialized management skills to the courts and to allow the judges to concentrate on the facets of their responsibilities for which they are best prepared: hearing and deciding cases.
7. Call upon bar associations and law schools to provide such trained management specialists.
8. Develop an individual calendar system so that individual judges are responsible for cases all the way through and there is an accountability for any "inordinate delays in particular cases."[12]

In the same report of the Bar Association's Committee on Crime Prevention and Control, the committee reported:

[11]Paraphrased from "Crime, Punishment, Violence: The Crisis in Law Enforcement," pp. 36–38.

[12]American Bar Association Special Committee, *New Perspectives on Urban Crime*, pp. iv, v.

> To function efficiently, any large and complex institution needs skilled administration, a fact that the courts have been terribly slow to recognize. Unlike hospitals, which in the last quarter century have increasingly entrusted their administration to management experts rather than practicing physicians, the courts have left the supervision of their business in the hands of the judges whose principal responsibility is—and should be—to hear and decide cases. As case loads continue to swell, the need to utilize trained court administrators becomes increasingly acute. Not only can they free judges to concentrate on their judicial responsibilities, but they can bring to the judiciary the type of management expertise rarely found in courts at the present time.[13]

Many of the recommendations of these various individuals and groups have been acted upon, such as the inauguration of sophisticated computer systems to cut down on time and duplication problems, improved calendar systems, diversion programs, and special quasi-judicial bodies to adjudicate and negotiate less serious crimes and civil cases. Among these recommendations, there was a call for more effective management of the system. A new professional has emerged from this call: the court administrator.

THE COURT ADMINISTRATOR

The court administrator is a trained court-house manager. Traditionally, the courts have survived management or near-management (or mismanagement in some cases, perhaps) under the direction of presiding judges of the courts. Most judges are trained in fields other than business management; they are educated and trained to practice law and may not have had any business or public management experience prior to entering the practice of law. The function of the judge is to devote full time and attention to matters in the courtroom and chambers. The judge cannot be expected to be all things to all people. Someone must supervise all of the support personnel who work in and about the courthouse, purchase supplies, program the computers, and juggle time schedules for maximum utilization of personnel and facilities within tight budgets. The result has been emergence of a professionally trained individual who carries the title of court administrator.

SUMMARY

In this chapter, we have examined the structure and functions of the courts component of the criminal justice system. We call this component the "process" unit because it is here that decisions are made, judgments are rendered, trials are held, and punishments and alternatives are decided on criminal activities for the purpose of assuring the most favorable disposition to reduce crimes.

The process a criminal offender goes through is of tremendous impor-

[13]American Bar Association Special Committee, *New Perspectives on Urban Crime*, p. 95.

tance to the student because it gives meaning to the "due process" guarantees assured the person who is processed through the system, and it is here that some semblance of justice for both offender and offended is meted out.

There are separate court systems for each of the sovereign states in the United States, and another separate federal court system. Even though the highest court of appeal, or the court of "last resort," is usually the highest appeals court within the state, the supremacy of the U.S. Constitution assures fair treatment at the hands of the justice system throughout the nation through an ultimate appeal to the United States Supreme Court.

EXERCISES AND STUDY QUESTIONS

1. Based on what you have studied in this chapter, draw a flow diagram on the progress of a misdemeanor case from arrest to final court disposition.

2. Draw a flow diagram on the progress of a felony case from arrest to final court disposition, being sure to include both the lower preliminary process as well as the trial.

3. Explain the relationships of the prosecutor and the defense attorney in a criminal trial.

4. Draw a chart of the court system in your state and in your county, and compare the chart with what you have read in this chapter. What are the differences? Similarities?

5. Which official is responsible for custody of the deceased in a homicide case?

6. Explain the phenomenon the author calls "judicial supremacy."

7. In the jurisdiction where you live, is there a justice court?

8. What is the function of a small claims court?

9. Describe the difference between a judge and a magistrate as described in this chapter.

10. When a grand jury determines that a person should be held to answer to a criminal charge, what does the district attorney file in the superior court?

11. Contrast and compare the coroner's inquest with the municipal court trial.

12. How does an administrative hearing compare with the criminal trial?

13. What is the substance and effect of the presentence investigation?

14. Describe the determinate sentence.

15. What is the indeterminate sentence?

16. What is the difference between "determinate" and "indeterminate?"

17. What is the purpose of a preliminary hearing?

18. Does an officer have the prerogative to choose when he will not accept a person arrested by another private person?

19. Are citations usually issued for felonies?

20. What is the purpose of bail?

21. What is the role of the judge in the issuance of a warrant?

22. May a police officer arrest a person suspected of a felony without a warrant?

23. Under what conditions would a bargained plea be acceptable?

RECOMMENDED SEMESTER/TERM PROJECT

1. Visit your local municipal court and follow a criminal case through the preliminary hearing to the felony trial in superior court. Prepare a chronicle of events as they unfold, outlining the original charge, the circumstances as they occur in scheduling, changing charges, motions, and the eventual results.

2. Draw a schematic chart on a felony and another on a misdemeanor case as they progress through the courts.

SUGGESTED FOR ADDITIONAL STUDY

For this chapter, refer to the Government Code, the Criminal or Penal Code, and other government publications for your own jurisdiction to contrast and compare the court system.

ADAMS, THOMAS F., *Criminal Justice Readings.* Pacific Palisades, Calif.: Goodyear Publishing Co., Inc., 1972.

BRISTOW, ALLEN P. and JOHN B. WILLIAMS, *A Handbook in Criminal Procedure and the Administration of Justice.* Beverly Hills: Glencoe Press, 1966.

——— *Determinate Sentencing—Reform or Regression.* Proceedings of the Special Conference on Determinate Sentencing, June 2–3, 1977, Boalt Hall, School of Law, University of California, Berkeley. Washington, D.C.: U.S. Department of Justice, National Institute of Law Enforcement and Criminal Justice, March, 1978.

FELKENES, GEORGE T., *Constitutional Law For Criminal Justice.* Englewood Cliffs, N.J.: Prentice-Hall, Inc., 1978.

LEWIS, MERLIN, WARREN BUNDY, and JAMES L. HAGUE, *An Introduction To The Courts and Judicial Process.* Englewood Cliffs: Prentice-Hall, Inc., 1978.

MAYERS, LEWIS, *The Machinery Of Justice, An Introduction to Legal Structure and Process.* Totowa, N.J.: Littlefield and Adams & Co., 1973.

RUBIN, H. TED, *The Courts: Fulcrum of the Justice System.* Pacific Palisades, Calif.: Goodyear Publishing Co., Inc., 1976.

WELLS, KENNETH M., and PAUL B. WESTON, *Criminal Procedure and Trial Practice.* Englewood Cliffs, N.J.: Prentice-Hall, Inc., 1977.

WESTON, PAUL B., and KENNETH M. WELLS, *The Administration of Justice* (2d ed.). Englewood Cliffs: Prentice-Hall, Inc., 1972.

WHEELER, RUSSELL, and HOWARD R. WHITCOMB, *Judicial Administration Text and Readings.* Englewood Cliffs: Prentice-Hall, Inc., 1977.

WRIGHT, R. GENE, and JOHN A. MARLO, *The Police Officer and Criminal Justice.* New York: McGraw-Hill Book Co., Inc., 1970.

9

Corrections

INTRODUCTION

Correctional institutions, including federal and state prisons, halfway houses, youth guidance centers, vocational training centers, juvenile halls and schools, city and county jails; probation agencies, including federal, state, and local; and parole agencies at both federal and state levels all make up the corrections component of the criminal justice system. In this chapter we shall examine all of those subsections of corrections.

The chapter will begin with an overview of the total corrections component, followed by a review of the goals and objectives of corrections. Then, we shall look at the various subunits through discussion of their basic structures and functions.

THE CORRECTIONS COMPONENT

When discussing corrections as a part of the criminal justice system, we begin with probation, progress on to institutions, then move along to parole. Although treated separately and in that order, it is difficult to separate them so completely in actual practice. The city or county jail may be the first stop for the criminal offender accused of crime. As a matter of fact, it usually is first in the chain of events in the life of the arrestee. Although not yet adjudged guilty of any wrongdoing, the accused is jailed by the police and "booked," or initially charged with the offense, which consists of searching, exchanging street clothing for jail clothing, bathing to reduce spread of disease, photographing and fingerprinting and logging necessary data in the arrest ledger and related documents (hence the term "booking"), and placement in the lockup, or cell. The jail serves as temporary storage facility pending release of the accused on bail, or until the trial. Later the accused may be determined guilty by the court, and will be required to serve out a prescribed sentence in the same jail as a sentenced prisoner.

Probation is the process involving conditional release in lieu of imprisonment—sometimes a combination of probation and a jail sentence may be prescribed instead of a longer prison sentence. The probation officer gets involved in the case before the punishment is prescribed, however. As an officer of the court, the probation officer conducts an investigation, usually called the presentence investigation, and submits a written report of the investigation to the judge. The report includes the officer's findings regarding the crime for which the subject is charged, previous criminal or delinquent record, if any, the subject's work and home environments and how he lives within them as a social being, prognosis for rehabilitation, and other information to help the judge determine how to sentence the accused. The probation report usually contains a recommendation to the judge as to how the probation officer believes the ends of justice will best be met, such as conditions of probation, length of sentence, and other suggestions, which the judge may or may not heed.

Parole is similar to probation, in that the process involves supervising convicted persons while at liberty, yet still within the jurisdiction of the court and the department of corrections. Parole is a form of "outpatient" aftercare during a conditional release from prison following a term in prison.

Briefly, that is corrections in a nutshell. Criticism of the processes involved have caused many people to carefully scrutinize this component of the system far more carefully than any other. The chief criticism is that "corrections does not correct offenders." There are essentially four reasons why the people want criminal offenders to be arrested and charged for their crimes. They are (1) rehabilitation of the criminal with assurance that he or she will not repeat the same or other crimes, (2) segregation of the offenders from society, (3) retribution, or punishment of the offender, and/or (4) revenge, or the satisfaction of getting retribution.

The real question so often asked is, "Does the corrections phase of criminal justice actually accomplish rehabilitation?" Comparing the people's objectives, following are the goals and objectives of corrections as seen by the practitioners in the field prepared by the Organization of State Correctional Services in the Control and Treatment of Crime and Delinquency, Board of Corrections for the State of California in 1967, and reproduced to serve simply as an example of how such a statement may be adapted as a guideline for action:

Goals of Corrections:

1. **Prevention.** To minimize the frequency with which law violators are recruited from the noncriminal population. Accordingly, the effectiveness of preventive efforts is measured by the volume of first offenses, that is, the rate of criminal recruitment.
2. **Correction.** To minimize the frequency which law violations are committed by persons who have prior records of criminality. Success of the corrective effort is, therefore, measured by various kinds of recidivism rates.

Objectives of Corrections:

Achievement of the goals of corrections requires establishment of more specific "targets" or "objectives" of the system. These objectives are:

1. **To assist the criminal and juvenile courts and the quasi-judicial parole boards to make effective decisions regarding disposition of offenders subject to the court's or parole board's jurisdiction.** This objective is accomplished by:
   - **(a)** Application of established standards in the determination of detention status of adults detained in jail and juveniles detained in juvenile hall.
   - **(b)** Clinical and investigative techniques culminating in reports with recommendations which evaluate the characteristics of the offender, the offense, and the feasibility of probation of other sentencing dispositions.
   - **(c)** Providing paroling authorities with information for the determination of sentence and of parole date and conditions, which information is based largely on evaluation of the attitudes, skills and demonstrated performance of the subject in a controlled environment and after progress in an appropriate rehabilitation or treatment program.
2. **To administer the sentencing dispositions of the courts by control of committed offenders in the institutions and/or on probation or parole.** This objective is accomplished by:
   - **(a)** Control in the institutions:
     - **(1)** Classifying inmates in accordance with security requirements.
     - **(2)** Maintaining safety and order within a secure perimeter.
     - **(3)** Providing for basic human needs and maintaining morale through good human relations.
   - **(b)** Control in the community:
     - **(1)** Classifying probationers and parolees in accordance with control requirements.
     - **(2)** Enforcing the conditions of parole.
     - **(3)** Investigating, evaluating, and reporting probation and parole performance.
3. **Prepare committed offenders for return to the community as useful persons by promoting and sustaining changes in attitude and behavior.** This objective is accomplished by:
   - **(a)** Providing programs in accordance with needs individually determined and reviewed.
     - **(1)** Work programs in the institution and on-parole employment compatible with his aptitudes, training, and consistent with his social and legal situation.
     - **(2)** Resocialization programs; to include both clinical and custodial aspects of the therapeutic community.
     - **(3)** Educational programs; consistent with appraisal of aptitudes, interests, and educational objectives.
     - **(4)** Spiritual programs; to include religious services and guidance.
     - **(5)** Medical service programs; to maintain good health and physical condition through medical and dental care.
     - **(6)** Leisure time programs; encouraging the use of leisure time for self-improvement and wholesome recreation.
   - **(b)** Developing and maintaining the offender's link to the community to the maximum extent compatible with control requirements.

(1) Encouraging legitimate communications with family, friends, and the community.
(2) Fostering contact with prospective employers and other persons concerned with vocational planning.
(3) Assisting in resolving personal problems of parents and dependents of the offender.

4. **Utilize incarcerated offenders' manpower and correctional facilities for the public benefit.** This objective is accomplished by:
   (a) Providing work for subjects in production of goods and repair of equipment for governmental use.
   (b) Providing subjects for work in:
      (1) Fire fighting.
      (2) Forestry and road maintenance operations.
      (3) Maintenance of beaches and parks and development of outdoor recreational areas.
      (4) Public assistance in civil defense and disaster work.
5. **Find the causes and the means for prevention and treatment of delinquency and criminal behavior and to participate in the development of criminal law.** This objective is accomplished by:
   (a) Conducting basic research in the behavioral sciences related to the causation of delinquency, crime, and the modification of deviant behavior.
   (b) Applying experimental program models designed to modify the behavior of wards, inmates, and parolees.
   (c) Evaluating program effectiveness through accepted research methods.
   (d) Communicating to the Governor, the Legislature, the Courts, and the public in general, analysis of the effects of the administration of criminal justice in the control of crime, and providing leadership towards the making of improvements.[1]

Keeping the needs of the public in mind, as well as the foregoing list of goals and objectives, let us look at the corrections system as it is today and as it should be.

PROBATION

The probation officer is either a federal or a county officer, depending on the jurisdiction of the case in which the defendant is involved. Although we shall briefly discuss federal probation later, this section generally refers to the local county probation officer and his department, an arm of the courts, with principal responsibilities as a correctional agency. The probation officer and his deputies serve at the pleasure of the superior court and function within the general policies and guidelines prescribed by that tribunal.

[1]Law Enforcement Assistance Administration, *Correctional Planning and Resource Guide* (Washington, D.C.: Government Printing Office, 1969) pp. 19–22.

Probation Defined Probation is a conditional imposition of supervised liberty in lieu of imprisonment in jail or some other institution, which continues for a specified period of time of good conduct. Probation may include a short term in confinement in a local jail followed by an extended period of this supervised freedom as a condition of suspension of a sentence to state prison. The objective of probation is to accomplish rehabilitation of the guilty offender through a series of supervised experiences and types of treatment without removing him from the social milieu. The process may be described as a means of protecting the community by contributing to the rehabilitation of an offender through constructive control. From the variety of definitions one may find, three factors seem to be constant: supervised liberty, threat of imprisonment as an alternative, and rehabilitation as an objective.

Probation is imposed by the judge in the same manner as he would impose a sentence of imprisonment in jail or state prison. It is one of the alternatives open to the judge when passing sentence, which he feels is the most appropriate course of action to lead to the eventual rehabilitation of the offender and to (hopefully) prevent him from repeating his criminal behavior. It is at the time the judge is contemplating the sentence that the probation officer or one of his deputies is assigned to the case. The judge orders a presentence investigation.

Presentence Investigation

There are at least four functions of the presentence investigation: (1) Compile all available data about the crime and the circumstances surrounding it, including any contributing or mitigating circumstances that might provide insight into the reasons for the crime; (2) find out as much as possible about the offender, his personal behavior characteristics, his family and work environment, and such other personal insights about the individual that will serve the judge in making his determination as to the most effective sentence to impose for the protection of the community and rehabilitation of the offender; (3) articulate the alternatives available to the court in the imposition of sentence; and (4) recommend to the court the alternative that the probation officer believes to be the better choice.

Uses of the presentence report, according to a Pennsylvania training manual, include:

1. A base of information to assist the court in determining the most appropriate disposition of the case.
2. Basis for case planning by the probation officer.
3. Source of information to institution when classifying offenders.
4. Resource for parole planning and supervision.

5. A base of information for referrals to noncorrectional human service agencies.
6. Source of information for correctional research.[2]

The probation officer provides a very critical service in the sentencing as well as the rehabilitative process when he conducts his investigation and presents his report to the court. The information he gathers, his interpretation, and his reporting of that information strongly influence the court in making the sentence determination.

The Sentence

Although prescribed maximum and minimum sentences are established by law and have considerable influence on the decisions made by judges, those judges do have wide discretionary powers in the sentencing process. They exercise the greatest power prior to a finding of guilty by making determinations as to exactly what charges are sustained by the evidence, and what charges will be tried, based upon decisions made at their own initiative and as a result of plea bargaining by counsel for the state and the defense. Misdemeanors are punishable by imprisonment in a county or city jail and/or a fine, or some lesser punishment, which may include straight probation. A felony conviction by a superior court carries a prescribed minimum and maximum sentence of imprisonment in prison, or the death penalty, a fine, or a combination of fine and prison. A federal felony is one which carries a punishment of imprisonment in a federal prison for one year or more.

Once the accused is found guilty, the judge sentences the accused. Under determinate sentencing law, the judge must follow certain guidelines in sentencing according to a formula; under indeterminate sentencing the judge sends the convicted person to prison "for the term prescribed by law." The sentence is then determined by a corrections board. But the judge is the key to the sentencing process, because it is the judge who determines whether sentences on multiple charges will run consecutively or concurrently, and the judge decides or verifies facts which make the circumstances surrounding the crime more or less serious, thereby directing which way the sentence will go. In a case when a judge finds an individual guilty of a felony, but sentences the accused to a straight jail sentence for thirty days with no accompanying probation or other restrictions, the judge has just changed the offender into a misdemeanant. He did not change the crime, but he did change the status of the criminal offender.

Although the stated purpose for imposition of sentence may be for the protection of the community and rehabilitation of the guilty offender, tra-

[2]Center for Law Enforcement and Corrections, *Probation, Parole, and Pardons: A Basic Course,* Training Module 6913 (University Park, Pa.: Pennsylvania State University, 1969), p. 14.

ditional demands on the courts have been that the sentence must also serve to isolate the criminal from the society he offended, and that there must be some revenge on the part of society for certain types of crimes. The offender must be required to "pay his debt" to society. The judge is responsive to the needs and demands of the community he serves, as well as to the justice system. In the final analysis, the decision the judge makes involves an intricate series of decisions that take into account the nature of the offense, the temper of the community, his own moral feelings about the offense, the legal constraints within which he must operate, internal and external pressures that are working on him at the time, the capacity to which the local jail and nearby prison may be extended, his own attitudes about the effectiveness of the alternatives to imprisonment, and the probation officer's presentence investigation report.

The Probation Process

The judge has weighed all of the factors presented to him following the findings of guilt, and he sentences the offender to probation. Although someone may argue about the semantics and state that probation is not a sentence, the threat of incarceration for all or part of a specified period of time stands throughout the duration of the probation. The similarity to a sentence ends at that point, and the probationary period has no resemblance to a similar period of time spent in custody in an institution. The conditions of probation are imposed by the judge, and the probation officer is required to enforce those conditions and to report infractions to the court. Terms of probation generally include the following restrictions and requirements:

1. Strict observance of all laws.
2. Developing and keeping good habits.
3. Maintaining a good work or school record.
4. Associating only with persons approved by the court and the probation officer.
5. Getting married or divorced or making other change in living arrangements with the approval of the probation officer prior to making the change.
6. Attending prescribed counseling or treatment sessions.
7. Abiding by all of the restrictions imposed by the judge who granted probation.
8. Reporting periodically as agreed with the court and the probation officer.

The terms may vary with the individual, and the variations should—ideally—correspond with the recommendations contained in the presentence report. Limitations do exist—realistically—because of the number of individuals who must be supervised by each probation officer. Part of the rehabilitative process involves the building of self-reliance and social responsibility, which includes living by established rules. Upon the successful completion of probation, the probation is automatically ended. A violation of probation must be brought to the attention of the court, and the discretion is again in the hands of the judge. He may order continuation of the probation; he may add restrictions; or he may revoke the probation and order the violator to go to jail or prison for the crime leading to his original conviction on the basis of his inability to perform his probation as required.

Except for recent breaks in the trend at the time of preparation of this manuscript, and at other times in history, this nation has seen continuous increases in the numbers of reported crimes in the Index offenses, as pointed out earlier in this text, and there has been a corresponding upward trend in arrest statistics. At the same time, however, another trend appears to be moving along. Populations, and average daily attendance at the many correctional institutions is showing a decrease. This is the result of many recommendations, and subsequent action on those recommendations for exploration in the use of alternatives to imprisonment for rehabilitative efforts. A 1972 California report to the attorney general stated:

> The trend is, simply stated, one of reducing the number of criminal offenders who are taken into close confinement and reducing the length of time served by those who are held in custody. The orientation of the decision makers toward this trend, and the various available programs, work together to produce a single result, to wit, a steady reduction in institutionalization and a comparable increase in community-based handling of offenders. The trend is nationwide and is clearly manifested throughout the California Department of Corrections, the California Adult Authority, the probation departments of the various California counties, and the court system.[3]

The President's Crime Commission made the following statement about community-based corrections, which includes probation as the principal process of this concept:

> With two-thirds of the total corrections caseload under probation or parole supervision today, the central question is no longer whether to handle offenders in the community but how to do so safely and successfully. Clearly, there is a need to incarcerate those criminals who are dangerous until they no longer are a threat to the community. However, for the large bulk of offenders, particularly the youthful, the first or the minor offender, institutional commitments can cause more problems than they solve.
>
> Institutions tend to isolate offenders from society, both physically and psychologically, cutting them off from schools, jobs, families, and other supportive influences and increasing the probability that the label of criminal will be indelibly impressed upon them. The goal of reintegration is likely to be furthered much more readily by working with offenders in the community than by incarceration.

[3]Task Force on Probation and Parole, *Report to Attorney General Evelle J. Younger* (Sacramento, Calif.: State Printing Office, 1972), pp. 4–5.

Additionally, other goals are met. One is economy. In 1965 it cost, on the average, about $3,600 a year to keep a youngster in a training school, while it cost less than one-tenth that amount to keep him on probation. Even allowing for the substantial improvements in salaries and personnel needed to make community programs more effective, they are costly. This is especially true when construction costs, which now run up to $20,000 for each bed in a children's institution, are included. The differential becomes even greater if the costs of welfare for the families of the incarcerated, as well as the loss of taxable income, are included.

Various studies have sought to measure the success of community treatment. One summary analysis of 15 different studies of probation outcomes indicate that from 60 to 90 percent of the probationers studied completed terms without revocation. In another study, undertaken in California, 11,638 adult probationers who were granted probation during 1956 to 1958 were followed up after 7 years. Of this group almost 72 percent completed their probation terms without revocation.

These findings were not obtained under controlled conditions, nor were they supported by data that distinguished among the types of offenders who succeeded or among the types of services that were rendered. But they are the product of a variety of probation services administered at different times and places and provide some evidence that well-planned and administered community programs can be successful in reducing recidivism. These findings, combined with the data from the national survey of corrections showing that probation and parole services are characteristically poorly staffed and often poorly administered, suggest that improvement in the quality of community treatment should be a major goal.[4]

Standard 1.2 of the American Bar Association Probation Standards stresses the desirability of a sentence of probation in these words:

Probation is a desirable disposition in appropriate cases because:

(i) it maximizes the liberty of the individual while at the same time vindicating the authority of the law and effectively protecting the public from further violation of law;

(ii) it affirmatively promotes the rehabilitation of the offender by continuing normal community contacts;

(iii) it avoids the negative and frequently stultifying effects of confinement which often severely and unnecessarily complicate the reintegration of the offender into the community;

(iv) it greatly reduces the financial costs to the public treasury of an effective correctional system;

(v) it minimizes the impact of the conviction upon innocent dependents of the offender.[5]

[4]President's Commission on Law Enforcement and the Administration of Justice, *Challenge of Crime in a Free Society* (Washington, D.C.: Government Printing Office, 1967), Chapter 6, "Corrections."

[5]Samuel Dash, "Challenge: Sentencing, Correction, Rehabilitation," from *Addresses and Papers of the National Conference on the Judiciary, Williamsburg, Virginia, March 11-14, 1971* (Washington, D.C.: Government Printing Office, 1971), p. 214.

Probation Subsidy

In 1963, the California legislature financed the State Board of Corrections in a study of probation services. As a result of that study, the State of California has been involved in a probation subsidy program since 1966. The basis for the program is the assumption that the most effective of professional services should be offered at the local level by community-based correctional services. In addition, it was felt that: (1) Crime and delinquency are products of the community and, therefore, resolution of the problems must be in the community; (2) local treatment has an advantage because the offender remains close to his family and social ties that bind him to conformity; and (3) local treatment is less expensive because it permits the offender to maintain financial self-sufficiency for himself and his family.[6]

The subsidy program costs one-sixth the expense of institutional treatment at the state level, according to Gerald Buck and Don Hallstrom. The state pays participating county probation departments a standard fee for each juvenile or adult who is retained at the local level instead of being committed to state institutions. A prerequisite for granting of funds is that the agency must be using techniques other than routine supervision, which may include the following: (1) employment of only the highest quality personnel, (2) reduction of the supervisor-caseworker ratio, (3) reduction of the caseload to fifty maximum, (4) diagnostic classification of cases and application of differential treatment based on individual needs, (5) more clerical assistance to free professionals from nonprofessional responsibilities, and (6) improved support services, such as training, research, psychological services, and volunteer services.

The Probation Department

The basic objectives of the probation department are to protect the community, to rehabilitate the offender and to protect children. With those objectives in mind, simplified as they are, the probation organization is structured in many ways quite similar to other bureaucratic organizational structures, which is unavoidable in government. The probation department is usually a county agency with its chief probation officer at about the same executive level as a police chief, sheriff, or other department head. The chief is selected by the presiding judge of the superior court, and serves in that capacity at the pleasure of the court. Usually all of the deputy probation officers are selected—and retain tenure—through civil service procedures.

[6]Information concerning the subsidy program and community-based treatment was compiled by two colleagues, Don Hallstrom and Gerald Buck, of the Orange County Probation Department, who are my coauthors on *Criminal Justice Organization and Management* (Santa Monica, Calif.: Goodyear Publishing Company, Pacific Palisades, California, 1974).

The small department will consist of one probation officer and possibly an assistant or deputy or two, all involved in field services, the primary task of the probation officer, which consists of presentence investigations and supervision of adult and juvenile probationers. The very large department will usually be divided into at least four basic units: (1) field services, (2) institutional services, including management of juvenile hall, camps, and other institutions, (3) administrative services, which handle the business and housekeeping affairs of the department, and (4) medical services, including medical, psychiatric, psychological, and dental services that the department provides.

The probation department operates in two fundamental ways: investigative and supervisorial. Within the framework of the agency, there are essentially two separate subsystems: criminal justice for adults and juvenile justice for youths who have not yet reached the age at which they are no longer considered juvenile. Investigative services are principally carried out for the court in the form of presentence investigations. Other investigations include placement of children in foster homes, financial ability of parents to pay for custodial services of children in juvenile institutions, and investigations related to casework. Supervisorial work involves field casework and operation of the various juvenile institutions. The structure of an agency usually shows two basic subdivisions of operational units within the probation department, adult and juvenile, along with another division involving the support services related to the actual operation of the probationary system.

Adult probation processes involve the presentence investigation, management of the county's parole program for conditional release from jail, counseling services for probationers, casework management of the many individuals who are on probation, and operation of many community-based rehabilitation programs that provide alternatives to imprisonment. Special educational and training programs are sometimes operated in cooperation with local colleges and occupational training schools to enhance the probationer's chances for greater employability and successful completion of probation. Use of probationers as volunteers in working with other probationers is a form of catharsis that is effective with some individuals. Referral of cases to other agencies and organizations also consumes a considerable amount of time and effort on the part of the probation department. Such referrals include cases involving alcoholics, drug-abusers, physically and socially handicapped, so-called "unemployable," medical and psychiatric services.

A form of probation that has met with varying degrees of success is the work furlough from jail, which requires the out-of-jail supervision of probation caseworkers when necessary. The probationer serves his time in jail, and at the same time goes out for specified hours during the day when he works on a regular job—which may be the same job he worked at before being sentenced to jail—and at regular wages. Sometimes the job is one found for the probationer by a probation officer, whose responsibility it is to monitor that individual while on the job to assure his presence on the job and his return to jail at the end of each working day. The cost to the county is less because the individual is able to continue supporting his family's needs while he serves out his sentence, which means that his family is not supported by welfare agencies during that time, and he is also employed upon his release from jail. This program may be just the moral boost the probationer needs on release from jail: a job and a source of income that he may not have had prior to his arrest and conviction, and an improved self-image.

Probation officers have told me that one of their greatest categories of probationers are "nonsupporting" fathers and husbands—men who have been placed on probation for nonpayment of support payments for spouses and/or children. One of the reasons why they have been placed on probation is because of their unemployability, or long histories of not working. The probation officers work very diligently at trying to find jobs for these men, and to help them keep the jobs they get. A very time-consuming task, they say, but essential if the welfare rolls are to be kept down.

Juvenile Probation Probation services for the juvenile involve a wide range of services. The casework responsibilities for the juvenile probationer are similar to those for the adult, with obvious differences because of the ages of the probationers. Other services in the juvenile category include investigations that involve dependency proceedings, matters that involve juveniles who are in danger of becoming delinquent, and investigations of juveniles who have been brought to the attention of the probation department because they violated a local, state, or federal law. Other services of the juvenile probation section are supervision and institutional services. Supervision of the dependent and the delinquent child involve different approaches because the dependent child has been the victim of criminal or negligent conduct on the part of his parents or some other person, and the delinquent child has been charged with some act that calls for behavior modification. The institutional services involve operation of the camps, training schools, and other institutions that provide custody of the dependent and delinquent children.

Investigations of juveniles are conducted for the assistance of the court in making a determination of the better course of action for the welfare of the child. In dependency matters, the court is concerned with placement of the child in the environment most appropriate for his needs to live a normal healthy childhood. The near-delinquent must have similar placement, perhaps, but his needs may be met adequately by keeping him in his own home and at the same time prescribing a program for him that might deter him from continuing in the direction toward delinquent behavior.

The Juvenile Detention Process

The juvenile is usually handled almost exclusively by the probation department once he or she has been detained by the police and taken or referred to probation. Let's track the juvenile offender through the process in the same way we did in the last chapter with the misdemeanor and felony violator.

The Offense Many juvenile acts of antisocial behavior, if committed by an adult, would be criminal violations. When a juvenile is the culprit, the child is dealt with informally at home, in school, the youth club, or other institutions or organizations that serve as operations bases for the child. An act of juvenile delinquency is sometimes defined as an act that would be classified as a crime if committed by an adult. Truancy, running away, and incorrigibility are not crimes, yet they are delinquent acts. Actually, as you can see, delinquent conduct extends beyond adult crime equivalents. Once the child commits a delinquent act, the process begins.

Prepolice Discretion The parents, teachers, minister, or friends and relatives may decide to handle the problem themselves, and the police are not involved, unless the police are the ones who observe the conduct and make separate decisions.

Police Intervention The philosophy of juvenile court laws is usually to make every effort to help the parents live up to their obligations and discipline their own children positively or negatively, depending on the circumstances. The police have five options: (1) do nothing; (2) counsel and release the child with no further action—no reports and no notification of parents; (3) counsel and release to parents, then make appropriate reports and consider the case closed with no further action recommended; (4) counsel and release to parents, with a follow-up report and recommendations for further action, including notification of the probation department by sending them copies of related reports accompanied by an application for petition—a document asking that the probation department petition the juvenile to court; (5) detain the child, notify parents, then take the child to juvenile hall intake for probation department disposition, accompanied by copies of reports and an application for petition. The police choose from the first three options more than half of the time, according to so many estimates and studies that it seems almost traditional. When the police decide to detain, the intake process at juvenile hall begins, which is similar to the jail booking process for the adult.

Intake A probation officer greets the child at the hall and receives a copy of the officer's report and application for petition. From that point on, the process involves the probation department and the juvenile court.

Since the philosophy of juvenile justice is to reunite parents and children as quickly as possible for family-unit and disciplinary considerations, the child will usually be released to parents after completion of the intake interview, even though the intake officer decides that the juvenile should appear later for a predetention and/or court hearing. The intake officer may hold the child in custody if there is an imminent danger to life and/or property, if the juvenile has violated conditions of probation, if there is likelihood that the child will flee, or if the officer determines that the child's own safety is in jeopardy if released.

The intake interview usually begins the investigation of the delinquent child. In many cases, the interview reveals enough information to the probation officer so that he may consider the matter in view of the report of the arresting officer, and make some sort of disposition on the case without carrying it further. The youth is counseled and released to his parents. Whether the information comes to the probation officer through the intake process, or from reports forwarded to the department for what the referring agent (usually a police officer, but it may come from a school or parents, or other agencies) believes to be the cause for action by the juvenile court.

The Juvenile Delinquency and Youth Crime Task Force Report describes the intake process:

> (intake is)...essentially a screening process to determine whether the court should take action and, if so, what action or whether the matter should be referred elsewhere. Intake is set apart from the screening process used in adult criminal courts by the pervasive attempt to individualize each case and the nature of the personnel administering the discretionary process. In adult criminal proceedings at the post-arrest stage, decisions to screen out are entrusted to the grand jury, the judge, or usually to the prosecutor.... At intake in the juvenile courts, screening is an important objective.[7]

The investigator must collect and document all of the available information concerning the juvenile's misconduct, the attitudes and background information on the child and his family, environmental influences, and the various other factors that have a direct and indirect effect upon the juvenile and his conduct. He must then make a decision as to what further action to recommend. The probation officer who investigates the case determines whether to proceed with formal court action or to take no further action. The officer's report contains recommendations for the judge, based upon the information he has accumulated and his assessment of the juvenile's likelihood for rehabilitation. The court relies heavily on the investigation and recommendations of the probation officer, and quite often takes what-

[7]President's Commission on Law Enforcement and the Administration of Justice, *Task Force Report: Juvenile Delinquency and Youth Crime* (Washington, D.C.: Government Printing Office, 1967), p. 5.

ever action the officer recommends. The importance of the intake process in the juvenile justice process is underlined by the Task Force:

> At the intake phase a great deal of juvenile misbehavior can be handled through alternatives other than adjudication. Community agencies and organizations such as social work agencies, Big Brother, employment facilities, school programs, and other viable resources can help the child rectify his problem and alleviate his negative situation. One of the primary considerations at intake should be the effect that labeling and the formal adjudication process will have on the youngster. Even though juvenile records are not public records, it would be naive to assume that there would not be a contaminating effect as a result of formal adjudication. Hence, the reason for attempting to make a referral other than formal adjudication in court.[8]

Prosecution Intervention In cases which involve the use of defense attorneys, or which might involve more than an informal court hearing, the county prosecuting attorney will be involved in the process to some extent. Since the Gault decision in 1967, particularly, the juvenile is assured of the same constitutional rights as the adult. In *Gault* v. *Arizona,* 387 U.S. 1, the Supreme Court ruled that a juvenile has a right to be informed of the specific charge against him, a right to counsel, a privilege not to incriminate himself, and a right to due process including cross-examination and confrontation of the witness. The prosecutor and defense attorneys will discuss merits of a case, discovery rules allow the juvenile and his attorney to know all the details of the case against him, and there is greater likelihood of plea bargaining. The prosecutor may advise the juvenile probation officer that there is no case, that the case should be changed to an alternative or lesser charge, or that a particular approach should be used to aid in prosecution strategy.

Detention Hearing If the probation officer at intake has made a decision to take the case further depending on advice and counsel of the prosecutor, the next step will be the detention hearing, which is similar to a preliminary hearing or an arraignment, depending on the jurisdiction. At that hearing, the decision of whether to call for a court hearing is made.

Court Hearing The purpose of this hearing is to determine the culpability of the accused juvenile by examining testimony and evidence. Although it may be somewhat more informal, the court hearing resembles a criminal trial. The judge or referee decides the fate of the juvenile, which may be one of the following: (1) release with a finding of no culpability (not guilty), (2) release to parents with no further action, (3) placed at home but under probation supervision, (4) detained in one of the juvenile institutions locally, (5) placed in a foster home, (6) remanded to a state correctional institution.

[8]President's Commission, *Task Force Report: Juvenile Delinquency and Youth Crime,* p. 5.

If the court finds the juvenile responsible for his or her delinquent acts, the child is usually declared a ward of the court and under its supervision for a prescribed length of time.

Supervision Supervision involves the process described earlier: supervised liberty for a specified period of time and with a list of conditions under which the probationer must perform. The caseworker meets and confers with the probationer in the office, in his home, and at various other places as often as practicable. He counsels the juvenile on family and personal problems, often extending his counseling to the family on matters relating to the juvenile and his problems. The officer attempts to identify referral needs and makes every effort to make those referrals to psychologists, employers, schools, youth organizations, and many other resources available to work toward the greatest degree of success with the child's rehabilitation. He also takes appropriate action on infractions of the conditions of probation, and he remands the violator back to the court for a new determination to be made as to how best to treat the child.

Institutional facilities operated by the probation department are basically of two types: (1) housing for dependent children, and (2) detention of juveniles for the treatment of delinquency. The children who are dependent upon the county because of abandonment or abuse, or for some other reason determined by the court, are returned to the custody of their parents or other responsible family adults as soon as possible, or they are placed in foster homes. Custodial, or detention, facilities include institutions most commonly known as juvenile halls, which are for the temporary detention of juveniles awaiting court appearance or placement in another institution, or placement in a foster home or the longer-term institutions, such as camps, ranches, and schools.

The temporary detention facilities provide housing on a more temporary and short-term basis. Consequently, the education and training they provide for the children are on a much more transient basis. In the other treatment institutions there is provision for educational progress, occupational training, various types of recreation and leisure-time activities, and after-care supervision to follow up whatever programs have been started while the juvenile is in the institution.

Federal Probation

The Federal Probation Service, through the Administrative Office of the U.S. Courts, provides probation and parole services for the ninety district courts in the fifty states, the District of Columbia, and Puerto Rico. The federal probation officer serves at the pleasure of the district court in essentially the same capacity as his counterpart who works as a deputy probation officer for the county. He engages in investigations and casework with individuals who have been adjudged guilty of federal offenses and who are placed on probation or parole.[9]

CORRECTIONAL INSTITUTIONS

Throughout the United States there is a vast network of jails, prisons, camps, farms, halfway houses, and private institutions. More than 1.3 million individuals are housed in thousands of institutions every day of the year, according to the Federal Bureau of Prisons.[10] Those prisoners are housed in federal, state, and local institutions, most of them in city and county jails. How many individuals are housed in each institution and the list of those places may be found in a several hundred page volume published by the U.S. Department of Justice.[11]

Figure 9-1 Group Counseling. California Rehabilitation Center at Corona.

Courtesy California State Department of Corrections.

[9]Richard G. Kleindienst, *Attorney General's First Annual Report, Federal Law Enforcement and Criminal Justice Assistance Activities* (Washington, D.C.: Government Printing Office, 1972), pp. 443–44.

[10]President's Commission, *Challenge of Crime in a Free Society,* p. 159.

[11]National Criminal Justice Information and Statistics Service, *Local Jails: A Report Presenting Data for Individual County and City Jails from the 1970 National Jail Census* (Washington, D.C.: Government Printing Office, 1973).

Local Jails

The local jails are maintained by the city police and county sheriffs across the nation, usually housing a handful to a few dozen inmates, many of them awaiting hearings and trials. Until found guilty in court, or by virtues of a plea of guilty, most of these "inmates in the waiting status" are still considered by law to be innocent until they are proven guilty. Their presumption of guilt by the arresting officers and the prosecutors causes them to be housed in the jail, but how to maintain their custody under maximum security conditions is a dilemma. Custody and transportation, and related matters concerning the feeding and control of these persons is the chief concern, while rehabilitative efforts are directed toward those who have been determined by the courts as guilty of some criminal conduct.

Short-term imprisonment with little or no attempt to rehabilitate the inmates describes the average jail. The prisoner who is serving a sentence of a few days may be assigned simple tasks that might attempt at keeping the individual busy to make the situation more tolerable for everyone concerned. For those whose sentences are somewhat longer, perhaps up to one year, there are work assignments both inside and outside the institution that they may take part in. In addition to keeping busy, the inmates may earn "good time" off their sentences for their conformance to the rules and participation in jail programs.

Efforts at rehabilitation in the county and city jail are necessarily short-term programs because of the nature of jail sentences, which are usually for terms of a few days to a few weeks. Any treatment programs must be brief and intensive in nature, and they must show some results in that short time, however slight those successes may be. The National Sheriff's Association *Manual on Jail Administration* discusses the short-term treatment program:

> Most jail personnel recognize the fact that the great majority of persons committed to their custody have some problems of a personal, social, and/or medical nature, that such problems vary according to the individual, and that the community and jail personnel should be doing far more to help resolve the problems of prisoners, if the real and sensible objective of the jail is to be accomplished. That objective is properly to confine, supervise, and help solve the problems that prisoners have so that they are less likely to come into further conflict with the law after release. If these functions of custody and treatment are effectively performed, future crimes by current prisoners will be reduced. Thus, the community will be a better and safer place in which to live for the prisoner and the citizens in the community.[12]

The treatment programs must help the jail inmates solve personal and

[12]National Sheriff's Association, *Manual on Jail Administration* (Washington, D.C.: National Sheriff's Association, Inc., 1970), p. 190.

social problems, and must address the problem of both the sentenced prisoners as well as those who are in custody while going through the various phases of the judicial process, still innocent in the eyes of the law but confronted by serious legal problems. The treatment activities are as varied as they are intense, and they must meet the needs of "the different types of inmates such as the pretrial, the first offender, the juvenile or youthful offender, the alcoholic or drug addict, the mentally or physically ill, and others."[13] Treatment programs include the obvious ones of medical and psychological, dental, and physical conditioning. Other treatment programs in the jail include counseling and guidance on a one-to-one relationship, therapy in groups or individual sessions for problem solving or behavior modification, educational programs to enable the inmate to experience genuine success in some significant way, religious participation, and an organized system of recreational activities. Occupational programs may be added to the list for the longer-term prisoners, although facilities and equipment are limited so that only a few basic occupational skills may be covered by an institution.

Housing and movement of the prisoners in jail are most challenging because of the transient nature of the institution. Booking and temporary housing until bail is raised for an early release, or placing in cells for overnight or a day or two while awaiting arraignment or trial involves classification and housing according to alleged charges, physical condition, criminal history, and age, not to mention special problems such as persons arrested for child molestation, drugs and intoxication, disorderly conduct, and the entire spectrum of criminal conduct that may involve special security problems. Once the individuals are placed, a continuous process throughout the day and almost without interruption, they must be processed through very thorough inspections and other procedures for security and health requirements. They are outfitted with jail clothes but must make frequent changes into street clothes for court appearances. Just the process of scheduling and moving the prisoners out of the jail into the maze of courtrooms according to some semblance of an organized pattern would challenge the mettle of a choreographer.

Visiting rights of attorneys and members of the family, inspection of visitors, arranging for privacy *and* security during visits, controlling the movement of people and prevention of smuggling contraband, providing supplies and equipment, such as paper, reference books, and a typewriter, for the inmate who chooses to handle his own defense, and special problems with the newsworthy prisoner are all individual problems that must be handled on a continuous basis in such a manner that it all occurs without incident and at a low visibility level. For the prisoner who is eventually sentenced to prison, the jailors transport them to the state prison or reformatory.

[13]National Sheriff's Association, *Manual on Jail Administration,* p. 190.

Juvenile Institutions

The two basic juvenile institutions are the home or house for dependent children, and the juvenile hall. Although their orientation is different, because the former involves children who are the victims of their circumstances, and the "hall" is for those who caused the circumstances leading to their detention, housing, control, movement, feeding, recreation, and most of the daily housekeeping activities are similar. These two facilities are for stays of short duration, where the children stay while waiting for placement in foster homes or return to their own homes, or—in the case of delinquent children—while their cases are studied and the court determines the most appropriate disposition for them. The delinquent children also may be placed in foster homes or returned to their parents or guardians although adjudged wards of the court, which means that they are remanded to the supervision of the probation department for behavior modification or other forms of treatment and rehabilitation.

For longer periods of custody, juveniles who have been remanded to the probation department or the state's Youth Authority (or similar agency), are placed in training schools, ranches, camps, or similar institutions. Although each type of institution is unique, their similarities are that they serve as the housing establishments for children under various degrees of supervision while efforts are made to develop in them a life style that will be carried on following their return to their own homes. Their schedules include educational programs, organized and individual recreation, work activities that may include organized occupational training programs, moral and spiritual counseling and guidance, and different types of treatment geared to their individual needs. Significantly important in the behavior modification process of delinquent children are the correctional personnel assigned to those institutions who serve as models for the children. Through their guidance and direction, the children are able to develop in a positive manner and live delinquency-free lives following their release from the institutions.

Community-based Treatment

Adults and juveniles who have been inducted into the criminal justice system may be directly introduced to processes in the system generally referred to as "community based," such as private counseling services or supervision by a probation officer, Alcoholics Anonymous, a youth organization, Big Brothers, day camps, or community centers for recreation and counseling services, training schools, educational programs, or places of residence where peer pressures serve to reinforce the legally and socially acceptable types of conduct. Others may be introduced to the community-based phase following a period of incarceration in an adult or youth institution. Such community treatment programs may include intensive sessions in transactional analysis or gestalt theory, behavior modification, or other forms of individual or group therapy. Methadone maintenance programs for drug users may be operating for the purpose of providing a legal source of drugs that substitute for heroin and other hard narcotics with an objective of gradually reducing the use of drugs and eventually total abstinence.

Some inmates of jails or penal institutions are allowed to pursue occupations in the community while they are serving their sentences. The work furlough program is a means by which the convicted prisoner may leave the jail or other institution for the time they work at their regular occupations, or at some other job found for them by the probation officer. Any violations may lead to cancellations of their participation in the program.

Variations of the work furlough program may include short-term "leaves," or approved absences from the institutions. Generally granted to the inmate of the institution whose term of custody is nearing an end, this type of a furlough program is designed to provide for the individual an opportunity to get out and look around, to find himself in relationship to other people in a posture of freedom, and to adjust to society gradually rather than to be suddenly evicted at the end of his term and to be totally disoriented to the world around him upon his release. Some persons become institutionalized and their release has such a traumatic effect on them that they willingly commit a new offense so that they might return to the security of prison or jail.

Neighborhood probation offices may serve as community centers for the probationers who live nearby, and such a base may provide for them a greater opportunity for success than having to visit a distant centrally located "concrete palace" in a civic center. For some individuals, a closer and more constant relationship with their probation or parole officers may provide for them the supervision most appropriate to their needs.

Halfway houses, either public or privately owned and operated, provide for the previously incarcerated individual the "institutional" feeling of security or control that has been his way of life for some time and at the same time provide for him opportunities to become socialized and reintegrated back into the community. Ongoing treatment programs continually operate, and the resident participates concurrently with his residency. The idealistic goal is that the individual will become both socialized and rehabilitated at about the same time as he is ready to leave the halfway house and return to his own community in what is hoped to be an improved condition so that he is less likely to repeat his criminal or delinquent behavior that got him into the system in the first place.

Many private organizations, particularly churches, may actively provide services aimed at the delinquent or near-delinquent child, and the feeling of belonging to some type of meaningful relationship with peers, and the comfort in knowing that they are wanted by someone else may provide for some the spiritual and moral strength that they may have lacked previously. Self-help organizations composed of former drug users, or burglars, or check passers, alcoholics, or persons with physical and emotional handicaps operate throughout the country with varying degrees of success in crime prevention. Goodwill Industries, The Salvation Army, rescue missions, and various societies and similar organizations have been quite active for many years.

Prisons and Penitentiaries

The state prison system is operated for the custody, rehabilitation, and other institutional corrections services for felons who serve longer sentences than those who are sentenced to county and city jails. Depending on the nature of the offense for which the person has been sent to the prison, the length of the sentence, the diagnostic evaluations of screening and placement personnel, special physical and/or mental problems, the individual's adaptability to the environment, the history of the offender, and many other factors, placement is made in a maximum, medium, or minimum security type of institution. The offender is introduced to the prison system by the judge when he pronounces sentence. In states that have the length of sentences determined by the court, the determination is made by the judge at the time of sentencing. Other states that have the *indeterminate sentence* provide that the judge sentence the prisoner "for the term prescribed by law."

The prisoner is transported to the diagnostic center, where he is tested for educational and vocational skills and knowledge, and he is studied to determine as much as possible about him so that he may be most effectively placed in the prison system. His offense and his background are studied so that efforts may be directed toward his rehabilitation. Following this evaluation, the inmate is placed in one of several different types of institutions. If the system uses the *indeterminate sentence,* it is at this point that the corrections board fixes the time of the sentence, or at least the time when the inmate may apply for parole. When a person is sentenced for the "term prescribed by law," the code describing the offense and the punishment sets both the minimum and the maximum, such as "not less than two nor more than five years in state prison." The judge has completed his part in the act by putting the process into motion. The corrections board now must study all of the facts and impressions presented to it, interview the inmate, and make a determination as to the most appropriate course of action with each individual.

The board may decide that the inmate must serve two years before he may apply for parole. Once that decision is made, there is little likelihood that he will serve less time, but he may serve more. Toward the end of the two years, the inmate's case is reviewed and the prognosis for his rehabilitation is studied; he is interviewed and questioned about his intentions and plans for parole. The board takes a vote and decides if he will be granted parole, or if he will be required to stay longer before his case will be reviewed again.

The institution in the system to which each person is sent depends on the term that he will serve, whether he has been in prison before, and which of the several programs will be most appropriate for his particular case. There are institutions of the more traditional type, designated as maximum, medium, and minimum security. The degrees of security are determined by the type of structure, security devices and systems, physical layouts of the institution and the escape probability, type of internal and peripheral controls, and the manner in which the inmates are housed and controlled. In the maximum security prison, the inmates are housed in separate or double cells that are locked to keep the prisoners from congregating; the buildings are made of impenetrable masonry or stone; the perimeter is enclosed by a high wall with double fences; and the entire complex is under the constant surveillance of armed guards. Medium security prisons are somewhere between the structure and character of that type of institution and those that are classified as minimum security institutions. The latter house their prisoners in dormitories in condomiunum-type settings, and they may be separated from the rest of the world by low fences, with gates that may not even be kept locked, except to keep out the curious.

Camps, ranches, and honor farms of various types, as well as the half-way houses mentioned earlier in this chapter may serve as minimum security facilities. Educational and occupational training programs are carried on in all of the institutions, as are a variety of treatment programs. The location of the institution, such as a forest area or prairie land, may have been selected so as to provide work assignments for the inmates that are directly related to the area, such as forestry and conservation programs of seeding and planting, or cattle ranching, or farming to produce much of the food consumed in the other institutions.

The President's Crime Commission, in its major report, *Challenge of Crime in a Free Society* described its concept of a model for correctional institutions:

> The Commission believes that there is, therefore, value in setting forth, in the form of a "model," the changes it sees as necessary for most correctional institutions. There will, of course, continue to be special offender problems that must be dealt with in other kinds of institutions. But in general new institutions should be of the sort represented by the model, and old institutions should as far as possible be modified to incorporate its concepts.
>
> The model institution would be relatively small, and would be located as close as possible to the areas from which it draws its inmates, probably in or near a city rather than a remote location. While it might have a few high-security

units for short-term detention under unusual circumstances, difficult and dangerous inmates would be sent to other institutions for longer confinement.

Architecturally, the model institution would resemble as much as possible a normal residential setting. Rooms, for example, would have doors rather than bars. Inmates would eat at small tables in an informal atmosphere. There would be classrooms, recreation facilities, dayrooms, and perhaps a shop and library.

In the main, however, education, vocational training, and other such activities would be carried on in the community-based resources. In this sense, the model would operate much like such programs as the Highfields and Essexfields projects. Its staff, like probation and parole officers, would be active in arranging for participation by offenders in community activities and in guiding and counseling them.

Some offenders might be released after an initial period of detention for diagnosis and intensive treatment. The model institution would permit correctional officials to invoke the short-term detention—overnight or for a few days—as a sanction or discipline, or to head off an offender from prospective trouble. Even if initial screening for classification indicates that long-term incarceration was called for, and an offender was, therefore, confined in another facility, the community-based institution could serve as a halfway house or prerelease center to ease his transition to community life. It could indeed serve as the base for a network of separate group homes and residential centers to be used for some offenders as a final step before complete release.

The prototype proposed here, if followed widely, would help shift the focus of correctional efforts from temporary banishment of offenders to a carefully devised combination of control and treatment. If supported by sufficiently flexible laws and policies, it would permit institutional restraint to be used only for as long as necessary, and in carefully graduated degree rather than as a relatively blind and inflexible process.

A final advantage of the concept suggested here is that institutions that are small, close to metropolitan areas, and highly diversified in their programs provide excellent settings for research and experimentation and can serve as proving grounds for needed innovations. Not only are they accessible to university and other research centers, but their size and freedom from restrictions foster a climate friendly to inquiry and to the implementation of changes suggested by it.

The Commission recommends:

Federal and State Governments should finance the establishment of model, small-unit correctional institutions for flexible, community-oriented treatment.[14]

The Federal Prison System

The federal system represents a comparatively small part of the total institution network, housing 5 percent of all prisoners in the United States.[15]

[14]President's Commission, *Challenge of Crime in a Free Society,* Chapter 6, "Corrections."

[15]Kleindienst, *Attorney General's First Annual Report,* pp. 15–16.

The Federal Bureau of Prisons, under the direction of the Attorney General's office, operates the federal prison system, which houses persons convicted for violations of federal laws. The system consists of all types of institutions from maximum security to halfway houses situated in the heart of metropolitan areas. As a part of the federal corrections system, members of the Federal Bureau of Prisons serve as a part of the Interagency Council on Corrections. The council is jointly chaired by officials of the Bureau of Prisons and the Law Enforcement Assistance Administration, and it coordinates all federal corrections programs, and makes policy recommendations in an effort to bring about improvements in the system. Participants in the council include members of the Civil Service Commission, the Office of Economic Opportunity, the Board of Parole, the Administrative Office of the U.S. Courts, Department of Labor, Housing and Urban Development Department, and the Department of Health, Education, and Welfare.[16]

After a reflective and analytical study of the prison system in the United States in 1972, the Annual Chief Justice Earl Warren Conference on Advocacy in the United States presented their final report: *A Program for Prison Reform.*[17] In that report, the Conference presented twenty recommendations for prison reform:

I

> Criminal sanctions can never be a cure for the ills of society. While at present they are considered necessary, and are regretfully imposed for lack of a constructive alternative, criminal sanctions are essentially negative responses to the failings of human beings, to the failure to correct basic malfunctions and inequalities in society, and to public demands for retribution.

II

> Prisons must be judged by their actual functioning rather than by their stated objectives. Experience has shown that prisons do not rehabilitate offenders. For all practical purposes, prisons are wholly punitive. Given this reality, they accomplish only three limited functions: Protection of society from a relatively small number of dangerous convicted persons for a limited period of time; possibly some deterrence of a limited segment of society at large; retribution for blameworthy acts. Furthermore, recidivism rates indicate that prison "caging" maladjusts prisoners, and thus actually exacerbates the crime problem.

III

> These limitations must be candidly recognized and the employment of imprisonment and other criminal sanctions must accordingly be sharply curtailed.

[16]Kleindienst, *Attorney General's First Annual Report,* p. 7.

[17]*A Program for Prison Reform,* the final report of the Annual Chief Justice Earl Warren Conference on Advocacy in the United States, June 9–10, 1972, sponsored by the Roscoe Pound—American Trial Lawyers Foundation, Cambridge, Massachusetts, pp. 9–16.

Indeed, the release of the majority of the prison population, coupled with the provision of community programs and services, would not increase the danger to the public, and ultimately would enhance public safety.

IV

Imprisonment should be a last resort. The presumption should be against its use. Before any offender is incarcerated, the prosecution should bear the burden of proving in an evidentiary hearing that no acceptable alternative exists. An equal burden should be required for the denial or revocation of "good-time," probation, and parole, which really are only other ways of imposing imprisonment.[18]

V

Nearly half[19] the present potential prison and jail population can and should be placed outside the criminal justice system by decriminalizing behavior which does not involve (a) the threat or use of force against another person or persons, (b) fraud, (c) wanton destruction of property, or (d) violent attacks against the government.

VI

Among the offenses which should be thus reviewed for immediate removal from the criminal law are alcoholism, drug addiction, adult-consenting sexual acts, such as homosexuality and prostitution, and gambling, all of which are usually "complainant-less."[20] It should also be recognized that further social, psychiatric and medical research may place certain forms of behavior now termed "criminal" into discernible, and possibly treatable, disease entities.

VII

The decriminalizing of offenses does not imply approval of such behavior or that society should ignore it. It recognizes that the criminal law and its agencies are inappropriate, often even exacerbating, to such behavior, and that what is required instead is a concurrent enlargement of available community resources in medicine, public health, vocational training, education, welfare and family counselling. It is important, however, that such "therapeutic" programs not be employed either as a guise under which another form of incarceration is im-

[18]Mr. Peter Preiser was of the opinion that the burden upon the Prosecution would be impossible to fulfill. Instead he suggested, "Accordingly, standards and criteria for the use of incarceration should be enacted by Legislatures, and before anyone is incarcerated, there should be an opportunity for a hearing. The same principles should be required for denial or revocation of parole."

[19]As pointed out by Mr. Hans W. Mattick, this estimate is based on an analysis of the FBI's *Uniform Crime Reports.* Professor Caleb Foote, on the other hand, believes a reduction of such size would require the adoption of all the prison-reducing recommendations in this report.

[20]District Attorney William Cahn was opposed to the removal of gambling and, to a lesser extent, prostitution from the criminal law. He regarded gambling, particularly, as a "corruptive influence on society" and a source of people's entering "the stream of criminal activity." He also was opposed to "legalization and decriminalization" in the area of narcotics addiction and drug abuse, both as to possession and the sale of drugs.

posed, or as a condition for the avoidance of imprisonment, both of which are often now the case.

VIII

We should further reduce our excessive reliance on prisons by making extensive use of alternatives to imprisonment, such as fines, restitution, and other probationary methods, which could at least as effectively meet society's need for legal sanctions.[21] However, such alternatives must be made available to all people who have committed similar offenses, so as not to become a means for the more affluent to buy their way out of prison. And, where some kind of confinement seems necessary, half-way houses, community centers, group homes, intermittent sentences, and other methods of keeping offenders within the community should be preferred to prison.

IX

Even where imprisonment is warranted, we should not normally resort to long sentences. Experience has proved that, beyond a certain length, they are self-defeating.[22] Therefore, those present statutory maximum sentences which are grossly disproportionate to any legitimate social purpose should be drastically reduced. Correspondingly, the average length of actual time served, which now exceeds that of other western nations, should likewise be greatly shortened.

X

The indeterminate sentence has not had the salutary effects predicted. Instead it has resulted in the exercise of a wide discretion, without the guidance of standards, and in longer periods of time served in prison. Those who are least able to mobilize social, economic and legal resources into the sentencing process thus become the victims of the harshest and most discriminatory sentences. On occasion, even the nonpoor may be victimized by an idiosyncratic judge with tendentious prejudices about race or life style. There should, therefore, be strict limitations on the judical and quasi-judicial exercise of discretion[23] in the fixing of terms of imprisonment, with firm guidelines based on reasonably definite factors such as past criminal record, maturity, and the mitigated or aggravated nature of the particular criminal act being weighed. By way of contrast, the definite sentence would automatically eliminate administrative parole board procedures which now consist largely of an untrammeled discretion which

[21]Several Conferees were of the opinion that fines and restitution without the threat of imprisonment would not be efficacious.

[22]This conclusion was based on the personal judgment of nearly every Conferee. However, Dr. E. Preston Sharp points out that "there is no clear evidence supporting either the negative or positive impacts of the length of a prisoner's incarceration. The major thrust should be to provide funds to support the long delayed and badly needed research capability."

[23]District Attorney Cahn was of the view that a strict limitation of discretion was insufficient and that "certain violations of the law should carry prison sentences as punishments without alternatives and without discretion." It was his position that such totally-fixed sentences would eliminate more clearly the necessity and the expense of the parole system. He also added that the prosecution should have nothing to do with sentencing.

reduce prisoners to little more than supplicants. The ultimate goal should be no indeterminacy whatsoever in sentences.[24]

XI

The presumption of innocence should pervade our system of criminal justice at all preconviction stages. But our present bail and release-on-recognizance systems do violence to that principle and are discriminatory and arbitrary.

Studies have demonstrated that most often bail is unnecessary and merely an unjustifiable impairment of the right of an accused to be free pending trial. Yet under our present practices half or more of accused persons are detained in jail pending trial.

Some members of the Conference recognized that short and specified pretrial custody may be required for society's protection in a few extreme cases, such as where a person is irrational and dangerous due to severe mental illness or when the state can establish the highly probable imminent occurrence of a specific dangerous crime of personal violence.[25]

But all agree that bail as a prevailing system should go. An end to it would, of course, also serve to further reduce prison and jail populations.

XII

The drastic reduction of our prison population would enable us to employ better our resources in the penal institutions which would remain.

Prison personnel must be adequately trained and compensated, and the racial and ethnic composition of the prison population should be taken into account in the formulation of staff recruitment policies.

XIII

We must take immediate steps to ensure respect for the rights which a democratic society must grant even to prisoners. Though he is suffering a punishment, a prisoner is still a citizen and a human being. Therefore, except to the extent absolutely necessary for custodial purposes, he should not be deprived of any of the individual rights recognized in a free society.[26] These include, but are not limited to, such basic dignities as freedom from racial discrimination, freedom from physical and mental brutality,[27] the right to adequate diet, clothing, and

[24]Mr. Henry J. Mascarello, while agreeing that imprisonment should be a last resort only, thought that it would be better achieved if sentences were indeterminate "leaving it up to a professionally-constituted parole board to decide (later and on the basis of more information) when the 'no other course' ceases to exist."

[25]District Attorney Cahn would also provide for custody (not bail) where the prosecution can "prove" substantial reason to believe defendant will not appear for trial.

[26]In the words of Mr. Robert L. Smith, "emphasis should be made on a justice or economic model which would force the correctional system to come closer to approximating the outside world."

[27]Dr. Irwin M. Greenberg comments, "In particular, solitary confinement should be abolished as a punitive measure. Enforced seclusion should only be utilized for the prevention of physical violence in cases where no medication can reduce the threat of such violence. It should be noted that recent research has indicated that therapeutic agents such as lithium carbonate may be highly useful in aggressive prisoners. In addition, it should be recognized that special sections for such prisoners, even in the absence of solitary confinement, only serve to promote aggressive behavior, and that too, should be abolished."

health care, the right to furlough or institutional accommodations to maintain social and familial ties, including being located as close to home as practicable, freedom from censorship of mail and other literature including law books, the right to participate in local and national elections, and the right to procedural and substantive due process to guarantee such rights.[28] Judicial, administrative, and legislative action to promote and develop these rights is imperative. The presumption should always be strongly in favor of full entitlement to such rights and not against them as is all too prevalent today.

XIV

As a further concomitant for the securing of such rights, prisoners should be permitted to organize, without fear of reprisal, for the purpose of effective expression and negotiation of grievances. Even in the absence of grievances, and as a method of avoiding abuses leading to grievances, there should be regular meetings between duly elected prisoners' representatives and prison authorities.[29]

XV

Under current practices, the initial sentencing, as well as the later parole hearing that determines the ultimate sentence, is usually conducted absent the right of a prisoner to present open proof, to cross-examine witnesses and probation officers, and to exercise the other elements of due process. The right to full due process should accompany the sentencing procedure through all its stages, including the denial of probation, or to any other decisional stage that substantially affects the term of imprisonment. Until such time as the present parole system is eliminated by short definite prison terms, due process should apply to both the initial granting and revocation of parole or good-conduct time. These events are now at least as critical in the sentencing process as is the original judicial decision.

XVI

Since most prisoners are without means to engage counsel for the protection of their rights, it is essential to the implementation of such rights that the availability of properly trained and experienced public defenders or private counsel, with adequate staff support, be assured to all. Such legal services should be available to challenge the conviction, to aid the prisoner with any civil problems, and to represent the prisoner in grievances against the institution.

[28]Interestingly, Mr. D. Lloyd Macdonald would specifically add to a "right to personality," commenting that: "The rapidly expanding medical and technological field of behavior modification through hormonal regulation, brain surgery, electric stimulation of the brain, and aversion therapy will soon allow corrections people to fundamentally change the behavior patterns and personality of persons in their custody. There is some promise in this, but the dangers are of profound dimensions for our social system. Any application of behavior modification techniques should be postponed pending full medical, jurisprudential and philosophical exploration of the implications. In any event, there ought to be an absolute bar against any use of such techniques without the inmate's consent and the concept of consent itself needs new attention and reformulation."

[29]District Attorney Cahn expressed a preference for an ombudsman concept as a means of dealing with grievances, rather than encouraging the organization of prisoners.

XVII

Like most other public institutions, prisons must be open to public scrutiny and not be hidden away beyond easy observation. To assure such high visibility, the press and other media, upon request, should have ready access to our prisons, provided that each prisoner's right to refuse interviews or exposure shall be respected.[30]

XVIII

The fact that rehabilitation is not a legitimate purpose of imprisonment does not imply that "helping" programs should be removed from prisons. The state has a duty to provide economic, social, educational and medical services in prisons, as well as in the communities, but since such services bear no relationship to the legitimate purposes of imprisonment, their acceptance by prisoners should be voluntary. Especially since there is no convincing evidence of the effectiveness of rehabilitative programs in prison, they should have no bearing whatsoever on the length of a prisoner's incarceration.[31]

XIX

Upon completion of their sentences, prisoners should return to full, lawful membership in society. No discrimination should be permitted against former offenders regarding work,[32] education, voting or other civil and human rights. Legislative reform in this regard should be undertaken, and existing agencies engaged in such functions as job placement and training should coordinate their efforts with those of the prison system. Changes should not have to await judicial intervention.

XX

To focus, as we have done in this Conference, on that portion of the criminal justice system which begins with judicial sentencing and terminates with restoration of civil and political rights is not to imply that other areas of our criminal justice system are not also in need of reform. Our entire criminal law should be reviewed periodically and systematically so as to keep it abreast of the contemporary needs of a free society.

PAROLE

The third part of the corrections component of the justice system is that phase in the process that follows imprisonment in the state and federal

[30]District Attorney Cahn would set out guidelines to avoid press "fishing expeditions" not directed toward specific complaints.

[31]A small minority—two—of the conferees were not ready to write off the value of prison rehabilitation programs. One of them believed the acceptance of such programs by prisoners should be mandatory. The other felt that the fault was with the imperfections in "previous rehabilitation programs."

[32]Except on the basis of explicit and narrowly-defined standards directly related to the circumstances of convictions for past offenses. (This qualification stressed by Messrs. Macdonald and Cahn.)

prison systems. There are county jail paroles, which are granted along similar lines with the same objectives, but parole generally involves the men and women who have already spent some time in prison and who are provisionally released for the last part of their prison sentences. During the time of his supervised freedom, the inmate-turned-parolee is still constructively in custody. Although the parolee has most of his constitutionally guaranteed rights throughout the term of his parole, he must perform according to certain standards and he is expected to subscribe to whatever treatment programs are made available to him.

Who is qualified for parole and at what point in time he may apply for consideration is generally the responsibility of the parole board, a body of individuals who have been selected from throughout the state and who have been appointed by the governor to serve for a specified period of time. In states which have a determinate sentencing law, such as California's Determinate Sentencing Act of 1976, the term of parole may be set at the time of sentencing in all but a few types of convictions, such as life sentences.

The board meets at regular intervals and reviews applications for parole. The amount of time demanded of the board's members depends on term-fixing policies, such as the indeterminate sentence when the inmate's term has no exact time when it must come to an end, except for those limitations imposed by the statutory maximum. To what extent the board actually gets involved in the process also dictates the amount of time necessary to carry out their duties. With the background information provided by the professional staff, and recommendations as to the suitability of the applicants for parole, the board makes the actual determinations whether or not to grant parole.

Factors in Determining Whether to Grant Parole

When the parole board reviews the individual cases of the applicants for parole, there are several factors they must take into consideration. Some of the factors are external, which involve the community's attitude and the response of the policeman, prosecutor, judge, and the victims of the crimes. Other factors are social, which involve the individual's ability to cope with the world around him. Still other factors are internal, and they involve the individual's prognosis for success once he is released. Considering many of the factors in a single listing, they include the following:

1. The nature of the offense for which the inmate was convicted.
2. The public sentiment in general, and their particular reaction to the individual being considered for parole.
3. Recommendations of the prosecuting attorney, the judge who issued the sentence, and the law enforcement officers who made the arrest.
4. The environmental factors leading to the individual's criminal involvement.
5. The inmate's personal history, and that of his family.

6. The individual's potential for continuing his education once released.
7. The employability of the inmate in some salable skill.
8. Plans and preparations for living and working arrangements on the outside.
9. Somewhere for the inmate to go where he will get the reinforcement or treatment he needs, such as a halfway house or other community resources that may be available to him.
10. The present attitude of the inmate towards himself and his behavior modification in relationship to the time when he was admitted to the institution.
11. The inmate's present state of mind, conduct, and adjustment as reported by the staff.
12. A counselor's evaluation of the candidate's likelihood to succeed on parole.
13. The individual's conduct during the interview, and his ability to convince the board that he is ready to go out on parole.
14. The decisions of the board whether or not to grant parole.

The board may sit as a total unit, or may break up into smaller groups for the purpose of interviewing candidates for parole, and they pass upon the applications. An advantage of parole, if it could be considered as an advantage, is that the inmate's reintegration into society is accomplished under the guidance and supervision of a parole officer, who is a specialist in behavior modification and who can initiate revocation proceedings if the parolee is not conforming to the conditions of his release. The individual who serves out his full sentence, or who is granted a discharge without parole, has no such supervision. Institutions have various effects upon the individuals, and a supervised transition period may be the far better course of action than a sudden implantation into what has become an alien world.

The basic functions of the parole official can be classified according to three major categories: (1) surveillance, (2) service, and (3) counseling.

Surveillance, as applied in parole, involves actual observation of the parolee under a variety of situations, often without his knowledge. The purpose of surveillance is to determine if the client is performing as he should even out of the presence of his probation officer. Surreptitious surveillance may be conducted to determine that the parolee is no longer in need of close supervision if he demonstrates sufficient internal controls. The process of surveillance may also determine that the parolee is associating with people who are negatively influencing him, and he may be found incapable of adjusting in conformance with the laws and the restrictions of his parole.

Services the parole officer provides include giving assistance in locating a new job or place to live, purchasing an automobile for transportation to work, channeling the parolee into community resource agencies that can help him in his reintegration into the community, and generally showing the parolee the way to solve his own problems. Supervision may be considered as a service, as it is through the parole officer that the parolee is going to demonstrate to the board that he is successfully accomplishing the objectives of his conditional release on parole.

Counseling is accomplished by the agency in a variety of ways, but most often involves the individual and his parole officer in one-to-one counseling situations. Other types of counseling may be attempted for parolee groups in an out-patient environment in which they hold sessions to address a host of problems. The function of the parole officer is to act as a change-agent, one who implements the modification of behavior and causes the parolee to redirect his own goals and values so that he will succeed on parole as an effective and self-respecting member of civilized society.
parole officer is to act as a change-agent, one who implements the modification of behavior and causes the parolee to redirect his own goals and values so that he will succeed on parole as an effective and self-respecting member of civilized society.

Since 1934, all of the states in the country have adopted an Interstate Probation and Parole pact, which provides for the movement of both probationers and parolees to another state to relocate families or to accept employment, or for some other legitimate reason. As a condition of this pact, the individual makes the application to make the move and then there is a transfer to a new probation or parole agency in the receiving state. Interstate agreements make this type of transfer possible. Families are reunited and employment opportunities for the parolee may be heightened. Conditions of such a transfer are that both states must agree to the transfer, and jurisdiction over the parolee is not relinquished in case there is a need to recall the parolee, such as in a case of parole violation.

Federal parole is managed by a federal parole board, and parolees are supervised by the Federal Probation Department, which handles both parolees and probationers for federal-law violators.

Parole Concepts

As a change-agent, similar to the probation officer, the parole officer is a caseworker specializing in behavior modification. The parole officer is responsible for facilitating reintegration of the parolee into society. The parole officer knows the parolee—his client—and the community, and attempts to provide positive reinforcement to the client and practical support in the reintegration process. The parole officer does what he can to change both the client and his environment so that they may adjust to one another.

The parole officer works with the parolee and his family as a unit, and attempts to aid them in readjusting to the family life and social life, utilizing as many resources at his disposal in the community as possible. The parole officer helps the client work out his educational and occupational goals, and helps him or her work toward accomplishment of those goals. The officer helps the client relocate if necessary, and helps the parolee find occupational counseling and assistance, leisure-time resources, family diagnostic services, financial and legal assistance, physical and mental health services, and home-finding. In general, the parole officer serves as a model for the client and shows him ways to experience successes, however slight they may be.

Herman Piven and Abraham Alcabes describe the "social worker" concept of the relationship of the probation-parole officer to his clients:

> The relationship of the social worker to the probationers and parolees on his caseload is a professional one. This means, first of all, that the offender is a "client" and that the focus of the relationship is on his needs, his concerns, and his situation. Secondly, the professional focus is limited to consideration of those factors which bear on the offender's problems and goals and about which the probation/parole officer can exercise his technical skills. Thirdly, the quality of the probation/parole officer's relationship to the offender must be one which accepts the offender as a worthy person and is devoid of the officer's personal judgment.[33]

In other words, say Piven and Alcabes, the "social worker" probation/parole officer's relationship with his client is guided by the following norms: (1) He provides a service; (2) there is a focus on problems that the officer has the skills to attack; and (3) there is an emotional neutrality on the part of the probation/parole officer.[34]

Two other caseworker approaches are discussed by the same authors, Piven and Alcabes, who have done extensive research in corrections. They are the "punitive" and the "protective" officers, whose methods of operation are described as follows:

> The punitive officer's supervision methods reflect his conception of offenders as malingerers and his goal of compelling conformity with ideal standards. The punitive officer's ongoing task is to define for the offender the full range of his social responsibilities.[35]
>
> ...The punitive officer relies upon negative sanctions to obtain conformity. He uses lectures, reprimands, and threats as devices to make the offender aware that the price of nonconformity is too high. (He uses threat of revocation, increased restrictions, and "shock-treatment" short-term jailing to emphasize his points.)[36]
>
> ...The protective agent does not adhere to a systematic theory of human behavior that identifies certain facts as relevant and others as irrelevant in controlling and rehabilitating an offender. Instead, attempting to "get to know" the offenders, he probes and proceeds or withdraws depending upon reactions. Unlike the punitive officer who restricts interviews with offenders to specific issues of conformity with social responsibilities, the protective agent has no

[33]Herman Piven and Abraham Alcabes, *A Study of Practice Theory in Probation/Parole* (Washington, D.C.: U.S. Department of Health, Education, and Welfare, 1971), p. 39.

[34]Piven and Alcabes, *A Study of Practice Theory in Probation/Parole,* p. 39.

[35]Piven and Alcabes, *A Study of Practice Theory in Probation/Parole,* p. 47.

[36]Piven and Alcabes, *A Study of Practice Theory in Probation/Parole,* p. 49.

analogous focus that prevents agent-offender interaction from developing more or less spontaneously.[37]

...In serving offenders, the protective agent sees his job as getting the offender to like him so that the probationer/parolee will accept his advice, and internalize his values. In protecting the community against offenders, his activities are similar to those of the punitive officer. In attempts to "rehabilitate" offenders the agent relies heavily on direct techniques; he finds a job *for* a man, he goes with him to apply for financial assistance, he loans him money out of his own pocket. Direct services are supposed to have two results. First, they value "problems" for the offender which block the offender's attempt to redirect his goals and to strengthen his internal controls. Second, they assist the agent's efforts to make the offender like him.[38]

Concerning the counselor role of the probation/parole officer, the objectives of the officer are to guide and direct the client to eventually develop a strong self-image and self-reliance. If the officer were to continue to make his decisions for him, there would be a reinforcement of the supportive role of the officer. To prolong the role of doing the individual's thinking and performing for him would prolong the term of parole or probation. The goals of probation and parole are to bring about behavior changes that are long-lasting and positive in harmony with social and legal requirements of crime-free behavior. Foremost among the obligations of the change-agent, then, is the task of stimulating the individual to think for himself. To illustrate that task, Piven and Alcabes have this to say:

Within the limits of the law, the right to ultimate choice of action resides with the client. When an offender tells the probation/parole officer that he wishes to marry, buy an automobile, change his place of employment, etc., the officer's obligation is to discuss the plan with the client by examining its probable consequences and alternatives, and with maximum considerations of the offender's views, feelings, capabilities, and goals.

When the offender has already made a choice and taken action, the officer may find it wise to review with him the meaning of the client's decision and help identify options that are still available. Whether a choice is being contemplated or has been made, the officer has an additional obligation: to allow and encourage the client to make the final decision.[39]

SUMMARY

The role of corrections, to paraphrase the word, is to correct certain modes of conduct and behavior in literally millions of individuals over a period of years. This, the third component of the criminal justice system,

[37]Piven and Alcabes, *A Study of Practice Theory in Probation/Parole,* p. 50.

[38]Piven and Alcabes, *A Study of Practice Theory in Probation/Parole,* p. 51.

[39]Piven and Alcabes, *A Study of Practice Theory in Probation/Parole,* p. 56.

addresses the problem of criminal and asocial behavior and attempts to show the individuals involved how to modify their own behavior so that the goals of crime-free behavior on their behalf may be reached. In this chapter we have covered the entire spectrum of correctional programs and different parts of the entire corrections component. There is no doubt that we have missed more than we have covered, but for the purpose of this text, it has been our intention to briefly explain each of the many correctional philosophies, agencies, and the roles that the individuals play in this important part of the administration of justice process.

Probation and parole, while perhaps addressing individuals with different degrees of sophistication in the ways of crime, are quite similar in their goals and objectives and in their methods of operation. The officers who fill these roles operate as behavior modification specialists, or change-agents. Through their own strong self-image they are responsible for providing a model for their clients, and for encouraging and assisting those clients to positively cultivate their own self-images and to undergo positive behavior modifications that redirect them back into the mainstream of social conformity. The approach of the caseworker is community-based, as are many of the other community-based treatment programs, including halfway houses, group counseling, and immersion in community-oriented social programs.

The institutions provide a multipurpose need of society. They serve to isolate certain individuals from the society they offended and committed crimes against, to hold them in some place where they may pay their "debt to society" or receive their punishment for their crimes. The penal institutions also protect society from those individuals who are not safe to society. Beside being responsible for providing the isolation and warehouse facilities, the institutions must also bring about some positive behavior changes, educational and occupational preparation, and some preparation for socialization in the society with which the criminal could not cope prior to his incarceration. There is a need for attitudinal and behavior changes on the part of individuals so that they may be reintegrated back into the society from which they originated.

EXERCISES AND STUDY QUESTIONS

1. What is the basic difference between probation and parole? Similarities?

2. Define a community-based corrections program. Give an example.

3. Describe how a presentence investigation is carried out, and explain its intended purpose.

4. List the different alternative types of sentences available to the court.

5. If you were the judge, what would be the restrictions you would impose on a probationer who had committed the crime of auto theft? Armed robbery?

6. How many different types of institutions are operated for juvenile delinquents?

7. What is the function of "juvenile intake"?

8. What is the average daily population of correctional institutions in the United States?

9. What efforts at rehabilitation are being made at the jail in your jurisdiction?

10. What is an indeterminate sentence, and how is it administered?

11. List and discuss the changes you would recommend to improve our present prison system.

12. What is the determinate sentence, and how is it administered?

13. List at least three conditions that would usually be imposed on a probationer.

14. What are the three basic objectives of the probation department?

15. What type of work is involved in probation field services?

16. Under what conditions may a police officer choose not to refer a juvenile violator to the probation department?

17. What are the advantages of a work-furlough program?

RECOMMENDED SEMESTER/TERM PROJECTS

1. Visit a correctional institution or jail. Interview custodial officers and their supervisors and review any material they provide. Prepare a paper describing the institution, explain the process a prisoner goes through from initial induction to release, describe its rehabilitation programs, if any, and then write your general impressions on the life of an inmate.

2. Visit your local probation or parole agency and interview at least three different officers with similar responsibilities. Based on the information you have about the different philosophies of probation/parole officers, ask them enough questions to determine which type of officers they represent (social, punitive, protective) and write an opinion paper on the strong points on each of the three approaches.

SUGGESTED FOR ADDITIONAL STUDY

ABADINSKY, HOWARD, *Probation and Parole Theory and Practice.* Englewood Cliffs, N.J.: Prentice-Hall, Inc., 1977.

ADAMS, THOMAS F., GERALD BUCK, and DON HALLSTROM, *Criminal Justice Organization and Management.* Santa Monica, Calif.: Goodyear Publishing Co., 1974.

AMERICAN CORRECTIONAL ASSOCIATION, *Correction Officers Training Guide.* Washington, D.C.: American Correctional Association, 1969.

CARNEY, LOUIS P., *Introduction to Correctional Science* (2d ed.). New York: McGraw-Hill Book Co., 1979.

CARNEY, LOUIS P. *Probation and Parole: Legal and Social Dimensions.* New York: McGraw-Hill Book Co., 1977.

DINITZ, SIMON, and WALTER C. RECKLESS, eds., *Critical Issues In the Study of Crime.* New York: Little, Brown, and Co., 1968.

FOX, VERNON, *Introduction to Corrections* (2d ed.). Englewood Cliffs, N.J.: Prentice-Hall, Inc., 1977.

KAY, BARBARA A., and CLYDE B. VEDDER, *Probation and Parole* (2d Ptg.). Springfield, Ill.: Charles C. Thomas, Publisher, 1971.

KILLINGER, GEORGE G., and PAUL F. CROMWELL, JR., eds., *Penology: The Evolution of Corrections In America.* St. Paul: West Publishing Co., 1973.

KILLINGER, GEORGE G., HAZEL KERPER, and PAUL F. CROMWELL, JR., *Probation and Parole in the Criminal Justice System.* St. Paul: West Publishing Co., 1976.

KLEGG, REED K., *Probation and Parole Principles and Practices.* Springfield: Charles C. Thomas, Publisher, 1975.

MORRIS, PAULINE, FARIDA BEVERLY, and JULIE VENNARD, *On License: A Study of Parole.* New York: John Wiley and Sons, 1975.

NEWMAN, CHARLES L., *Personnel Practices in Adult Parole Systems.* Springfield: Charles C. Thomas, Publisher, 1971.

______, *Sourcebook on Probation, Parole, and Pardons* (3d ed.). Springfield: Charles C. Thomas, Publisher, 1970.

SMITH, ALEXANDER, and LOUIS BECLIN, *Introduction to the Probation and Parole.* St. Paul: West Publishing Co., 1976.

WEST, D. J., ed, *The Future of Parole. Commentaries on Systems in Britain and the U.S.A.* London: Gerald Duckworth and Co., Ltd., 1972.

10

Selection, Education, and Training for Criminal Justice

INTRODUCTION

Selection procedures for most criminal justice agencies are similar because of government/civil service standardized procedures. Educational requirements all differ, and so do training programs because of the many different skills required of the various practitioners. In this chapter, we shall review some of the selection procedures that are common to most civil service positions, with additional screening devices because of the sensitive and confidential nature of the work. Then, a brief look at educational and training programs for a few selected positions in the system.

Certain procedures and models outlined in this chapter are based upon California programs. The purpose is obviously because of my own orientation and is in no way intended to represent a superior point of view, It is my hope that the student and professor alike will use the material in this chapter as a base for further study of local programs and procedures. This will make it easier to objectively study the similarities and differences in programs and to eventually adopt those items that "fit" and supplant those that do not fit with programs and techniques that do.

The first section of this chapter will review the typical selection process in step-by-step order.

THE SELECTION PROCESS

The Position Announcement

The position announcement is usually widely disseminated, and it should reflect the following information: position description, general duties and responsibilities, any special talents or proficiencies that are required (type sixty words a minute, fly fixed wing aircraft, operate a motor vehicle, special language requirements) and special qualifications desired (work with the public under trying circumstances, knowledge of competitive sports rules, able to relate well with people of various ethnic cultures) and any unusual requirements, such as night work.

The civil service announcement will list educational minimums, experience requirements, physical requirements (including height, weight, color perception, no disabilities) when specifically related to the job demands, and any other local considerations that may have been mandated, such as local residence or other similar matters. The announcement should also list a brief but concise description of the position and expectations of the individual who fills it. It is wise to read that description carefully and to inqure of the employing agency any additional information about the position. The candidate should be confident that he is qualified for the position and that he knows precisely what the position is.

Certain affirmative action guidelines and timelines or specific needs of the agency to have representation from specific segments of the community may be reflected or announced in the publication announcing the position opening. For example, recent large volumes of immigrants from one specific area of the world with distinctive cultures and languages may be an excellent reason for singling out specific nationality heritage so that the agency will be truly representative of the city or county it serves.

The Application Form

The employing agency may actually use two separate forms: an application, and a personal history statement. The application is usually brief, asking for a sketch of the individual's physical and personal characteristics, work history, and educational background, accompanied by a listing of references and other data that will aid the personnel agency in performing a cursory background preemployment check. The second form goes into much more detail, and it may include a request for certain data and supporting documents beyond the scope of the application form. For example, if the employer is aggressively seeking candidates in compliance with any equal opportunity and/or affirmative action requirements, it will be necessary for the employing agency to determine the racial or ethnic origin of the candidate. The surname, as you know, does not always accurately reflect one's heritage as it may have been changed by marriage, adoption, or court action, or it simply may not give a clue as to ethnic origin.

The applicant should be careful to read every question and to address the question by responding accurately. It is easy to volunteer information that is not requested or to answer a question in such a manner that the explanation may raise doubts as to an individual's qualifications. For example: the question "Have you ever been convicted for any crime other than a minor traffic violation?" may induce a response of "No, but I was picked up for questioning once in a bunch of burglaries but the police couldn't prove anything." Actually what might have happened is that the individual had no involvement in such a crime but was interviewed because he had been observed in the area at about the time the crimes were committed. The response as written could stimulate all sorts of interpretations. Of course, an investigation will be conducted—or should be, but what would you think if you read that response and were to make a value judgment as to whether you would employ the applicant for a position of public trust? Be truthful, but only answer the questions.

From my own experience in the business of conducting background investigations as well as performing certain personnel responsibilities for a criminal justice agency, I have found that many applicants somehow have the feeling that a background check does not extend beyond state lines or back very far into an individual's past. Be assured that those feelings are not based on fact. The person conducting the background investigation develops a biography on the candidate, which spans most of the entire lifetime and has no geographical boundaries. A good background investigator will know the candidate better than the candidate himself when the investigation has been completed.

The Written Examinations Used as a device to screen the number of candidates down to a number that the personnel agency can work with, as well as a determinant of the intellectual capacity and learning capability of the candidate, the written examination usually consists of a battery of tests. Most examinations are objective type, with multiple choice responses for standardization of scoring and rank-ordering the candidates. Usually included is some form of general intelligence test, an adaptability test, and other examinations to test for the specific items listed on the position description. If the job announcement states that a basic knowledge of legal procedure is necessary, the applicant may rest assured that some of the test battery will address itself to a determination of the candidate's knowledge of legal procedure.

Special talents, such as unique memory capabilities, will also most likely be tested. Personality and interest inventories may also be included in the battery because of the agency's desire to seek candidates who are not only qualified to perform the required tasks, but who are likely to stay on the job and to grow within the profession because of strong interests as well as knowledge and adaptability. In short, the test battery should test for those qualities and proficiencies stated on the position announcement.

Recent affirmative-action hiring practices have brought about some dramatic changes in psychological-intelligence testing as a part of the selection process. The test must not be merely used as a device to "whittle down" the number of candidates. First, the tests must be designed to determine knowledge and skills necessary to perform the tasks required. Second, artificial barriers in the test, such as obscure bits of knowledge that sometimes cause grade spreads in testing, must be deleted unless it can be shown that there is a relationship between the test and the job. Failure to conform to acceptable guidelines will lead to lawsuits and/or withdrawal of federal financial support, and, in some cases, criminal prosecutions.

The Oral Interview

The candidates who pass the written portion of the series of screening devices are next scheduled for oral interviews. Although they are expected to be experts in the profession for which the screening is being conducted, the interviewers may or may not be professional interviewers. In many instances, these individuals have never met each other before this day of the interviews. Their own personal philosophies may differ, and there may be a general concept of what type of person they are looking for to fill the position, but each interviewer may base his decisions upon his own background and experiences. The point of this information is that the oral interview is unpredictable and quite subjective, except in cases when the board members have worked as a team before and they have structured the interviews with a consensus of their value systems operating to make an objective evaluation of each candidate and to rank-order the candidates according to some system.

The oral interview is a type of role-casting, not unlike the procedure used to select actors to play a role in a play. The written examination has been used to determine the candidate's knowledge and adaptability. The oral interview is the time when the members of the board may look for a self-image (particularly if they are confident that their own attributes are the key to successful performance on the job), and to make some value judgment as to whether the candidate would be believable in the role for which he applied. For example, the candidate should "look the role," mannerisms and speech should have certain characteristics that will immediately impress the public that the candidate has the ability to perform the job with authority, and the candidate's responses to the interviewer's questions must indicate that his/her personal philosophy is in harmony with the philosophical viewpoints of the members of the interview board. This may not be stated in the job specifications, but you may rest assured that most interviews are subjective in their appraisals of individual personality traits.

The oral interview usually lasts from thirty to forty-five minutes, but the first one or two of those minutes may be the most critical. From that point on, the members of the board may ask questions and seek responses that confirm their initial impressions about the candidate. According to scientific standards, this may not be a valid method of testing. The point is that—valid or not—the method is relied upon quite heavily and the candidate should be prepared to perform as well as possible, knowing that he is being judged as a whole person from a subjective standpoint. The public does it every day in every single contact the officer makes. Initial impressions are important indeed!

Keeping in mind the subjective nature of the oral interview, the candidate should bear in mind that there are essentially two basic features of the test: (1) the initial impression the interviewee makes upon the interviewer, and (2) the candidate's ability to handle himself well in oral exchange with three or four expert interviewers. There are basically three types of interviews: unstructured, nondirected, and structured. The unstructured interview is usually under the control of the interviewers, but there has been no advance planning and it varies from interview to interview. The nondirected interview is actually dominated and controlled by the candidate, who is allowed to take the conversation wherever he wishes for it to go. The structured interview is directed and controlled by the interviewers as a team. They ask a series of specific questions of all of the candidates and evaluate the responses and the conduct of the candidates according to some sort of agreed-upon criteria. By using this method, it is possible to compare the candidates and to rank-order them according to the criteria established by the interview board in advance.

The interview board usually looks for the following qualities in candidates from their own subjective points of view during the brief interview: judgment, leadership potential, motivation, ability to communicate effectively, analytical ability, initiative, and overall personality. Some interview boards are required to use rating forms with points assigned to each quality, or an overall percentage point system, and points are assigned by the interviewers to each of the items listed above, plus overall appearance, experience in this or a related field of work, speech, education, physical and emotional fitness.

Although they do not necessarily appear in the following order, questions in an oral interview for almost any position in any profession, including the many agencies of the justice system, will probably include the following:

- In a short paragraph or two, tell the board who you are.
- Why do you believe you are qualified for the position, and (sometimes) why are you better qualified to fill the position than those who are competing with you?
- What do you plan to be doing five or ten years from now?
- What is your ultimate goal in life? What are your intermediate goals, if any?
- Why did you choose this particular occupation-profession?
- Why did you apply to work at this particular agency?
- Have you applied other places? If so, if you were called at the same time to go to work at this place and another, which offer would you accept?
- What do you know about this specific position for which you are applying?
- Have you inquired about this agency and what do you know about it?
- Why do you want this particular position? Why this occupation as a choice?
- Do you believe that you are qualified for this position? Why?
- What are your strongest assets in relation to this position?

- What are your weaknesses or how might you not perform well in one or more areas of the position?
- What have you done to prepare for this position? What have you done, or will you do to compensate for those weaknesses?
- What characteristics are most essential to this position?
- How do you believe you compare with those requirements?
- What is your ultimate goal in life—professionally or otherwise?
- What would you change about this position if you had the authority to implement change?
- How do you perceive yourself in the role for which you are applying in relationship to the roles of the other agencies in the system?

There are various hypothetical situations that may be contrived by the interview board to test for the individual's ability to make value judgment decisions. It would be wise for the candidate to project himself into the position for which he is applying, then to spend some time listing some of the problems or other situations that may arise. Once the list is compiled, the next step would be to contrive as many exigencies as possible and anticipate the alternative plans of action that may solve the problem. The benefit of such an exercise might be that the candidate had rehearsed at least one of the hypothetical problems presented by the interview board. With such preparation, the "extemporaneous" response of the candidate would certainly put him in good stead with the board.

In oral interviews, the exact answer the candidate gives is of less importance than the board's impressions about how much thought the candidate gave to his answer, his or her reasoning behind the answer, and explanations which demonstrate effectiveness in argumentation and debate.

The oral board is usually required to assign each candidate a percentage score, 70 percent usually considered as a passing score. They are also required to state reasons why they rate individuals low, and why they do not recommend for hiring. The reasons must be job-related, but at best their subjectivity still prevails. These are some of the reasons why candidates have either been rejected, or why they have been rated low in specific categories:

- Personal appearance: Cosmetic personal appearance may strike the board as detracting from eligibility to perform effectively, such as malformed facial or body features, a permanent scowl, toothless grin. Skin blemishes, or unwashed or poorly-groomed appearance, sometimes accompanied by disagreeable body odor. Inappropriate facial hair. Stained teeth, or other appearance that indicates lack of care for personal hygiene and/or no care for personal appearance.
- Personal appearance: Clothing may be inappropriate for the occasion, may be in need of cleaning or laundering, or obviously not attuned to reality, such as tennis or lounging clothing for an interview.
- Poor presentation of self, such as lack of poise or self-confidence, overly self-conscious, timid, arrogant, conceited, too hesitant in reacting to the board members or their questions.

- Lack of social sensitivity, irritating mannerisms, such as picking on self or clothing, making sounds with mouth, cracking knuckles, not being concerned about board member's allergy to cigarette smoke.
- Poor eye contact with the board members, or no eye contact at all.
- Closed-mindedness, indicated in the way questions are answered.
- No preparation for a career, and less for this particular position.
- Academic deficiency for this particular position.
- Lack of preparation for the interview.
- Lack of vitality, apparent lethargic appearance.
- No sense of humor, inability to laugh at his own mistakes.
- Prejudice showing in talk or actions.
- Expresses moral standards which are at odds with those required by the job.
- Indicates no great interest in the job—never asks questions of board.
- Inability to answer the questions correctly.
- Inability to communicate effectively, not persuasive.
- Unwilling to work at lesser job as a start—wants to be instant boss.
- "Wet-fish" handshake.

Although you may find only some or none of these disqualifying factors on any published list, one or more of them may have a direct or subconscious effect on one or more of the oral board members, and the candidate will be rejected, perhaps for some other stated reason.

Physical Agility Qualifications

Certain occupations in the justice system require a certain type of physical specimen as well as one who can perform well in psychological and oral interviews. The juvenile hall group supervisor or police officer fall within this category. Brute strength is not as necessary as agility and endurance. The deliberate antagonist or the individual who physically resists arrest or some other form of custody, such as an attempt to escape, is occasionally encountered. They must be handled quickly and effectively, because any prolongation of the altercation will most certainly lead to greater injury to all participants. An individual who is in excellent physical condition and who is then trained by his agency to perform well in weaponless combat situations can usually handle most situations well, provided the odds against him are not too great. The candidate's physical condition may be tested simply by a medical exam, or by both a medical exam and an agility performance test.

The agility test usually starts off with a few basic tests to determine muscular development and coordination, which may include sit-ups and push-ups, and other feats that can be shown as job-related in terms of endurance, agility, or strength. The test usually includes an obstacle course, with a realistic time limit, which may include one or more of the following: short sprint, balance walk on top edge of a fence, crawling through pipes, under low beams, over hurdles, changing directions around obstacles, jumping over simulated culverts filled with water, and various other job-related feats.

Every part of the course has a realistic counterpart in actual street police duties. Picture the following examples taken from actual experiences: (1) The petty thief captured in the act outside the stadium during a sporting event who ran when an attempt was made to handcuff him. He disappeared among the long row of parked automobiles. (2) The escaping armed robber who alighted from his wrecked car, vaulted a cinder-block wall, jumped on another, ran along the fence, then jumped off into another yard before finally being captured. (3) The car thief who jumped out of the car, dropped down into a drainage ditch, crawled through a culvert underneath the freeway, and escaped across an open field. (4) The frightened juvenile who—for fear his parents would punish him for being out after curfew—sprouted wings and "flew" as though his feet were not touching the ground. In all of these situations, what must the police officer do? Subdue them? Shoot them? Fire warning shots into the air? No. In most cases, the officer is justified only to the extent that he may chase and capture them, using only what force is necessary. The problem is catching them. Success in passing an agility test serves to predict the candidate's agility to take part in chases such as those described.

Medical Examination

Whenever a new employee goes to work, the employer assumes legal responsibility for his physical well-being while actually on the job. He is obligated to provide safety training and safe devices with which the employee must work. The nature of law enforcement and corrections work, particularly, involves certain hazards that cannot be avoided by safety equipment as in a shop. The gun-crazed madman bent upon killing everyone who gets in his way, the high-speed chase of the traffic violator, the parolee who knows that this violation will lead to his lifetime return to prison, and many other situations that involve emotional trauma take a heavy toll even from the healthy officer. The officer who had high blood pressure (hypertension) or ulcers prior to entering the service is a liability who will certainly worsen as a result of the emotional stresses attendant to even the routine aspects of the work. No matter how badly he or she may wish to be accepted for employment or how favorable he may look otherwise, an early medical retirement must be expected. Therefore, the decision must be in favor of the agency and the candidate rejected.

Because every agency is autonomous in many respects, it has—or may have—different medical requirements. The following is an example of a typical list of medical standards for a police officer:

1. **Height: There may be a minimum or maximum, but it cannot be discriminatory because of race or sex.**

2. Weight must be proportionate to height.
3. Vision and eyes: 20/20 each eye, corrected. Color vision must be normal. Rejection for impaired depth perception, impaired eyelids that interfere with vision or do not protect eye from exposure, and other impairments, such as ulcers, corneal scars, or cataracts.
4. Hearing and ears: ability to hear a whispered voice at fifteen feet with each ear.
5. Nose, sinuses, and mouth: a variable minimum amount of teeth, with some requirement as to appearance and ability to masticate properly. Rejection for speech impediment, deformity of mouth or lips, pyorrhea, acute or chronic sinusitis, enlarged tonsils and adenoids, or nasal obstructions.
6. Skin: must be free from gross disfigurements or blemishes. A candidate may be disqualified for obscene tattoos.
7. Extremities: must be in excellent condition. Disqualification for recurring dislocations; loss of joints from certain fingers, particularly the thumb and index finger; and healed fractures of bones that inhibit or limit the strength or use of any limb. X-rays may be ordered.
8. Cardiovascular: pulse limits 50 to 90. Blood pressure not to exceed 140/90. Candidates rejected for history of heart disease or heart damage, past or present syphillis.
9. Respiratory: chest x-ray and skin test for tuberculosis recommended. Disqualification for any acute or chronic disease of the respiratory system.
10. Gastrointestinal: rejection for any acute or chronic disease of stomach, including existing or history of ulcers. Other disqualifying features: diseases of the intestines, liver, pancreas, spleen, and gall bladder, or hemorrhoids —other than minor—until repaired.
11. Genitourinary system free from acute or chronic disease.
12. Disqualified for disabling disease or demormity of the bone structure. Of particular interest to the medical examiner: the spinal structure, the feet, and any presence of arthritis.
13. Neurological and psychological: rejection for any acute or chronic organic disease or history of epilepsy, vertigo, or paralysis.
14. General: on completion of the medical examination and the accompanying chemical analysis that the doctor may order, he may pass the candidate as qualified for the position, or he may reject the candidate for any cause or defect that he believes would impair the health or inhibit the usefulness of the candidate if accepted.

The list above is merely representative, of course, and examining physicians for some agencies may have very extensive check lists and manuals covering any disqualifying feature in the medical phase of the selection process. There are so many possibilities that lead to early retirement, that medicals are very thorough, and if there is any doubt as to qualification, the decision is made in favor of the agency. Any disqualifying characteristics must be shown to actually handicap the candidate from performing the full duties of a peace officer. For positions other than public-safety personnel, such as clerical, the medical requirements may simply state "must be in perfect physical health, as determined by a physician."

Personality Evaluation

This phase of the selection process is usually conducted by a licensed psychiatrist, or a psychologist. Although limited to the selection of police officers and sheriff deputies, the practice could be extended to include many of the other positions in the system. It is imperative that the officer be free from psychological or emotional problems that would adversely affect the ability to function with objectivity and with a maximum effectiveness. There is no place among the police ranks for the individual who is mentally or emotionally "out of synch" with the general society and with reality. Masochistic and sadistic tendencies are not acceptable, as are many other characteristics that the psychiatrist or psychologist and the selection board agree are disqualifying. Certain fears—or phobias—may be so great as to make it impossible for the police officer to function effectively. Some of those fears may be of high places, pain, being in a closed place, or fear of fear. The psychopath, sociopath, or person suffering from any other mental or neurological disorder should be screened out, and such a screening process cannot be accomplished exclusively by a pencil and paper test. Therefore, only an expert can handle this phase of the selection process.

The psychiatric exam usually consists of a battery of tests including the Minnesota Multiphasic Personality Inventory, the Rorschach Ink Blot Test, and several others, which may be the Thematic Apperception Test, one on mental maturity, possibly an intelligence inventory, and others personally selected by the examining professional. The final phase of the psychological or psychiatric screening usually includes a personal interview and subjective evaluation.

The role of this professional is to recommend to the selection board or committee whether the candidate does or does not possess the qualities tested for. Although the final decision is usually left to someone else, the psychiatrist or psychologist may be authorized to pass or fail the candidate. Even this method of psychological selection is not perfect because many latent tendencies are not identified, but it is considered an invaluable tool in the selection process because the *obvious* misfit is obvious only to the psychiatrist in many cases. An example of the value that the psychiatric test may have is the candidate who is passed as acceptable and later becomes disgruntled with the department's policies. In one Southern California city several "hate" letters were given to the psychiatrist who had originally examined all of the policemen then on the job. From his files, the doctor collected several samples of written material from previous tests and compared them with the writing style of the anonymous letters. He provided the chief of police with a list of possible suspects, which later was narrowed down to the true culprit. Although the latent personality trait involving anonymous letter writing did not reveal itself at the time the officer was admitted into the ranks, it did later and the end result was removal of an unfit policeman. There are many other examples, both positive and negative, but the one cited was clearly unique.

Fingerprints

Any time a person applies for a position with any governmental agency he is fingerprinted and sometimes photographed. Whenever a person is arrested for any offense he *may* be fingerprinted, but when a person is "booked" into jail for any offense he is *usually* fingerprinted. Whenever a person is committed to any state or federal institution he is fingerprinted. Private corporations involved in sensitive productions involving government contracts fingerprint all applicants. Whenever fingerprints are taken by any of the foregoing agencies, they are classified by the individual agencies for their own files, then one set is mailed to the Federal Bureau of Investigation central clearing house and another set mailed to the respective state clearing houses. At each of the many clearing houses, each set of fingerprints is classified and a record of the prints' owner added to a cumulative file maintained on each individual. Because there are no two sets of fingerprints alike, the prints are a positive means of identification, and a single individual may have a fingerprint record under more than one name.

Whenever an agency submits a set of fingerprints to a clearing house such as the FBI, that agency sends back by return mail the cumulative list showing all the times that individual has been fingerprinted for any reason under any name. For example, a "rap sheet" (a chronology of the times and places a person has been fingerprinted) on a single individual may read as follows: At age fourteen, Jerome Ford was committed to a farm for delinquent boys in Virginia for a series of delinquent acts. At age seventeen, Jerry enlisted in the U.S. Navy at Bethesda, Maryland. At age twenty-three, our subject was arrested for auto theft in Chicago and used the name of Jerry F. Queenbury. At age twenty-seven, Mr. F. changed his name in a lawful court procedure in Seattle to Jerrold Fillmore Quick. Finally, our subject—true name Quick—applied for a job as a policeman in San Francisco under his true name. As far as we know from the information furnished in this account, the subject has been fingerprinted in Virginia, Maryland, Illinois, and California under three different names. Although his name has been changed, his fingerprints have not. When the San Francisco Police Department sends the candidate's fingerprints to the FBI and the California Bureau of Criminal Identification and Investigation, they will receive replies from both of those agencies. The "rap sheets" will show the dates, the reason for the taking of prints, plus the name given at the time, and the disposition—if provided by the contributing agency—of each particular incident, such as "released, no complaint filed."

In addition to what we already know, the information sheet from the FBI may also show Mr. Quick as an applicant for the position of policeman in San Diego and Eureka. He had either forgotten or deliberately failed to mention when making his application in San Francisco that he had applied at the other two agencies. A check with those agencies might possibly reveal that Quick actually did become a member of one of those departments and was dismissed two months later for the use of excessive force or extorting money from prisoners.

In the case of some juvenile arrests, individual agencies maintain fingerprint files but—because of the tender age of the children—do not submit them to state or federal agencies. In an actual case worked by the author, one young candidate's background checked perfectly except for a lapse of about three years during which time the candidate's mother was married to one of her several husbands in one of the Southern states. Although the FBI reported no fingerprint record on the candidate, a copy of his fingerprints was mailed to police departments in the two largest cities where the candidate had lived during that specific three-year time span. As a result of those inquiries, one of the two agencies reported that the candidate had been arrested under another name as one of the leaders of an auto theft ring that had operated in that state for several months until they were apprehended transporting one of the cars across the border. Had the check not been made, the candidate would—no doubt—have been appointed to the ranks of the police department. For some reason, fingerprints taken at the time of that arrest never found their way to the department's files. That state had a general policy of not requiring submission of juvenile prints, thus there were no fingerprints in the state clearing house either.

Polygraph

Polygraph operators theorize that virtually everyone has at least one skeleton in his closet. Verified deceptive patterns are noted in replies to such questions as: Did you ever steal anything in your life?, Did you ever cheat on a test in school?, or Did you ever tell a deliberate lie to hurt someone else? Doctor Kinsey's reports on the sexual behavior of the American male and female further bears this theory out with respect to our social mores. If this device—the polygraph—is utilized as a part of the selection process, a great deal of discretion and good judgment must be exercised. Indiscriminate use of polygraph files could be devastating. The examiner must be absolutely above reproach, and there must be no question as to his professional competence. His examination should pertain only to those character traits that directly relate to the applicant's suitability for the police service.

When preparing a set of questions for polygraph examination for pre-employment screening, it is first necessary to determine exactly what type of person the chief administrator wishes to employ. Although there may be a sexual and/or moral revolution going on elsewhere, the private lives of officers and other employees in the criminal justice professions are open books to the citizens who pay the bills, and reputations of the agencies are dependent upon the good reputations of their employees. Personal lives do not seem to be kept personal by some individuals, and any open display of sexual promiscuity, drug use, or any other excessive deviations from the accepted mores of the community may cause disqualification of the candidate. There is absolutely no place in the organization for a burglar, a robber, or a thief. Many other traits must be identified and evaluated. The examiner must determine whether a single act of theft or certain acts of moral indiscretion at some time in the candidate's lifetime makes him a thief or robber. Individual departments utilize their polygraph examination phase of the selection process differently. A personal inquiry of each department's personnel division would be necessary in order to ascertain their specific utilization of the polygraph. As a scientific aid to interviewing, the polygraph may be rejected by some employee unions as unfair or menacing, therefore unacceptable.

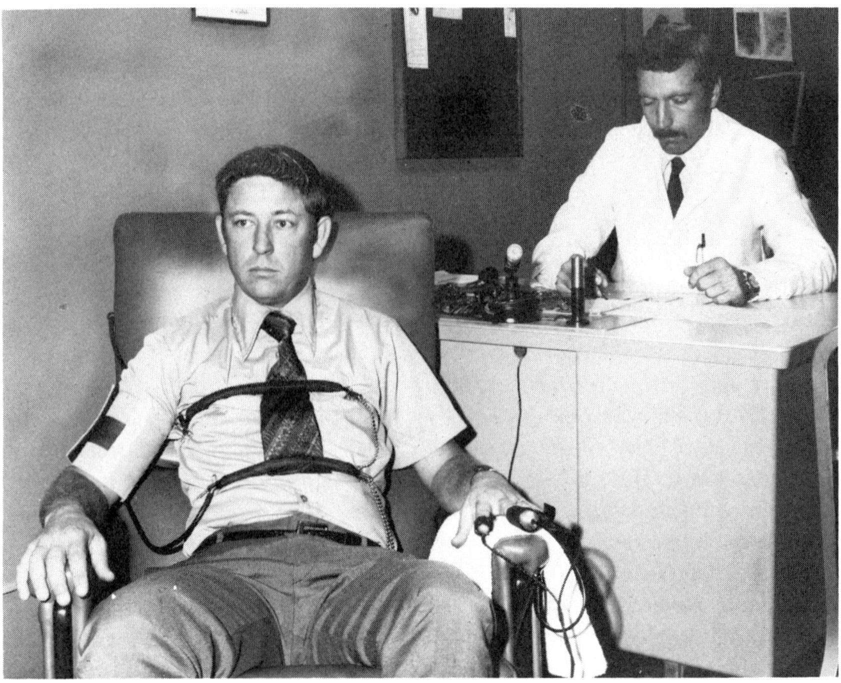

Figure 10-1 The Polygraph Examination. The polygraph is a valuable aid to the investigation. Posed by Officers J. Birkes (left) and R. Lindley.

Courtesy Police Department, Santa Ana.

The Background Investigation

The initial application submitted by the candidate is usually relatively brief compared with the personal history statement required by the department personnel unit. The form is actually an autobiography in question and answer form, and it is used as the basis for the background investigation. The investigation is primarily conducted for the purpose of screening out the undesirable applicants who have derogatory personal histories. Secondarily, the investigation provides the administrator with a complete biography of each employee including special talents and training. Typical questions asked in the personal history statement form will be listed in the following paragraphs, along with a discussion of the background investigation and how they are related.

1. *Other names.* List all other names you have used or been known by, including nicknames, maiden name, adopted name, other. State during what period(s) of time each other name was used. School attendance and work records often reflect a variety of names for many reasons. Either in practice or by law, married women may have more than one married name because of more than one marriage, and sometimes people temporarily adopt the names of relatives they are living with to avoid confusion in sending messages home to parents and guardians.

2. *Description of your automobile(s).* As a matter of routine, automobile license numbers are checked against outstanding warrant files and vehicles wanted for other purposes, including stolen cars and/or license plates. Another purpose for requesting this information is that the selection committee can discover something about the owner's personaltiy from the type of vehicle he or she drives. Some individuals live far beyond their means, which may lead to embarrassment to the agency. Some neighbors who are good sources of information about the candidate only know their neighbors by the description of the car they drive.

3. *Education record.* This category includes high school, college, vocational, and trade schools. Personal visits to these institutions are made by the investigators, if possible, or mail inquiries are made to determine scholastic records in addition to sociability, participation in sports and other school events, and citizenship records. Scholastic grades are naturally of interest to the background investigator. When compared with the intelligence quotient of an individual, it is often possible to determine something about the drive and perseverance he may or may not possess. An individual with an extremely high IQ who made Cs and Ds may prove less desirable as a potential employee than the average IQ with a scholastic record of As and Bs or "just average" attained by the student who diligently applied himself and made the best of what he had in the way of natural ability.

4. *Degrees, credentials, certificates* you hold. Pilot's license, radio licenses, teaching credentials, special certificates, and degrees reflect both

the training and capabilities of the individual, including special language skills.

5. *Disciplinary action record* while in school, including scholastic probation. This information aids in determining behavior patterns, which may affect a public servant's ability to cope with various problems involved.

6. *Employment record,* including all places of employment during the candidate's lifetime, and periods of unemployment. Name and address of employer, type of business, dates of employment, high salary, position and duties, name of immediate supervisor, and reason for leaving. When possible, the investigator makes a personal contact with all previous employers (out-of-town employers are questioned by mail) for the purpose of talking with fellow workers and supervisors and looking through the candidate's work records. Rating while on the job, sickness histories, and all other relevant data are collected and evaluated.

7. *Military record,* if any, including duty assignments, rates or ranks held, any disciplinary action, and type of discharge as well as the actual dates of service is requested—another employer, of course.

8. *Relatives.* List relatives, their names, places of residence, occupations, and additional information that will sufficiently identify them. Criminal offenders in a candidate's family may have sufficient influence over him that he might possibly be placed in an untenable position of having to yield to pressures to take preferential actions for family harmony, such as "clearing" criminal records by removing or altering records from the files or possibly exerting official influence to gain special favors. Community reputation of the entire agency also depends upon the individual reputations of all of its employees.

9. *References.* Some agencies require only four or five references. This is of no value to the investigator because the candidate invariably lists the family physician, a clergyman, an attorney, possibly a so-called influential citizen, and perhaps a casual acquaintance who is a deputy district attorney or chief of police. These people are not likely to condemn or negatively criticize the candidate because they know nothing about his personal life; most are no more than slightly acquainted. Some agencies require ten to fifteen references who have knowledge of the candidate's reputation, who know him socially, and who have knowledge of his professional or occupational capabilities. Armed with this list of people who have personal knowledge of the candidate's personal and occupational characteristics, the investigator attempts to find out as much as he can about exactly what the candidate is "made of." He also inquires as to the identity of other people who may know him. Out-of-town reference letters are usually mailed to the references and a few confidential questions asked in an effort to glean from as many sources as possible the maximum amount of information that can be amassed.

10. *Medical record.* List all surgery or serious illnesses during the candidate's lifetime. Nature of illnesses and/or purpose for any surgery and the

names of hospitals and doctors are required. These items are checked out very carefully because the employer assumes liability for the candidate once appointed. Some permanent disabilities are discovered that otherwise may have been overlooked by the medical examiner or omitted from the original application by the candidate. Along with this question there will usually be others pertaining to sick leave history and any history of the candidate's having been a recipient of any disability allowance for sickness or injury, including medical retirement from another retirement system.

11. *Sources of income.* List additional sources of income, such as earnings by spouse. At first glance, an individual's expenditures may appear to be in excess of his income, and the investigator may draw the conclusion that the subject is on the verge of having his wages attached or going into bankruptcy. Good credit is mandatory for the police employee, and the candidate must have the self-control to live within his means. The total income presents a true picture of the candidate's fiscal status.

12. *Debts and credit.* List outstanding debts and credit references. Other questions along the same line may call for a statement regarding whether or not the candidate has ever been refused credit and any other data relevant to the candidate's credit record.

13. *Previous residence(s).* List all places of residence during the candidate's lifetime. Out-of-town places of residence are checked out by the local police having that particular jurisdiction if the agency's investigator cannot drive the distance and conduct his own investigation. All cities and counties in which the candidate lived are either visited in person by the investigator, or a letter of request for investigative assistance is sent to those that are too far distant. Police, court, and school files are searched for any record of the candidate; the local credit bureaus' records are checked, and personal contacts are made with former employers, teachers, neighbors, friends, and anyone else who may have known the candidate. Personality and character traits of the candidate are the object of this phase of the investigation. Many police agencies have established such a favorable working relationship that a request sent by the Santa Ana, California, Police Department Personnel Division to another police department even as far away as New York City or Houston results in the initiation by that agency of an investigation that yields as comprehensive a report as is required.

14. *Marital status,* name of spouse and children, if any, and vital statistics on all aspects of the marital and familial situation of the candidate, including former marriages are requested.

15. *Traffic record.* List all traffic citations and/or traffic arrests (not including parking tickets), *including* those received while under the age of eighteen. The question calls for the date and place, charge or violation, and the disposition (fine, forfeited bail, jail). The driving record of a potential policeman is most essential because virtually all police agencies require their

officers to possess a valid driver's license and their normal duties include driving department vehicles under both routine and emergency conditions. A poor driving record will disqualify the candidate who has proved to be an insurance liability, accident-prone, or citation-prone. Police officers who violate the traffic laws are subject to the same treatment—citation or arrest—given the nonpolice violators. Each member of a police agency, or any agency that pools its motor vehicles, is covered by the automobile insurance regardless of which vehicle he operates. What that means to the agency in terms of cost is that a lone negligent operator who is allowed to drive the vehicles will cause the agency's insurance policy to go up considerably for the entire fleet. It would be an economic impossibility, much less an unwise decision, to employ one or more individuals with poor driving records. If your own insurance premium payments go up fifty percent after you have a traffic collision or receive two or three citations, just imagine the increase for an agency that has a fleet of one hundred vehicles. There are other reasons, of course, for rejecting a candidate with a poor driving record. A department is responsible for all its agents.

16. *Police record.* Other than traffic (covered in 15 above), have you ever in your lifetime been arrested, held by the police for investigation or questioning, or otherwise been under investigation by the police? Complete details are required, including the nature of the incident, time, place, and disposition. The background investigator secures copies of all reports, if available, and he looks into the nature of the charge, including recontacting victims, and interviews the original investigating or arresting officer. In many cases, deliberate omission of information that should be included in response to this question is sometimes a serious matter. An example of deliberate omissions or falsification of the personal history statement is the case of the twenty-five-year-old candidate who listed that he had never been questioned by the police under any circumstances. His background investigation revealed that he had been caught stealing some items from an automobile at the age of fourteen, was severely reprimanded by the police officer, and was released to his parents. Other than the one incident when he was arrested and released as a child, the candidate's background was excellent. When the personnel investigator later questioned the candidate about the incident, the candidate denied anything of that nature ever taking place. He was given an opportunity to refresh his memory and make any changes on the form that he wished to make before being considered for the position. He chose to continue his denial of the act, even when the investigator suggested that it had occurred when he was about fourteen and in a specifically named city when he lived at a certain address in that city. The candidate continued to adamantly maintain that he had never been contacted by the police for any reason, and finally conceded with a great deal of reluctance that such an incident had taken place when he was confronted with a copy

of the arrest report. He was disqualified—not for the act of theft at age fourteen, but for *falsifying his personal history statement.* What would prevent that individual from perjuring himself in court to cover an error in judgment?

17. *Other applications.* If you have applied for employment with any other police agency, list the date of application, name, and location of the agency, and the status of the application (accepted, not accepted, or pending). The purpose for this question is to aid in the investigation and evaluation of the subject. Another agency may already have conducted a thorough background investigation and some duplication will be avoided, and the opinions of other qualified police practitioners will help in what amounts to a reevaluation of the candidate for a similar position.

The final part of the statement is an agreement by the candidate that he understands the terms of the probationary appointment procedure, that he also understands a thorough background investigation will be conducted, and that he will be disqualified for any deliberate falsification or omissions.

Proof of Good Character

Proof of good character is defined in New York Police Department's notice of examination as follows:

> Proof of good character will be an absolute prerequisite to appointment. The following are among the factors which would ordinarily be cause for disqualification: (a) conviction of a misdemeanor or an offense, the nature of which indicates lack of good moral character or disposition toward violence or disorder; (b) repeated conviction of an offense, where such convictions indicate a disrespect for the law; (c) repeated discharge from employment where such discharge indicates poor performance or inability to adjust to discipline; (d) addiction to narcotics or excessive use of alcoholic beverages; (e) discharge from the Armed Forces other than the standard honorable discharge. In accordance with the provisions of the administrative code, persons convicted of a felony are not eligible for positions in the uniformed forces of the police department. In addition, the rules of the city civil service commission provide that no person convicted of petty larceny, or who has been dishonorably discharged by the Armed Forces shall be examined, certified, or appointed as a patrolman.[1]

Selection Interview

Following the background investigation, the next step in the selection process is to schedule the candidate for a selection interview. The interview is usually conducted by at least one staff officer charged with the responsi-

[1]George P. McManus, Project Director, *Police Training and Performance Study,* New York Police Department, Project 70-4 (Washington, D.C.: Government Printing Office, 1970), p. 31.

bility for selecting only the best-qualified candidates. In all but the largest departments it is most desirable for the chief administrator to take an active part in the selection interviews. In any event, the final decision and responsibility is his. The successful candidates are appointed and launched on their careers.

Probation

Public agencies that provide their employees with the protection and many other benefits of a civil service system have a six-month to two-year probationary period that precedes attainment of permanent status, or tenure. The purpose of the probationary period is to give the employee a breaking-in period during which he determines whether he and the job are suited for each other and to serve the employing agency as the final—and most important—part of the selection process. During the probation, the employee may be terminated by the agency for unsuitability with no right to appeal his dismissal. The decision of the department head in the case of any probationary termination is final.

EDUCATION FOR THE JUSTICE SYSTEM

Development of a universal body of knowledge is one of the prime requisites of a profession. Throughout the justice system there have been many professions, particularly the legal profession, and there have been professional individuals scattered throughout in virtually all of the components of the system. As for universality of knowledge about any part of the system, the development of such knowledge has been somewhat piecemeal and far from universal. During the past few years, particularly since the advent of federal financing of program development and of loans and grants to the students who specialize in law enforcement, corrections, or other components of the justice system through the Law Enforcement Assistance Administration, we have witnessed the phenomenal growth of administration of justice educational programs. From just a dozen or so in the 1950s, the college and university programs have literally mushroomed to approximately one thousand such programs in the U.S. today. Not all institutions offer degree programs, and may have only a few representative courses, but the offerings are bona fide academic courses.

Although the financial boost from LEAA loans and grants substantially contributed to the growth of criminal justice education and the improvement of the programs through tuition payments to the institutions with the loan and grant money, the "G.I. Bill" should not be relegated to a back seat. That wonderful financial aid program has made the "impossible dream" of a college education for millions of veterans come true.

Along with the proliferation of programs throughout the nation, we have witnessed the development of courses by the thousands. Many courses were designed to meet local needs only, with little or no thought given to what the other colleges and universities were doing, particularly in other states. Most of the agencies in law enforcement and the courts, and many of the correctional programs, particularly in juvenile corrections, are operated by local government, with a comparative few operated by state government. Colleges and universities, each with their own local advisory boards and committees, develop their educational programs in accordance with the objectives that are most relevant and important to them. As they have developed during the phenomenal growth period, the courses and the programs have grown in their own unique patterns.

During recent years, educators responsible for the overall criminal justice system, including administrators, instructors, professors, department and division chairpersons, deans, and leaders in the related professional organizations, began to look toward some sort of standardization. Not only must the students move from the two-year junior or community colleges into the upper classes of the four-year colleges and universities, but many students move back and forth within the lower undergraduate levels from one four-year college to another, from four-year colleges to community colleges, and vice versa. They also move from community or junior college to other institutions of the same sort at other parts of the state, and quite often from one state to another. Recognizing this transient nature of our students for whatever reasons there are, there has been at least a consensus that standardized curricula and courses must be developed. Although we are a far way from implementing standardization on a nationwide level, there has been some progress within the states.

The following few pages will illustrate the results of some of those efforts at standardizing at least the general educational base in general education and in criminal justice education, and some of the areas agreed upon by a majority of educators and practitioners as to how the student should be prepared for the professions in criminal justice.

General Education Base

Fundamental to the collegiate preparation of any student is the broad general education base. The individual who is preparing for professional development in the justice system must have a large portion of his educational preparation in subjects that are certainly related to his overall academic needs, but which do not fall in the category of Administration of Justice education. Basic subjects include communications skills: English Grammar, English Composition, and Public Speaking. Anything beyond the minimum requirements largely depend on the individual proficiencies and interests of the students. For the purpose of maintaining an excellent physical condition there should be some involvement in sports and/or recreation activities and instruction. The individual who is planning a career in corrections and who is also planning to start at the entry level as group supervisor in a juvenile institution should take courses in officiating competitive sports, and as many different kinds of sports and recreation classes as possible. He will be involved in directing the activities of youths under his guidance during their leisure time as well as at other times of the day and days of the week on the job.

First Aid is important, and it may be required of all students along with courses on personal grooming and health, and a college orientation class, but if an applicant misses it in college there is no doubt that he will be required to take it in the academy of any law enforcement agency. Certain health education courses may be required by the state or the institution as being essential to the base education required for a college degree.

Natural Science, either a physical science or a biological science, depending on college requirements should also be studied. For those interested in criminalistics, Chemistry is important. For other students there is little direct relationship to the needs of the student for performance on the job. The science course he takes should be whichever one he wishes for personal interest.

Social Science courses may be required, such as a U.S. History course and American Government Institutions. In addition to those courses, there are many others in the social sciences that would prove most worthwhile both in the *required* and in the *elective* categories. Special Ethnic Studies courses should be considered, particularly by the student who plans to work in areas in which there is a significant representation of some ethnic heritage other than his own. Sociology and Cultural Anthropology are a must for the individual who is planning to specialize in probation or parole work. Child Development and Human Services courses would likewise be directly related to the objectives of the change-agent, or the caseworker. The Social Sciences include a diverse range of courses of instruction in Psychology that should also be worked into the student's program as much as possible. Child Psychology, Social Psychology, and Abnormal Psychology are just three of the outstanding courses that would enhance the student's knowledge and awareness of the problems he will be facing in the world of the justice system.

Humanities includes an array of course selections that will serve to enrich the student's educational progress. The types of courses that would directly relate to the student's professional choice may include Philosophy, Logic, Art, Music, Theater Arts, Foreign Language, or additional courses in Speech or Written Communications. Not only should the student be concerned with fulfillment of his personal life and leisure time, but he may also become occupied in a position in which he is expected to either direct or show others how to make healthy and productive use of their leisure time.

Special courses that should be considered as electives may include Typing, Shorthand, Journalism, Participative Sports, Band or Chorus or other artistic participation type class, Supervision, Business Management, Bookkeeping, Accounting, Computer Science, and as many other electives in the Social Sciences, particularly Sociology and Psychology. All of these courses, which are not classified as "Administration of Justice" or "Criminology," or "Police Science," or "Correctional Science," or any other justice system-oriented programs, make up approximately two-thirds to three-quarters of the student's total two-year, and then four-year college or university education. Administration of Justice courses should be complete and comprehensive, but they should not dominate the entire educational program. As a matter of fact, many of those courses listed above are directly related to justice administration and round out the essential body of knowledge and proficiencies that the college-prepared professional must master.

Administration of Justice[2] The student's major course of study for any one of the justice system's components will include at least one-fourth to one-third of his total program in specialized courses under the umbrella of some title representative of the "total system" encompassing most of the components of the justice system. Although there was originally a stronger emphasis on each of the more specific categories of police science, corrections, court administration, criminology, or law enforcement, it seems that the "umbrella concept" has been the principal thrust during recent years. This could be, in part, the result of insistence by the Law Enforcement Assistance Administration that many sources of funding would be meager unless any educational program would address the educational needs of the "total system."

In California during the fiscal year 1971 to 1972 a task force was created by the Community College Chancellor's Office in cooperation with a state justice educators' association.[3] The purpose of the task force was to reevaluate the curricula for criminal justice educational programs with a view to design a basic core curriculum that would serve as a common base for educational programs leading to two-year degrees in the several different options in the fields of criminal justice.

The members of the task force agreed that criminal justice education—and educators—must recognize at least these two premises:

[2]Although this portion of the chapter emphasizes the California Community College approach because of the author's direct involvement in the California experience, it is not intended that the student or instructor consider it from a "superior versus inferior" viewpoint in comparison with any other system. It is simply presented here as an example of an approach to the educational preparation for the justice system.

[3]California Association of Administration of Justice Educators, Inc. The task force was chaired by Professor Robert Blanchard of Riverside and members included J. Winston Silva of the California Community College Chancellor's Office, Robert Ferguson of Saddleback College in Mission Viejo, Paul Howard of Bakersfield, Al Nottingham of Modesto, and myself, Tom Adams of Santa Ana.

1. Subsystems are no longer in a position to function in a vacuum of isolation from one another, lacking concern for the impact the operation of one subsystem has on the other.
2. It is of paramount importance that all system members have a deep sensitivity and understanding of human beings and the society in which they exist. This understanding should include the origin and styles of deviant behavior and current theories and treatment of these human weaknesses.[4]

Historically, there had been considerable isolationism among the various criminal justice professions in philosophy, in training, in education, even an elitist attitude in some cases. Such isolation has led to separatism and suspicion, a distrust and/or disrespect of one group of professionals in the system by another group. When keeping this historical fact in mind, it seemed most logical that a series of courses should be developed that would serve as a core body of knowledge and skills shared by practitioners in all segments of the criminal justice system.

With a clearly defined set of objectives in mind, the committee carefully studied the current course offerings, selected the major stores of knowledge and specific proficiencies that appeared to be common to the total justice system. The committee's conclusions were based upon their study of the existing courses, the needs of the several types of agencies within the system, and a consensus of the input of their colleagues throughout the state. The effort was cooperative, and the results were five courses now referred to as the five core courses for Administration of Justice.

1. INTRODUCTION TO THE ADMINISTRATION OF JUSTICE

Course Description. The history and philosophy of administration of justice in America; recapitulation of the system; identification of the various subsystems; role expectations and their interrelationships; theories of crime, punishment, and rehabilitation; ethics, education and training for professionalism in the system.

Course Goals:

1. Provide a knowledge of the various agencies encompassing the administration of justice system and the interrelationship between them.
2. Develop the ability of the student to recognize the administration of justice agency best suited to his or her talents and aspirations.
3. Develop an appreciation of the complexity of the total system and the importance and dignity of being a part of the system.

2. PRINCIPLES AND PROCEDURES OF THE JUSTICE SYSTEM

Course Description. An in-depth study of the role and responsibilities of each segment within the administration of justice system: law enforcement, judicial,

[4]From the statement of philosophy, *Task Force Report, Five-Core Curriculum, Part I*, July, 1972.

corrections. A past, present, and future exposure to each subsystem procedures from initial entry to final disposition and the relationship each segment maintains with its system members.

Course Goals:

1. Provide the student with a knowledge of the procedures involved in the justice system from arrest to release.
2. Develop skills in applying this knowledge to an understanding of the operation of the justice system.
3. Develop an appreciation of the necessity for the justice system to operate as a cooperating entity so the most effective handling of cases can be provided.
4. Develop an ability to utilize the material presented in this course in making appropriate, discretionary decisions as to how to proceed while operating as a member of the system.

3. CONCEPTS OF CRIMINAL LAW

Course Description. Historical development, philosophy of law, and constitutional provisions; definitions, classification of crime, and their application to the system of administration of justice; legal research, study of case law, methodology, and concepts of law as a social force.

Course Goals:

1. Provide the student with a knowledge of the historical development of law and the philosophy of law.
2. Familiarize the student with the U.S. Constitution and integrate constitutional provisions with the fundamentals of law.
3. Introduce the student to basic legal definitions and concepts that provide a foundation for law.
4. Develop within the student an appreciation for the value of case study and legal research as a means of interpreting court decisions in relation to the written statutes.

4. LEGAL ASPECTS OF EVIDENCE

Course Description. Origin, development, philosophy, and constituional basis of evidence; constitutional and procedural considerations affecting arrest, search, and seizure; kinds and degrees of evidence and rules governing admissibility; judicial decisions interpreting individual rights and case studies.

Course Goals:

1. Provide the student with a working knowledge of the rules of evidence, the various kinds of evidence, and the admissibility of evidence.
2. Develop in the student the ability to evaluate the various kinds of evidence available in a given case in order to determine its admissibility in court.
3. Develop an appreciation of the value of all kinds of evidence and the need to use proper procedures and techniques so as to maintain the value and admissibility of evidence.

4. Develop the skill in handling case material so that evidence admissibility will not be destroyed by improper techniques or procedures.
5. Impress upon the student the knowledge that legally admissible evidence is the end product of all the work and effort of the crime investigator, and that it is essential that he possess a sound knowledge of the rules of evidence.

5. COMMUNITY RELATIONS

Course Description. An in-depth exploration of the roles of the administration of justice practitioners and their agencies. Through interaction and study, the student will become aware of the interrelationships and role expectations among the various agencies and the public. Principal emphasis will be placed upon the professional image of the system of justice administration and the development of positive relationships between members of the system and the public.

Course Goals:

1. Acquire a broad base of information regarding the social and ethnic structure of the community and the variety of cultural influences.
2. Develop an awareness of the many real and/or imagined problems of the various segments of the community in relationship to the criminal justice system. This shall be accomplished by means of an opinion survey, survey of available literature, lectures, and guest appearances.
3. Participate in discussions and group projects to acquire an awareness of the social and personal needs of the various individuals and groups of individuals in the modern society that may have previously been foreign to the awareness and experience of the students.
4. Identify conflicts in principles and philosophies of individuals or groups of individuals that contribute to confrontations and physical conflict with different segments of the criminal justice system.

Following development of the core courses that would serve as a base of general knowledge and skills, the next phase the task force tackled was that of developing "tracks," or options, for the specialist education, depending on the occupational goals of the individual students in law enforcement, corrections, the courts, crime laboratory, and private security. Sets of courses for each of these options were developed. In California, most of the participating community college criminal justice departments have adopted the core concept, and those are transferrable from any community college to another, and from community college to state universities and state colleges, as well as most private colleges and universities.

The course titles in the various options should include, at the lower division college level, with a view to continuation at the upper division and graduate levels with a minimum of conflict or repetition, the following:

1. Law Enforcement. Substantive law, field enforcement services, principles of investigation.

2. Court Services. Judicial processes in the state, civil practice, court enforcement principles, court administration.
3. Corrections. Fundamentals of crime and delinquency, institutional and field services, counseling and interviewing.
4. Crime Laboratory Assistant, or Physical Evidence Technician. Physical Evidence, Evidence Photography, Evidence and the Laboratory.
5. Private Security Services. Security Services System, Business and Retail Security, Industrial Security.

There are many excellent programs throughout the United States. To mention a few and to exclude all the others would give me more enemies than allies. However, the trend appears to be toward (1) a strong background in general education requirements for a degree with a broad-base education, (2) a common core of subjects basic to all components of the criminal justice system, and (3) special elective courses for each of the special areas, such as Traffic and Public Safety, Corrections, Police Management, Business Administration, Commercial and Business Security, Juvenile Justice, Patrol Operations, Laboratory Services, Computer Services, Criminal Investigation, and others.

Not even touched upon in this section are those highly specialized areas, such as the coroner, who may employ doctors as examiners and pathologists; attorneys who serve as advocates and judges, scientists with special laboratory skills, and business managers.

TRAINING AND EDUCATION

Skills development and indoctrination to the routine activities of the occupation are usually assigned the label *training;* while the orientation to philosophy, theories and concepts of the role through intellectualization processes are usually assigned the label *education.* Although it is virtually impossible to distinguish the two in many respects, recent attempts have been made in order that they may be handled differently. A simplified distinction might be to designate training as the process of instructing the individual on how to do the job and providing him with the basic information about the job, and *education* as the process of providing him with a body of knowledge on which he may base his decisions when he is performing the job. While training is generally directly related to the tasks to be performed by the practitioner, the education that he receives should be on a broad base so that he not only understands his own role in society, but that of others who surround him and with whom he interacts.

Charles Tenney defined training in this manner:

> A particular subject may be determined to be of the *training* variety if it is directed primarily to the mastery and application of particular rules, to the development of particular mechanical skills in the operation of particular items

of equipment, or to the development of a skill in the performance of particular maneuvers concerning which little or no discretion is involved.... In other cases, the *manner* in which a course is taught and its *content* will determine its training character.... In either case, whether because of the nature of the subject matter itself or because of the manner in which it is taught, little attention is given to the questions of policy, of discretion, or of alternative methodologies.[5]

In 1973, the following statements were published by the National Advisory Commission on Criminal Justice Standards and Goals in their Standards 12.1 and 12.2:

Standard 12.1:

Development, Implementation, and Evaluation of Criminal Justice Education and Training Programs

In selecting and placing personnel with the necessary skill and knowledge to fulfill efficiently and effectively the objectives of the criminal justice system, criminal justice agencies, and agencies of education should undertake the following activities:

1. Identify specific and detailed roles, tasks, and performance objectives for each criminal justice position in agencies of various jurisdiction, size, and locale and in relation to other positions in the criminal justice system and the public. These perceptions should be compared with actual practice, and an acceptable level of expected behavior established.
2. Establish clearly the knowledge and skill requirements of all criminal justice positions at the operational, support, and management level on the basis of roles, tasks, and performance objectives identified for each position.
3. Develop educational curricula and training programs only on the basis of identified knowledge and skill requirements; terminate all unnecessary programs.
4. Develop implementation plans that recognize priorities and constraints and use the most effective learning techniques for these education and training programs.
5. Develop and implement techniques and plans for evaluating the effectiveness of education and training programs as they relate to on-the-job performance.
6. Develop for all criminal justice positions recruitment and selection criteria that incorporate the appropriate knowledge and skill requirements.
7. Develop techniques for a continuous assessment of education and training needs as they relate to changes in social trends and public needs on a national and local basis.
8. Require all criminal justice personnel to possess the requisite knowledge and skills prior to being authorized to function independently. Require personnel

[5]Tenney, *Higher Education Programs in Law Enforcement and Criminal Justice PRI-2*, p. 8.

already employed in these positions to obtain the requisite knowledge and skills within a specified period of time as a condition of continued employment.[6]

Standard 12.2:

Criminal Justice System Curriculum

Criminal justice system curricula and programs should be established by agencies of higher education to unify the body of knowledge in criminology, social science, law, public administration, and corrections, and to serve as a basis for preparing persons to work in the criminal justice system.

The following factors should be included in the development of curricula and programs:

1. A range of associate arts program through graduate offerings should be established as rapidly as possible.
2. Care should be taken to separate the academic nature of the curricula from training content and functions best performed by police, courts, and corrections agencies.
3. Liaison should be established with criminal justice agencies to insure that theoretical content keeps pace with rapid new developments in the field.[7]

TYPES OF TRAINING PROGRAMS FOR CRIMINAL JUSTICE

Following the new employee's appointment and prior to actual exposure to the job that he will be performing on a regular basis he is given some sort of agency orientation and indoctrination. He is instilled with the pride of membership in this organization in particular and the profession in general. It is, indeed, a proud time, and he is to be reminded that his newly designated power has a set of tremendous responsibilities accompanying that power, and he is given an outline of his limitations as well as the scope of his responsibility. Following that brief induction session, and possibly concurrent with his actual on-the-job participation, the new employee's experiences begin.

Interns and Cadets

As professionalization of the entire field of law enforcement and criminal justice evolves into reality, the academic requirements will doubtlessly

[6]National Advisory Commission on Criminal Justice Standards and Goals, *Report on the Criminal Justice System* (Washington, D.C.: Government Printing Office, 1974), p. 168.

[7]National Advisory Commission on Criminal Justice Standards and Goals, *Report on the Criminal Justice System*, p. 170.

increase. Education is a means to an end, however, not an end in itself. Knowing a job and knowing *about* a job are two different situations. You do not learn to swim without getting into the water, nor can you learn the job of *being* a policeman without "getting into the water." During the past several years, various police agencies and colleges have cooperated in a variety of programs that provide to the preservice student practical on-the-job training while still attending college. Two of the more popular programs are internship and cadet training.

How to stimulate and maintain the interest of the young high school graduate during the interim between graduation and entry to the justice system, which may be a few years because of school commitments, has always been a problem. Rather than to leave a young person's decision to enter law enforcement to chance, it is more desirable to help the student make a choice while still in high school through career guidance programs. It is then necessary that we encourage him for the next few years. The ultimate goal would be entrance into the ranks of law enforcement as an officer, a deputy, or an investigator. But there must be some intermediate goals that are attainable along the way. Without these goals, there is frustration and in many cases a redesignation of goals. Internship and cadet training provide those intermediate goals and emotional satisfaction as well. Additional incentives may be provided in the form of assured acceptance into the sponsoring agency at the completion of the training and financial assistance in the form of nominal pay on an hourly basis.

Internship, or work experience programs, have been in operation within two-year and four-year college programs for many years. The student is usually required to attend at least a half-time school schedule and to take a major in the law enforcement program. Some schools include young ladies in their program, but their utilization by cooperating agencies is on a much more limited basis. The student enrolls for the internship, or work experience, course for a specific number of credits (or units) and is required to work and/or observe at a specified cooperating agency for a minimum number of hours. This particular type of course usually does not involve financial remuneration for the student.

Approval of the intern is dependent upon successful completion of a series of entrance examinations and a thorough background investigation conducted by some agencies, and other agencies call for little more than a brief oral interview. In exchange for his hours of work observation, the student receives the credits and grades characteristic of all other college courses. He may be required to prepare periodic reports to both the agency and the college professor in charge of the program and to the agency intern coordinator.

The *cadet training program* is similar to the internship program, but there is usually an employer-employee relationship between the student and the agency for which he performs. On-the-job supervision in a cadet program is usually the primary responsibility of the employing law enforcement agency. It is possible to assign the cadet to a wide variety of duties throughout the agency in nearly every area except actual enforcement or investigative assignments.

A student attending classes, on a full-time or three-quarter schedule may be scheduled for a twenty-hour week during the school year and a full schedule during school vacation when the officers would be taking their vacations. The most practical method of selection of cadets is to have them go through the identical series of exams and the entire selection process as if they were applying for the policeman position. Later, when the cadet reaches the age or the point in his or her academic career when a full-time work schedule and a position as police officer is the cadet's next step in a career, the candidate need take only a new medical exam and interview because all of the other screening steps have been completed.

An advantage to completing the selection examination process at the beginning of the cadet's employment in that capacity is that the individual who obviously will not gain eventual employment as a law enforcement officer will know it at that time rather than having the misfortune of spending four years in college only to find out—with degree in hand—that he is not qualified for the job.

In order to assure the agency that the program is actually going to produce officers or agents for that agency instead of professional student-cadets, the cadet could be required to sign an agreement that he or she will apply for the officer or agent position within a reasonable time (specifically stated in the agreement) after he reaches a specified age or completes college, whichever occurs first, and that failure to do so will result in termination as a cadet. This technique would assure a turnover of cadets, limiting their membership to future police officers or investigators only.

Supplementing a paid internship or cadet training program, some colleges use their police science students in a variety of paid police-type activities. Some of those activities include on-campus traffic control, crowd control, and general security. Still another incentive to the future police officer student is the requirement that they wear distinctive uniforms while in class and on campus. Esprit de corps runs high when the students are well trained and strictly disciplined. Entrance into this select group of students should be difficult, with summary expulsion for those who disobey the rules or fail to perform as required.

Basic Training

The classroom setting with instructors drawn from within the organization to introduce the new employees to the manipulative and procedural functions of his job provides the employee with the basic tools that he must have to function effectively. The classroom instruction may or may not be mixed with field experiences or some laboratory training. This training may last from ten to twenty hours to as much as twenty or more weeks of intensive training in an academy setting. Many police-training leaders have agreed for many years that 400 hours should be a minimum length of a basic academy. The subjects and the hours devoted to each may vary, but if there is a state agency that monitors police academies, there will be a minimum time and specific objectives for each course. Examples of topics covered and time devoted to each subject of some academy programs follow.

WICHITA, KANSAS, 1977

1.	Criminal Investigations	91
2.	Defense Tactics	16
3.	Dynamics of Effective Patrol Services	52
4.	Experiential Learning	128
5.	First Aid	40
6.	Legal Aspects of Law Enforcement	33
7.	Orientation to Police Enterprise	25
8.	Outside Agencies	28
9.	Police Response to Community Social Problems	50
10.	Police Weapons	44
11.	Supportive Services	6
12.	Traffic Safety and Enforcement	29
13.	Writing Skills for Effective Communication	30
14.	Youth Services	11
	Testing	28
	Review	13

HAWAII POLICE DEPARTMENT, 1977

1.	Police Defensive Driving	12
2.	Traffic-Driver Audit	4
3.	Explosive Ordnance	8
4.	Criminal Law	22
5.	Narcotics	4
6.	Traffic Administration and Procedures	30
7.	Physical Training	22
8.	Criminal Investigation	50
9.	Criminalistics and Scientific Aids	10
10.	Arrest, Search and Seizure	12
11.	Supervision and Leadership	4
12.	Communications	4
13.	Police Community Relations	4
14.	Juvenile Delinquency and the Police	12
15.	Crisis Intervention	40

16. First Responders Course (Life Support) 40
17. Firearms.......... 26
18. Counterfeit Money.......... 4
19. Alcohol, Tobacco, and Firearms 4
20. Organized Crime 2
21. Police Surveillance.......... 2
22. Techniques of Observation 2
23. Introduction to Law Enforcement.......... 4
24. Self Defense for Police Officers 18
25. Breathalyzer Training.......... 24
26. Techniques and Mechanics of Arrest 3
27. Miranda Ruling 2
28. Civil Liabilities 4
29. Examinations 20
30. Duty Manual.......... 4
31. Police Organization and Management.......... 2

DENVER, COLORADO, 1977

1. History and Orientation, Academy
   Administration of Justice 60½
2. Basic Law 58
3. Police Procedures.......... 174½
4. Skill Training
   Communications, Driving, Firearms, Self Defense.......... 176½
5. Community Relations 46½
6. Roll Call and Inspections.......... 17½
7. Supervised Group Study 5
8. Field Training Officer Seminar 2
9. Crime Prevention 30
10. Child Abuse 3
11. Charting and Drawing Crime Scenes 2
12. Criminal Justice System.......... 1
13. Organized Crime 2
14. Labor Relations, Accident Review Board 1
15. Fingerprints.......... 3
16. Narcotics 5
17. Medical Examiner 2
18. Civil Procedures 1
19. Special Assignments.......... 3
20. I.D. Picture Mug Shots 1½
21. S.I.B. Inspection 2
22. Commentary Driving Exercise/Mobile Radio Use.......... 6
23. Observation Rides (State, City, Radio) 16
24. Field Problems, Patrol, Stops, Traffic.......... 20
25. Review, Course and General.......... 4½

26.	Sudden Infant Death	1
27.	Deaf Awareness	3
28.	Motor Pool Procedures	½
29.	First Aid	24
30.	On the Job Training	40

CALIFORNIA, 1978 (POST Minimum Standards, All Agencies)

1.	Professional Orientation	10
2.	Police Community Relations	15
3.	Law	45
4.	Laws of Evidence	15
5.	Communications	15
6.	Vehicle Operations	15
7.	Force and Weaponry	40
8.	Patrol Procedures	90
9.	Traffic	30
10.	Criminal Investigation	45
11.	Custody	5
12.	Physical Fitness and Defense Techniques	40
13.	First Aid and CPR	15
14.	Examinations (Written and Performance)	20

Basic training for correctional personnel varies considerably, because there is such a variety of positions within the corrections category, including the parole and probation officer, and the correctional officer. The latter is usually required to have the least amount of academic college preparation prior to entry, in many cases only the high school diploma or its equivalent. Probation and parole officers are usually required to have at least a baccalaureate degree prior to entry.

Brewer and Blair listed a nine-part base of knowledge that should be common to all three categories of correctional personnel, regardless of their respective positions or prior academic preparation: (1) Introduction to the System, (2) Concepts of the Correctional System, (3) Communications, (4) Dynamics of Human Behavior, (5) Personal and Cultural Norms, (6) Mental and Physical Health Influence on Behavior, (7) Influence of Groups on Behavior, (8) Change and the Learning Process, (9) Resources. The charts prepared by Brewer and Blair are comprehensive in their presentation of the duties, skills, knowledge, and other data essential to a training program for the various professionals in the corrections component of the criminal justice system.[7]

[7]Donald D. Brewer and Carol Ann Blair, *In-Service Training for Probation, Parole, and Correctional Personnel: A Plan for Action* (Washington, D.C., Law Enforcement Assistance Administration, 1968).

Class of Duties	On-the-Job Technical	Skills in	Conceptual Knowledge of
I. Supervision of Groups of Inmates Specific duties	Counts Feeding Protective utensils Prevent waste Movement Issues Org. Work Crews	Observation Instruction Information giving Use of group leadership Discipline Motivation	Causes of behavior Group dynamics and interaction Process of change Learning process Values, roles, attitudes Communication Discipline Motivation Authority
II. Supervision of Individual Specific duties	Reports Search Contraband	Observation Instruction Information giving Interpretation of rules Relationship Listening Discipline Motivation	Causes of behavior; group dynamics and interaction Process of change; learning process, values, roles, attitudes, communication; discipline; motivation; authority; Individualized behavior; Deviant behavior; Interpersonal relationships helping process Meaning of untruth, stealing Meaning of loss of freedom Meaning of and use of work Family functioning; separation
III. Security Specific duties	Visiting procedure Outside perimeter Firearms Self-defense Assist defense of another Fire procedures Arrest, seize and search	All skills in I and II plus First Aid Securing evidence Giving testimony Predicting and preventing altercations	All areas in I and II plus Use of knowledge to predict behavior and to recognize "danger signals" in behavior of individual and groups
IV. Administrative Duties Specific duties	Censoring process Operate and inspect safety devices Process of transporting prisoners Care of equipment	Public Interpretation Use of resources—institutional and community Identification of problems	Organization Philosophy and mission Legal rights and responsibilities Criminal Justice System

I. *Supervision of Individuals*
   A. *Personal counseling for rehabilitation*
      1. Employment counseling
      2. Personal problems, social, physical, emotional
      3. Training—education
      4. Marital and family
      5. Management—home, financial
      6. Social functioning

   → Resource information; Referral procedure

   B. *Enforcement*
      1. Interpretations of rules and regulations
      2. Reporting systems
      3. Revocation procedures
      4. Dismissal procedures
      5. Follow-up procedures

   → Knowledge of rules and regulations

II. *Investigation*
   A. *Pre-sentence (Probation)*
      1. Collects information on
         a. Criminal record
         b. Employment, school history
         c. Family history
         d. Medical and psychological history
         e. Community reputation
         f. Collateral contacts and records
      2. Prepares report
         a. Organizes information
         b. Makes diagnosis and plan
         c. Makes recommendations

   → Location of records; Where information is available; Specific format of reports; Scope of content; Sample reports

   B. *Parole report*
      1. Collects information on
         a. Current family situation

   → See above

Interviewing
Recording
Organization of information
Establishing and maintaining relationships
Observations
Referral
Using community resources
Assessment—diagnosis
Prognosis—forecasting
Interpretation
Motivation
Information giving
Listening
Individualization
Empathy
Using authority
Communication—oral, written
Self-analysis
Problem solving

See above

Helping Process
Interpersonal relationships
Measuring of behavior
normal deviant
Personality development
Process of change
Basic learning theory
Social systems
Socio-cultural concepts
Values systems
Role theory
Family functioning
Group dynamics
Attitudes
Self-awareness
Authority—limit setting
Diagnosis
Social planning
Organization of community
Vocational guidance
Basic medical knowledge
Basic psychiatric knowledge
Behavior and illness
Narcotics
Alcoholism
Communication: written, oral, non-verbal

See above

Figure 10-2 Custodial Officers Duties, Skills, Knowledge.

Source. Donald D. Brewer and Carol Ann Blair, *In-Service Training for Probation, Parole, and Correctional Personnel: A Plan for Action* (Washington, D.C.: Law Enforcement Assistance Administration, 1968), p. 42.

Duties	On the Job Technical	Skills in	Knowledge of
b. Availability of employment c. Institution adjustment d. Medical and psychological evaluation e. Social adjustment 2. Prepares report a. Organizes information b. Makes prognosis c. Makes recommendations			
III. *Officer of Court or Parole Board* A. *Function as "arm" of Court or Board* B. *Implementation of Court order* C. *Liaison* 1. With court 2. With enforcement officials 3. With attorneys 4. With other correctional divisions	Specific tasks Court procedures Board procedures Rules and regulations Rights and responsibilities	All above plus official behavior	All above plus Criminal Justice System Legal processes Political systems
IV. *Community Interpretation* A. *Develop resources i.e. jobs, housing, etc.* B. *Utilize community resources.* C. *Interpret program to public* D. *Interpret individual to public*	Resource information Use of existing printed material	Public speaking Public writing "Salesmanship"	Community attitudes
V. *Administration* A. *Maintain records and reports* 1. Individual 2. Administrative B. *Caseload management* C. *Personnel management* D. *Budget and expenditure* F. *Training and instruction*	Scope of content Format Forms Resources available Rules and regulations Accountability	Organization of work Assignment of work Basic budget formulation Basic statistical analysis Handling personnel problems On-the-job training and instructions Determining training needs	Basic management techniques Supervisory methods Basic personnel management O-J-T techniques

Figure 10-3 Probation and Parole Officers Duties, Skills, Knowledge.

Source. Donald D. Brewer and Carol Ann Blair, *In-Service Training for Probation, Parole, and Correctional Personnel: A Plan for Action* (Washington, D.C.: Law Enforcement Assistance Administration, 1968), pp. 50–51.

On-the-job-training Technical	Basic "floor of knowledge"	Skills Training	Institutes	Formal Education
Resource information Referral procedure Knowledge of rules and regulations Location of records Specific format of records Locating information Scope and content of reports Sample reports Court procedures Board procedures Rules and regs. of court or board Right to repeal of court or board Accountability	Introduction Concepts of correctional system Communication Dynamics of human behavior Personal and cultural norms Mental and physical health and behavior Change—the learning process Resources	Examples: Interviewing Referral process Recording Official behavior Public interpretation Case load management Problem solving techniques Training others	Examples: Narcotics Alcoholism Mental problems Guidance for Employment Organization of conventions	A.B. degree in Social Welfare-Corrections sequence Masters degree with field placement in corrections
This technical knowledge is always taught within the setting to which the employee is assigned.	This can be taught within the setting if there is the professional capability, It can also be taught by a specially employed Institution. This would also be the base for new employees.	These skills can be taught by a university team to assure that basic conceptual knowledge is included. Content will be based on the duties to which the skills relate.	These are thought of as periodic institutes within the academic setting with the goal of enrichment of the employee.	These are given within a properly accredited institution.

Figure 10-4 Training for Probation and Parole Personnel.

Source. Donald D. Brewer and Carol Ann Blair, *In-Service Training for Probation, Parole, and Correctional Personnel: A Plan for Action* (Washington, D.C.: Law Enforcement Assistance Administration, 1968), p. 56.

Escort Training

Following the basic training, the new employee is now equipped with the knowledge and fundamental proficiencies to do the job, and he is ready for the application phase of his learning process. He must be able to identify the situation and interpret what he must do in his role in the justice system that will correctly address that problem. He is assigned to work with a teammate, a more experienced member of the same organization who has been selected because he performs well on the job, but also because he has the interest and ability to function as a tutor. The relationship is one similar to that of journeyman-apprentice. At the beginning, the tutor demonstrates how to perform the tasks, then he directs the novice to perform them under his surveillance. They discuss the concepts and the actual procedures. This

Figure 10-5 Roll Call Training in Progress.
Courtesy Police Department, Lawton, Oklahoma.

procedure goes on until the trainee is able to function effectively and correctly with the tutor looking on and offering only an occasional word of advice or direction. At some time when the tutor feels confident that his charge can "solo," he steps aside and the newly trained employee is on his own. He will continue to be subjected to some supervision and occasional "check-rides" with a senior officer or perhaps another tutor or two to make sure that he has assimilated all of the essential knowledge and improved his basic skills.

In-Service Daily Training

A specific period of time may be set aside each day for a training session during which the supervisors and training personnel may present formal or informal instructional material to bring the employees up to date on new laws, procedures, new information, or to have some sort of refresher training to assure maximum efficiency on the job. A short film or videotape may be used, or a ten-minute lecture accompanied by some sort of testing to assure the instructor that the information was digested or that the new technique has been mastered by the recipients of the training. Such training is usually related to current problems or current or future needs. Otherwise, the student-practitioners will get little—if any—benefit from the training.

Training Bulletins and Home-Study Material

Professional journals provide excellent sources of information for the professional in the justice system, and libraries will yield more valuable information. The agency may select certain items of interest and essential knowledge for certain individuals or for the entire department membership, and duplicate and disseminate them for home study.

Role Playing as a Training Device

Developed by psychiatrists as a variation of psychodrama in which individuals may act out their feelings and thoughts, utilization of role playing is a form of rehearsal-training that may be quite effective. Simulations of real situations that have occurred, or that frequently occur, or that may never have happened yet, but are anticipated, provide an excellent vehicle for realistic training. The simulation is presented to the student under controlled conditions when the individual is put under artificial stress so that he must make critical decisions, yet be afforded the luxury of making his mistakes while he is performing during the training session rather than in actual situations. The objective is to provide the individual with a series of experiences so that when he is confronted with a real situation under stress he may act as one who has been through similar experiences before, and he should perform with greater confidence and skill.

Seminars and Symposia

Problem-solving groups representing the various agencies of the justice system may meet and discuss their respective problems, and may exchange ideas on their perceptions of the other person's responsibilities. This type of training stimulates greater understanding and cooperation among members of the several components of the justice system. Many of the problems are common to more than one component, and joint symposia creates an awareness that one is not unique in his need for assistance and understanding. This particular method of training session is utilized for problem solving and exchange of information.

Regional Training Centers

All of the components of the justice system have continuous needs for training for both general and special needs. Although the actual course content may vary, the media and facilities, equipment, and support personnel may all be provided at some centrally located resource center. Such a pooling of talents and resources appears to be the trend throughout the nation. Only the largest agencies are able to support such a center by themselves, but when operated under a joint powers agreement, costs are prorated and it is possible for the smaller agencies to benefit from the more advanced forms of training.

Specialized Training

With pooled resources such as those found at regional centers, training programs have been developed to serve agency needs of the many components of the justice system beyond the orientation and apprenticeship levels. Specialized training programs are available for prosecuting attorneys, newly appointed judges, court administrators, as well as many of the different tasks performed by members of corrections and law enforcement professions. The supervisory, mid-management, and executive positions are also recognized by such training courses and seminars in first-line and middle-management supervision, and executive development. Concurrent with management training programs for the incumbents, lower-ranking individuals who have demonstrated promising talents are sent to management training programs and are programmed through a series of learning experiences as a part of a planned executive development schedule.

SUMMARY

What is education and what is training may be a topic for discussion, and there may be some disagreement on definitions, but there is no disagreement that both are equally important and that they are inseparable. In the preceding pages we have covered principles and practices of both education and training, and have briefly touched upon some of the specific developments that have occurred during the past decade. The first part of the chapter was devoted to the selection methods and philosophies of many contemporary criminal justice agencies. The material contained in the pages of this chapter should serve as a basis for closer scrutiny by the student who is preparing to seek admittance into one of those agencies, and who intends to launch a career in the criminal justice field.

EXERCISES AND STUDY QUESTIONS

1. What is the difference between education and training, as explained in this chapter?

2. Why is there a difference between the application form and the personal history statement?

3. What is the purpose for such a thorough background investigation used by a criminal justice agency prior to employment as a candidate?

4. According to the statement of philosophy, what is the reason for having all Administration of Justice students take "core" courses prior to branching out with one of the tracks that are available to him?

5. The type of training the author called escort training is employed by the prosecuting attorney in which manner when a new prosecutor is placed on the job?

6. Is the internship a valid means of preparing students for criminal justice occupations? Can you explain why you responded to that question as you did?

7. Explain the reason for such a heavy emphasis on liberal arts for Administration of Justice students who are preparing to be police officers.

8. After you have examined the course descriptions of the five core courses, comment on whether you believe those five topics should be core courses, and explain the reasoning for your comment.

9. What courses would you suggest as electives for each of the three justice system components of law enforcement, judicial process, and corrections?

10. List Humanities courses that should be recommended for students preparing for (1) probation officer, (2) federal investigator, (3) group supervisor in juvenile hall, (4) deputy sheriff. If you chose different courses for each of those positions, explain why.

11. For what types of personality characteristics do you believe an individual who is applying for a juvenile probation officer should be excluded if he were screened by a psychologist? Why?

12. Take the position in criminal justice that you would be personally interested in as a potential employee, analyze the qualities that you believe essential for that position, then prepare about six questions you would ask candidates for that position. Try it out on a fellow student and see if you agree on the answers.

13. In addition to those items listed in the text as reasons why candidates are not selected, add three to five more reasons you can think of.

14. In the city where you live, does your police department have a cadet or intern program? What positions do they have for students to work part time?

15. What emphasis, if any, do you believe the police should put on human-relations training in a basic academy?

RECOMMENDED SEMESTER/TERM PROJECTS

1. Go through a basic recruit academy syllabus for a police department, or a basic training manual for use to train probation or parole agents to list those items that the individual must demonstrate knowledge and skill. With that information, prepare a field training guide that a senior officer or agent would take with him while breaking in a new officer during escort training. In your guide, describe the purpose for the guide, and how to use it.

2. Choose two different entry-level positions for the criminal justice professions, such as group supervisor in a youth camp and a police officer. Go through your college catalog, and list those courses you would recommend for each of the two candidates. Explain your reason for choosing each course, and tell how each will enhance the individual's performance on the job.

SUGGESTED FOR ADDITIONAL STUDY

American Correctional Association, *Manual of Correctional Standards* (3d ed.). New York: American Correctional Association, 1966.

Commission on Peace Officers Standards and Training, *Performance Objectives for the POST Basic Course.* Sacramento, Calif.: Commission on Peace Officers Standards and Training, 1977.

______, *POST Prescribed Curricula.* Sacramento, Calif.: Commission on Peace Officers Standards and Training, 1978.

Governor's Commission on Crime and Delinquency, *Performance Objectives for the New Hampshire Police Academy.* Concord: Governor's Commission on Crime and Delinquency, 1977.

Joint Commission on Correctional Manpower and Training, *Manpower and Training in Correctional Institutions.* Washington, D.C.: Government Printing Office, 1969.

PIVEN, HAROLD, and ABRAHAM ALCABES, *Probation/Parole: Pilot Study of Correctional Training and Manpower.* Washington, D.C.: Government Printing Office, 1967.

STINCHCOMB, JAMES D., *Opportunities In Law Enforcement and Related Careers.* Skokie, Ill.: National Textbook Co., 1976.

11

Ethics, Professionalism and the Community Image

INTRODUCTION

Someone said, "The proof of the pudding is in the eating." What does that have to do with criminal justice? Just this: individuals and agencies can have their codes of ethics and be true professionals in every sense of the word, but it will all be for naught unless the community accepts them as professionals. Not only must the criminal justice practitioner be a living example of professionalism, free from the taint of suspicion, and completely ethical in all transactions, but that individual must be all of those things *in the eyes of the public.*

In this chapter we shall explore the subjects of professionalism and ethics, as well as techniques in gaining public recognition through development of the correct community image.

ETHICS AND PROFESSIONALISM

The many thousands of men and women who occupy the hundreds of classifications of positions in the justice system and its many components serve the public in what I believe to be a position of trust and responsibility. Power vested in these individuals by law is far exceeded by the public's acceptance of their authority. Many of these people are held in awe by the publics they serve, and the responsibility to those "publics" is compounded by the pressure to restrain one's self where no external pressures are applied. For example, to the bewildered first-time law violator the police detective who questions him is about ten-feet tall and has total power over his freedom. The investigator has the burden of responsibility to remind the violator that he has the guaranteed right to refuse to answer questions even though he—the investigator—is earnestly seeking those answers. The judge in the courtroom cannot find a person guilty just because the accused person's hair or clothing style is different from that of the judge. The decision must be based solely on the evidence presented to the judge in a legally prescribed manner, and it can happen that the judge will find someone not guilty even though he may privately or "intuitively" believe that person to be guilty. It is the judge's responsibility to remind the accused as well as the prosecutor and defense attorney that he is innocent until *proven* guilty even though the circumstances may indicate that it is an "open and shut case."

Every individual who is employed within the justice system must adhere to the principles of the codes of ethics of the respective components of the system. Such an individual should not divest himself of his individuality and his personal consciousness of mitigating circumstances that may surround certain actions requiring his intervention, but he must act within the propriety of the ethical requirements of his profession. These codes of ethics may bear the title of Judicial Ethics and may describe the conduct of *judges,* but they apply to every member of that component of the system because they are directly responsible to the same principles and ethics as the judge as his agents and as his direct affiliates. If one of the occupational participants in one of the system's components finds that he cannot operate effectively within the constraints of certain ethical requirements, then he should seek a position in another occupation that will be more compatible with his own philosophy.

The ethical requirements of the law profession provide that an attorney should competently represent his client. If a client is known to be guilty by his own admissions, his attorney is still compelled to provide for his client competent legal services, which may lead to a jury's finding of *not guilty.* The police officer may witness a criminal act that he feels should not be considered a crime, yet he must effect the arrest because of his ethical requirement to serve the *public good* as determined by the legislative branch of government. The probation officer may personally believe that a particular religious philosophy has such a carnival-like aura about it that it is in total disharmony with his personal convictions, yet he is ethically required to try every approach toward the rehabilitation of his client and that may include referral to the spiritual guidance offered by that specific sect.

Professionalism goes along inseparably with ethics. As a matter of fact, one of the requisites of a profession is that it must have a code of ethics and that there must be some provision for the enforcement of those ethical requirements. Professionalization in the justice system has grown immensely in the past few decades, and many new professions have emerged within the system.

The justice system is providing a series of services for the public, and it must maintain an open line of communications with the individuals in that public to have an exchange of ideas as to the needs and wishes of both practitioner and public. It is a multidirectional communications requirement. I use the word *individual* to emphasize the distinct individuality of the practitioners in the justice system as well as the individuality of the public, which is actually a conglomeration of many publics: the taxpaying public, the parent public, the law-violating public, the law-abiding public, the middle-class public, the rich public, the poor public, the advantaged public, the disadvantaged public, and many composite publics representing two or more classifications of publics. The mere explanation of "public" becomes complex, as it also involves "community," which may be similarly discussed to emphasize the intense individuality of the people who make up the public or the community.

If we expect the people to understand *what* we are doing and *why,* it is our responsibility to explain it to them. After all, it is their interests that we are looking after. Professional prosecutors, judges, police officers, parole and probation officers, court administrators, investigators, and other individuals working in the field of criminal justice have been employed to perform their services in accordance with their respective proficiencies and their discretionary powers. The work is not one for amateurs, and most of the people in the community know that. When the many jobs are being done correctly in an acceptable manner, the general public does not attempt to interfere. There are detractors, of course, and those who will criticize regardless of what is being done, or how.

It is when the police officer, or the judge, or the prosecutor "pulls a boner," or a series of errors that the publics begin expressing their concern. If we are to expect the people who comprise the publics to be able to tell the difference between correct and incorrect procedure, there must be an ongoing educational and informational process so that the people have the information and knowledge that they need. If the justice system provides this information correctly, the agency relationships with the community are enhanced and it is possible to have actual community involvement as well as understanding.

PROFESSIONALISM

A profession does not suddenly become a profession by proclamation. Although the word has been used in so many different ways, in this chapter the term will apply to those positions that meet the criteria outlined in the paragraphs that follow.

Profession Defined and Discussed

Textbook and dictionary definitions vary, but there seems to be a general agreement on certain factors that distinguish a particular occupation as a profession. Those factors include:

1. A common body of specialized knowledge.
2. Minimum education requirements prior to entry into the profession.
3. Free exchange of information between individuals and their departments.
4. Careful and rigid preemployment screening.
5. A code of ethics.

6. Recognition by the public.
7. Decision-making responsibility and authority.

A closer analysis of these seven factors may provide greater insight into many of the occupations in the justice system and enable you to determine whether certain occupations qualify for the classification of *profession*.

1. A Common Body of Specialized Knowledge Approximately one thousand educational institutions in the United States offer one or more different programs of education leading to two-year associate degrees, baccalaureate degrees, graduate degrees and doctorates in fields related to the justice system. At the two-year level, a core curriculum may be offered that provides the common body of specialized knowledge in administration of justice, followed by the student's choice of which one of several tracks he wishes to follow. Tracks include Crime Lab Assistant, Business and Industrial Security, Law Enforcement, Judicial Process (Courts), or Corrections. The growth of libraries in criminal justice fields, and the diverse backgrounds of their authors further attest to the "body of knowledge" concept.

An interesting phenomenon occurs within the justice system educational process: The core at college-entry level provides a common base of information to all participants in the several programs; the students then branch off into tangents related to their own needs and interests; and this is followed by a general transition back toward a second common body of knowledge in organization, management, administrative problems, the overall aspects of public administration, and community-agency cooperation.

2. Pre-entry Education Requirements There seems to be considerable variance on this qualification. Graduation from high school with no college history at all may be considered sufficient for entry into any of the occupations in prisoner control and in law enforcement. Other occupations, such as judges and lawyers, must have advanced professional degrees, and yet others, such as probation and parole, may require baccalaureate degrees prior to entry into the profession, but that degree may be in any major and/or minor. It appears that there is considerable room for "professional" growth in pre-entry education requirements for virtually all of the justice system professions with the exception of attorneys and judges. Many proponents for advanced education for justice system components encourage support to baccalaureate level degrees for police officers as well as for other professionals in related agencies.

3. Free Exchange of Information between Individuals and Their Departments Trade secrets are zealously guarded by competing manufacturers of soaps and toys, but what would be the result if the first doctor to successfully transplant a kidney or some other vital organ would forever keep his secret? A true professional is one who makes a discovery that serves mankind in such a beneficial way that it saves lives, or changes lives, and then shares that information with colleagues by writing papers and conducting a series of lecture-demonstrations. He attempts to disseminate the information, and he assists others in developing the technique so that they may duplicate his successes and may even improve upon them. For example, consider human-organ transplants and the free flow of information among the doctors who perform these miracles of medical science.

In the field of justice administration, the probation officer who develops a technique in which he experiences any degree of success in behavior modification has a professional obligation to tell his colleagues about his new technique. A free-flowing exchange of information throughout the several professions in the justice system is essential to the perpetuation of those professions. Unfortunately, there are some individuals in every profession who may be so greedy, or insecure, or may have some unfulfilled need that they guard their secrets and refuse to share them. The true professional who selflessly devotes his life to the service of others seems also to have the personality characteristics that involve the same selfless exchange of information.

4. Careful and Rigid Preemployment Screening There is a variety of methods of selection utilized by many different agencies. Under the watchful eyes of their respective Peace Officers Standards and Training Commissions, police officers of the several states that have mandated professional standards are subjected to a series of rigid tests. Only a small percentage of candidates who apply are successful in gaining appointments. Law schools and state bar examinations are as much a screening process as a learning process, and many aspirants to the legal profession have failed to successfully complete the process, or have had their completion delayed because of some deficiency in their qualifications.

The testing process includes intelligence surveys, attitude and personality screening devices, endurance and agility tests, rigid training schedules, and a probationary period—all designed to eliminate all but the best qualified for the positions involved. Background investigations are conducted for the purpose of determining the candidate's reputation, which is so important to all of the justice system, and to find out whatever possible about the candidate's past performance and attitudes both in his public and his private life.

5. A Code of Ethics Standards of conduct and specified principles for professional performance provide for the individual a set of guidelines that he may follow as a form of self-discipline, a practice that is essential to any professional person. Within the profession there must also be a prescribed enforcement procedure to assure compliance with the codes of ethics and to assure some form of punitive and corrective action to be taken upon violators of the codes. In this chapter we shall look at some of the codes of ethics found in the justice system.

6. Recognition by the Public Each of the several professions within the justice system, and other occupations and paraprofessions (or "subprofessions"), is usually viewed separately by the public and holds its own distinctive position of influence in its relationship with the people it serves. A true test of whether a particular calling has attained professional status is to determine how well it is accepted by the public.

7. Decision-making Responsibility and Authority All professionals, such as those in medicine and law, must make independent decisions based upon their assessment of the situation that confronts them, their education and experiences with similar encounters, the confidence and trust others put in him to make critical decisions, and the authority allowed them to make such decisions. About this particular process involving the police officer, James Q. Wilson made these observations:

> Formally, the police are supposed to have almost no discretion: by law in many places and in theory everywhere, they are supposed to arrest everyone whom they see committing an offense or, with regard to the more serious offenses, everyone whom they have reasonable cause to believe has committed an offense. In fact, as all police officers and many citizens recognize, discretion is inevitable partly because it is impossible to observe every public infraction, partly because many laws require interpretation before they can be applied at all, partly because the police can sometimes get information about serious crimes by overlooking minor crimes, and partly because the police believe that public opinion would not tolerate a policy of full enforcement of all laws all the time.
>
> In almost every public organization, discretion is exercised...but the police department has the special property...that within it discretion increases as one moves *down* the hierarchy.[1]

The Organization's Responsibility to the Professional

Part of the public's acceptance of an individual and his occupation as a professional involves the manner in which his own organization accepts him and presents him to the public. There are certain factors that comprise the agency's responsibility to the individual. Those factors include the following:

1. Competent Leadership The executives and management people in the organization must provide enlightened leadership to the professionals who must respond to their leadership. A good leader must be a model for those he leads, and professional leaders should be no exception. As is common among emerging professions, the "old guard," the professionals who perhaps had less formal training and education, but who, nevertheless, stimulated

[1]James Q. Wilson, *Varieties of Police Behavior: The Management of Law and Order in Eight Communities* (Cambridge: Harvard University Press, 1968), p. 7.

the growth and development of the newcomers to the profession, are finding themselves surrounded by individuals of lower rank who have more formidable-looking credentials. The mark of a competent leader is the ability to utilize the talents of subordinates to their maximum potential. Rather than look upon the relative newcomers as threats, the "Abe Lincolns" of the criminal justice professions can lend their wisdom and experience to the "new breed," and enhance their total value and effectiveness of the profession. No individual is a good leader if his or her subordinates will not or cannot respond to, and accept, that leadership.

There are many leaders in the criminal justice system with very impressive credentials in addition to the valuable wisdom and experience. Those individuals, too, should encourage the growth and progress of their followers. Suspicion and distrust will gnaw away at the roots of the agency and will eventually cause its destruction. Someone once said that a tree at Gettysburg withstood cannonballs and many seasons of bad weather, but finally let the little things—the termites—destroy it. The "little things" can also destroy a profession.

The leader should maintain an attitude conducive to the encouragement of academic progress and experimentation that accompany professional growth and development, and should refrain from overshadowing his subordinates' accomplishments by his own display of skills and talent.

2. More than Adequate Facilities Although government operations involve public approval for any type of construction, and then once the decision is made to build, someone who offered to do the work at the lowest bid is chosen, it should be borne in mind that the "bargain basement" is not always the best place to find a bargain. Functional, spacious, and comfortable quarters must be modern and well equipped. Furniture and office equipment, and other operating equipment should be maintained in excellent working condition and nothing should be allowed to fall into a state of disrepair.

Although there are many offices and other facilities in criminal justice that maintain 40- to 45-hour weeks, many agencies, such as police and sheriffs' departments, jails, crime laboratories, their personnel, and their equipment all operate around-the-clock. A week actually goes by in less than two days, comparatively speaking. The 168-hour week times 52 means that the police station and its contents gets 8,736 hours of use in the same year that a regular business office gets 2,346 hours of use. A year goes by about every three months. Even the copy machines wear out four times as fast!

3. Good Equipment The vehicles, weapons, office equipment, uniforms or other special clothing, and all of the additional equipment that the professional uses should be in excellent shape and capable of serving the purpose for which they are maintained. Special safety equipment should be purchased or provided by the agency.

4. Training and Educational Assistance Schedules should be arranged as closely as possible to allow agency members to attend class whenever possible. Arrangements should be made, as nearly as possible, for the agency to at least address the needs of its employees in attempting to upgrade themselves both academically and ethically. In-service training must be arranged, and continuous efforts should be made to make training meaningful and actually productive in accordance with real needs. Schedules should be arranged so that the interested employees may continue their educational pursuits without the work and the school attendance interfering with each other. Financial incentives are used by many agencies to stimulate interest in continuing one's educational pursuits. An example of pay incentive for college education for police officers would be an added 2½ percent for two years of college, 5 percent for a baccalaureate degree, and 7½ percent for a master's degree.

5. Recognition Individual employees should have a team spirit and strive to present an image of the department that will enhance the individual's status with colleagues and the public. Although it may not be wise to emphasize private gain as an end result, there should be realistic incentives and rewards that will encourage the employees to earn recognition for extra efforts toward improvement of techniques in performing one's tasks. Constructive changes that lead to actual improvement are healthy, but changes that are made strictly for the sake of change may lack the same vitality.

Although it is more traditional that all press releases and other information come from the office of "Chief Goodfellow," there is no valid reason why certain individuals below the rank of chief cannot be named as officers who "broke an impossible case," "successfully prosecuted the Bonnie and Clyde of this generation," or who developed a new management tool utilizing electronic data processing. For many years it was hard to believe that the FBI had anyone intelligently leading the organization except the late John Edgar Hoover. The press releases read as though he was the only person in the entire organization who was working. To illustrate my point, would you please do as much research as you want and name one high-ranking leader in the history of the Federal Bureau of Investigation (other than Hoover, that is).

6. Remuneration Professional people must be paid wages appropriate to professional positions. Pay should be comparable to the performance as well as the competence and skill of the professional who is being paid. Unfortunately, civil-service rules tend to reward the mediocre and the individuals who contribute a great deal more to their professions are paid no more than those who retired on the job and spend their time counting the hours until they can stay home and work in their gardens or whatever they plan to do after they retire. If a second language proficiency is sufficient to merit a pay increment, so should a proficiency in operating an airplane, a helicopter, or other special motor vehicle equipment, or participation in a special enforcement team that requires continual exercise and skills practice to retain proficiency.

The Individual's Responsibility to the Profession

"Dedication to the profession" should describe the professional's attitude and actions. If he is to earn for himself and his colleagues the status of a professional, he has certain obligations to his employing agency and, above all, to the profession itself.

1. *Positive attitude.* The chronic complainer and the drone have no place in the administration of justice. The individual's attitude must be one of optimism and enthusiasm. By his own enthusiasm, he will generate the same feeling in the people with whom he works.
2. *Industriousness.* The highly individualized professional should be able to work on his own. Success in any profession requires intelligence and energy. Criminal justice is no exception. Energy, too, is infectious. One enthusiastic person can stimulate an entire work force under the right circumstances.
3. *Loyalty.* The professional must be loyal to his profession and the leaders of his organization as he is to his God, his country, and his community. Misplaced loyalty, such as that which causes one to lie and "cover" for a fellow employee who is violating the law or ethical standards of the profession, should be avoided at all costs. Loyalty is for the common good of the people.
4. *Competence.* The individual must achieve and maintain minimum performance standards. The "twenty-year company man" may or may not be a true professional. Practice itself does not necessarily "make perfect." *Perfect practice makes perfect.*

ETHICS

Every profession has its canons, or code of ethics that it uses to identify its principles, its goals, and general rules of ethical conduct. Such an instrument is used as a self-management tool that acts as a gauge by which an individual may measure his own standards and mode of operation. Development and maintenance of some sort of uniformity in minimum standards of conduct by all members of the profession involve the utilization of a statement of ethics to articulate what those standards are and how they may be maintained. The errant member of the profession who fails to adhere to the minimum standards and to the codes of conduct stated in the canons may be reminded by his peers of such standards, and his deliberate or continued violation of those standards may ultimately be utilized as a means of denying the individual the privilege of continuing his practice in the profession.

The several components of the justice system have their respective canons and codes of ethics. Because there are so many individual professions within the system, there are many more than the few that you will find in this chapter. For example, attorneys have canons of ethics; court administrators, legal secretaries, court reporters, and many others likewise have their own special codes of ethics. In this chapter, we shall discuss the Law Enforcement Canons and Code of Ethics, the Canons of Judicial Ethics, and the Declaration of Principles of the American Correctional Association. Each of these represents the types of professional statements and standards that are characteristic of the several professions represented in the justice system.

Law Enforcement Canons and Code of Ethics

LAW ENFORCEMENT CODE OF ETHICS

As a Law Enforcement Officer, my fundamental duty is to serve mankind; to safeguard lives and property; to protect the innocent against deception, the weak against oppression or intimidation, and the peaceful against violence or disorder; and to respect the Constitutional rights of all men to liberty, equality and justice.

I will keep my private life unsullied as an example to all; maintain courageous calm in the face of danger, scorn, or ridicule; develop self-restraint; and be constantly mindful of the welfare of others. Honest in thought and deed in both my personal and official life, I will be exemplary in obeying the laws of the land and the regulations of my department. Whatever I see or hear of a confidential nature or that is confided to me in my official capacity will be kept ever secret unless revelation is necessary in the performance of my duty.

I will never act officiously or permit personal feelings, prejudices, animosities, or friendships to influence my decisions. With no compromise for crime and with relentless prosecution of criminals, I will enforce the law courteously and appropriately without fear or favor, malice or ill will, never employing unnecessay force or violence and never accepting gratuities.

I recognize the badge of my office as a symbol of public faith, and I accept it as a public trust to be held so long as I am true to the ethics of the police service. I will constantly strive to achieve these objectives and ideals, dedicating myself before God to my chosen profession... law enforcement.[2]

CANONS OF POLICE ETHICS

Article 1. Primary Responsibility of Job

The primary responsibility of the police service, and of the individual officer is the protection of the people of the United States through the upholding

[2]Adopted in 1956 by the California Peace Officers Association, and in 1957 by the International Association of Chiefs of Police.

of their laws; chief among these is the Constitution of the United States and its amendments. The law enforcement officer always represents the whole of the community and its legally expressed will and is never the arm of any political party or clique.

Article 2. Limitations of Authority

The first duty of a law enforcement officer, as upholder of the law, is to know its bounds upon him in enforcing it. Because he represents the legal will of the community, be it local, state or federal, he must be aware of the limitations and prescriptions which the people, through law, have placed upon him. He must recognize the genius of the American system of government which give to no man, groups of men or institution, absolute power, and he must insure that he, as a prime defender of that system, does not pervert its character.

Article 3. Duty to be Familiar with the Law and with Responsibilities of Self and other Public Officials

The law enforcement officer shall assiduously apply himself to the study of the principles of the laws which he is sworn to uphold. He will make certain of his responsibilities in the particulars of their enforcement, seeking aid from his superiors in matters of technicality or principle when these are not clear to him; he will make special effort to fully understand his relationship to other public officials, including other law enforcement agencies, particularly on matters of jurisdiction, both geographically and substantively.

Article 4. Utilization of Proper Means to Gain Proper Ends

The law enforcement officer shall be mindful of his responsibility to pay strict heed to the selection of means in discharging the duties of his office. Violations of law or disregard for public safety and property on the part of an officer are intrinsically wrong; they are self-defeating in that they instill in the public mind a like disposition. The employment of illegal means, no matter how worthy the end, is certain to encourage disrespect for the law and its officers. If the law is to be honored, it must first be honored by those who enforce it.

Article 5. Cooperation with Public Officials in the Discharge of their Authorized Duties

The law enforcement officer shall cooperate fully with other public officials in the discharge of authorized duties, regardless of party affiliation or personal prejudice. He shall be meticulous, however, in assuring himself of the propriety, under the law, of such actions and shall guard against the use of his office or person, whether knowingly or unknowingly, in any improper or illegal action. In any situation open to question, he shall seek authority from his superior officer, giving him a full report of the proposed service or action.

Article 6. Private Conduct

The law enforcement officer shall be mindful of his special identification by the public as an upholder of the law. Laxity of conduct or manner in private life, expressing either disrespect for the law or seeking to gain special privilege, cannot but reflect upon the police officer and the police service. The community and the service require that the law enforcement officer lead the life of a decent and honorable man. Following the career of a policeman gives no man special prerequisites. It does give the satisfaction and pride of following and furthering an unbroken tradition of safeguarding the American republic. The officer who reflects upon this tradition will not degrade it. Rather, he will so conduct his private life that the public will regard him as an example of stability, fidelity, and morality.

Article 7. Conduct Toward the Public

The law enforcement officer, mindful of his responsibility to the whole community, shall deal with individuals of the community in a manner calculated to instill respect for its laws and its police service. The law enforcement officer shall conduct his official life in a manner such as will inspire confidence and trust. Thus, he will be neither overbearing nor subservient, as no individual citizen has an obligation to stand in awe of him nor a right to command him. The officer will give service where he can, and require compliance with the law. He will do neither from personal preference or prejudice but rather as a duly appointed officer of the law discharging his sworn obligation.

Article 8. Conduct in Arresting and Dealing with Law Violators

The law enforcement officer shall use his powers of arrest strictly in accordance with the law and with due regard to the rights of the citizen concerned. His office gives him no right to prosecute the violator nor to mete out punishment for the offense. He shall, at all times, have a clear appreciation of his responsibilities and limitations regarding detention of the violator; he shall conduct himself in such a manner as will minimize the possibility of having to use force. To this end he shall cultivate a dedication to the service of the people and the equitable upholding of their laws whether in the handling of law violators or in dealing with the lawabiding.

Article 9. Gifts and Favors

The law enforcement officer, representing government, bears the heavy responsibility of maintaining, in his own conduct, the honor and integrity of all government institutions. He shall, therefore, guard against placing himself in a position in which any person can expect special consideration or in which the public can reasonably assume that special consideration is being given. Thus, he should be firm in refusing gifts, favors, or gratuities, large or small, which can, in the public mind, be interpreted as capable of influencing his judgment in the discharge of his duties.

Article 10. Presentation of Evidence

The law enforcement officer shall be concerned equally in the prosecution of the wrongdoer and the defense of the innocent. He shall ascertain what constitutes evidence and shall present such evidence impartially and without malice. In so doing, he will ignore social, political, and all other distinctions among the persons involved, strengthening the tradition of the reliability and integrity of an officer's word.

The law enforcement officer shall take special pains to increase his perception and skill of observation, mindful that in many situations his is the sole impartial testimony to the facts of a case.

Article 11. Attitude Toward Profession

The law enforcement officer shall regard the discharge of his duties as a public trust and recognize his responsibility as a public servant. By diligent study and sincere attention to self-improvement he shall strive to make the best possible application of science to the solution of crime, and, in the field of human relationships, strive for effective leadership and public influence in matters affecting public safety. He shall appreciate the importance and responsibility of his office, and hold police work to be an honorable profession rendering valuable service to his community and his country.[3]

CANONS OF JUDICIAL ETHICS

Canon 1. A judge should uphold the integrity and independence of the judiciary.

Canon 2. A judge should perform the duties of his office fairly and diligently.

Canon 3. A judge may engage in activities for the improvement of the law, the legal system, and the administration of justice.

Canon 4. A judge should regulate his extrajudicial activities to minimize conflict with his judicial duties.

Canon 5. A judge should avoid impropriety and the appearance of impropriety in all of his activities.

Canon 6. A judge should publicly report compensation received for quasijudicial and extrajudicial activities.

Canon 7. A judge should not engage in political activity except to the extent necessary to obtain or retain judicial office through an elective process.[4]

Declaration of Principles of the American Correctional Association

PREAMBLE

The American Congress of Correction, to reaffirm the basic ideals and aspirations of its membership, to encourage a more enlightened criminal justice in our society, to promote improved practices in the treatment of adult and juvenile offenders, and to rededicate its membership to the high purposes stated by its founding leaders in 1870, does adopt this revised Declaration of Principles.

Principle I

The prevention and control of crime and delinquency are urgent challenges to the social sciences. The growing body of scientific knowledge, coupled with the

[3]Composed in 1957 by a Committee of the International Association of Chiefs of Police, Inc. consisting of the following: Andrew J. Kavanaugh, Franklin M. Kreml, and Quinn Tamm.

[4]Presented by United States Supreme Court Chief Justice Warren E. Burger at Williamsburg, Virginia, in March, 1971. Prepared by a Committee of the American Bar Association in February, 1971, this was presented as the sixth draft of that document. Taken from: *Addresses and Papers of the National Conference on the Judiciary, March 11-14, 1971 at Williamsburg, Virginia* (Washington, D.C.: Government Printing Office), *Justice in the States,* p. 25.

practical wisdom and skill of those professionaly engaged in society's struggle with the problem of criminality, provide the soundest basis for effective action.

Principle II

The forces for the prevention and control of crime and delinquency ultimately must find their strength from the constructive qualities of the society itself. The properly functioning basic institutions—such as the family, the school and the church, as well as the economic and political institutions—and a society united in the pursuit of worthwhile goals are the best guarantees against crime and delinquency. The willingness of the society to maintain a rationally organized and properly financed system of corrections, directed toward the reclamation of criminals and juvenile delinquents, is a prerequisite of effective control.

Principle III

Both punishment and correction are at present our methods of preventing and controlling crime and delinquency. Further improvement and expansion of the correctional methods should be the generally accepted goal, fully in line with the spirit of the penal reform of the past century and our current correctional progress.

Principle IV

Traditionally, violators of the criminal law have been differentiated into those who are mentally sick and should be handled as such and those who are considered criminally responsible. The best legal and psychiatric knowledge should be employed to define this distinction.

Principle V

Until the guilt of the suspected offender has been established in the course of due process of law, he should be considered innocent and his rights as a free citizen should be respected, except for such restraints as are indispensable to insure the proper investigation and trial.

Principle VI

If, as a result of a miscarriage of justice, an individual has been made to suffer, he should receive reasonable indemnification.

Principle VII

The correctional facilities, comprising both institutional and noninstitutional treatment—probation and parole—should be planned and organized as an integrated system under a central authority responsible for guiding, controlling, and vitalizing the whole.

Principle VIII

The variety of treatment programs corresponding to the different needs of the offenders suggests a diversification of correctional institutions resulting in a system of specialized institutions so classified and coordinated and so organized in staff and program as to meet the needs of those offenders who present specific problems. The spirit of continued experimentation with new types of institutions and agencies which show promise of more effective results should be encouraged and supported.

Principle IX

Repeated short sentences imposed for recurring misdemeanors or petty offenses, are ineffective, both as means of correction and as a punitive deterrent. These sentences often are a contributing factor in the career of the petty recidivist. An integrated system of control by means of special institutional facilities and community supervision is essential for the solution of this problem. Further research and experimentation with agencies and institutions of other than the conventional type offer the greatest promise.

Principle X

The architecture and construction of penal and correction institutions should be functionally related to the programs to be carried on in them. The great variety of existing programs, to be further diversified in the future, indicates the need for a similar variety and flexibility of architectural design and type of construction. The building standards and technological advances of the day should be reflected in these institutions. The current scepticism about inordinately large institutions suggests the desirability of institutions of moderate size, which may be more costly to build and operate, but which lend themselves better to the fulfillment of the objectives of a good correctional institutional program.

Principle XI

The organization and administration of correctional institutions and agencies is one of the more complex areas of public administration and deals with one of the most involved of social problems. It is essential that the administration of the correctional agencies meet the highest standards of public administration and that all employees be selected in accordance with the best available criteria and serve on the basis of merit and tenure systems.

Principle XII

The special and complex problems characteristic of criminal and delinquent behavior imply the need for suitable personality traits and specialized skills on the part of the personnel and hence the need for special professional education and training of a high standard, including preservice and continued in-service training.

Principle XIII

Correctional institutions and agencies can best achieve their goal of rehabilitation by focusing their attention and resources on the complete study and evaluation of the individual offender and by following a program of individualized treatment.

Principle XIV

The sentence or disposition determining the treatment for the offender should be based on a full consideration of the social and personality factors of the particular individual.

In the many jurisdictions these investigations may be made at different levels, so long as the essential information is available to the court or treatment authority at the time crucial case decisions are to be made.

Principle XV

A punitive sentence should properly be commensurate with the seriousness of the offense and the guilt of the offender. Inequality of such sentences for the same or similar crimes is always experienced as an injustice both by the offender and the society. On the other hand, the length of the correctional treatment given the offender for purposes of rehabilitation depends on the circumstances and characteristics of the particular offender and may have no relationship to the seriousness of the crime committed. In a correctionally-oriented system of crime control, the indeterminate sentence administered by qualified personnel offers the best solution.

Principle XVI

The principles of humanity and human dignity to which we subscribe, as well as the purposes of rehabilitation require that the offenders, while under the jurisdiction of the law enforcement and correctional agencies, be accorded the generally accepted standards of decent living and decent human relations.

Their food, clothing and shelter should not be allowed to fall below the generally accepted standards, and they should be afforded the conventional conveniences made possible by our technological progress. Their health needs—both physical and mental—should be met in accordance with the best medical standards. Recreation should be recognized as a wholesome element of normal life.

Principle XVII

Religion represents a rich resource in the moral and spiritual regeneration of mankind. Especially trained chaplains, religious instruction and counseling, together with adequate facilities for group worship of the inmate's own choice, are essential elements in the program of a correctional institution.

Principle XVIII

Rewards for conformance to the highest values of our culture should be given precedence over fear of punishment in guiding the development of human character in correctional systems as well as in society at large. Enlightened self-interest must be emphasized and made operative at all times.

Principle XIX

No law, procedure or system of correction should deprive any offender of the hope and the possibility of his ultimate return to full, responsible membership to society.

Principle XX

Moral forces, organized persuasion and scientific treatment should be relied upon in the control and management of offenders, with as little dependence upon physical force as possible.

Principle XXI

The task of evaluating the individual offender and developing the most appropriate treatment program must draw upon all the available knowledge and professional skill represented by sociology, psychology, psychiatry, social case work and related disciplines. Specialists and technicians from these fields must be welded into a diagnostic and treatment team by competent administrators, so that the disciplines they represent may become the core of the correctional treatment program.

Principle XXII

To assure the eventual restoration of the offender as an economically self-sustaining member of the community, the correctional program must make available to each inmate every opportunity to raise his educational level, improve his vocational competence and skills, and add to his information meaningful knowledge about the world and the society in which he must live.

Principle XXIII

To hold employable offenders in correctional institutions without the opportunity to engage in productive work is to violate one of the essential objectives of rehabilitation. Without in any way exploiting the labor of involuntary confines for financial gain, or unduly interfering with free enterprise, it is not only possible but imperative that all governmental jurisdictions give full cooperation to the establishment of productive work programs with a view to imparting acceptable work skills, habits, attitudes and work discipline.

Principle XXIV

Some of the criminal law violators who are found by the courts to be criminally responsible, but who are abnormal from the point of view of the modern disciplines of psychiatry and psychology, are in need of psychotherapy. Diagnostic and treatment facilities for such mentally abnormal offenders should be further developed at the appropriate stages of the correctional process.

Psychiatric and psychological services should be provided for the presentence investigations of the courts; out-patient clinics for the use of the noninstitutional treatment agencies—probation and parole; and psychiatric and psychological services within the penal and correctional institutions, even to the extent of developing special institutions for this type of offender.

Principle XXV

Recent research in the community aspects of the institutional populations suggests the importance of the group approach to the problem of correctional treatment. There is a need for more attention to the implications of this new method as well as the need to support and promote experiments and demonstration projects.

Principle XXVI

The exercise of executive clemency in the pardon of criminals is a question of great delicacy and difficulty. The use of this power should be limited largely to cases of wrongful conviction, or of excessive sentences constituting injustice, or, in rare instances, where extreme hardship is involved and executive dispensation is warranted. The practice of releasing large numbers of prisoners by executive clemency is generally condemned. The use of executive clemency or pardon to restore civil rights to a fully rehabilitated person who has established a record of responsible living for a period of years is, on the other hand, to be commended.

Principle XXVII

Suitable employment for a discharged or paroled offender is one of the major factors in his rehabilitation and the regaining of his lost position in society. The most forceful efforts and comprehensive methods should be exercised to secure such work. An understanding, favorable attitude and the participation of organized labor and management should be actively sought.

Principle XXVIII

Probation has come to be accepted as the most efficient and economical method of treatment for a great number of offenders. To enhance the achievement of the full potentialities of probation, mandatory exceptions to the use of probation with respect to specific crimes or to types of offenders should be eliminated from the statutes.

Current research indicates great possibilities for developing specific types and degrees of probationary supervision adapted to the needs of the individual offender.

Principle XXIX

With a few possible exceptions, all offenders released from correctional institutions should be released under parole supervision, and parole should be granted at the earliest date consistent with public safety and the needs of rehabilitation. Decisions pertaining to an individual's parole should be made by a professionally competent board. The type and degree of supervision should be adapted to the needs of the individual offender.

Principle XXX

The collection and publication of criminal statistics designed to provide information on the extent and nature of criminality and juvenile delinquency and on the various phases of the correctional process is indispensable for the understanding of crime and for the planning and evaluation of correctional and preventive measures.

Such statistics are necessary and should be developed on the national, state and local levels and should consist of statistics of the offenses known to the police, arrest statistics, judicial statistics, probation, institutional and parole statistics as well as criminal career records.

Principle XXXI

Research and the scientific study of the problems of juvenile delinquency and criminality and of the methods of dealing with these are essential prerequisites for progress. Through its educational, research and governmental institutions society should sponsor, finance and carry out both basic and applied research in this area. The law enforcement and correctional institutions and agencies should lend their support, take initiative and themselves engage in appropriate research as an indispensable part of their effort to improve their performance.

Principle XXXII

In a democracy the success of any public agency, including that of correctional institutions and agencies, depends in the final analysis on popular support. An adequate financial base, emphasis on the adequacy of personnel and, in general, insistence on an alert and progressive administration in corrections is the responsibility of the public and a function of its enlightened concern with crime and delinquency problems.

Principle XXXIII

The correctional process has as its aim the reincorporation of the offender into the society as a normal citizen. In the course of noninstitutional treatment the offender continues as a member of the conventional community. In the course of his institutional stay constructive community contacts should be encouraged. The success of the correctional process in all its stages can be greatly enhanced by energetic, resourceful and organized citizen participation.[5]

THE COMMUNITY IMAGE

Community Relations

Mere use of the words seems to imply that some sort of human interaction is involved, that there is some face-to-face, give-and-take interfacing on a "no-host" basis. In this environment of informality and spontaneity the objective of community relations activities is to achieve a mutual understanding between the people in the community and the justice system people who serve them. There can be no single program or activity that is expected to meet this objective. The process is continuous, it is diversified, it is fluid and interrelated with the entire agency's activities, and it involves people in these activities as individuals.

[5]American Correctional Association, *Manual of Correctional Standards* (College Park, Md.: American Correctional Association, 1959), pp. XIX–XXIV. The document was first prepared by the American Prison Association in 1870. It was revised and reaffirmed in 1930 and again in 1960 by the American Correctional Association.

Self-evaluation Before an agency attempts to widely disseminate details of its activities, there should be a careful study of those activities to determine that they are well defined and well done. The image that the agency wishes to present should be one that involves both facilities and personnel. Personal conduct should be pleasant and inoffensive. When one has to exercise his authority to accomplish a task it is possible to speak confidently and forcefully without taking on an officious air that will sound pompous and more of a caricature rather than a serious act. Roles are important to social interaction, and it is important that the actors in their respective roles do convincingly look the parts they are playing. Their dress, personal grooming, physical appearance, and mannerisms must be representative of the roles they play if the people are to accept them in those roles.

The building and its offices should be pleasant and nonthreatening, and certain parts of the building should be designed to evoke appropriate responses. For example, the courtroom has many traditions and its design tends to cause its occupants to act in a more subdued manner than they would act in the hallway. The raised bench and the traditional positions for the people who spend their days in the courtroom perpetuate the ceremonial atmosphere of the room and tend to encourage dignified and "courtly" conduct.

Cultural Awareness Every racial or ethnic culture is steeped in rich tradition that distinguishes that culture from all others, however subtle the differences may seem. Genuine sincerity in attempts to develop an understanding in a culture other than one's own is an admirable trait. It is not enough for a justice system practitioner to refrain from demonstrating prejudicial views, or to be tolerant of others; what he must do is to actually make it a point to develop his own awareness of the cultures and traditions of people with whom he works and for whom he serves in his public service occupation. Along with this understanding, it is extremely important that there be a deliberate avoidance of the use of "trigger words," or those words that tend to evoke the ire of those to whom the words may apply—by inference if not by actual intention.

Professional Conduct Both on and off the job, the professional should continue to play the role, which means that he or she is under close observation by everyone who knows him or her as a representative of the justice system. There is a quiet dignity to the professional when the role is cast in the theater. The public that is responsible for payment of a professional's salary similarly expects the "real-life" players to possess similar qualities. If those qualities are unrealistic and need modification, then it is time that the actual players bring about that change.

An objective, impartial attitude may be reflected in the individual's actions, and he must refrain from a display of personal involvement in someone's personal problems that present themselves to him while he is working. A calm and detached manner is far more effective than subjective emotionalism. Gratuities and special favors should not be accepted because of the ethical considerations involved, in addition to other considerations. The justice system practitioner must be approachable and a good listener, and should avoid being a "busybody" or meddler.

Community Assistance If we are to effectively serve the community on the basis of real needs that the people have identified to the different components of the justice system, we must have the community's assistance. Use of advisory committees to determine the temper and priorities that exist in the eyes of the community is an effective method for getting feedback from the community. Careful selection of community representatives is critical. Unless the selection method is designed to choose true leaders in the community, the agency doing the selecting may discover that it is creating its own "community representatives" who represent no one but themselves. Such a selection may also tend to alienate those so-called leaders from the community they are supposed to represent, while a true leader in the community would probably not suffer from alienation. In fact, his position may be strengthened by such an affiliation, because the people he represents would be confident that he would not serve as a "rubber stamp" for anyone.

Volunteers The use of volunteers or similar aides in some paraprofessional capacity stimulates community interest in many of the criminal justice operations that would otherwise go unnoticed. The utilization of interns, cadets, or community service representatives within the agency also provides financial assistance to students who are preparing for professional positions within the system. The individual who is employed by an agency and who finds that his work is rewarding and challenging does not have to be sold on the value of his input nearly as much as if he were on the outside looking in.

Political Activity Partisan political activity on the part of the public servants in the justice system is a dangerous game to play. One of the disadvantages is whatever one does in the line of his normal responsibilities may be interpreted through partisan viewpoints. There are other ways to engage in political activity, however, that will produce a positive effect on the system's community image. When a particular law is unenforceable, for example, or is ambiguous and impossible to interpret objectively, then it would be most desirable to have someone in the system to speak out in behalf of either changing the law or eliminating it completely. If enforcement of a particular law is unpopular, it may not be eliminated, but an officer may advise (through his department) the legislature of the problems encountered in that law's enforcement. The legislators could then study the law in light of the feedback they receive from the enforcement officers, and take whatever steps they believe necessary. The *intent* of the law may be to solve a certain type of social problem or to respond to some sort of pressures on legislatures to make the law. If, after a careful study, the legislators decide that the law should continue to be enforced, then it would be their responsibility to "sell" the idea to their constituents, who are the same constituency served by the justice system.

Community Participation by Agency Members. As private individuals, the police officer, or court clerk, or parole officer, or any other people in the justice system professions and paraprofessions have private lives to lead as neighbors, parents, spouses, and they may worship if and how they choose, hold memberships in whatever organizations they wish, and actively participate in community affairs. Such activity and membership should be extended whenever possible to get maximum community involvement.

Address Criticism The stoic position of certain agencies in the face of criticism must give the leaders of those agencies a certain feeling of satisfaction in knowing that the criticism is incorrect and they are secure in the knowledge that what they are doing is correct. Unfortunately, however, there are many people who believe that one's refusal or failure to deny certain accusations is the equivalent to confessions of culpability, or tacit admissions. Sometimes the charge itself causes damage, and then a stand of silence may reinforce that damage. Any criticism or accusations of improper conduct should be carefully studied, and accompanied by careful self-analysis at the same time to determine the degree of truth or accuracy—if any—of the charges. The sources of rumors and gossip, and false accusations should be ferreted out and identified. Then it is advisable to attempt to widely disseminate the true facts that will answer the distorted facts, or the lies that have been circulated. There are times when the accused may use the press media as a platform for widely disseminating proclamations of his innocence and to plead for the sympathy on the part of the public, while at the same time the prosecutor must remain silent and present the evidence only in court to assure the accused his constitutionally guaranteed right to a fair trial, due process, and his posture of innocence until he is proven guilty.

Communicators Are Essential By both oral and written methods, it is necessary that the police officer, the judge, the attorney, or any other professional in the justice system have the ability to communicate effectively. An articulate man or woman can win a conviction with the support of sufficient evidence, prevent a riot, arbitrate a family dispute, settle complaints, and accomplish many of the agency's objectives through the use of persuasive communications.

Public Relations

As used in this chapter, the term *public relations* implies more of a formalized one-way communicative process in which the justice system and its operants present their agencies to the public at an advantage through the media of mass communications and in personal presentations, but less on a give-and-take basis than through community relations processes. The public relations process involves press agentry, salesmanship, image building, and all of the other techniques that most business and industrial enterprises employ to present their products or services in the best possible light. Presidents are elected, milk regains its popularity, books are sold, colleges become internationally famous, entertainment celebrities attain stardom, and justice system agencies gain *acceptance* when they employ public relations methods. The individual who becomes the greatest in any profession gains that stature because he: first, does something that causes the world to know of his unusual talents and accomplishments; second, he continues to demonstrate his greatness; and, third, his feats are publicized so that the world will know of him and his stature of greatness. Without the correct type of publicity, for example, the Los Angeles Police Department would be just another name on a list of names. Think about it; even a church has a bell to remind people of its existence. "It pays to advertise" is not a hollow slogan.

It is necessary to continually strive for public recognition and to try to get extensive dissemination of information about an agency's efforts if the public is to understand what a criminal justice agency is doing. Each actor must play his role in a convincing manner, and there should be some concerted effort to continuously be active in matters of public relations. It is not unusual for any agency of any size that can support the expense to employ a full-time public relations expert. Among his other responsibilities, the program developed by such an expert would include the following:

1. *Publication of policies and philosophies of the department.* Whenever the agency in question takes a stand, such as a hard line by the courts on violators of pedestrian right-of-way in which many people have lost their lives during a recent period of time, the public should know of the court's attitude on the matter. A statement by the judge that he believes his actions will serve to deter more deaths, and that he intends to send some people to jail for the offense should be publicized and may help solve the problem. A police department might advertise that citations will be issued for all littering violations and might help to keep the city cleaner. A prosecutor whose philosophy is to aggressively seek out and prosecute violators of consumer fraud laws should educate the public through publicity on the types of activities that might be used to bilk them out of their money; at the same time the criminals are publicly notified that they should either comply with the laws or find their victims elsewhere.

2. *Regular publications.* Annual reports, budget statements, special information bulletins, printed brochures, and press releases may all be used to an advantage by agencies of the justice system, provided the materials are factual, accurate, and interesting. A well-written press release about some item of public interest will quite probably be printed by at least one of the

Figure 11-1 Community relations activities (above) of the police department include community involvement.

Courtesy Police Dept., St. Louis, Missouri.

Figure 11-2 The officer in this photo is accepting printed material from Mr. Darling and Councilman Fischer for the "Officer Bill" program which involves the children of San Jose.

Courtesy Police Dept., San Jose, California.

papers and is likely to be used by the other media as well. Editors often keep a ready supply of filler material—stories and items of interest that do not have to be dated—that can be used to fill a space or time frame when the opportunity presents itself. The material is of extra value if someone does not have to rewrite it.

3. *Radio and television appearances.* This is an excellent opportunity for the introduction of a new procedure or what might amount to a "crack-down" on some type of criminal activity. Sometimes an opportunity like a radio or television interview is the chief executive's only opportunity to explain a procedure or a philosophy in his own words without modification.

4. *Personal visits to the homes of new residents.* New arrivals to a community are often visited by representatives of several of the local merchants, sometimes by a young lady operating a welcome wagon, armed with free gifts and introductory discounts. Such an opportunity may be used by the local police department or sheriff in providing the new resident some printed information about procedures for reporting crimes or for home protection. Some departments have their "beat officers" visit the new residents so that the officers and the people may get acquainted. The personal touch has a salutory effect, providing the visit is timed right and the resident is not sensitive to the visit. The uniformed officer and the visibly-marked car may be alarming to some people, but if such a practice is commonplace, then there should be no embarrassment by having a police car parked out front.

5. *Public speaking programs.* Entertainment committee chairmen are hard pressed for original and entertaining programs for their organizations. It is not unusual for the chairman for some breakfast or luncheon club to call his local police department, sheriff, or district attorney with a fervent plea for a speaker to fill in for some other speaker who had to cancel at the last minute. Speeches and programs may be prepared well in advance by the agency's public relations officer, who can call on a specialist in some area virtually at the last minute. Armed with the standard prepared material, the expert can embellish and expand, and once again sell his department.

There are many different types of special occasions when the justice system may comfortably take part in ceremonies without being out of place, such as Law Day, Armed Forces Day, and Labor Day events. Shortly before heavy shopping seasons, a program on bad checks and shoplifting is quite popular with merchants and other businessmen. Vacation time calls for special presentations on driving and security tips for the motorist or traveler. Special problems created by natural weather phenomena, such as snow and ice, or flash floods, provide an excellent opportunity for the agency to perform genuine public services and at the same time score successfully for the image of the agency.

How does one sell a prison to a group of local businessmen? It may be necessary to assure them that the institution is not unfairly competing for their markets, and at the same time demonstrate the skills and talents of convicted prisoners who are in need of employment to assure their success on parole once released. An example of the type of public relations work that may be done with some success may be to have a professional burglar demonstrate how easy it is to break into the average home, but how difficult a certain local security product makes the task of committing burglary. In order to avoid getting into the middle of what might be a condition of fierce competition between two neighboring manufacturers, it may be an effective public relations device to have the inmates who have been convicted for burglary serve as an advisory board or "testing laboratory" for certain security device manufacturers. Various other types of criminal specialties may be used as topics for crime prevention seminars and public relations programs. It will serve as an informative tool for the public and a form of catharsis for the participants who may use his public-speaking tour as a rehabilitation tool.

A series of well-prepared, half-hour programs involving interesting visual aids and other multimedia supplements to the prepared speech by a well-trained agency representative can do a great deal of good for the agency. The nature of the business—jails and institutions, law enforcement, the courts, and field casework—makes it somewhat difficult to allow public access into some institutions (impossible in some cases) or to ride along during the average work day. Motion pictures, videotapes, and slide programs can be used as a vehicle to transport the audience on a vicarious tour through the labyrinths of the institution that stands at the outskirts of town, and such a tour may serve to dispel some of the myths about what goes on inside the walls. Some of the community residents may become so interested in some phase of a rehabilitative process, for example, that they may volunteer to help with the program.

6. *Positive action programs.* An ethnic minority may be aggrieved about alleged or real problems of discrimination. While carefully avoiding any "showcase" attempt to display a fair and unbiased attitude on the part of the department, it may be possible to make positive efforts to employ representatives of the minority population, or to direct a series of programs to specifically overcome whatever barriers or difficulties that may have existed. Sometimes a mere shifting of priorities in the agency's public relations program may solve a problem that may exist because one facet of the program was incorrectly placed on the priority list. This is one occasion when the utilization of an advisory committee would be helpful.

7. *Participation in youth activities.* The agency may sponsor a youth organization as an extension of its own regular responsibilities, such as an explorer post, youth athletic league, or youth employment service. Positive results may be obtained by a genuine display of interest in the community as a responsible part of that community.

8. *Enlist spokesmen.* Within the community it is not difficult to encounter someone who feels strongly about the police, or the courts, or pro-

bation in a positive way. They are genuinely concerned that innuendos and unfounded slander about the agency or any of its members may be perpetuated beyond our wildest imagination. There are times when such a spokesman who speaks from a vantage point outside the agency will have a greater effect than some agency representative, who may be accused of "whitewashing" a situation because of his protective attitude from inside the agency.

9. *Rumor control.* When emotions are keyed up and tempers flare some inconsequential incident may run rampant and almost spontaneously get out of control like a brushfire in a dry canyon. By suggestion, and sometimes by deliberate implantation at the appropriate time, unfounded bits of information might be disbursed and then the rumors begin to fly, grossly exaggerated bits of lies and half-truths. The damage is sometimes irreparable. If possible, indigenous leaders of the community should be informed of the facts and—if a rumor control procedure has been established—they may be able to squelch the rumor before its gets too far.

10. *Attempts to overcome community indifference.* Sometimes an antagonistic individual is easier to cope with than one who displays no interest in a situation at all. Special interest groups, both pro and anticriminal justice system, are vocal and manage to be heard. What is really difficult is to prod the indifferent and apathetic people in the community into expressing their likes or dislikes. If the entire community is to be served, then it is imperative that we find out how and what the community at large is thinking. Surveys, questionnaires, and other forms of opinion analyses may be utilized to determine community standards for courtroom documentation that a certain type of entertainment, for example, is contrary to local mores. Personal visits to the homes and businesses of many of these silent residents may prove beneficial both to the agency and to the people they are serving.

11. *Public image.* It is important to establish a businesslike operation and present an image to the public that convinces them that their justice system is operating efficiently and that their taxes are well spent. Telephone courtesy and personal contacts in office reception areas should be as important to the criminal justice agency as it is to the automobile sales agency, which considers every caller or visitor a potential buyer. There is a difference between an individual who speaks with authority and the one who speaks as an officious martinet who mouths words in such a manner that he evokes resentment and anger. People should be treated with courtesy and respect, and with dignity.

SUMMARY

Professionalism involves more than the completion of a college baccalaureate program. There is a personal commitment also involved, which extends beyond the normal "job requirements" of any occupation. A common body of knowledge is essential to provide the base for the profession, a minimum educational requirement is imposed to assure acquisition of that body of knowledge, and along with the assimilation of information and development of proficiencies required of the profession there is a free exchange of information concerning techniques and procedures, including what might be considered in business and industry as "trade secrets." A true professional zealously exchanges information as the possessor of a trade secret zealously guards its confidentiality. Selection of individuals who are to become members of a profession, and regulation of the membership through enforcement of rigid professional standards are prime requisites for professionalism. Many of the occupations in the justice system already meet the specifications of true professions according to the prerequisites discussed in this chapter, and as illustrated in their codes of ethics or statements of principles. Many other occupations are emerging as professions.

Ethics of professionals include attitudes as well as personal and public commitments to service. There is a general preparation statement in the code of ethics, which involves an attitude of "service above self," or "equal service to all people," or—as stated in the Law Enforcement Code of Ethics —"my fundamental duty is to serve mankind; to safeguard lives and property; to protect the innocent against deception, the weak against oppression or intimidation, and the peaceful against violence or disorder; and to respect the Constitutional rights of all men to liberty, equality, and justice." Other aspects of professionalism that are articulated through the media of statements of principles and codes of ethics involve selflessness, exemplary morality, serving as a model to aspirants to the same profession and an example of the profession to the community. Use of one's professional status to gain special favors, gratuities, or positions of advantage is similarly forbidden by one's professional membership. In addition to the profession itself recognizing certain individuals as "professionals," there is an extremely important consideration: public acknowledgment.

As with any business or government operation, the criminal justice agency must have a good public relations program, and it must involve itself with the community it serves as *a part of* that community rather than *apart from* the community. As continuously pointed out in this chapter, if there were two words to describe community and public relations they would be "Effective Communications."

EXERCISES AND STUDY QUESTIONS

1. What are the factors that distinguish a *calling* as a *profession?*
2. Do you agree with the statement that professionals should not zealously guard trade secrets as one would do in business and industry?
3. Why is it so important that individuals in the justice system pro-

fessions be so careful about the conduct of their private lives?

4. What are the preentry educational requirements for the profession you have selected for your occupational goal?

5. Regarding the decision-making prerogative of a professional, is it wise to extend this prerogative to the field police officer and allow him to make the decision whether to prosecute someone for a felony?

6. Continuing with the decision-making prerogative of a professional, what types of constraints should be imposed upon the police officer, the prosecuting attorney, the judge, the probation officer?

7. List at least three things that the agency should provide for its employees in recognition of their professional stature.

8. How would you distinguish between a true professional compared with another type of employee?

9. Give an example of how acceptance of a gratuity could later "backfire."

10. Explain the general theme of each of the professional ethics and/or principles of each of the three components of the justice system: law enforcement, judicial process, and corrections.

11. In the jurisdiction where you live, are all of the criminal justice practitioners considered professionals? Which ones are not and why? Which ones are, and why?

12. What is your opinion about the higher ranking officer's disparity in academic achievement compared to some of their newer officers relative to their leadership potential? Do you believe that a superior education is essential for leadership?

13. What can be done as a pay incentive to encourage employees to attend college on their own time?

14. If an employee observes another employee with the same agency violate ethical standards which are also a violation of departmental rules and regulations, where should his loyalty lie?

15. Define *public relations.*

16. Define *community relations.*

17. Now that you have defined the two terms, what is the difference, if any?

18. Why is it imperative that an agency self-evaluate?

19. Give an example of how an officer of a police department may demonstrate his desire to gain cultural awareness.

20. In what way would you utilize an advisory committee to assist in the operation of a medium security prison?

21. In what capacity would you place a volunteer citizen in a probation department?

22. How may a police officer engage in politics and not involve himself in partisanship?

23. If you were a police officer visiting a new resident on your beat, what types of information about the department do you believe he should have?

24. What could a superior court judge do to improve his community image?

25. In what ways could the district attorney improve his community image?

26. To what extent do you believe a deputy sheriff can ethically become involved in an election campaign for the position of sheriff?

RECOMMENDED SEMESTER/TERM PROJECT

1. Write a ten-page paper on professionalism: what it is, how one become a professional, and how it relates to the field of criminal justice.

2. Develop a five-point plan for a community relations program for each of the following: probation department, police department, sheriff's department, and the district attorney. Prepare the plan as though you had been employed as the public relations expert for each of these departments and your plan is intended to solve the major communications problems with the community.

SUGGESTED FOR ADDITIONAL STUDY

ADAMS, THOMAS F., *Criminal Justice Reading.* Pacific Palisades, Calif.: Goodyear Publishing Co., Inc., 1972. A section of this book of carefully selected readings is devoted to police professionalism.

American Correctional Association, *Manual of Correctional Standards.* College Park, Md.: American Correctional Association, 1959.

COFFEY, ALAN, EDWARD ELDEFONSO, and WALTER HARTINGER, *Human Relations; Law Enforcement in a Changing Community* (2d ed.). Englewood Cliffs: Prentice-Hall, Inc., 1976.

HEWITT, WILLIAM H. and CHARLES L. NEWMAN, *Police Community Relations. An Anthology and Bibliography.* Mineola, N.Y.: The Foundation Press, 1970.

KLEIN, HERBERT F., *The Police—Damned If They Do—Damned If They Don't.* New York: Crown Publishers, 1968.

LAFAVE WAYNE R., *Arrest: The Decision to Take a Suspect into Custody.* Boston: Little, Brown, and Company, 1965.

MCDOWELL, CHARLES P., *Police in the Community.* Cincinnati: The W. H. Anderson Company, 1975.

PARKER, L. CRAIG, JR., and ROBERT D. MEIER, *Interpersonal Psychology for Law Enforcement and Corrections.* St. Paul: West Publishing Co., 1975.

RADELET, LOUIS A., *The Police and the Community.* Beverly Hills: Glencoe Press, 1973.

REISS, ALBERT J., JR., *The Police and the Public.* New Haven: Yale University Press, 1971.

SKOLNICK, JEROME, *Justice Without Trial: Law Enforcement in Democratic Society.* New York: John Wiley & Sons, Inc., 1966.

TROJANOWICZ, ROBERT C., and SAMUEL DIXON, *Criminal Justice and the Community.* Englewood Cliffs: Prentice-Hall, Inc., 1974.

WILSON, JAMES Q., *Varieties in Police Behavior: The Management of Law and Order in Eight Communities.* Cambridge: Harvard University Press, 1968.

WILSON, O. W., *Police Planning* (2d ed.). Springfield, Ill.: Charles C. Thomas, 1962.

12

Justice Administration—Where Do We Go From Here?

INTRODUCTION

Progress in the entire criminal justice system, as presented in this text is absolutely essential if our modern society is to keep from strangling itself. In this chapter, it would be impossible to enumerate all of the innovations in administration and the related fields. What we will cover are some of the highlights, beginning with the President's Crime Commission study and all of its reports that were released for public ingestion in early 1967. Prior to that time the police, the courts, corrections, and all of the related agencies and their processes were of little concern to anyone except those who were directly involved with the system.

The "business" of criminal justice is similar to many other businesses that deal in services. The significant difference is that none so directly and dramatically affect the lives and reputations of many of the individuals we contact. A decision has tremendous impact, whether it be to arrest or release, file a complaint or not file, cite or not cite, shoot or not shoot, or simply prepare and file a report.

Recognizing the need for innovation and improvement, the criminal justice practitioner must first identify and analyze the problem. Once he has done that, he can address the problem. By now, it seems, we have identified enough problems to keep us busy for at least the next century. As a serious student of criminal justice, it will be your responsibility to finish this chapter, which is in progress while the book is going into print. We shall articulate some of the challenges that have been identified, recommendations to meet those challenges, and a few highlights of what types of programs and projects have already been undertaken.

THE CHALLENGE OF CRIME

On July 23, 1965, President Lyndon B. Johnson assembled together a panel of people representing divergent views and a variety of backgrounds and created a committee with a single objective: to study the criminal justice system for the purpose of making a series of recommendations for improvement of the system. Officially named the President's Commission on Law

Enforcement and Administration of Justice, the commission, its consultants, and its staff compiled in a series of publications, task force reports, and its major publication, *Challenge of Crime in a Free Society,* a wealth of information that previously had been available to the people in a piecemeal fashion. Little of the information was new, just the method of collecting and disseminating it and putting it into focus.

The President's Crime Commission made more than two hundred recommendations for change in every facet of the criminal justice system. Not only did the commission recommend action to be taken by the public segment of our society but also the private segment in a massive cooperative effort. All of these publications are available for nominal prices through the U.S. Government Printing Office and should find their way into your library.

For the purpose of this chapter's theme, some of the commission's most significant recommendations are recounted. Study the recommendations carefully and compare them with the actual policies and procedures of the various agencies in your own city, county, and state.

CRIME IN AMERICA

The Commission Recommends:

- Those cities that have not already done so should adopt centralized procedures for handling the receipt of reports of crime from citizens and institute staff controls necessary to make those procedures effective.
- The present index of reported crime should be broken into two wholly separate parts, one for crimes of violence and the other for crimes against property.

JUVENILE DELINQUENCY AND YOUTH CRIME

The Commission Recommends:

- Efforts, both private and public, should be intensified to:
  - Prepare youth for employment.
  - Provide youth with information about employment opportunities.
  - Reduce barriers to employment caused by discrimination, the misuse of criminal records, and maintenance of rigid job qualifications.
  - Create new employment opportunities.
- To the greatest feasible extent, police departments should formulate policy guidelines for dealing with juveniles.
- All officers should be acquainted with the special characteristics of adolescents, particularly those of the social, racial, and other specific groups with which they are likely to come in contact.
- Custody of a juvenile (both prolonged street stops and station house visits) should be limited to instances where there is objective, specifiable ground for suspicion.
- Every stop that includes a frisk or an interrogation of more than a few preliminary identifying questions should be recorded in a strictly confidential report.

- Police forces should make full use of the central diagnosing and coordinating services of the Youth Services Bureau. Station adjustment should be limited to release and referral; it should not include hearings or the imposition of sanctions by the police. Court referral by the police should be restricted to those cases involving serious criminal conduct or repeated misconduct of a more than trivial nature.
- Communities should establish neighborhood youth-serving agencies—Youth Services Bureaus—located if possible in comprehensive neighborhood community centers and receiving juveniles (delinquent and nondelinquent) referred by the police, the juvenile court, parents, schools, and other sources.
- Juvenile courts should make fullest feasible use of preliminary conferences to dispose of cases short of adjudication.
- The movement for narrowing the juvenile court's jurisdiction should be continued. (Specifically, the commission recommends a list of changes, primarily limiting the jurisdiction of the juvenile court to only those acts of a juvenile that would be criminal acts if committed by an adult.)
- Counsel should be appointed as a matter of course wherever coercive action is a possibility, without requiring any affirmative choice by child or parent.
- Notice should be given well in advance of any scheduled court proceeding, including intake, detention, and waiver hearings, and should set forth the alleged misconduct with particularity.
- Adequate and separate detention facilities for juveniles should be provided.
- Legislation should be enacted restricting both authority to detain and the circumstances under which the detention is permitted.

THE POLICE

The Commission Recommends:

- State legislatures should enact statutory provisions with respect to the authority of law enforcement officers to stop persons for brief questioning, including specifications of the circumstances and limitations under which stops are permissible.
- The police should formally participate in community planning in all cities.
- Police departments in all large communities should have community-relations consisting of a headquarters unit that plans and supervises the department's community relations programs. It should also have precinct units, responsible to the precinct commander, that carry out the programs. Community relations must be both a staff and a line function. Such machinery is a matter of the greatest importance in any community that has a substantial minority population.
- In each police precinct in a minority-group neighborhood there should be a citizen's advisory committee that meets regularly with police officials to work out solutions to problems of conflict between the police and the community. It is crucial that the committees be broadly representative of the community as a whole, including those elements who are critical or aggrieved.
- It should be a high-priority objective of all departments in communities with a substantial minority population to recruit minority-group officers and to

deploy and promote them fairly. Every officer in such departments should receive thorough grounding in community-relations subjects. His performance in the field of community relations should be periodically reviewed and evaluated.

- Every jurisdiction should provide adequate procedures for full and fair processing of all citizen grievances and complaints about the conduct of any public officer or employee.
- Police departments should develop and enunciate policies that give police personnel specific guidance for the common situations requiring exercise of police discretion. Policies should cover such matters, among others, as the issuance of orders to citizens regarding their movements or activities, the handling of minor disputes, the safeguarding of rights of free speech and free assembly, the selection and use of investigative methods, and the decision whether or not to arrest in specific situations involving specific crimes.
- Each municipality, and other jurisdiction responsible for law enforcement, should carefully assess the manpower needs of its police agency on the basis of efficient use of all its personnel and should provide the resources required to meet the need for increased personnel if such a need is found to exist.
- Basic police functions, especially in large and medium-sized urban departments, should be divided among three kinds of officers, here termed the "community service officer," the "police officer," and the "police agent."
- Police departments should recruit far more actively than they do now, with special attention to college campuses and inner-city neighborhoods.
- The ultimate aim of all police departments should be that all personnel with general enforcement powers have baccalaureate degrees.
- Police departments should take immediate steps to establish a minimum requirement of a baccalaureate degree for all supervisory and executive positions.
- Until reliable tests are devised for identifying and measuring the personal characteristics that contribute to good police work, intelligence tests, thorough background investigations, and personal interviews should be used by all departments as absolute minimum techniques to determine the moral character and the emotional and intellectual fitness of police candidates.
- Police departments and civil service commissions should reexamine and, if necessary, modify present recruitment standards on age, height, weight, visual acuity, and prior residence. The appointing authority should place primary emphasis on the education, background, character and personality of a candidate for police service.
- Police salaries must be raised, particularly by increasing minimums. In order to attract college graduates to police service, starting and maximum salaries must be competitive with other professions and occupations that seek the same graduates.
- Salary proposals for each department within local government should be considered on their own merits and should not be joint with the demands of other departments within a city.
- Promotion eligibility requirements should stress ability above seniority. Promotion "lists" should be compiled on the basis not only of scores on

technical examinations but on prior performance, character, educational achievement and leadership potential.

- Personnel to perform all specialized police functions not involving a need for general enforcement powers should be selected for their talents and abilities without regard to prior police service. Professional policemen should have the same opportunities as other professionals to seek employment where they are most needed. The inhibitions that civil service regulations, retirement plans, and hiring policies place on lateral entry should be removed. To encourage lateral movement of police personnel, a nationwide retirement system should be devised that permits the transferring of retirement credits.
- All training programs should provide instruction on subjects that prepare recruits to exercise discretion properly, and to understand the community, the role of the police, and what the criminal justice system can and cannot do. Professional educators and civilian experts should be used to teach specialized courses—law and psychology, for example. Recognized teaching techniques such as problem-solving seminars should be incorporated into training programs.
- Formal police training programs for recruits in all departments, large and small, should consist of an absolute minimum of 400 hours of classroom work spread over a four- to six-month period so that it can be combined with carefully selected and supervised field training.
- Entering officers should serve probation periods of, preferably, eighteen months and certainly no less than one year. During this period the recruit should be systematically observed and rated. Chief administrators should have the sole authority of dismissal during the probation period and should willingly exercise it against unsatisfactory officers.
- Every general enforcement officer should have at least one week of intensive in-service training a year. Every officer should be given incentives to continue his general education or acquire special skills outside his department.
- Every state, through its commission on police standards, should provide financial and technical assistance to departments to conduct surveys and make recommendations for improvement and modernization of their organization, management, and operations.
- Every medium- and large-sized department should employ a skilled lawyer full time as its legal adviser. Smaller departments should arrange for legal advice on a part-time basis.
- Police departments must take every possible step to implement the guiding organizational principle of central control. Specialist staff units for such matters as planning, research, legal advice, and police personnel should include persons trained in a variety of disciplines and should be utilized to develop and improve the policies, operations, and administration of each function.
- Every department in a big or medium-sized city should organize key ranking staff and line personnel into an administrative board similar in function to a corporation's board of directors, whose duty would be to assist the chief and his staff units in developing, enunciating, and enforcing departmental policies and guidelines for the day-to-day activities of line personnel.

- Every department, regardless of size, should have a comprehensive program for maintaining police integrity and every medium- and large-sized department should have a well-manned internal investigation unit responsible only to the chief administrator. The unit should have both an investigative and preventive role in controlling dishonest, unethical, and offensive actions by police officers.
- Police departments should commence experimentation with a team-policing concept that envisions those with patrol and investigative duties combining under unified command with flexible assignments to deal with the crime problems in a defined sector.
- A comprehensive regulation should be formulated by every chief administrator to reflect the basic policy that firearms may be used *only* when the officer believes his life or the life of another is in imminent danger, or when other reasonable means of apprehension have failed to prevent the escape of a *felony* suspect whom the officer believes presents a serious danger to others.
- States should assume responsibility for assuring that area-wide records and communications needs are provided.
- In every metropolitan area the central city or the state should provide laboratory facilities for the routine needs of all the communities in the area. State or multistate laboratories and the FBI laboratory should continue to provide the necessary research to make available to all laboratories more sophisticated means of analysis.
- Specialized personnel from state or metropolitan departments should assist smaller departments in each metropolitan area on major investigations and in specialized law enforcement functions.
- Each metropolitan area and each county should take action directed toward the pooling, or consolidation, of police services through the particular technique that will provide the most satisfactory law enforcement service and protection at lowest possible cost.
- Police standards commissions should be established in every state, and empowered to set mandatory requirements and to give financial aid to governmental units for the implementation of standards.

THE COURTS

The Commission Recommends:

- Felony and misdemeanor courts and their ancillary agencies—prosecutors, defenders, and probation services—should be unified.
- As an immediate step to meet the needs of the lower courts, the judicial manpower of these courts should be increased and their physical facilities should be improved so that these courts will be able to cope with the volume of cases coming before them in a dignified and deliberate way.
- Prosecutors, probation officers, and defense counsel should be provided in courts where these officers are not found, or their numbers are insufficient.
- The states and federal government should enact legislation to abolish or overhaul the justice of the peace and U.S. commissioner systems.
- Each state should enact comprehensive bail reform legislation....
- Each community should establish procedures to enable and encourage police departments to release, in appropriate classes of cases, as many arrested

persons as possible promptly after arrest upon issuance of a citation or summons requiring appearance.

- Prosecutors and defense counsel should in appropriate cases share information they secure independently at all points in the process when such sharing appears likely to lead to early disposition.
- Police, prosecutors, bar associations, and courts should issue regulations and standards as to the kinds of information that properly may be released to the news media about pending criminal cases by police officers, prosecutors, and defense counsel. These regulations and standards should be designed to minimize prejudicial statements by the media before or during trial, while safeguarding legitimate reporting on matters of public interest.
- States should reexamine the sentencing provisions of their penal codes with a view to simplifying the grading of offenses, and to removing mandatory minimum prison terms, long maximum prison terms, and ineligibility for probation and parole. In cases of persistent habitual offenders or dangerous criminals, judges should have express authority to extend prison terms. Sentencing codes should include criteria designed to help judges exercise their discretion in accordance with clearly stated standards.
- The question whether capital punishment is an appropriate sanction is a policy decision to be made by each state....

CORRECTIONS

The Commission Recommends:

- Parole and probation services should be available in all jurisdictions for felons, juveniles, and those adult misdemeanants who need or can profit from community treatment.
- Every state should provide that offenders who are not paroled receive adequate supervision after release unless it is determined to be unnecessary in a specific case.
- Probation and parole services should make use of volunteers and subprofessional aides in demonstration projects and regular programs.
- Probation and parole officials should develop new methods and skills to aid in reintegrating offenders through active intervention on their behalf with community institutions.
- Case loads for different types of offenders should vary in size and type and intensity of treatment. Classification and assignment of offenders should be made according to their needs and problems.
- Correctional authorities should develop more extensive community programs providing special, intensive treatment as an alternative to institutionalization for both juvenile and adult offenders.
- Federal and state governments should finance the establishment of model, small-unit correctional institutions for flexible, community-oriented treatment.
- Graduated release and furlough programs should be expanded. They should be accompanied by guidance and coordinated with community treatment services.
- Local jails and misdemeanant institutions should be integrated into state correctional systems. They should not be operated by law enforcement agencies. Rehabilitative programs and other reforms should be instituted.

- Wherever possible, persons awaiting trial should be housed and handled separately from offenders.
- Universities and colleges should, with governmental and private participation and support, develop more courses and launch more research studies and projects on the problem of contemporary corrections.

ORGANIZED CRIME

The Commission Recommends:

- At least one investigative grand jury should be impaneled annually at each jurisdiction that has major organized crime activity.
- Congress should enact legislation dealing specifically with wiretapping and bugging.
- Every attorney general in states where organized crime exists should form in his office a unit of attorneys and investigators to gather information and assist in prosecution regarding this criminal activity.
- Police departments in every major city should have a special intelligence unit solely to ferret out organized criminal activity and to collect information regarding the possible entry of criminal cartels into the area's criminal operations.
- The prosecutor's office in every major city should have sufficient manpower assigned full time to organized crime cases. Such personnel should have the power to initiate organized crime investigations and to conduct the investigative grand juries mentioned above.
- The federal government should create a central computerized office into which each federal agency would feed all of its organized crime intelligence.
- Groups should be created within the federal and state departments of justice to develop strategies and enlist regulatory action against businesses infiltrated by organized crime.
- Private business associations should develop strategies to prevent and uncover organized crime's illegal and unfair business tactics.
- Enforcement officials should provide regular briefings to leaders at all levels of government concerning organized crime conditions within the jurisdiction.

NARCOTICS AND DRUG ABUSE

The Commission Recommends:

- Research should be undertaken devoted to early action on the further development of a sound and effective framework of regulatory and criminal laws with respect to dangerous drugs. In addition, research and educational programs concerning the effects of such drugs should be undertaken.
- The enforcement and related staff of the Bureau of Customs should be materially increased.
- The enforcement staff of the Bureau of Narcotics should be materially increased. Some parts of the added personnel should be used to design and execute a long-range intelligence effort aimed at the upper echelons of the illicit drug traffic.

DRUNKENNESS OFFENSES

The Commission Recommends:

- Drunkenness should not in itself be considered a criminal offense. Disorderly and other criminal conduct accompanied by drunkenness should remain punishable as separate crimes. The implementation of this recommendation requires the development of adequate civil detoxification procedures.
- Communities should establish detoxification units as part of comprehensive treatment programs.
- Research by private and governmental agencies into alcoholism, the problems of alcoholics, and methods of treatment should be expanded.

SCIENCE AND TECHNOLOGY

The Commission Recommends:

- Police call boxes should be designated "public emergency call boxes," should be better marked and lighted, and should be left unlocked.
- Whenever practical, a single police telephone number should be established, at least within a metropolitan area and eventually over the entire United States, comparable to the telephone company's long-distance information number.
- Frequencies should be shared through the development of larger and more integrated police mobile radio networks.
- Police departments should undertake data collection and experimentation programs to develop appropriate statistical procedures for manpower allocation.
- A National Criminal Justice Statistics Center should be established in the Department of Justice. The center should be responsible for the collection, analysis, and dissemination of two basic kinds of data:
    - Those characterizing criminal careers, derived from carefully drawn samples of anonymous offenders.
    - Those on crime and the system's response to it, as reported by the criminal justice agencies at all levels.
- A federal agency should be assigned to coordinate the establishment of standards for equipment to be used by criminal justice agencies and to provide those agencies technical assistance.
- The federal government should encourage and support the establishment of operations research staffs in large criminal justice agencies.
- A major scientific and technological research program within a research institute should be created and supported by the federal government.
- Criminal justice agencies, such as state court and correctional systems and large police departments, should develop their own research units, staffed by specialists and drawing on the advice and assistance of leading scholars and experts in relevant fields.[1]

[1]President's Commission on Law Enforcement and the Administration of Justice, *Challenge of Crime in a Free Society* (Washington, D.C.: Government Printing Office, 1967).

RESULTS

What is your opinion of each one of those recommendations individually? What do you believe to be their general value and effect? Following this series of recommendations, we have seen the implementation of literally dozens of these recommendations. Certainly not to be ignored are the significant advances made by individual criminal justice agencies for decades in a successive progression of events prior to the commission's study and recommendations. In fact, many of those recommendations were based on ongoing programs within specific agencies contacted during the commission's fourteen months of operation. However, it cannot be denied that both personal and financial attention toward the problems of the criminal justice system were much more generous following the commission's reports.

LAW ENFORCEMENT ASSISTANCE ADMINISTRATION

One of the more visible results of the recommendations of the President's Crime Commission was the establishment of the Law Enforcement Assistance Administration.[2] *Law Enforcement,* in the context of the Omnibus Crime Bill of 1968 and the Law Enforcement Assistance Act, is the term used to describe all of the components of the systemm of justice administration, including the fields of law enforcement, corrections, and the courts. Congress established LEAA to channel funds to states through their respective State Planning Agencies, and to carry out certain other activities involving research and improvement of law enforcement systems. The funds available through this source have amounted to several billion dollars for local agency support.[3]

The Attorney General's Annual Report explains the background of the Law Enforcement Assistance Administration:

> The Law Enforcement Assistance Act of 1965 (P.L. 89-197) established a program of funding research and demonstration projects to improve law enforcement, crime prevention and administration of criminal justice.
>
> The policy of providing Federal funds for state efforts in law enforcement and criminal justice received strong endorsement in 1967 from the President's Commission on Law Enforcement and Administration of Justice. That Commission said it perceived a need for a Federal assistance program "on which several hundred million dollars annually could be profitably spent over the next decade."
>
> Basic Act. The following year, Congress established the nation's first large-scale comprehensive program attacking crime and delinquency. That

[2]Law Enforcement Assistance Administration, *3rd Annual Report of the Law Enforcement Assistance Administration Fiscal Year 1971* (Washington, D.C.: Government Printing Office, 1972), p. 3.

[3]Fiscal reports from the LEAA are available for review each year as public records.

program was embodied in the Omnibus Crime Control and Safe Streets Act of 1968 (P.L. 90-351).

Congress said in that Act that it found "a high incidence" of crime that threatened the "peace, security, and general welfare" of the nation. It said that law enforcement needed to be better coordinated, intensified, and more effective at all levels of government. Further, Congress found that "crime is essentially a local program that must be dealt with by state and local governments if it is to be controlled effectively."

Congress said its declared policy was "to assist state and local governments in strengthening and improving law enforcement at every level by national assistance."

It said the Act had the threefold purpose to: "(1) encourage States and units of general local government to prepare and adopt comprehensive plans based upon their evaluation of State and local problems of law enforcement; (2) authorize grants to States and units of local government in order to improve and strengthen law enforcement; and (3) encourage research and development directed toward the improvement of law enforcement and the development of new methods for the prevention and reduction of crime and the detection and apprehension of criminals."

The Act further called for special efforts in the areas of organized crime and civil disorders; it established a National Institute of Law Enforcement and Criminal Justice to conduct research; it established an academic assistance program to further education among law enforcement personnel; it directed LEAA to collect, evaluate, publish and disseminate statistics and other data on the condition and progress of law enforcement in the nation; and it authorized expenditures of $100,111,000 for the first two years, FY 1968 (or the portion thereof remaining) and FY 1969.

The Act was approved by the Senate on May 23, 1968, and by the House of Representatives on June 6, 1968. It was signed into law by the President on June 19, 1968. Congress approved appropriations for FY 1969 on August 9, 1968, and on October 21, 1968, LEAA formally came into being as the first Administrators took office under recess appointments. By December 19, 1968, all states had established State Criminal Justice Planning Agencies (SPA).

Congress amended the basic Act in the Omnibus Crime Control Act of 1970 (P.L. 91-644), which was signed into law by the President on January 2, 1971.[4]

An Ongoing Program

Literally billions of dollars previously not available to the several components of the justice system are being poured into their jurisdictions to fulfill research, training, and operational needs, as well as special crime-related projects to meet the demands caused by the growing problems of

[4]President's Commission, *Challenge of Crime in a Free Society,* p. 5.

crime and its prevention, criminals and their rehabilitation, and the system and its management. Just a listing of the many topics covered in the President's Crime Commission Report of 1967 indicates the scope of projects that LEAA funding would be directed toward during the next few years.

To enumerate names, dates, and places in this chapter would date this publication because of the constantly changing picture in this category. Rather than specifically list new products, changes in procedures, innovative programs, or recent studies, what we shall do is list some of the topics that were listed in the commission's recommendations in which significant changes may or may not have taken place during the past few years. Filling in the details of precisely what has been done—if anything—will be left to you, the reader.

- Improvements in crime reporting procedures.
- Policy guidelines for dealing with juveniles.
- Police referrals to the youth services bureau of delinquents and near-delinquents.
- Neighborhood police youth services bureaus.
- Separate detention facilities for juveniles.
- "Stop and frisk" legislation and guidelines.
- Police involvement in community planning.
- Innovative community relations programs.
- Citizens advisory groups to work with police agencies.
- Recruitment of officers from minority group heritage.
- Guidelines for officers in matters in which the officer has wide discretionary powers.
- Different levels of entry into police service.
- Recruitment of police officer candidates on college campuses.
- Educational upgrading for police entrance and promotion requirements.
- Improved selection methods.
- Modifications of physical requirements for police service.
- Pay and promotion on the basis of ability and merit.
- Lateral movement of qualified police personnel.
- Upgrading of training to include discretionary decision making.
- Minimum of 400 hours basic training combined with additional time for actual training in the field.
- One week refresher training at least once a year.
- Probationary period for minimum of one year to eighteen months.
- Establishment of procedures to process and investigative grievances and complaints about the conduct of any department employee.
- Internal affairs units to assure honesty and integrity of personnel.
- Team-policing concept for maximum effectiveness.
- Improvement in utilization and deployment of manpower.
- Consolidation of some police services to improve service with economy.
- Community detoxification centers for alcoholics.

- Standardization of information releases about arrested persons and pending cases to assure a fair trial for defendants.
- New methods for probation and parole.
- Community-based treatment centers for criminal offenders.
- University and college involvement in criminal justice education and training.
- Special intelligence units to ferret out and combat organized crime.
- Consolidation and coordination of police information systems and computerization where applicable.
- Establishment of research and development units in local, state, and federal agencies of criminal justice.

During the early stages of development of the newly formed Law Enforcement Assistance Administration and at about the same time when the requests for funding had begun to gain momentum, that agency produced several documents relating to guidelines on the process of making applications for funding. Among those documents was the *Correctional Planning and Resource Guide.*[5] The following statement appeared in the introduction:

> To be comprehensive, law enforcement planning must include all elements of the criminal and juvenile justice system. Further, comprehensive planning will require interrelating of the separate law enforcement elements—police, courts, corrections, the criminal law and a variety of environmental factors and conditions. Among these are population growth and characteristics, socioeconomic conditions, employment, education, mental and physical health.[6]

Referring to the President's Commission on Law Enforcement and the Administration of Justice, previously referred to also as the President's Crime Commission, the *Guide* continues:

> Despite the seriousness of the crime problem today and the increasing challenge in the years ahead, the central conclusion of the Commission is that a significant reduction in crime is possible if the following objectives are vigorously pursued:
>
> *First,* society must seek to prevent crime before it happens by assuring date collection methods and set up an audit system.
> by strengthening law enforcement, and by reducing criminal opportunities.
>
> *Second,* society's aim of reducing crime would be better served if the system of criminal justice developed a far broader range of techniques with which to deal with individual offenders.
>
> *Third,* the system of criminal justice must eliminate existing inequities if it is to achieve ideals and win the respect and cooperation of all citizens.
>
> *Fourth,* the system of criminal justice must attract more people and better people—police, prosecutors, judges, defense attorneys, probation

[5]Law Enforcement Assistance Administration, *Correctional Planning and Resource Guide* (Washington, D.C.: Government Printing Office, 1969).

[6]LEAA, *Correctional Planning and Resource Guide,* p. 1.

> and parole officers, and corrections officials with more knowledge, expertise, initiative, and integrity.
>
> *Fifth,* there must be more operational and basic research into the problems of crime and criminal administration, by those both within and without the system of criminal justice.
>
> *Sixth,* the police, courts and correctional agencies must be given substantially greater amounts of money if they are to improve their ability to control crime.
>
> *Seventh,* individual citizens, civic and business organizations, religious institutions, and all levels of government must take responsibility for planning and implementing the changes that must be made in the criminal justice system if crime is to be reduced.
>
> Essential to the achievement of these objectives is the need to overcome the fragmentation, disunity and operations of programs at cross purposes by the multitude of agencies and jurisdictions which are essential supports to law enforcement and corrections.[7]

Criminal Justice Standards and Goals

On October 20, 1971, the National Advisory Commission on Criminal Justice Standards and Goals was appointed by Jerris Leonard, administrator of the Law Enforcement Assistance Administration. The commission's objective was to formulate for the first time a set of national standards and goals for criminal justice components to reduce and prevent crime at the state and local levels. LEAA's funding to those programs would be related to the efforts by those thousands of local and state agencies to accomplish those standards and goals. Approximately fifteen months and 1.75 million dollars later, the commission had produced six volumes covering its findings and recommendations. Following are excerpts from those recommendations enumerated in one of the volumes, *Report on the Criminal Justice System.*

- **1.1** Crime-oriented planning. Planning agencies and coordinating councils should analyze problems and implement programs to meet crime-reduction objectives.
- **1.2** Improve linkage between planning and budgeting by developing more effective budget programs and master plans.
- **1.3** Set minimum standards for grants and subgrants and fund according to agencies' adoption of the minimum standards.
- **3.1** Coordination of information systems. Assist agencies in development of date collection methods and set up in audit system.
- **3.2** Each state should establish a criminal justice information system and have it interface with other state agencies and local agencies within each state. Information would contain wanted persons, identifiable stolen

[7]LEAA, *Correctional Planning and Resource Guide,* p. 3.

items, criminal history files with arrest status of offenders, vehicle and driver files, Uniform Crime Report data, other activities on criminal violators, and general improvement in hardware to accomplish all this.

3.3 Criminal justice components at local levels to receive assistance in developing their respective information systems with their unique needs and

3.4 have the capability to interface and exchange vital information.

4.1 Police information systems to include dispatch information and date which shows case information through to final disposition.

4.2 Crime analysis capability using information on modus operandi of offenders, field interviews, arrests, crime reports, incident reports, dispatch information, traffic collision and citation activity.

4.3 Identification through information system of the manpower needs of each agency through analysis of allocation and assignments of patrol and specialist personnel, and striving for maximum utilization of available human resources.

4.4 Information system to study response time and be developed so that officers' needs in the field for information should be provided within certain established minimum times, such as two-minute maximum time for officer in the field with a potential danger, such as a field interview or car stop.

4.5 Every agency should participate fully in the Uniform Crime Reporting program.

4.7 Audit procedures should be established to assure accuracy and completeness in taking appropriate crime and incident reports.

5.1 A court information system that retains and provides information unique to each case and defendant. Include sufficient data about the defendant to make decisions on sentencing, setting bail, continuances, past history, criminal record.

5.2 Calendar management in the courts. Scheduling of judges, facilities and the principals involved in the proceedings. Setting up a system assuring accountability.

6.1 Development of a Corrections Information System for offender accounting, decisionmaking, research, response to questions.

6.5 Develop a system of maintaining current data on status and location of all offenders in institutions, on probation and parole, and in community diversion programs.

6.7 Evaluating the performance of the system. Overall system performance reviewed to assure compilation and dissemination of data on recidivism and other performance measures. The purpose is to determine program effectiveness in corrections goals.

7.6 Security of computerized files. Should be separate from all other files and available only to those criminal justice personnel who have a need for such information.

12.1 Criminal justice educational and training programs update.

13.1 Criminal code update for any state not having done so within previous ten years.

13.4 Corrections laws should be revised to promote effective, fair prison administration, relevant staff and inmate education, modernized prison industries.

13.6 Procedural law revision. Same as changes in substantive laws, any state not having done so within previous ten years should update and revise codes of criminal procedure.

13.8 Continuing education on the new codes at all levels and components of law enforcement, courts, corrections.[8]

TRENDS FOR THE FUTURE

The past few years have witnessed literally thousands of studies and experiments in all of the areas of justice administration. Because a texbook is a semipermanent document once the manuscript is submitted to the publisher and many innovations at the time of the writing may have been tried or abandoned, or modified many times, or may have become "traditional" by the time the text reaches the classroom, this particular section of the book must necessarily be open-ended. You, the reader and student, are challenged to write the conclusions for this chapter based on your inquiries of your local justice system agencies and your research on what has become of the crime commission's recommendations and the many thousands of studics and innovations in methods and equipment that have occurred since that commission's report was first disseminated.

To stimulate the further study of this tremendous boon to the system, following is a brief list of just a few of the LEAA funded projects, and other projects that have been carried out concurrently with other funds as sources of support during recent years. From your local criminal justice agencies, find out what they have been doing and see what you can add to the list. As a part of your participation in writing this chapter in the annals of criminal justice, prepare a paragraph about each item on this list and then discuss them in class with your instructor and fellow students.

Law Enforcement

- Enlightened, more "humanistic" approaches to personnel management.
- Changes in weaponry, including nonlethal projectiles and tear gas that can be directed toward its target more selectively.
- Computer-based information systems.
- Hand-held portable radios for foot beat officers.
- Tracking systems for radio-equipped police cruisers.
- Atomic research in criminalistics.
- "Systems" approach to police training, defining objectives based on task analyses and teaching toward those objectives with prescribed minimum performance levels.

[8]National Advisory Commission on Criminal Justice Standards and Goals, *Report on the Criminal Justice System* (Washington, D.C.: Government Printing Office, 1973).

- "Civilianizing" certain police positions that do not require peace-officer powers or qualifications, such as clerical and statistical positions.
- Changes in entrance requirements, such as the height, dental, and visual acuity restrictions.
- Entry into police service at different levels, depending on experience, education, and age factors.
- Lateral transfer of experienced personnel from one agency to another without loss of rank, longevity, or retirement benefits.
- Building security studies.
- Family crisis intervention experiments.
- Ultra-high frequency radio equipment and teleprinters in vehicles.
- Organized crime task forces that work cooperatively to address a mutual problem.
- Electronic analysis and retrieval of criminal histories, providing information about crimes and the people who commit them.
- Law enforcement education program, including loans and grants to students.
- Disadvantaged persons trained for law enforcement.
- Police corruption and organized crime.
- Law enforcement standards laboratories for study of new equipment.
- Police air mobility in helicopters and fixed-wing aircraft.
- Electronic surveillance and intelligence equipment.
- Unification of services, consolidating several smaller agencies into one metropolitan agency.
- Police legal advisors.
- Universal police emergency telephone number: 911.
- Alarm systems evaluation and improvement.
- Private police and their training.

Corrections

- Prison legal-aid programs.
- Training for jail and prison personnel.
- Uniform inmate grievance procedures.
- Father's day and special family activities, conjugal visits.
- Probation subsidy as an alternative to imprisonment.
- Short-term leaves prior to parole, with an objective of making the reintegration process an easier transition.
- Alcoholic detoxification centers.
- Correctional supervision and management training.
- Modifications in correctional facility architecture.
- Parole decision-making.
- Community-based corrections.
- Drug abuse rehabilitation.
- Parole computerized data bank.
- Juvenile corrections studies.
- Reduced case loads.
- Success predictability for parolees.
- Special casework approaches.

- Summer excursions for juvenile probationers and near-delinquents.
- Interagency cooperative projects in training and casework management.

Courts

- Bail reform studies.
- Bail investigation and "recognizance releases" pending hearings and trials.
- Use of hearing officers or commissioners to relieve load on judges.
- Reduction of delays on pretrial procedures.
- Court administrators to replace judges for court management.
- Executive training for court administrators.
- Uniform codes and standards.
- Recruitment and training of prosecutors.
- Specialized training for judges.
- Improvement in court paper-work procedures.
- Automated transcription systems.
- Improvements in court security.
- Selection and utilization of juries with less delay.
- Automated records for the courts.
- Extension of public defender services for the indigent.
- Consolidation and coordination of court bailiff responsibilities.
- Statewide court systems, including phasing out of the justice court.

BENCHMARKS OF PROGRESS

Several years after the President's Crime Commission report and recommendations and then the Commission on Standards and Goals, many millions of dollars had been spent, and thousands of reports from throughout the country indicated that the Law Enforcement Assistance Administration had been at work. But, has it done any good? Has there really been any improvement in the criminal justice system? If so, just exactly what had been accomplished to date? And, did the American people get their money's worth? In an effort to get answers to some of those questions, I surveyed several hundred agencies in law enforcement, corrections, and the courts.

With no attempt to analyze for you the significance of their responses, following are some of the questions that were asked of chief executive officers, personnel and training officials, and other practitioners in the various components of criminal justice. It is my suggestion that, as a student, you visit your local agencies and then, as an outside project for the class in which you are using this text, prepare your own analysis of where the system is now compared with where you believe that it should be. Then prepare your own recommendations for future action, if any.

The questions asked in the survey will precede the responses written by the individuals identified by general position title, such as chief executive officer, personnel director, training director.

Chief Executive Officer

QUESTION: What major changes and/or improvements have been made in your agency during the past decade as a direct or indirect result of the Omnibus Crime Bill (1968)?

RESPONSES: Law Enforcement

- Increased ability to use technological advances in the law enforcement field via the use of LEAA funds; i.e., microfilm recording system.
- Statistical evaluation of patrol procedures and a reduction in response time through the use of paraprofessionals.
- Updated and advanced technological equipment.
- Word-processing equipment and training for complete typewritten reports for the entire department.
- Institution of a modern communication center complete with a multichannel UHF radio system.
- Acquisition of a multifaceted mobile crime-scene van for detailed crime-scene investigations.
- Burglary and robbery-reduction programs which include portable alarm and surveillance equipment.
- Regional crime laboratory.
- Team-policing concept.
- More involvement with the community through neighborhood watch crime prevention units.
- Development of an operational automated vehicle-locator system.
- Greater emphasis on higher education.
- Statewide standards and training unit.
- Personal radio equipment for officers working on foot.

RESPONSES: Corrections

- Seven new federal prisons have been built. They are new and modern and rely on technology rather than bars and concrete to contain inmates.
- Broadly expanded role and responsibility regarding corrections as a part of the entire criminal justice system.
- Increased research efforts.
- Improved preservice and in-service corrections training.
- Establishment of community service centers throughout the state to assist ex-offenders.
- Improved vocational and educational programs in institutions.
- Improved rehabilitation programs in institutions, i.e., counseling.
- Creation of a research and planning unit.
- Creation of three work release centers—adult males.
- Training unit on a statewide basis for correctional personnel.

RESPONSES: Courts (Attorneys General)

- The establishment of the Organized Crime Prevention Unit on a local level.

- The establishment of the Career Criminal or Major Violator's Unit which is now being tested in various prosecutors' offices.
- One state's attorney reported no change.
- Witness Assistance Program.
- County Fraud Squad.
- Added more attorneys and investigators through LEPA and LEAA grants.

QUESTION: What major changes and/or improvements do you believe will take place in your agency during the next five years?

RESPONSES: Law Enforcement

- Increase in manpower.
- Increase in department office space and facilities, new administration building, training center, precinct stations.
- Return to high level of community involvement.
- Progressive changes in methods of criminal investigation.
- Increased effectiveness due to more efficient manpower deployment.
- Greater accountability of personnel (zone patrol).
- Reduction of specialized units in police department.
- Elimination of most minor types of calls and investigations.
- Improved scientific crime-solving techniques.
- Computer-aided dispatching and communications center.
- More paraprofessionals in nonpolice street assignments.
- More specialization in professional law enforcement tasks.
- Subjection to increased political influence.
- Development of a customized neighborhood team-policing program.

Comment Quotes from Police Chiefs:

- Irvine, California: "Police departments continue to operate separately rather than using regional approach. County and local government need to force P.D.'s to work together via joint funding."
- Gainesville, Florida: "I believe that any police agency that could have taken advantage of federal funding and did not probably set their own agency back anywhere from five to ten years. Federal funding has opened up a world of improvement in various small agencies across the nation, allowing them to improve their communications system, their records system and their entire overall investigative ability for the fact that they are able to fund and buy special equipment that they would have never been able to obtain through their own city government."

QUESTION: What major changes and/or improvements do you believe will take place in your agency during the next five years?

RESPONSES: Corrections

- More humane prisons will be built—and smaller, housing no more than 550.
- Flat sentencing legislation will be passed by Congress.
- Expanded programs of work, education, and training for inmates.
- The building of new medium-security structures.

- The expansion of community-based programs.
- Increased vocational training to present inmate population.
- Work-release supervision.
- Training of correctional officers greatly improved.

QUESTION: If you will, please describe how training in your own agency and your area of criminal justice has changed since about 1965.

RESPONSES: Training Directors, Law Enforcement

- Courses of all types are more involved and directed toward a more intelligent officer.
- Officers are better educated and more experienced, and training programs are geared for this higher level.
- More people attending college under LEEP.
- Attendance at academy is mandated by law.
- More job-related training with role-playing emphasized.
- Practical field exercises and on-the-job training has been increased.
- Programs are brought up to date by the state agency which regulates academy training.
- More representatives from other agencies in the criminal justice system have participated in our programs to give our officers an even greater understanding of their role and how others fit into the picture of law enforcement.
- Much more behavioral science.
- Crisis intervention.
- Training in 1965 consisted of a six-week program with no examination process. Real improvement began in 1971. Increase of academy program to 14 weeks, examination process, followed by four weeks in the field on-the-job training and evaluation in the field.
- We now spend more time in courses dealing with human relations, communications, minority group relations, handling abnormal people, and other courses where there may be a chance of conflict between a police officer and the people with whom he works.
- Switch to use of regional academies as opposed to putting on our own training. We have observed many positive aspects of this type of training, chief among which is the intense, close relationships of our trainees fostered by the live-in format of the academies.
- Training is being recognized as important as an ongoing operation as opposed to something received at initial employment only.

RESPONSES: Training Directors, Corrections

- In 1969 a state law was enacted requiring that all police officers, probation and parole officers, and correctional officers receive 160 hours of basic training during their first year of employment (Kansas). In July, 1974, we began providing 80 hours of annual instruction to correctional officers (required by statute).
- Prior to 1974 the Missouri Division of Corrections Training was geared toward custody. Since May of 1974 the curriculum has been revised to include all personnel within the division.

- Our correctional training since 1965 has focused primarily on our correctional officers. With the ever-changing laws relating to rights of inmates, it is necessary to keep our officers up to date on rights of inmates, handling of prisoners, holding down writs, and grievance procedures.
- Training has changed from a local-unit concept of orientation training to both academy-type training and local unit in-service type training at all levels of operation.
- We are doing a great deal more in-house training, and that training has been standardized throughout the Bureau of Prisons. In the past, each institution developed its own program(s) and the quality varied widely. There is an attempt to blend in-house training, delivered by correctional professionals with experience and the respect of their peers, with consultant services from academia. There has also been, successfully in my opinion, an attempt to train *all* new employees—regardless of job type or specialty—together with emphasis on both custody and program (treatment) responsibilities. This appears to have reduced the custody versus treatment personnel attitudes that used to prevail. In corrections, generally, there has been a recognition—reflected in training—that correctional personnel are different from "normal" law enforcement personnel such as police. (Dennis Hubbard, Chief, Training Program Development, Federal Bureau of Prisons.)

QUESTION: What changes, if any, have taken place in the selection process for your agency during the past several years since 1965?

RESPONSES: Personnel Directors, Law Enforcement

- Physical agility and polygraph testing, lower height standards.
- All entry-level exams have been currentized to reflect EEOC/Federal and state guidelines on job-relatedness.
- More emphasis has been placed on documenting each selection as to the qualifications of those concerned with emphasis also on EEOC principles.
- Psychological and psychiatric examinations, extensive medical and background investigations; weight and height requirements eliminated; high-school completion required; greater attempts to recruit and the giving of pretests. (Jersey City Police.)
- Elimination of two-year residency requirement.
- Have gone from one-to-one preemployment interview to panel-of-three oral examination.
- Age requirements have changed.
- Like so many other public and private agencies, Affirmative Action has impacted heavily on our recruitment and selection procedures. Our testing procedures are therefore closely monitored to insure that they are free from any bias that would restrict minorities or women from competing in the examination process.
- Improved techniques and more thoroughness in conducting background investigations.
- Increased attention to job-related testing process, validity of testing process.
- The entrance level test for police officer is now job-related. Tests used previously were general aptitude tests.

- Raising the educational requirement from a high-school diploma to an Associate Degree in Criminal Justice (Dearborn, Michigan).

RESPONSES: Personnel Directors, Corrections

- New test in accordance with EEOC standards.
- The addition of physical agility test.
- Increase in minimum experience and education requirements.

In the actual study excerpted in the previous few pages, each of the several officials in the many departments queried were asked to respond to a series of questions. Obviously, what you have just seen is a very small portion of that survey. What you did see, however, is that the professionals in the fields of criminal justice know what their well-defined objectives are, and many agencies are on their way working toward accomplishment of those objectives.

EXEMPLARY PROJECTS

A recent publication of the National Institute of Law Enforcement and Criminal Justice (NILECJ) highlighted twenty-nine exemplary projects funded during the past several years by the Law Enforcement Assistance Administration. These projects were designated "exemplary" because they qualified in the following five areas:

1. Goal achievement: Overall effectiveness in the reduction of crime or improvement in the operations and quality of the justice system.
2. Replicability: Adaptability to other jurisdictions.
3. Measurability: Formal evaluation data or other conclusive evidence of product achievement (minimum of one year's results).
4. Efficiency: Demonstrated cost-effectiveness.
5. Accessibility: Willingness of project staff to provide information to other communities.[9]

The twenty-nine exemplary projects were classified under the following general headings:

1. Community Involvement... encouraging citizens to join the effort to reduce crime and improve criminal justice in their communities.
2. Law Enforcement... applying innovative techniques to prevent crime, increase arrests, and improve the efficiency of existing operations.
3. Prosecution... focusing on target crimes and career offenders to improve case preparation and increase conviction.
4. Adjudication and Defense... implementing improved management practices for the benefit of all participants in the judicial process.

[9]Material for this and all subsequent related text matter is taken from publication regarding a program of the NILECJ, Law Enforcement Assistance Administration, U.S. Department of Justice, *Exemplary Projects* (Washington, D.C.: Government Printing Office, 1978).

5. Corrections... exploring new directions in the institution and the community.
6. Juvenile Programs... providing positive new directions to youth in trouble.
7. Alternate Service Delivery... easing the burden on criminal justice agencies by providing mechanisms for delivery of selected services to the public.

Following are summaries of those twenty-nine projects.

(a) Community Involvement

(1) Stop Rape Crisis Center, Baton Rouge, Louisiana

In 1974 a group of Baton Rouge women, representing a cross section of the community, mounted an offensive against rape. They identified two key problems: the low priority given rape cases by the community's law enforcement agencies and the lack of supportive social services for rape victims. They brought their findings to the District Attorney who helped them design a comprehensive program to improve enforcement and prosecutorial techniques while minimizing the victim's trauma.

While many features of the Louisiana program are typical of rape crisis centers, Baton Rouge goes beyond the standard approach in several important ways:

- Its status as a section of the District Attorney's Office helps to ensure that adequate prosecutorial resources are devoted to rape cases. This status also contributes to the remarkably high degree of support for the project from local law enforcement agencies.
- Its emphasis on coordination. The city police and the county sheriff participated in planning the center; as a result, standard operating procedures in both law enforcement agencies ensure that the center is an integral part of the processing of virtually every reported rape.
- The cooperation of local judges, who collaborate in a system of "vertical prosecution," in which each rape case is assigned to a particular judge and prosecutor from arraignment through trial. This case assignment system minimizes the burden on the victim and helps to maintain her cooperation as the case proceeds through the legal process.
- The involvement of the medical community and the provision of free medical service to the rape victims. Local doctors participated in developing the center's medical component, and a representative of the medical profession remains personally involved in the administration of medical services to rape victims. In addition, 12 physicians volunteer their time on a rotating on-call basis and two local hospitals have set aside examination rooms expressly for rape victims.
- Involvement of the community at large. Trained volunteer counselors staff the 24-hour crisis telephone line which connects calls directly to counselors without an intervening answering service. To assist police investigation of rape cases, the center agrees to preserve a victim's anonymity. If a victim chooses not to report the crime officially, she is encouraged to provide information about her assailant to the volunteer counselor.

The women who serve as volunteer counselors also act as the victim's personal escort, accompanying her through every phase of the prosecution of her case. In addition, 19 volunteers from the community serve on the center's advisory board. Members include representatives from law enforcement and social service agencies, two local universities and other community groups.

Neither the victim nor the taxpayer is asked to bear the cost of these services. The volunteer counselors and doctors help the project keep operating costs below 40,000 dollars per year.

(2) Community Crime Prevention Program (CCPP), Seattle, Washington

The Seattle CCPP is demonstrating that crime rates can be lowered if the citizens of a community are willing to participate in crime prevention. The goals in Seattle are to mobilize citizen concern over a rapdily rising residential burglary rate and turn it into citizen action to attack the problem.

The four principal tactics used in organizing a neighborhood—residential security inspection, property marking, block watches, and informative materials—are not original. The CCPP's success in applying them has come from careful coordination, the commitment of full-time staff, the cooperation of the Seattle Police, and the cultivation of a sense of community in the neighborhoods.

A rigorous evaluation of the CCPP provides evidence of the project's success in meeting its goals.

- Two victimization surveys show burglary rate reductions in participating households ranging from 48 percent to 61 percent.
- Citizen reports of burglary have risen from 51 percent to 76 percent of actual burglaries committed.
- A higher proportion of calls made to police are burglary-in-progress calls.
- The decrease in burglaries among CCPP participants has not meant an increase among nonparticipants, or in adjacent neighborhoods.
- The program met or exceeded its goal of involving 30 percent of the households in each target neighborhood.

The CCPP was initially developed and directed by the city's Law and Justice Planning Office, using LEAA block grant funds. Its success has led to its incorporation into the city's Department of Community Development.

(3) Rape/Sexual Assault Care Center (R/SACC), Des Moines, Iowa

Rape and sexual assault are crimes that create special difficulties for both the victim and the criminal justice system. Fear of harassment and humiliation during the medical examination and legal investigation inhibits many victims from even reporting the crime, much less pursuing the case through the legal process. In handling these crimes, criminal justice agencies often must cope with irrational laws, incomplete physical evidence, and uninformed public attitudes.

The Des Moines Rape/Sexual Assault Care Center has devised a single, comprehensive program to deal with these multiple problems. The beneficiaries of the program are not only the victims, but the legal system, the medical community, law enforcement agencies and the general public. A small staff (victim-contact worker, project coordinator, secretary, and special prosecutor) work in cooperation with a 70-member board of directors who represent local medical, social, governmental, and law enforcement agencies. The center's activities include:

- Twenty-four-hour telephone and personal contact service, including compassionate assistance to the victim during the medical examination and prosecutor's interview.
- Referral services to a wide network of community agencies that can give specialized help to the victim.
- In-service training for medical and criminal justice professionals who deal with rape victims.
- Public education to replace existing ignorance and misinformation with the facts about sex crimes.

From the time the center was created in October 1974, until its designation as an exemplary project in June 1976, police clearance rates for rape cases rose from 50 percent to 69 percent. Even more significant changes were seen in the special prosecutor's office, where victims showed an increasing willingness to press charges. Before the program began, charges were filed in only a third of cases where the offender was identified; that figure had jumped to three-fourths of those cases by June 1976. An equally dramatic rise in conviction rates occurred: While only 40 percent of the cases tried in the preproject period resulted in conviction, the figure rose to 65 percent in the project's first year and to 82 percent in the second year.

Contributing significantly to the improved record or convictions are legislative changes in the 1974 Iowa Criminal Code that disallow any irrelevant testimony involving the victim's past sexual history and eliminate the requirement for corroboration beyond the physical evidence and the victim's testimony. These reforms were stimulated by the individuals who went on to create the Rape/Sexual Assault Care Center as a necessary step in gaining the victim cooperation so essential to successful prosecution of rape cases.

Since R/SACC was named an exemplary project, it has expanded its services to provide peer counseling through an ongoing support group for women who have been assaulted. Additional LEAA funding has permitted one staff member to travel around the state assisting other communities in developing similar rape assistance centers.

(4) Volunteer Probation Counselor Program, Lincoln, Nebraska

Lay volunteers in Lincoln are successfully counseling high-risk probationers—misdemeanants of ages 16 to 25 with an average of 7.3 previous arrests and convictions.

A one-year comparative analysis of recidivism in the volunteer counselor program and a control regular probation program showed these results:

	Volunteer, %	Control, %
New nontraffic offenses	15	63.7
Multiple new offenses	10	52.2

The volunteer program has three main features that contribute to its success:

- Screening: only those volunteers with appropriate motivations and resources are selected.
- Training: an extensive program emphasizes both general counseling skills and crisis intervention techniques.
- Matching: the ability of a volunteer to respond to the particular needs and interests of the individual probationer determines assignments.

The program has recently expanded to serve alcohol and drug abusers and older offenders.

(b) Law Enforcement

(5) Hidden Cameras Project, Seattle, Washington

Like many urban areas, Seattle recorded a dramatic increase in robbery during the last decade. Between 1966 and 1975, the number of reported robberies jumped from 650 to more than 2,000—a 224 percent increase. At the same time, clearance rates remained consistently low—approximately 25 percent. Because robbery often results in injury as well as financial loss to the victim, the city made it a priority "target crime."

The Seattle Law and Justice Planning Office decided to focus on commercial robbery for three reasons: First, potential targets could be readily identified through police crime reports. Second, commercial robbers were believed to be repeat offenders, so that any arrests would have a telling effect on robbery rates. Third, since commercial robberies were widely publicized, they engendered a disproportionate amount of fear among the public.

In 1975 the Seattle Police Department installed cameras in 75 commercial establishments that had been identified as high-risk robbery locations. The cameras were hidden in stereo speaker boxes and activated by removing a dollar "trip" bill from the cash drawer. The project director, who is on call 24 hours a day, seven days a week, immediately retrieves the film, develops prints, and distributes them to police within hours to aid in the identification, apprehension and prosecution of robbery suspects.

The city's Law and Justice Planning Office conducted a rigorously controlled experiment to measure the project's impact on arrests, convictions, and the overall commercial robbery rate in Seattle. The results are compelling:

- The overall clearance rate for robberies of businesses equipped with hidden cameras was 68 percent, compared to a 34-percent clearance rate for the control group of businesses without the hidden cameras.

- Fifty-five percent of all hidden camera cases were cleared by arrest, compared to only 25 percent of control group cases.
- Forty-eight percent of the robbers at hidden camera sites were eventually identified, arrested and convicted, compared to only 19 percent of control-group robbers.
- Commercial robbery in Seattle declined by 38 percent in the one-year period following project onset; noncommercial robberies increased by 6.7 percent in that same period.
- Case processing time from arrest to conviction was approximately one month shorter for hidden camera cases than for control-group cases.

The Seattle project is relatively simple, straightforward and inexpensive, requiring only one staff member. It requires technical skills which are widely available or easily learned. As an even greater plus, it is likely to be greeted warmly by local merchants in any community. Seattle plans to make the camera project a permanent part of the city's anticrime program.

(6) Street Crime Unit (SCU), New York City Police

SCU fills the gap between routine, visible police patrol and after-the-fact criminal investigations. The unit focuses on street crimes—robbery, personal grand larceny, and assault. Its primary strategy employs officers disguised as potential crime victims placed in an area where they are likely to be victimized. A plainclothes backup team waits nearby, ready to come to the decoy's aid and make an arrest. Careful screening of applicants, extensive training and close liaison with precinct commanders are marks of SCU's able management. Here is its 1973 record:

- Three thousand, five hundred and fifty-one arrests (85 percent felonies).
- Seventy-six percent of robbery arrests led to conviction.
- Ninety-five percent of grand larceny arrests led to conviction.
- Average man days per arrest: 8.2 (departmental average for all uniformed officers: 167).
- Cost: nominal increase per arrest and conviction, due to equipment costs.
- Risk: virtually no increased danger to police or citizens.

The unit's impressive performance is continuing. In 1974 SCU made 4,423 arrests, of which 90 percent were felonies. More recent statistics show a conviction rate of 90 percent.

(7) Central Police Dispatch (CPD), Muskegon County, Michigan

The Central Police Dispatch consolidated the radio dispatch services of nine law enforcement agencies. Until CPD, the agencies' service was limited, confused, inefficient, and costly:

- Eight of the nine departments operated on a single radio frequency, independently of each other.
- Only four of the nine departments had around-the-clock dispatch service seven days a week.

- Nearly 10 percent of the combined personnel in the agencies were assigned to dispatch services.

By pooling the radio dispatch resources of the agencies, CPD provides all nine departments with around-the-clock, seven-day service, eliminates confusion and duplication, and reduces the number of dispatch personnel required. Use of civilians as dispatchers adds to the cost savings. The centralized service also helped implement the 911 emergency system in sparsely populated areas.

CPD has met and surpassed most of the relevant standards recommended by the National Advisory Commission on Criminal Justice Standards and Goals. In fact, by 1975 the program had implemented many of the commission's recommended 1980 standards.

Spurred by the success of this initial cooperative effort, the nine agencies have pooled their resources to create a central narcotics unit and a crime prevention bureau.

(8) Police Legal Liaison Division, Dallas, Texas

The Dallas Police Legal Liaison Division successfully integrates two parts of the criminal justice system that often operate in isolation—the police and prosecutor. Since 1973, Assistant City Attorneys have been on call 24 hours a day to advise Dallas police officers on case preparation. In addition, the attorneys provide regular training for police in the elements of various offenses, proper search and seizure procedures, and other aspects of the law.

To reduce the number of cases "no-billed" or dismissed due to police error, project attorneys have established a case review system. All prosecution reports are reviewed for legal sufficiency before they are submitted to the district attorney's office. The result? The number of "no-bills" due to police error dropped from 13.8 percent to 4.3 percent from September 1973 to September 1975. Similarly, felony dismissals resulting from police error were reduced from 6.4 percent to 2.6 percent during the same period.

Increased convictions, although important, are not the only measure of the project's success. More informed decisionmaking by police in such sensitive areas as arrest and search and seizure means greater respect for the constitutional rights of individuals.

The project was included in the Dallas city budget at the expiration of its LEAA High-Impact grant.

(c) Prosecution

(9) Connecticut Economic Crime Unit, Chief State's Attorney's Office, Wallingford, Connecticut

Prosecution of economic crimes is particularly difficult. In recent years, efforts to upgrade the investigation and prosecution of such crimes have resulted in creation of special units in many jurisdictions. Two of these efforts—in Seattle and San Diego

—have previously been named Exemplary Projects. The Connecticut Economic Crime Unit was the first statewide program aimed at pinpointing and combatting economic crime and consumer fraud.

The Economic Crime Unit operates in conjunction with an Economic Crime Council, composed of representatives of virtually every regulatory, enforcement, and prosecutorial agency in the state. Marshalling statewide expertise and resources through monthly meetings of the Economic Crime Council, the Chief State's Attorney's Office has succeeded in mounting a comprehensive offensive against the white-collar criminal. Connecticut's unique, centralized approach means the ECU can collect evidence and present cases that might otherwise have been unprosecutable.

The results:

- In two years of operation, the Connecticut ECU has successfully prosecuted 100 percent of its 86 tried cases.
- Almost 100,000 dollars over the unit's operating expenses have been returned to victims and the state in restitution and fines.

In addition, the Connecticut ECU provides ongoing, statewide police training programs designed to teach police officials and line officers the applicable statutes for prosecution and how to identify various consumer-fraud schemes. The unit has also organized a successful public awareness campaign that includes wide distribution of consumer alert bulletins, publication of a citizen's handbook on economic crime, and direct liaison with the classified advertising departments of all major newspapers in an attempt to prevent publication of false advertising. These programs are highly regarded as deterrents to white-collar crime in Connecticut.

(10) Major Offense Bureau (MOB), Bronx County, New York

In The Bronx, New York, special prosecution efforts against habitual and violent offenders have dramatically reduced the time that potentially dangerous criminals remain free in the community awaiting trial. The average time between arrest and trial of repeat offenders has been cut from 400 to 90 days. Equally important, most of those indicted have been convicted, sentenced, and imprisoned.

These results have been achieved by creation of a Major Offense Bureau in The Bronx district attorney's office. Staffed by 10 experienced assistant district attorneys, the bureau uses an objective screening procedure to isolate those cases that deserve priority treatment. The screening mechanism—a modified version of the case weighting system developed by the Washington, D.C. Exemplary Project PROMIS (Prosecutor's Management Information System)—ranks cases according to the seriousness of the crime, the offender's criminal history, and the strength of the evidence.

Eligible cases are immediately referred to an assistant district attorney who is responsible for the case throughout the entire judicial process. Special trial sessions that hear only MOB cases virtually eliminate scheduling delays.

In its first 30 months, MOB successfully demonstrated its ability to speed up case processing while developing complete, well-prepared cases, as the following statistics show:

- Ninety-nine percent of the indictments were voted and presented to the Supreme Court within 3 days of arrest compared to the usual time lapse of several weeks.
- Ninety-two percent of those indicted were convicted.
- Ninety-four percent of those convicted were sentenced to prison, compared to less than half of a group whose cases were processed traditionally.
- Sentences ranged from 3 to 10 years.

The Bronx approach to processing serious felony cases also permits substantial economies by reducing pretrial detention, repeated court appearances, and duplication of effort by prosecutors.

(11) Fraud Division, King County (Seattle) Prosecutor's Office
(12) Fraud Division, San Diego County District Attorney's Office

Economic crimes and consumer frauds—which bilk millions of dollars from unsuspecting citizens—are the special targets of these divisions.

King County focuses on major economic crimes. Enlisting the investigative expertise of other agencies whenever possible, King County's Fraud Division has logged an impressive record of success: In the first two and one-half years of operation, 95.5 percent of the division's cases were successfully prosecuted representing more than 3.4 million dollars in economic losses.

The San Diego Fraud Division works with a larger staff and deals with *all citizen complaints* (15,251 during 1974) concerning fraud. A vast number of cases were settled outside the courts, either through in-house investigative teamwork or use of the small claims courts. Like Seattle, San Diego also prosecutes major impact cases, involving economic losses totalling millions.

(13) Prosecutor Management Information System (PROMIS), District of Columbia

PROMIS uses an automated management information system to select high priority cases in the U.S. Attorney's Office, Superior Court of the District of Columbia, for intensified pretrial preparation by a special team of attorneys. Pending cases are ranked daily according to four criteria: (1) seriousness of offense; (2) defendant's criminal record; (3) strength of evidence; and (4) age of case or number of continuances.

PROMIS also helps the prosecutor's office to:

- Spot scheduling and logistical impediments.
- Maintain evenhandedness in using prosecutorial discretion.
- Analyze and research the problems of screening and prosecuting criminal cases.

During its first 19 months of operation, the conviction rate for cases receiving special preparation was 25 percent higher than that for cases routinely processed.

(d) Adjudication and Defense

(14) One Day/One Trial: Jury System, Wayne County, Michigan

Trial by jury is increasingly perceived as an excessive burden to jurors, according to a recent survey. Wayne County, Michigan, courts have adopted a promising alternative to the lengthy jury term. As the name implies, under the One Day/One Trial System, jurors are eligible for service for only one day. If they are chosen, they serve for the duration of the trial. If they are not selected, they have fulfilled their obligation for the year.

The system taps seven times as many citizens for jury duty, makes better use of their time, and saves money for the courts.

Computers are used to maintain a current list of all registered voters for easy access when jury pools are drawn. A personal-history questionnaire, sent to all prospective jurors, "prequalifies" them. Every morning, as new jurors convene in the assembly area, a 16-minute slide program acquaints them with the legal process and their roles as jurors. Standbys are notified by telephone the evening before if they need to appear.

Two numerical indexes show that jurors are being used more efficiently. Where the number of juror days served greatly exceeds the number of trials or the number of trial days, much of the jurors' time is spent sitting and waiting to be impaneled on a jury. In Wayne County both ratios decreased substantially—25 percent and 32 percent, respectively. In addition, jury costs per trial were cut from 862 dollars to 646 dollars.

Perhaps the most significant success of the program is that more people are sharing both the duties and benefits of jury duty.

(15) Creighton Legal Information Center (CLIC), Omaha, Nebraska

Comprehensive collections of legal materials are often scarce in rural areas. Criminal justice personnel in Nebraska sometimes travel up to 300 miles to obtain the legal documentation necessary to support an argument—a costly procedure, both in time and money.

The Creighton Legal Information Center provides a central library research facility for judges, prosecutors, defense counsel, and police. Student researchers from the Creighton University Law School compile well-documented legal memoranda on topics requested by users. An average of 8.8 student hours are required to prepare each legal memorandum, at no cost to the requestors. The findings are summarized in a newsletter, published by the center, and the complete document filed for future reference. The project also has prepared a deskbook for Nebraska judges on criminal procedure and sentencing alternatives.

Users report that CLIC services have significantly improved the quality of cases argued before Nebraska's rural courts. During the first 14 months of CLIC's operations, 66 percent of the judges from the eligible rural counties had used its services at least once. All said they would use them again.

CLIC has a sophisticated monitoring and evaluation system to tailor project activities to user needs. The project's comprehensive documentation includes analysis instructions, computer programs, and management control forms.

Under an LEAA grant, CLIC has provided technical assistance to replicating agencies in 13 states; requests for technical assistance are still pending from about eight others.

(16) Administrative Adjudication Bureau (AAB), New York State Department of Motor Vehicles

The AAB streamlines the traffic and criminal adjudication process by removing most traffic offenses from the criminal courts in New York City, Rochester and Buffalo.

Besides removing the unsafe driver from the streets more promptly, the bureau's direct and fast disposition of traffic cases has meant:

- Significant reduction in the criminal court case backlog: 20 judges and 9 courtrooms relieved of traffic cases.
- Time spent by police at traffic hearings cut in half.
- More uniform application of sanctions.
- Discouragement of scofflaws.

The AAB's method combines three basic elements: (1) merger of the licensing agency with the traffic offense adjudication agency; (2) the services of highly-trained adjudicators; and (3) use of computerized information.

In the fiscal year ending March 31, 1975, the AAB returned 7.5 million dollars to the treasuries of the jurisdictions where traffic offenses took place, a sum representing the excess of fines collected over its operating expenses. This total represents a 25 percent increase in returns compared to the previous court system.

(17) The Public Defender Service (PDS) of the District of Columbia

PDS has successfully overcome the traditional barriers faced by public defender services—high caseloads and poorly paid and inadequately trained attorneys.

PDS provides quality representation to the indigent defendant from arrest to release through:

- Limited caseloads.
- Individualized and continuous client representation.
- An ongoing training program beginning with a special six-week program for new staff attorneys.
- Effective management and administration patterned after large law firms.
- Use of supportive services, such as psychiatric evaluations, counseling, and other rehabilitation services.
- Service to the legal profession and the justice system by sponsoring practice institutes and encouraging law reform.

(e) Corrections

(18) Montgomery County Work Release/Prerelease Center (PRC), Montgomery County, Maryland

Finding a job can be a difficult and stressful situation for anyone. For the newly released offender, it could be an insurmountable obstacle to becoming a productive member of the community. The Montgomery County Work Release/Prerelease Center helps to ease the transition from incarceration to freedom by assuring that its clients have employment, housing and cash savings at the time of release.

Montgomery County PRC is a coeducational, residential, community-based correctional facility serving sentenced offenders within six months of their release or parole hearing, pretrial detainees, and selected probationers and parolees. The program involves extensive supervision, counseling services, social awareness instruction, and work or education release from the center.

With the assistance of a Work Release Coordinator, all PRC residents obtain jobs shortly after their arrival (unless they intend to enroll in a full-time academic or vocational training program). All employed residents—full time or part time—pay up to 200 dollars a month for their room and board. Many residents also pay fines, restitution, legal fees, and family support.

Each resident's activities at the center are prescribed by a contractual agreement developed prior to his or her arrival at PRC. A triphased furlough/release plan allows increasing privileges as the resident demonstrates responsible behavior through adherence to his contract and PRC rules.

PRC has had significant impact on the recidivism rates of its clients. During the three-year study period, a total of 407 residents successfully passed through the program. A one-year followup study showed that under 20 percent were rearrested subsequent to leaving the program. Less than 1 percent were arrested for new crimes while assigned to the center.

PRC has also succeeded in marshalling community support in Montgomery County. The center has gained the acceptance and support of both neighbors and local civic groups and its funding was completely assumed by the county government upon termination of its LEAA grant.

(19) Ward Grievance Procedure, California Youth Authority

Left unresolved, even minor problems can fester within the confines of a prison, spawning hostility and even open confrontation between inmates and staff. To alleviate the problem, the California Youth Authority has created a formal but easy-to-use method for resolving inmate grievances in California's youth institutions. Both wards and staff participate in the procedure, which works this way:

Any inmate with a grievance is entitled to an open hearing conducted by ward and staff representatives. If the decision is unsatisfactory, the grievant may appeal to higher levels within the Youth Authority, and ultimately to an outside review panel, chaired by a professional arbitrator. Volunteer arbitrators are identified with the assistance of the American Arbitration Association. At each level, grievances are responded to in writing, within strict time limits.

In the 19-month period from September 1973 to April 1975, 85 percent of the cases were resolved, approximately 10 percent had been withdrawn prior to the hearing, and another 5 percent were still pending at the time of reporting. In 70 percent of the cases, the disposition has been in favor of the grievant either totally or through some sort of compromise. Only 24 percent of the grievances were denied. In these cases the reasons were clearly set forth in writing, thus clarifying official policy. Most of the grievances are resolved at the first level of review—the ward staff committee meeting. Only 2 percent of the grievances required outside arbitration.

Training—for wards, staff, and management—is a key to the project's success. Another special feature contributing to its effectiveness is the involvement of the wards themselves. Ward grievance clerks process complaints, manage paperwork, and often represent grievants.

The California Youth Authority's collaborative approach to resolving problems has paid off in terms of effectiveness and acceptance of the grievance procedures. The process has recently been expanded to include parolee as well as inmate grievances.

(20) Parole Officer Aide Program, Ohio Adult Parole Authority, Columbus, Ohio

Ex-offenders represent an untapped reservoir of talent for the corrections system. Their own experience behind bars often gives them a special rapport in dealing with offenders. Recognizing this fact, the National Advisory Commission on Criminal Justice Standards and Goals recommended that, "Correctional agencies should take immediate and affirmative action to recruit and employ capable and qualified ex-offenders in correctional roles."

The Ohio Parole Officer Aide Program exemplifies the benefits of such action. Carefully screened and trained ex-offenders work under the supervision of a Senior Parole Officer, handling caseloads and developing job opportunities for parolees. Their performance to date has met professional standards.

The program reaps a double dividend. The added manpower permits more individualized attention to an important need of parolees—finding a job. At the same time, the program provides an employment opportunity for ex-offenders in positions that offer career potential. More than half of the parole officer aide positions have now become permanent civil service positions, with the remainder scheduled for conversion in the near future. Educational advancement is not overlooked. Each aide is allowed up to 10 hours leave a week to attend school, and a number are currently enrolled at both the college and graduate school level.

(21) Community-Based Corrections Program, Polk County (Des Moines), Iowa

The Des Moines program coordinates four services for defendants and convicted offenders: pretrial release on own recognizance, pretrial supervised release, probation, and residence at Fort Des Moines, a correctional facility offering work and educational release. Synchronizing the four components to a unified system eliminates overlapping and splintered administration. Equally important, it provides flexibility in responding to a wide range of client needs.

In 1973, the Des Moines project saved the county and state correctional systems an estimated 454,229 dollars. The pretrial components also saved defendants an estimated 154,000 dollars for the cost of bail bonds, and enabled many of them to retain their jobs and support their families.

Of the 246 clients released by the Fort Des Moines correctional facility before 1973, only 53 (21 percent) were charged with indictable offenses during an average 19-month period following release. In particular, recidivism data show that the correctional facility deals effectively with those clients with high-risk characteristics such as prior convictions, unemployment, and drug or excessive alcohol use. The high-risk clients were charged with no more new offenses after release than were relatively low-risk clients with no prior convictions, more substantial employment history and a relatively minor history of drug or alcohol use.

Because of the Des Moines Program's demonstrated success, the Iowa State Legislature voted to assume total funding of the project and adopted "community-based corrections" as the model for future Iowa correctional programs.

(f) Juvenile Programs

(22) Community Arbitration Project, Anne Arundel County, Maryland

In 1973, the juvenile intake office of Anne Arundel County, Maryland, faced heavy backlogs of relatively minor cases that impaired its ability to deal with youngsters in more serious trouble with the law. Delays in resolving cases were frequent. A child accused of a first or second misdemeanor offense typically waited four to six weeks before official action was taken on his case. By that time, the incident was no longer fresh in the youngster's mind, making it difficult to reinforce the concept of accepting responsibility for the consequences of his actions.

The offender's parents and the victim were only marginally involved as the case proceeded. Many victims were never informed of the final disposition of the case. As a result, both parents and victims felt powerless and ineffective.

Most important, case dispositions often were unsatisfactory. Because of caseload pressures, many offenses received only cursory attention. Or cases were sent for formal adjudication—a process that may alienate the youngster and result in an unnecessary stigma. Public dissatisfaction with the county's juvenile justice system was increasing.

In 1975, the county devised an alternative to the system. The Community Arbitration Project is designed to alleviate the burden on the juvenile court while still impressing on the young offender the consequences of his or her behavior.

Under the program, juvenile misdemeanants are issued a citation which records the offense and schedules a hearing to arbitrate the case seven days later. The suspect's parents and the victim receive copies of the citation and are asked to appear at the hearing. The right to counsel is made clear to the youngster and his parents.

Although the hearing is informal, it is held in a courtroom setting to enhance the child's understanding of the meaning and importance of the procedure. The Juvenile Intake Commissioner—an attorney with experience in juvenile cases—serves as arbitrator. The commissioner hears the complaint and reviews the police report. If the child admits committing the offense and consents to arbitration, the commissioner makes an informal adjustment, sentencing the child to a prescribed number of hours of community work and/or restitution, counseling, or an educational program. The case is left "open," to be closed within 90 days upon a positive report from the child's field-site supervisor. If the offense is serious, if the child denies his involvement, or if the child or his parents so request, the case may be forwarded to the state's attorney for formal adjudication.

In two years since project inception, 4,233 youths have gone through the program. Nearly half of their cases were adjudicated informally; only 8 percent were referred to the state's attorney. In addition, a comparison was made of the recidivism rates of a sample of CAP clients and a sample of traditionally processed juveniles. As illustrated in the following table, the results for CAP clients are impressive.

Differences in recidivism were particularly significant for property offenders.

CAP has been fully funded by the State of Maryland's Juvenile Services Administration since April 1977.

Recidivism of CAP Clients and Control Group

	Percent Recidivist	Number of Rearrests per Client	Number of Cases
Traditional processing	14.3	.659	342
CAP	9.8*	.415**	482

*Difference significant at p = .07
**Difference significant at p = .01

(23) Project New Pride, Denver, Colorado

Project New Pride is a successful attempt to help juveniles, most with lengthy records of prior arrest and conviction, to break out of what could become a lifetime pattern of crime by instilling a sense of self-pride. The project integrates education, employment, counseling, and cultural education—services which are usually highly specialized and fragmented. Intensive application of this service integration approach is the key to the success of New Pride.

The program accepts Denver County residents 14 to 17 years old, who have had a recent arrest or conviction for burglary, robbery, or assault related to robbery, and who have at least two prior convictions for similar offenses.

A unique feature of the program is its pioneering work with youth with learning disabilities. Tests administered to project youth in the first two years of operation showed that 71 percent of New Pride participants had learning disabilities. The Learning Disabilities Center has recently received a separate grant and will be able to serve an increased number of clients.

The effect on the 160 clients who have completed the New Pride program has been significant.

- The nonstatus offense rearrest rate for New Pride clients during a 12-month period in the community was 27 percent. The rate for a control group was 32 percent.

- Seventy percent of clients have been placed in full- or part-time jobs, and the rearrest rate for employed clients was one-third the rate for unemployed clients.

New Pride has also pointed up the potential economic advantages to the community. The cost of incarcerating a youth in Colorado is estimated at 12,000 dollars a year. New Pride spends 4,000 dollars per year to keep a youngster out of institutions.

Originally funded under LEAA's Impact Cities program, New Pride is now an established program of the Colorado Division of Youth Services.

(24) Community-Based Adolescent Diversion Project, Champaign-Urbana, Illinois

In these two adjacent communities, the university and the criminal justice system have joined forces in a successful new approach to helping juveniles in trouble. Youngsters who have contact with the police that would normally lead to the juvenile court and the prosecutor are referred instead to the project.

Undergraduates at the University of Illinois fill volunteer roles in the project for academic credit in psychology. The students receive training and supervision by experienced psychologists as an ongoing course activity.

Each youngster is assigned to a student volunteer for a 4½-month period. After assessing the youngster's problems and needs, the student develops a program for the youth using one of two innovative techniques.

The youngster may sign a contract with a parent or a school teacher that spells out specific obligations that each party must fulfill. The contractual agreements involve real-life issues such as curfew hours and household chores.

Or the student may use the child advocacy approach, introducing the youngster to educational, welfare, health, mental heath, and vocational resources in the community and encouraging their use.

The project's diversion power is evident in the following comparisons between 24 participants and a control group of 12:

Number of Police Contacts (Academic Year 1974–1975)

	One Year Prior to Project	During Project
Participants	2.21	0.46
Control group	2.25	2.25

Number of Court Petitions Filed (Academic Year 1974–1975)

	One Year Prior to Project	During Project
Participants	0.13	0.08
Control group	0.25	0.75

The project's experimental phase ended in 1975 and it is now operated by a community group working with the university students.

(25) 601 Juvenile Diversion Project, Sacramento, California

The 601 Project of the Sacramento Probation Department provides short-term family-crisis counseling in lieu of juvenile court processing for status offenders, truants, runaways, and unmanageable youngsters. Youths and their families meet with 601 project counselors, usually within 2 hours of referral, to work out the delinquency problem together. In cases where the youth cannot reasonably return home at once, temporary accommodations elsewhere are sought, with the consent of both parents and child.

In October 1976, the project was relocated to Neighborhood Alternative Centers staffed by graduate student volunteers as well as regular probation officers.

The original 601 program (the name derives from the relevant section of the California Penal Code) has been expanded to include selected cases of criminal conduct, such as petty theft and possession of drugs. The basis for this expansion lies in the project's first-year record:

	Project Cases	Control Cases
Petitions filed	3.7%	19.8%
Repeat offenses (within 1 year)	46.3	54.2
Juvenile hall detention	13.9	69.4
Average detention time (nights)	0.5	4.6
Average case handling time (hours)	14.2	23.7
Average case cost	$284	$526

(26) Providence Educational Center (PEC), St. Louis, Missouri

At the time of exemplary designation, PEC was funded under LEAA's Impact Cities Program and focused on diverting youth with relatively serious offenses from training school incarceration. Currently, PEC also accepts youth referred through the juvenile court's status offenders diversion program. All referrals to PEC must be certified by the state as having behavioral disorders or learning disabilities.

PEC's program allows most youths to remain in their homes while participating in intensive education and counseling in an "alternative school" setting. Teams of professionally trained counselors, educators, and social workers devise an individual program for each child, who "graduates" when he or she has achieved the 8th-grade reading level required for high school admission in St. Louis and/or demonstrates adequate social functioning—usually after 9 months from referral. PEC can accommodate 75 youths in its educational program.

In September 1974, the Student Work Assistance Program (SWAP) was launched, allowing youngsters to spend three hours studying at PEC and three hours working in the community each day.

PEC has received continued funding from the Juvenile Court, the Junior League, the Mayor's Office of Manpower, LEAA, St. Louis Commission on Crime and Law Enforcement, and other local civic and service organizations.

(27) Neighborhood Youth Resources Center (NYRC), Philadelphia, Pennsylvania

This center provides a wide range of services for youngsters living in a high-crime, inner-city area of Philadelphia. Open 12 hours a day, NYRC offers:

- Crisis intervention, or immediate short-term aid.
- Individual plans for long-term comprehensive assistance.
- Counseling and educational assistance to groups of youngsters.
- Referrals to cooperating agencies and careful monitoring and followup.
- Legal representation.

Emphasizing its role as a community center, NYRC also sponsors recreational and cultural programs, counseling for youth on probation, and legal education for neighborhood residents.

Evidence of NYRC's impact emerges in a comparison of arrest rates (per thousand) for target and nontarget area boys within two precincts. The arrest rates for boys in the target group were significantly lower in the felony, lesser misdemeanor, and status offense categories.

	9th District		23rd District	
	Target	Nontarget	Target	Nontarget
Felonies	9.1	51.3	4.2	17.3
"Victimless" misdemeanors	19.7	24.6	2.3	12.0
Status offenses	31.5	82.5	2.3	18.5

(g) Alternative Service Delivery

(28) Mental Health-Mental Retardation Emergency Service, Inc. (MCES), Montgomery County, Pennsylvania

Police are on duty around the clock. As the only available service agency during many hours of the day, they must cope with a variety of social problems, among them psychiatric and drug/alcohol emergencies that may not be criminal offenses but nevertheless pose a threat to the victim and the community. Few jurisdictions have developed alternatives to arrest and detention for people in such circumstances. One that has is Montgomery County, Pennsylvania.

MCES is a private, nonprofit corporation and a fully licensed and accredited psychiatric hospital which supplements police services by assuming the burden of psychiatric and drug/alcohol emergencies. MCES offers a comprehensive 24-hour placement alternative for police by providing:

- Telephone "hot-line" assistance.
- Specially equipped emergency vehicle.
- Crisis Intervention Outreach Team.
- Psychiatric evaluation.
- Detoxification.
- Short-term hospitalization.
- Referral to other agencies for continuing care.

To further assist police in handling these emergencies, MCES formed a Criminal Justice Liaison Network by placing trained mental health workers in selected police departments.

Since MCES opened its doors in February 1974, 30 percent of its client contacts have been criminal justice referrals. Of 152 criminal justice referrals examined by MCES in a three-month period from June through August 1976, 103 (68 percent) resulted in either no charge or charges being dropped. In many of the 34 cases in which charges were brought, citations had been issued prior to MCES referral.

Another measure of MCES's assistance to the county police is the amount of police time saved by the transportation service. MCES staff logged 970 hours transporting clients between January 1975 and April 1977.

Upon receiving accreditation, MCES moved to a third-party billing system. In 1976 third-party payors provided 70 percent of the program budget, and in the first quarter of 1977, 97 percent of billings was provided by third-party payors (i.e., private and public health benefit plans).

(29) Citizen Dispute Settlement Program ("Night Prosecutor"), Columbus, Ohio

Currently there is widespread interest in the development of informal approaches to the resolution of minor disputes as alternatives to arrest or court action. One of the first such programs to be initiated was the Night Prosecutor Program, begun in Columbus, Ohio in the fall of 1971. The Columbus program provides an out-of-court method of resolving neighborhood and family disputes through mediation and counseling. The emphasis is on a lasting solution to an interpersonal problem rather than a judgment of right and wrong. The program also serves as a forum for bad check cases, and spares prosecutors, police, judges and courtroom staff the workload of minor cases. The average cost per case handled by the program is about 20 dollars compared to 100 dollars for prosecution and trial.

Cases are screened and referred by the local prosecutor's office for a hearing within a week after the complaint is filed. Law students trained as mediators meet with the disputants during convenient evening and weekend hours to help them solve their problems without resorting to formal charges and court procedures. Counseling is provided by social work graduate students.

During the year 1976:

- Six thousand and four-hundred-twenty-nine cases scheduled—3,478 actually heard (excluding an additional 10,196 bad check cases).

- Criminal affidavits filed in only 2 percent of all cases scheduled.
- Cost per case: approximately 20 dollars (contrasted to an estimated 100 dollars for processing a criminal misdemeanor, from filing an affidavit to completion of a court trial).

The basic concept of the Columbus program has been replicated in a number of jurisdictions, many of which are experimenting with the use of different groups as mediators (e.g., professional people or trained lay citizens) and varying placements of the program with or outside the criminal justice system.

SUMMARY

In this chapter we have merely scanned the trends in justice administration in the United States, particularly some of the things that have taken place during the turbulent and extremely demanding years of the past decade. Since the inauguration of the Law Enforcement Assistance Administration and State Planning Agencies, and the infusion of billions of dollars previously not available for research, education, and training, we have witnessed thousands of experiments and innovations. At the present time we are in a constant state of modification and realignment. The nature of law enforcement and criminal justice agencies as community service organizations, which must be responsive to the changes of the demands of society, has made it necessary for such dynamic efforts to evaluate and reevaluate, modify, change or retain, and to generally update the system to best serve the needs of the people. We have merely exposed you to the data. Now it is your responsibility as the student to complete the chapter.

EXERCISES AND STUDY QUESTIONS

1. Visit your local police agency. From your observations, list at least three positions currently being filled by sworn police officers that could be handled just as well—if not better—by civilian counterparts.

2. In class, discuss the relative merits of internship training programs for college students.

3. What is "lateral entry," and of what value is it to the professional?

4. When the author stated that there is a "more humanistic approach to criminal justice management," what did he mean?

5. What was the purpose for creation of the President's Crime Commission?

6. What is the purpose for the Law Enforcement Assistance Administration?

7. What dramatic improvements have been made in the local law enforcement picture where you live as a direct or indirect result of the special funding made possible through the Law Enforcement Assistance Administration?

8. What is "community-based corrections," and what is different about it when compared with institution-based corrections?

9. Is there any difference in the operation of the courts in your jurisdiction as a result of funding through LEAA or other sources?

10. What do you believe the minimum academic standards should be for each of the entrance-level positions in the criminal justice components of law enforcement, court administration, and corrections?

11. From your personal observations, and from the opinions of some of your friends, have there actually been any improvements in the criminal justice system in your own community and in the state in which you live? What improvements?

RECOMMENDED SEMESTER/TERM PROJECTS

1. From the recommendations of the President's Commission on Law Enforcement and the Administration of Justice listed in this chapter and in the commission's report, and the many standards listed by the National Advisory Commission on Criminal Justice Standards and Goals, choose any twenty of those recommendations and/or standards. Write your own justification for each that you choose. Then visit as many criminal justice professionals as you can, interview them, find out if they agree with your justifications. Also, determine to what extent, if any, those recommendations are being carried out and if the standards are in actual existence.

2. Prepare your own list of Criminal Justice Standards and Goals as you see them. List them in order of priority, then justify each one and discuss the reasons for your topics listed.

SUGGESTED FOR ADDITIONAL STUDY

President's Commission on Law Enforcement and the Administration of Justice, *Challenge of Crime in a Free Society.* Washington, D.C.: Government Printing Office, 1967.

National Advisory Commission on Criminal Justice Standards and Goals, *Report on the Criminal Justice System* and related reports. Washington, D.C.: U.S. Government Printing Office, 1973.

Index

D

E

F

N

O

T